SOCIOLOGICAL
METHODOLOGY
1999

SOCIOLOGICAL METHODOLOGY 1999

VOLUME 29

EDITORS: Michael E. Sobel and Mark P. Becker

ADVISORY EDITORS: Kenneth A. Bollen

Jacques A.P. Hagenaars

Edgar Kiser

Calvin Morrill

Martina Morris

Susan A. Murphy

Trond Petersen

Elizabeth Stasny

Ross M. Stolzenberg

Kazuo Yamaguchi

MANAGING EDITOR: Kathleen J. Meyer

An official publication by Blackwell Publishers for

THE AMERICAN SOCIOLOGICAL ASSOCIATION

FELICE LEVINE, *Executive Officer*

Library of Congress Catalog Card Information
Sociological Methodology, 1969–85
    San Francisco, Jossey-Bass. 15 v. illus. 24 cm. annual. (Jossey-Bass behavioral science
    series)
        Editor: 1969, 1970: E. F. Borgatta; 1971, 1972, 1973–74: H. L. Costner;
        1975, 1976, 1977: D. R. Heise; 1978, 1979, 1980: K. F. Schuessler;
        1981, 1982, 1983–84: S. Leinhardt; 1985: N. B. Tuma

Sociological Methodology, 1986–88
    Washington, DC, American Sociological Association. 3 v. illus. 24 cm. annual.
        Editor: 1986: N. B. Tuma; 1987, 1988: C. C. Clogg

Sociological Methodology, 1989–1992
    Oxford, Basil Blackwell. 4 v. illus. 24 cm. annual.
        Editor: 1989, 1990: C. C. Clogg; 1991, 1992: P. V. Marsden
        "An official publication of the American Sociological Association."
        1. Sociology—Methodology—Year books.   I. American Sociological
        Association.   II. Borgatta, Edgar F., 1924– ed.

HM24.S55   301'.01'8   68-54940
                            rev.
Library of Congress   [r71h2]

British Cataloguing in Publication Data
Sociological Methodology. Vol. 29
7   1. Sociology. Methodology
        301'.01'8

ISBN 0-631-21789-4
ISSN 0081-1750

REVIEWERS

David L. Banks
McKinley L. Blackburn
Michael W. Browne
Michael Chernew
Jan de Leeuw
Norman Denzin
David Draper
Scott Eliason
Noah Friedkin
Roger Gould
Shelby J. Haberman
Jacques A. Hagenaars
Robert M. Hauser
Ronald Kessler
Edgar Kiser
Jacob A. Klerman
Joseph B. Lang
Stanley Lieberson
James G. Mackinnon

David Madigan
Calvin Morrill
Martina Morris
Trivellore E. Raghunathan
Stephen W. Raudenbush
Mark Reiser
Garry Robbins
John Skvoretz
Tom A. B. Snijders
Jose Soltero
Ross M. Stolzenberg
Thomas R. TenHave
Peter van der Heijden
Jeroen K. Vermunt
Stanley Wasserman
Marty Wells
Nanny Wermuth
Xihong Lin
Kazuo Yamaguchi

CONTENTS

CONTRIBUTORS

Vincent Buskens, Interuniversity Center for Social Science Theory and Methodology (ICS), Utrecht University

Katherine Faust, Department of Sociology, University of South Carolina

Zvi Gilula, Department of Statistics, Hebrew University of Jerusalem

Martin Karlberg, Biostatistics & Clinical Information Systems, Astra Arcus

Yiching Lin, Department of Economics, Arizona State University

John L. Martin, Department of Sociology, Rutgers University

Stephen W. Raudenbush, Department of Educational Studies, University of Michigan

Mark Reiser, Department of Economics, Arizona State University

Nicole J. Saam, Institute of Sociology, University of Munich

Robert J. Sampson, Department of Sociology, University of Chicago

John Skvoretz, Department of Sociology, University of South Carolina

L. Andries van der Ark, Department of Social Sciences, Utrecht University

Peter G.M. van der Heijden, Department of Methodology and
    Statistics, Utrecht University

Jeroen K. Vermunt, Faculty of Social and Behavioral Sciences,
    Tilburg University

James A. Wiley, Survey Research Center and Department of Sociology,
    University of California at Berkeley

Kazuo Yamaguchi, NORC, University of Chicago

SUBMISSION INFORMATION FOR AUTHORS

Sociological Methodology is an annual volume on methods of research in the social sciences. Sponsored by the American Sociological Association, its mission is to disseminate material that advances empirical research in sociology and related disciplines. Chapters present original methodological contributions, expository statements on and illustrations of recently developed techniques, and critical discussions of research practice.

Sociological Methodology seeks contributions that address the full range of problems confronted by empirical work in the contemporary social sciences, including conceptualization and modeling, research design, data collection, measurement, and data analysis. Work on the methodological problems involved in any approach to empirical social science is appropriate for *Sociological Methodology*.

The content of each annual volume of *Sociological Methodology* is driven by submissions initiated by authors; the volumes do not have specific themes. Editorial decisions about manuscripts submitted are based on the advice of expert referees. Criteria include originality, breadth of interest and applicability, and expository clarity. Discussions of implications for research practice are vital, and authors are urged to include empirical illustrations of the methods they discuss.

Authors should submit five copies of manuscripts to
Professor Michael E. Sobel, co-Editor
Sociological Methodology
University of Arizona
Department of Sociology
Social Sciences Building, Room 400
Tucson, AZ 85721

Manuscripts should include an informative abstract of not more than one double-spaced page, and should not identify the author within the text. Submission of a manuscript for review by *Sociological Methodology* implies that it has not been published previously and that it is not under review elsewhere.

Inquiries concerning the appropriateness of material and/or other aspects of editorial policies and procedures are welcome; prospective authors should correspond with the editors by E-mail at either *sobel@ u.arizona.edu* or *mbecker@mich.edu*.

IN THIS VOLUME

FOREWORD

A central concern in sociology is the manner in which individual behavior is conditioned by those structures in which individuals are located. Two very different approaches to this topic are taken in the first two chapters. The next four chapters describe new methods and models for categorical data, with emphasis on the latent class model. The remaining three chapters present advances in describing and modeling aspects of social networks.

Chapters 1 and 2 feature different approaches to studying units embedded in larger structures. In Chapter 1, Raudenbush and Sampson consider the problem of how to quantitatively assess ecological (social) settings such as neighborhoods or schools. Because administrative data (for example, census data or official crime statistics) are of little help in describing social/organizational processes such as neighborhood social control or cohesiveness, using systematically observed ecological data (for example, gang graffiti, density of liquor stores, density of advertising, number of abandoned cars) is important for assessing the social and physical conditions of the environments in which subjects are located. The authors focus on statistical models for evaluating the quality of such ecological assessments. Specifically, they use hierarchical statistical models to quantify sources of uncertainty in systematic social observation. These models take account of three sources of variation: (a) item inconsistency within a face-block (observed neighborhood), (b) face-block variation within neighborhood clusters (NC), and (c) temporal variation. Parameters in the hierarchical model (intra-NC correlations, NC level reliabilities, face-block reliability and inter-scale correlations) are tied to assessments of the ecological data. Raudenbush and Sampson also discuss how these measures can be used to inform the design of future research.

In Chapter 2, Saam uses a probabilistic model of attitude change among elites that draws upon variables from both the micro and macro levels of analysis. The model, which originates in statistical physics, has received only limited attention from previous social researchers. Using the model, Saam simulates the history of coup d'etats in Thailand over a recent sixty year period.

In Chapter 3, Reiser and Lin propose a goodness-of-fit test for a latent class model for dichotomous items, to be used when the cross-classification of counts in the observed table is too sparse to comfortably use the usual asymptotic theory. Like a similar test proposed in the psychometrics literature for the factor analysis of dichotomous variables, the test here is indirect because the fit of the model is assessed by comparing the bivariate (as versus full joint distribution) distributions of the observed data with the bivariate distributions predicted under the model. If the second order observed marginals are not adequately reproduced under the model, the model for the underlying table is inadequate and the test will appropriately reject the null hypothesis. However, the failure to reject the null using this test provides only weak evidence supporting the model under consideration. That is because the model under consideration is but one of a potentially large number of models for which the maximum likelihood estimates of the aggregated cell counts are congruent with the corresponding expected counts. Reiser and Lin do, however, present simulation results indicating that there are some settings under which their proposed test performs well, both in terms of test size and power, when compared to other procedures routinely used. They also illustrate the utility of the proposed test using an extremely sparse cross-classification (1826 empty cells) of symptoms of anxiety and depression.

In Chapter 4, Wiley and Martin consider latent class models for sets of binary items that arise from a generalization of Guttman scaling. In a deterministic Guttman scale, the items are linearly ordered. However, due to measurement errors, respondents to a survey (intelligence test) do not always respond using one of the permissible response patterns. Thus, researchers such as Andrich, Proctor, and Goodman developed probabilistic models which account for response patterns not permitted under deterministic Guttman scaling. Wiley and Martin begin with a generalization of Guttman scaling in which a set of items is only partially ordered. As before, due to measurement error, respondents do not always respond using one of the permissible response patterns. The authors then introduce a latent class model that accounts for the response patterns not permitted under deterministic scaling. To illustrate the utility of the approach, they model a set of items concerning attitudes toward welfare. They also dis cuss the limitations of their approach and suggest topics that future researchers might find it useful to address.

In Chapter 5, van der Heijden, Gilula, and van der Ark consider the relationship between multivariate versions of correspondence analysis and the latent class model. For two discrete variables, under suitable conditions, a number of relationships between correspondence analysis and the latent class model have been obtained; for example, the row and column scores in correspondence analysis can be related to conditional probabilities of class membership in the latent class model. For higher way tables, latent class analysis is a model for the unobserved table cross-classifying the observed data by class membership, while joint correspondence analysis models the separate bivariate distributions implied under the latent class model. A number of relationships analogous to those obtained in the case of a two way table are obtained. The authors also comment upon the relationship between the latent class model and the more conventional multivariate correspondence analysis.

In Chapter 6, Vermunt considers nonparametric models for contingency tables where one or more of the variables is ordinal. In contrast to restricting the table probabilities parametrically, as in log-linear and log-bilinear models, for example, the models here are specified by imposing linear equality and/or linear inequality constraints on the table probabilities and/or their logarithms. The class of models thus obtained include log-linear models because these can also be specified by means of linear equality constraints on the logarithms of the table probabilities, but they do not include log-bilinear models. Vermunt also shows how a number of other familiar models (for example, marginal homogeneity for a square table) can be obtained within this framework, and he also introduces models that are not so familiar to social researchers (for example, a model for stochastically ordered marginal distributions in a square table). Vermunt discusses an algorithm for estimating (most of) the models by maximum likelihood and he shows how the bootstrap can be used for hypothesis testing (the usual asymptotic theory for parametric models for contingency tables does not apply in general). To illustrate the flexibility of the frame-work, a number of examples are considered.

Chapters 7 through 9 report advances in social network research. In the first of these, Karlberg considers testing for transitivity in directed graphs. Here the problem is to develop suitable measures of transitivity and to compare the values of these measures in an observed graph to the distribution of values under a suitable null distribution. Although previous workers recognized the utility of using the uniform distribution with in-degrees and outdegrees equal to those in the observed graph as a null dis-tribution, it was not feasible to do so until recently. Karlberg takes advantage of recent advances in sampling from this distribution to estimate the crit-ical values associated with several possible measures of transitivity. He then considers the power of these measures under a suitable alternative data generating model; the simulated results from this exercise lead him to favor using the local average transitivity measure.

In recent work on one-mode networks, where ties are between en-tities of a single type, statistical models allowing for limited forms of de-pendence between units (nodes) have been proposed and estimated using pseudo-likelihood methods. In Chapter 8, Skvoretz and Faust carry these developments over to affiliation networks, where ties are between entities of two types, for example, actors and events. Specifically, they modify triad models for one-mode networks to apply to affiliation networks taking into account the fact that in affiliation networks it is not possible to have a triad with three edges or to distinguish between two stars with two actors and one event and two stars with two events and one actor.

In prior work on the efficiency (amount of time) of information flow through a given network, Yamaguchi proposed a Markov chain model (termed the transit model) in which an actor who passes information to another actor no longer retains that information. While this assumption is sometimes reasonable, actors often retain the information they transmit. Thus, in Chapter 9, Buskens and Yamaguchi extend the transit model to allow for retention, for the case where an actor transmits information in any period to at most one other actor and the case where an actor is per-mitted to transmit information to more than one actor. They consider a number of dyadic and global measures of the amount of time it takes for information to spread through the network, and they empirically study the dependence of these measures on the other network properties, using a set of connected networks with seven actors.

ACKNOWLEDGMENTS

We are especially grateful to the reviewers and advisory editors, who have given generously of their time to help in the production of this volume. Kathleen Meyer is the managing editor of *Sociological Methodology,* and Stephanie Argeros-Magean is the copy editor. Janet Cronin was responsible for proofreading and corrections, and Roberta Spinosa-Millman coordinated production at Blackwell. *Sociological Methodology* is sponsored and supported by the American Sociological Association.

ECOMETRICS: TOWARD A SCIENCE OF ASSESSING ECOLOGICAL SETTINGS, WITH APPLICATION TO THE SYSTEMATIC SOCIAL OBSERVATION OF NEIGHBORHOODS

Stephen W. Raudenbush*
Robert J. Sampson†

This paper considers the quantitative assessment of ecological settings such as neighborhoods and schools. Available administrative data typically provide useful but limited information on such settings. We demonstrate how more complete information can be reliably obtained from surveys and observational studies. Survey-based assessments are constructed by aggregating over multiple item responses of multiple informants within each setting. Item and rater inconsistency produce uncertainty about the setting being assessed, with definite implications for research design. Observation-based assessments also have a multilevel error structure. The paper describes measures constructed from

Revision of a paper presented at the annual meeting of the American Society of Criminology, San Diego, November 1997. The research reported here was supported by the Project on Human Development in Chicago Neighborhoods (PHDCN), with funding from the National Institute of Justice and the John D. and Catherine T. MacArthur Foundation. We thank Felton Earls, Albert J. Reiss Jr., and Steven Buka for their essential role in the design of PHDCN, and Richard Congdon for the programming of all computations. Meng-Li Yang checked the derivations and computed all results. We would also like to acknowledge the helpful comments of anonymous reviewers.
    *University of Michigan
    †University of Chicago

1

*interviews, direct observations, and videotapes of Chicago neigh-
borhoods and illustrates an "ecometric" analysis—a study of bias
and random error in neighborhood assessments. Using the observation data as an illustrative example, we present a three-
level hierarchical statistical model that identifies sources of error
in aggregating across items within face-blocks and in aggregating across face-blocks to larger geographic units such as census
tracts. Convergent and divergent validity are evaluated by studying associations between the observational measures and theoretically related measures obtained from the U.S. Census, and a
citywide survey of neighborhood residents.*

This paper addresses the challenge of assessing the social and physical properties of ecological settings, especially the neighborhood. Most published research on neighborhoods relies on data collected by administrative agencies for other purposes, principally the U.S. decennial census. Measures gleaned from the census typically cover socio-demographic factors such as poverty, family structure, unemployment, and racial composition. Other sources of administrative data often aggregated to the neighborhood level include government crime reports (e.g., the FBI's Uniform Crime Reports), vital health statistics (e.g., rates of infant mortality; suicide), records of social-service agencies (e.g., public assistance caseloads), and school records (e.g., dropout rates; average test scores).

Although much can be gained from these administrative sources, they are not helpful in revealing unofficial behavior (e.g., undetected crime, disorder) and the social-organizational processes that lie behind neighborhood demography. Mayer and Jencks (1989) have argued that if neighborhood effects on social outcomes exist, presumably they are constituted from social processes that involve collective aspects of community life. To date, however, theories emphasizing collective processes such as neighborhood social control and cohesion have rarely been translated into measures that directly tap hypothesized constructs. Common sources of administrative data also poorly capture the physical properties of neighborhoods such as the markings of gang graffiti, the density of liquor stores, and abandoned cars.

A key focus of this paper is on the statistical methods needed to evaluate the quality of such ecological assessments. Two data collection strategies will be considered: (1) the neighborhood survey and (2) the direct observation of physical conditions and social interactions occurring within neighborhoods. We concentrate primarily on the second approach, as it is the more novel of the two and illustrates all of the basic principles involved in assessing reliability and validity. However, we shall briefly review work on the neighborhood survey and compare measures generated from survey work with those derived from direct systematic observations.

1. FROM PSYCHOMETRIC TO "ECOMETRIC" STANDARDS

It is tempting to describe the problem at hand as the need to understand "the psychometric properties of ecological measures." But this awkward phrasing merely reveals the individualistic bias of modern social science, underscoring the need to take ecological assessment seriously as an enterprise that is conceptually distinct from individual-level assessment. Ecological constructs need not be merely the aggregate of individual ones, and thus we seek to understand what we call the "ecometric" rather than psychometric properties of ecological measures. We show that "ecometric assessment," while borrowing tools from the rich tradition of psychometrics, has its own logic.

Moreover, without a coherent strategy for evaluating the quality of ecological assessments, a serious mismatch arises in studies that aim to integrate individual and ecological assessments. The assessment of individual differences, building on decades of psychometric research, employs measures that have withstood rigorous evaluation. This is especially true of measures of cognitive skill and school achievement, but it extends as well to measures of personality and social behavior. These measures have been thoroughly evaluated in many studies; each scale includes many items; ill-performing items have been discarded; and psychometric properties have been found to hold up in many settings. Without comparable standards to evaluate ecological assessments, the search for individual and ecological effects may overemphasize the individual component simply because the well-studied psychometric properties are likely to be superior to the unstudied ecometric ones.

The history of psychometrics is indeed instructive to our case. Beginning in the early years of this century, educational psychologists, statisticians, and others launched a new realm of applied social science destined to have a profound impact on modern society: the assessment of human ability and personality. An enormous demand arose for standardized tests that seemed to offer a meritocratic basis for selecting persons for advanced schooling, for employment, and for specializations within the armed forces. The testing movement that resulted made permanent contributions to statistical methodology, including correlational and factor analysis, and produced a branch of applied statistics called *psychometrics* that has come to dominate thinking about the reliability and validity of measurement in social science.

In contrast, until recently there has been no parallel effort to create a scientific basis for the methodological assessment of human ecological settings such as neighborhoods and schools. While there have been many studies of organizational climate (cf. Pallas 1988), one rarely encounters a rigorous evaluation of the reliability or validity of such measures, nor are standard errors of measurement associated with them. Measures of organizational climate, ironically, have historically been studied psychometrically at the level of the individual respondent rather than "ecometrically" at the level of the organization, even when the analysis used the organization as the unit of analysis in structural models (Sirotnik 1980). As part of a larger study of individual and ecological correlates of social behavior, we are engaged in a multipronged effort to assess neighborhoods as important units in their own right. In approaching the problem of ecometric assessment, we borrow, integrate, and adapt three analytic strategies that are prominent in modern psychometrics: (1) item response modeling, (2) generalizability theory, and (3) factor analysis.

Item response models conceive the probability of a correct response to an item on a test as a function of the ability of the examinee and the difficulty of the item (Lord 1980; Rasch 1980). Assuming all items represent the same ability domain, difficult items will be answered correctly less often than will easy items. Similarly, given the difficulty of the item, more able examinees will obtain a correct response with higher probability than will less able examinees. If the model is sensible, it will generate an interval scale along which every item and every examinee can be located. A visual examination of this "item map" provides useful clues about the construct validity of the test, because one can assess whether the empirically estimated item difficulties conform to cognitive theory regarding the sources of item difficulty. It is also possible to identify misfitting items (e.g., difficult items frequently solved by persons of low ability) and misfitting persons (e.g., able persons who frequently miss easy items). Such analyses form a basis for discarding poor items and assessing the overall quality of the scale. The analysis produces a measure of scale reliability and a standard error of measurement for each examinee (Wright and Stone 1979).

Generalizability theory enables the study of multiple sources of measurement error in an assessment (Cronbach et al. 1972; Brennan and Kane 1979). Suppose, for example, that an examinee is asked to write an essay on Saturday morning and that the essay is rated by a single rater. Possible error sources would be day of week, time of day, the specific task (e.g., the topic chosen for the essay), and the rater. A generalizability study might assess persons on several days of the week and times of day and on varied tasks, with essays read by multiple raters. Such a study would provide not only a summary measure of reliability but also an estimate of the magnitude of each component of error. It would presumably influence future assessments. For example, if tasks and raters produce large error variance, future assessments might require essays on several topics, each to be rated by two raters, thus averaging over task and rater errors, and achieving an acceptable level of reliability. However, the design of future assessments would depend heavily upon their use. For example, if the writing task were used as part of a program evaluation, it might be cheaper to sample more examinees in each comparison group rather than to hire more raters or to require more tasks per examinee. A generalizability study would specify the sample size per group required to achieve a given reliability of the program group mean.

Factor analysis enables a determination of the interrelationships among measures. Often studies collect data on a fairly large number of measured variables. However, these variables may in fact reflect variation in a smaller number of latent variables or factors. Confirmatory factor analysis enables one to test *a priori* hypotheses about the associations between underlying factors and observed variables (Joreskog and Sorbom 1988). Often a factor analysis lays the basis for a parsimonious representation, and this can be particularly important in the case of ecological measurement. Typically the sample size of ecological units is small and the intercorrelations among ecological variables high. Thus a parsimonious representation of variation at the ecological level may be essential for meaningful analysis and interpretation.

With this backdrop in mind, we now turn to the description of two forms of ecological assessment that are not yet standard in social science. We begin with a brief consideration of survey-based measures of ecological settings, where experience has accumulated rapidly in recent years. Building on the survey approach, we then turn to an extended treatment of the more novel technique of systematic social observation.

2. ASSESSING SURVEY-BASED MEASURES OF
ECOLOGICAL SETTINGS

The problem of measuring high school climate provides a useful lead-in to considerations of using survey questionnaires to assess neighborhoods. Raudenbush, Rowan, and Kang (1991) analyzed national survey data yielding questionnaire responses from 15 to 30 teachers in each of about 400 schools. Dimensions of climate included teacher control over the conditions of instruction, teacher collaboration, and administrative support. Multiple Likert scale items tapped each of these constructs. The investigators used a three-level hierarchical statistical model to assess sources of measurement error.

At the first and lowest level of aggregation, item responses within a given scale varied within a teacher around that teacher's "true perception." The source of variation at this level was item inconsistency. At the second level, the "true perceptions" on each scale varied among teachers within a given school around the school's "true score." Here the variation reflected individual variation in perceptions. At the third and highest level of aggregation, school "true scores" varied around a grand mean. This analysis strategy enabled Raudenbush et al. (1991) to estimate (1) the reliability with which teacher perceptions vary; but more importantly, (2) the reliability of the school-level measures of each aspect of climate; and (3) the correlation structure at the teacher level and at the school level among the three climate dimensions.

The analysis just described was in fact a generalizability analysis, laying the groundwork for assessing how adding items to each scale or sampling more teachers per school would increase the reliability of assessment of either persons (teachers) or ecological units (schools). The analysis showed that adding items was far more useful in improving teacher-level reliability than in improving school-level reliability. Viewing teachers as raters of the school, school-level reliability relies principally upon the degree of rater agreement and the number of raters per school. The analysis thus aids in determining the needed sample size of teachers per school to achieve a given school-level reliability on each climate dimension and helps in allocating resources between investing in more data collection per teacher (through more items) or more teachers per school. The analysis also involved a multilevel principal components analysis that revealed the number of reliably varying dimensions of school climate, in addition to, and distinct from, the number of reliably varying dimensions of teacher perceptions. A further extension might have involved multilevel factor analysis (Muthen 1991, 1997).

A similar logic may be applied to the use of interviews to measure social organizational aspects of neighborhoods. Sampson, Raudenbush, and Earls (1997) used a multilevel research design (described below) to construct and evaluate measures of neighborhood social organization. Within each of 343 Chicago neighborhoods, between 20 and 50 households were selected according to a multistage probability sample. The total sample size was 8,782, with a response rate of 75 percent. Within each household, a randomly chosen adult was interviewed concerning conditions and social relationships in the local neighborhood. Sampson et al. (1997) employed a three-level hierarchical model (formally presented in Raudenbush and Sampson [forthcoming]) to investigate the statistical properties of neighborhood measures of social cohesion and informal social control. The analysis yielded estimates of item inconsistency within each scale, interrater agreement on each scale, and an overall estimate of the reliability of measurement of each scale.

This analysis is extended in Table 1, which displays five scales that tap theoretically relevant aspects of the physical and social properties of neighborhoods as perceived by Chicago residents. The table also includes the items composing each scale, the interrater agreement, and the scale reliability at the neighborhood level. Interrater agreement is measured by an intraneighborhood correlation coefficient (ICC)—that is, the ratio of between-neighborhood variance to the sum of between- and within-neighborhood variance, where the variance attributable to item inconsistency has been removed. In essence, these ICCs capture the extent to which assessments of the "ego-defined" neighborhood, as conceived by the individual rater, are correlated within the physical spaces defined *a priori* as neighborhoods.

Table 1 reveals that the ICCs are modest, ranging from .13 for informal social control to .36 for social disorder. Because these correlations are variance ratios, it is clear that in no case does most of the variation in ratings lie between neighborhoods. The relatively modest ICCs are similar to those found in other studies looking at contexts such as schools and even families. Duncan and Raudenbush (1997:10) advise caution in interpreting small ICCs, as effect sizes commonly viewed as large translate into small proportions of variance in individual outcomes explained by neigh-

TABLE 1
Selected Variables from the PHDCN Community Survey (8,782 respondents,
343 neighborhood clusters)

Scale	ICC	Reliability
Social Disorder	.36	.89
Litter		
Graffiti		
Vacant or deserted houses		
Drinking in public		
Selling or using drugs		
Teenagers/adults causing trouble		
Perceived Violence	.25	.82
Fights in which a weapon was used		
Violent arguments between neighbors		
Gang fights		
Sexual assaults		
Robbery		
Social Cohesion	.24	.80
Close-knit neighborhood		
Helpful people		
People get along with each other		
People share the same values		
People can be trusted		
Social Control	.13	.74
Neighbors are willing to do something about:		
children skipping school		
children painting graffiti		
children showing disrespect to adult		
someone being beaten or threatened		
keeping the fire station open		
Neighborhood Decline	.18	.75
Personal safety worse		
Neighborhood looks worse		
People in neighborhood less helpful		
Level of police protection worse		

borhood membership. In fact, neighborhood effect sizes as large as .8 of a standard deviation difference can give rise to an ICC as low as .14. Therefore a small correlation among neighbors does not rule out a large effect size associated with a measured difference between neighborhoods (Duncan and Raudenbush 1997:11).

Although the interrater agreement appears modest, only a moderate sample size of raters per NC is required to achieve reasonably high interrater reliabilities at the neighborhood level. This association between sample size of raters and reliability is graphed in Figure 1, for informal social control (which has the lowest interrater agreement) and social disorder (which has the highest interrater agreement). The curves for the other three measures lie between the two curves in Figure 1 because their interrater agreements are neither as low as that for informal social control nor as high as that for social disorder. It is clear that sampling 20 raters per neighborhood produces interrater reliabilities ranging from .70 to .90 while 40 raters yields reliabilities ranging from .83 to .95. The curves make vividly clear the diminishing returns to investments in raters beyond a given number to yield acceptable reliability.

Further analysis revealed some redundancy among the scales. For example, the correlation between social control and social cohesion, disattenuated for measurement error, was $r = .88$. This result was conceptually sensible. Informal social control taps the extent to which neighbors can be relied upon to intervene to protect the public order. Without some degree of social cohesion, which involves neighbors knowing and trusting

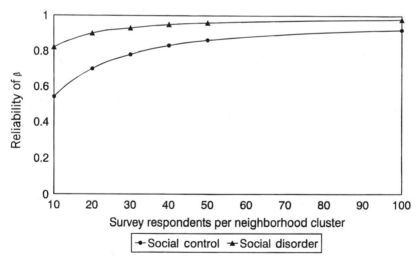

FIGURE 1. Reliabilities of community survey measures of social disorder and social control.

each other and having shared values, informal social control would appear impossible. And the exertion of such informal control would likely enhance social cohesion: people get to know each other by working together for common goals. The two sets of items appeared closely linked to the larger notion of collective efficacy (Sampson et al. 1997). Thus the two measures were combined to create a more parsimonious, reliable, and readily interpretable measure of an ecological construct with strong theoretical connections to crime reduction.

The two examples of ecological assessment just described involved paradigm examples of generalizability theory. In both cases, measurement error was decomposed into variation attributable to item inconsistency and rater inconsistency. This strategy provided the basis for assessing the needed sample size of raters (and of items, though not emphasized in the second example) in future studies. The two cases varied from standard generalizability theory in that multiple measures were simultaneously assessed; in this way, both analyses are easily amenable to multilevel factor analyses. The methodology linking latent variable analysis with multilevel modeling and the assessment of indirect associations (Raudenbush and Sampson forthcoming) can be applied to the sort of nested neighborhood-level designs now appearing in the social sciences (e.g., Elliott et al. 1996; Cook et al. 1997; Brooks-Gunn et al. 1997).

On the other hand, neither of these survey-based examples provided independent or "objective" assessments of the ecological environment based on direct observation. Moreover, instead of a serious item response analysis, in both cases Likert-scale (ordinal) responses were treated as interval-level data. This practice, certainly open to criticism, is widespread and will often cause little trouble when large numbers of item responses are aggregated to produce a scale score. However, a serious item response analysis is not only better grounded theoretically, it also produces information relevant to future scale construction and to interpretation of effect sizes (Wright and Masters 1982). We thus turn to the assessment of direct observational measures, illustrated with the use of item response analysis. The approach is similar to that used in the two survey-based measures described above in that generalizability and factor analysis also come into play.

3. SYSTEMATIC SOCIAL OBSERVATION

Direct observation is fundamental to the advancement of science. With this in mind, more than 25 years ago in an early volume of *Sociological*

Methodology. Albert J. Reiss Jr. (1971) advocated systematic social observation (hereafter, SSO) as a key measurement strategy for a wide variety of social science phenomena. Reiss (1971:4) defined systematic observation to include explicit rules which permit replication. He also argued that the means of observation, whether a person or technology, must be independent of that which is observed. As his main example, Reiss described systematic observations of police-citizen encounters but noted as well the general application to physical conditions and social interactions within neighborhood settings (see also Reiss 1975). In particular, SSO provides measures independent of the perceptions of survey respondents and can tap aspects of the social and physical environment that survey respondents have difficulty describing accurately. The key disadvantage of observational methods in neighborhood research, of course, is that they cannot capture the theoretical constructs that require resident perspectives. Thus, for example, assessing resident perceptions of social cohesion and social control (Sampson et al. 1997) requires survey methods. If researchers rely entirely on observations, there is a danger that they will misinterpret the significance of observable conditions such as physical disorder, building conditions, and land use. Nevertheless, when used in conjunction with survey-based methods, direct observation can provide an independent source of data that can strengthen inferences about neighborhood social organization and its consequences. For example, Sampson and Raudenbush (1998) have tested the association between social control and cohesion, as tapped by survey methods, and neighborhood disorder, as indicated by independent observation. This strategy avoids reliance on resident reported disorder, which would possibly create a "same-source" bias.

Despite the potential of observation for providing quantifiable, objective, and replicable measures of physical and social structure, published examples of systematic social observation at the neighborhood level are relatively infrequent. We believe one of the primary reasons has been methodological uncertainty on how to properly conduct and assess systematic observations. A major exception and an advance in systematic observational study was provided by the research program of Taylor and colleagues in Baltimore (Taylor, Shumaker, and Gottfredson 1985; Taylor, Gottfredson and Brower 1984; Covington and Taylor 1991). Using observations conducted by teams of trained raters walking in the neighborhood, Taylor et al. (1985) assessed 20 percent of the occupied street blocks in 66 Baltimore neighborhoods. They identified two physical dimensions of neighborhoods that stood out empirically: physical decay and nonresidential land use. These two dimensions were reliable in terms of individual-level standards (e.g., Cronbach's alpha and interrater reliability) and were related as expected to independent measures of perceived disorder and fear of crime derived from neighborhood surveys. A smaller-scale version of systematic observation based on interviewer ratings in a neighborhood survey was also used in Taub et al. (1984).

Building on the conceptual framework of Reiss (1971) and the techniques of Taylor and colleagues (1984, 1985), the Project on Human Development in Chicago Neighborhoods initiated in 1995 a combined person-based and video-taped approach to collecting systematic observations of neighborhood social and physical disorder. This substantive focus drew on considerable theory and past research indicating that physical and social disorder provide important environmental cues to residents and potential predators alike (Skogan 1990). After describing the sample design and data collection, we present a generalizable model for how to properly assess such observational techniques.

3.1. Sample Design

Chicago's 865 census tracts were first combined into 343 neighborhood clusters (NCs). The overriding consideration in the formation of NCs was that they should be as ecologically meaningful as possible, composed of geographically contiguous census tracts, and internally homogeneous on key census indicators. The resulting ecological units contained about 8000 people, much smaller than Chicago's 77 community areas but large enough to approximate local neighborhoods. Geographic boundaries (for example, railroad tracks, parks, and freeways) and knowledge of Chicago's neighborhoods guided this process.

The 343 NCs in Chicago were then stratified by seven levels of ethnic mix and three levels of SES. Within strata, 80 NCs were sampled with the aim of obtaining a near balanced design, thus eliminating the confounding between ethnic mix and socioeconomic status (SES). However, there were two empty cells (low SES, predominantly European-American; and high SES, predominantly Hispanic). Also, the largest stratum was low SES and predominantly African-American, containing 177 NCs, generally characterized by concentrated poverty, racial segregation, and other forms of disadvantage. The final design randomly sampled four NCs within cells that had at least four, all NCs within cells having fewer than four, with an over sampling of the largest and most disadvantaged cell.

In the first wave of the PHDCN's longitudinal study, approximately 6500 young people have been sampled and assessed within the resulting 80 NCs. Data gathered by means of the systematic observations and neighborhood survey will provide explanatory variables to be used in conjunction with information about individual and family characteristics to account for variation in the developmental trajectories of these young people.

3.2. Instruments and Data

Between June and September 1995, observers trained by the National Opinion Research Center (NORC) drove a sport utility vehicle at a rate of five miles per hour down every street within the 80 sample NCs. The composition of the vehicle included a driver, a videographer, and two observers. The unit of recorded observation was the face-block: the block segment on one side of the street. For example, the buildings across the street from one another on any block comprised two separate units of observation. An advantage of this microlevel of coding is that observations can then be pieced together to form higher levels of aggregation desired by theory or as suggested by patterns in the data.

As the NORC team drove down the street, a pair of video recorders, one located on each side of the vehicle, captured social activities and physical features of both face-blocks simultaneously. Also at the same time, the two trained observers—one on each side of the vehicle—recorded their observations onto an observer log for each face-block. Additionally, the observers added commentary when relevant (e.g., about unusual events such as a drug bust) by speaking into the videotape audio. Using these procedures, the SSO team produced Hi-8 videotapes, observer logs, and audiotapes for every face-block in each of the 80 sampled NCs. In all, 23,816 face-blocks were observed and video-recorded for an average of 298 per NC.

NORC collected data on 14 variables in the 23,816 observer logs with an emphasis on land use, traffic, the physical condition of buildings, and evidence of physical disorder. The observer log data were easily transformed into machine readable data files as they were entered on scannable forms. By contrast, because of the expense of first viewing and then coding the videotapes, a random subsample of all face-blocks was selected for coding. Specifically, in those NCs consisting of 150 or fewer face-blocks, all face-blocks were coded. In the remaining face-blocks, sample sizes were calculated to approximate a balanced design as closely as possible in order to maximize statistical power for comparisons of NCs. A total of 15,141 face-blocks were selected for videotape coding, for an average of 189 face-blocks per NC. From the videotapes, 126 variables were coded, including detailed information on physical conditions, housing characteristics, businesses, and social interactions occurring on each face-block (NORC 1995). Coders were trained in multiple sessions, including an intercoder reliability training where 90 face-blocks were independently double coded, differences resolved, and coding procedures revised. Moreover, as a check on quality control, a random 10 percent of all coded face-blocks were recoded by new observers, and the results compared. This test produced over 98 percent agreement (for full details see NORC 1995; Carter et al. 1996).

3.3. *Measures and Scales*

Given the focus of this paper on methodological issues in evaluating ecological measures, we have selected two scales for illustrative analysis. The first is a scale intended to capture the level of physical disorder, represented by items indicating the presence or absence in the street, sidewalk, or gutter of empty beer bottles; cigarettes or cigars; drug paraphernalia; condoms; garbage; abandoned cars; and various types of graffiti. Although some of the scales were measured initially on an ordinal scale, the data behaved essentially as dichotomous items, coded for analysis as 1 = presence and 0 = absence of the indicator of disorder.

Table 2 gives the frequency distribution of the items. The variation in sample size reflects the fact that six of the ten items were taken from the observation log and thus have nearly complete data. The other four variables were derived from the videotapes, and are thus based on the reduced subsample selected for coding. Note that the items behave essentially as one might expect. Less serious indicators of disorder (presence of cigarettes and garbage) arise more frequently than do indicators that might be regarded as more serious (drug paraphernalia and condoms) with the presence of beer bottles arising with moderate frequency. An exception occurs in the case of graffiti: political graffiti is very rare, though not necessarily indicative of severe disorder.

The second scale is intended to capture direct evidence of social disorder. All items were coded from videotape. They include presence of adults loitering, public drinking, peer gangs, drunken adults, adults fight-

TABLE 2
Frequency Distribution of SSO Item Responses, Face-Block Level

Variable	Category	Frequency
Physical Disorder		
Cigarettes, cigars on street or gutter	no	6815
	yes	16758
Garbage, litter on street or sidewalk	no	11680
	yes	11925
Empty beer bottles visible in street	no	17653
	yes	5870
Tagging graffiti	no	12859
	yes	2252
Graffiti painted over	no	13390
	yes	1721
Gang graffiti	no	14138
	yes	973
Abandoned cars	no	22782
	yes	806
Condoms on sidewalk	no	23331
	yes	231
Needles/syringes on sidewalk	no	23392
	yes	173
Political message graffiti	no	15097
	yes	14
Social Disorder		
Adults loitering or congregating	no	14250
	yes	861
People drinking alcohol	no	15075
	yes	36
Peer group, gang indicators present	no	15091
	yes	20
People intoxicated	no	15093
	yes	18
Adults fighting or hostilely arguing	no	15099
	yes	12
Prostitutes on street	no	15100
	yes	11
People selling drugs	no	15099
	yes	12

ing, prostitutes, and drug sales. In general, indicators of social disorder are present far less frequently than are indicators of physical disorder (see again Table 2). Activities viewed as indicative of serious disorder (prostitution, drug selling, adults fighting) are again especially rare. Indicators that are somewhat less severe are also somewhat less rare (drinking alcohol, presence of peer gangs), though they remain very rare. One item—adults loitering—is the least severe and occurred with much higher frequency than did any other item.

A simple visible inspection of two scales suggests that the physical disorder scale will behave better "ecometrically" than will the social disorder scale. First, it has more items (10 versus 7). Second, and more important, the physical disorder items appear to range widely in severity; several occur with large frequency, several others with modest frequency, and several are comparatively rare. In contrast, the social disorder indicators all occur with extremely rare frequency except one: adults loitering or congregating. The concern is that the social disorder scale will be dominated by this single item. Even that item has a low frequency, so that the overall scale may well lack reliability. In the next section, tools are developed to more formally test these intuitions.

4. A MODEL FOR UNCERTAINTY IN SYSTEMATIC SOCIAL OBSERVATION

Let us now consider how to adapt tools found useful in psychometrics to the problem of evaluating measures of ecological settings, here obtained through systematic social observation of neighborhoods. First, it will be desirable to understand how the items function within each construct and to use this information to build an interval scale for each. In the analogy with ability testing, each face-block is an "examinee," each indicator of disorder is an "item," and a "correct response" occurs when a face-block achieves a "yes" on that item. In this setting, item "difficulty" is the severity of the indicator of disorder, and face-block "ability" is its summary score on the disorder measure.

Second, it is essential to recognize that if the goal is to assess neighborhood clusters (NCs), there will be at least three components of measurement error: (1) item inconsistency within a face-block; (2) face-block variation within NCs, and (3) temporal variation. Temporal variation is an obvious problem in the case of measuring social disorder. The probability of finding adults loitering or drinking or finding peer gangs hanging out, or of seeing prostitution or drug deals will clearly depend on the time of day on which a face-block is observed. Thus it will be necessary to estimate and adjust for time of day. Fortunately, time of day varied substantially within every NC because of the time required to complete the observation. The attempt to model and estimate each component of error variation is consistent with generalizability theory in psychometrics.

Third, the item response model must allow for randomly missing data because only a random sample of the face-blocks yielded data coded from the videotapes. The hierarchical logistic regression model we describe below makes use of all available data.

Fourth, we are interested in the association between the constructs of physical and social disorder, adjusting for measurement error. This is akin to a confirmatory factor analysis in which ten items reflect physical disorder, seven items reflect social disorder, and the aim is to understand the association between physical and social disorder conceived as latent variables or factors.

To achieve these three goals, we formulate a three-level hierarchical logistic regression model. The level-1 units are item responses within face-blocks, the level-2 units are face-blocks, and the level-3 units are NCs.

4.1. Level-1 Model

The level-1 model represents predictable and random variation among item responses within each face-block. This is a standard one-parameter item response model and might be termed a Rasch model with random effects.[1] However, it will contain two dimensions (physical and social disorder) rather than the single dimension in classical applications of the Rasch model.

Let Y_{ijk} be an indicator taking on a value of unity if indicator i of disorder is found present in face-block j of neighborhood k, with $Y_{ijk} = 0$ if not; and let μ_{ijk} denote the probability $Y_{ijk} = 1$. That is,

$$Y_{ijk} | \mu_{ijk} \sim \text{Bernoulli} \; ;$$

$$E(Y_{ijk} | \mu_{ijk}) = \mu_{ijk}, Var(Y_{ijk} | \mu_{ijk}) = \mu_{ijk}(1 - \mu_{ijk}) \; . \tag{1}$$

[1] An important advantage of the random effects approach is that data from all face-blocks, even those with a zero on every item, contribute to the analysis. In contrast, a standard fixed effects Rasch analysis would exclude such cases.

As is standard in logistic regression, we define η_{ijk} as the log-odds of this probability. Thus we have

$$\eta_{ijk} = \log\left(\frac{\mu_{ijk}}{1 - \mu_{ijk}}\right) . \tag{2}$$

The structural model at level 1 accounts for predictable variation within face-blocks across items. It views the log-odds of finding disorder on item i as depending on which aspect of disorder is of interest (physical or social) and which specific item is involved. Let D_{pijk} take on a value of 1 if item i is an indicator of physical disorder, 0 otherwise; and let $D_{sijk} = 1 - D_{pijk}$ similarly indicate whether that item indicates social disorder. Then we have

$$\eta_{ijk} = D_{pijk}\left(\pi_{pjk} + \sum_{m=1}^{9} \alpha_{mjk} X_{mijk}\right) + D_{sijk}\left(\pi_{sjk} + \sum_{m=1}^{6} \delta_{mjk} Z_{mijk}\right) ,$$

$$\tag{3}$$

where

$X_{mijk}, m = 1,\ldots,9$ are nine dummy variables representing nine of the ten items that measure physical disorder (each taking on a value of 1 or 0); $Z_{mijk}, m = 1,\ldots,6$ are six dummy variables representing six of the seven items that measure social disorder.

In fact, we "center" each X and Z around its grand mean. This enables us to assign the following definitions:

π_{pjk} is the adjusted log-odds of finding physical disorder on a "typical item" when observing face-block j of NC k;
π_{sjk} is the adjusted log-odds of finding social disorder on a "typical item" when observing face-block j of NC k;
α_{mjk} reflects the "difficulty" or "severity" level of item m within the physical disorder scale;[2] similarly, δ_{mjk} reflects the "difficulty" or "severity" level of item m within the social disorder scale.

---

[2]The interpretation of these coefficients as "difficulty" or "severity" requires that they be multiplied by -1.

Using the analogy of educational testing, π_{pjk} and π_{sjk} are the pair of abilities being measured and each α and δ reflects item difficulty. These item difficulties could, in principle, be allowed to vary across face-blocks or NCs; however, in the absence of theory that might predict such variation, they will be held constant in the interest of parsimony. Thus $\alpha_{mjk} = \alpha_m$ and $\delta_{mjk} = \delta_m$ for all j, k. Note that one item within each scale must serve as the "reference item" (it is not represented by a dummy variable). This item is defined to have a difficulty of zero and all other item difficulties are compared to it.

One benefit of explicitly representing the item difficulties in the model is that face-block measures of disorder, π_{pjk} and π_{sjk}, are adjusted for missing data. In the current data set, missing data arise because of the expense of coding the videotapes, leading to the decision to code just a random subsample of face-blocks within NCs. Face-blocks not sampled will have data from the observation log but not the coding log. No bias arises because the coded face-blocks constituted a representative sample of face-blocks in the NC. Nevertheless, controlling the item difficulties enables all of the data collected to be effectively used in the analysis.

4.2. Level-2 Model

The level-2 model accounts for variation between face-blocks within NCs on latent face-block disorder. Each is predicted by the overall NC level of disorder and the time of day during which the face-block was observed:

$$\pi_{pjk} = \beta_{pk} + \sum_{q=1}^{5} \theta_{pqk}(\text{Time})_{qjk} + u_{pjk}$$

$$\pi_{sjk} = \beta_{sk} + \sum_{q=1}^{5} \theta_{sqk}(\text{Time})_{qjk} + u_{sjk} . \qquad (4)$$

$(\text{Time})_{qjk}$ for $q = 1,\dots,5$ are five time-of-day indicators (specifically, they indicate 7:00 to 8:59 AM; 9:00 to 10:59 AM; 11:00 AM to 12:59 PM; 1:00 to 2:59 PM; and 3:00 to 4:59 PM, where the omitted group is from 5:00 to 6:59 PM).

θ_{pqk} and θ_{sqk} are regression coefficients that capture the time-of-day effects on observing physical and social disorder within NC k. In principle, these could be allowed to vary over NCs, but for parsimony we shall hold them constant: $\theta_{pqk} = \theta_{pq}$ and $\theta_{sqk} = \theta_{sq}$ for all k. Note that the model allows different time-of-day effects for the social disorder items than for the physical disorder items. Driving this decision is the fact that certain observable social interactions (e.g., adults drinking) are much more likely to occur later in the day than early in the day while physical evidence such as the presence of graffiti should not be so sensitive to time of day. The model can also be elaborated to allow time-of-day effects to vary across items. Thus the "item difficulties" in equation (3)—the α and δ coefficients—could be separately modeled as a function of time of day. We forgo this option to reduce the complexity of the model, particularly in light of the low frequency associated with many of the items (Table 2). β_{pk} and β_{sk} are the "true" scores for NC k on physical and social disorder, respectively, adjusting for time of day.

The random effects u_{pjk}, u_{sjk} are assumed to be bivariate normally distributed with zero means, variances τ_{pp} and τ_{ss}, and covariance τ_{ps}. The variances will be large when face-blocks vary greatly within NCs on their levels of disorder.

4.3. Level-3 Model

The third and final level of the model describes variation between NCs, the key units of measurement, on physical and social disorder. We have simply

$$\beta_{pk} = \gamma_p + \upsilon_{pk}$$

$$\beta_{sk} = \gamma_s + \upsilon_{sk} \tag{5}$$

where γ_p and γ_s are the grand mean levels of physical and social disorder in Chicago neighborhoods and the random effects υ_{pk} and υ_{sk} are assumed to be bivariate normally distributed with zero means, variances ω_{pp} and ω_{ss}, and covariance ω_{ps}. The variances will be large when NCs vary greatly on their levels of disorder.

Estimation.   Combining equations (2)–(5), our task is to estimate the nonlinear mixed model

$$E(Y_{ijk} | \mu_{ijk}) = \text{Prob}(Y_{ijk} = 1 | \mu_{ijk}) = \mu_{ijk} = (1 + \exp\{-\eta_{ijk}\})^{-1} \tag{6}$$

with

$$\eta_{ij} = D_{pijk}\left(\gamma_p + \sum_{q=1}^{5} \theta_{pq}(\text{Time})_{qjk} + \sum_{m=1}^{9} \alpha_m X_{mijk} + u_{pjk} + v_{pk}\right)$$

$$+ D_{sijk}\left(\gamma_s + \sum_{q=1}^{5} \theta_{sq}(\text{Time})_{qjk} + \sum_{m=1}^{6} \delta_m Z_{mijk} + u_{sjk} + v_{sk}\right). \quad (7)$$

For purposes of illustration in the pages to follow, all model parameters were estimated simultaneously by penalized quasi-likelihood or "PQL" (Breslow and Clayton 1993) using an algorithm described in detail by Raudenbush (1995) and implemented in Version 4 of the HLM program (Bryk et al. 1996). The advantages and disadvantages of this approach relative to alternative approaches are discussed in Appendix A. That appendix also provides a sensitivity analysis based on a better approximation to maximum-likelihood estimates.

4.4. Measurement Properties to Be Estimated

The three-level hierarchical logistic regression model described above can be viewed as an item response model embedded within a hierarchical structure in which the secondary units of measurement, the face-blocks, are nested within the units of primary interest, the NCs. It extends the usual item response model also in allowing for multiple characteristics to be measured—in this case, physical social and physical disorder, rather than a single, unidimensional trait—and in allowing for randomly missing responses.

Fitting the model produces considerable information of interest in assessing the quality of the measures. The item difficulties have been mentioned above and their use in creating and interpreting a scale will be illustrated in the next section. Other key quantities are described below.

Intra-NC Correlations. The variance estimates within and between NCs yield an estimated "intra-NC correlation" on each measure that expresses the consistency of disorder across face-blocks. Consider the physical disorder items. If we substitute equation (5) into equation (4), we have a combined model for π_{pjk}, the latent trait being measured for face-block j of neighborhood k:

$$\pi_{pjk} = \gamma_p + \sum_{q=1}^{5} \theta_{pq}(\text{Time})_{qjk} + u_{pjk} + v_{pk}. \quad (8)$$

This leads to the following definition of the intra-NC correlation for physical disorder:

$$\rho_{NCp} = \text{Corr}(\pi_{pjk}, \pi_{pj'k}) = \frac{\text{Cov}(\pi_{pjk}, \pi_{pj'k})}{[\text{Var}(\pi_{pjk}) * \text{Var}(\pi_{pj'k})]^{1/2}}$$

$$= \frac{\omega_{pp}}{\omega_{pp} + \tau_{pp}} . \tag{9}$$

Here face-block pjk and face-block $pj'k$ are two different face-blocks within the kth NC. The intra-NC correlation for social disorder is, of course, analogous. The intra-NC correlation in equation (9) represents the proportion of variation in the true latent traits that lies between NCs. By definition, such variation excludes item inconsistency. By conceiving η_{ijk} as a latent variable following a logistic distribution, it is also possible to define an intra–face-block correlation and an alternative intra-NC correlation that would incorporate item inconsistency (see Gibbons and Hedeker 1997:1533).[3] Large intra-NC correlations imply that face-blocks within NCs are comparatively similar and that NCs vary considerably.

NC-level Reliabilities. Closely related to the intra-NC correlation is the internal consistency reliability of NC measurement. It depends on the intra-NC correlation but also on the number of face-blocks sampled, the number of items per scale, and the item difficulties. An approximation to the reliability for NC k, in the case of physical disorder, is given by

$$\lambda_{pk} = \frac{\text{Var}(\beta_{pk})}{\text{Var}(\hat{\beta}_{pk})} \approx \frac{\omega_{pp}}{\omega_{pp} * \dfrac{\tau_{pp}}{J_k} + \dfrac{1}{n_k J_k \omega_k}} , \tag{10}$$

where

λ_{pk} is the internal consistency of the physical disorder measure for NC k;
n_k is the average number of items per face-block in NC k ($n_k = 10$ if videotapes for all face-blocks in that NC are coded);
J_k = the number of face-blocks sampled within NC k;
w_k is the average within NC k of $\mu_{ijk}(1 - \mu_{ijk})$ on physical disorder items.

[3]The latent trait π_{pjk} is what we seek to measure more and more accurately as we add items to the scale, and the intra-NC correlation indexes the relative importance of NC variation and face-block variation within NCs on this trait. This is different from the intra-NC correlation on a measure based on a fixed number of items.

This conception of internal consistency can be motivated as follows. Suppose we use only the data from NC k to estimate β_{pk} and we regard that estimate as our measure of β_{pk}, the true level of physical disorder in NC k. Equation (10) is then the proportion of the variance in the estimates that is attributable to variance in the trait of interest; it is also the correlation between two such estimates derived from independent random samples of face-blocks. This approach to measurement reliability in an ecological setting is a direct extension of the approach used by Raudenbush et al. (1991) to measure school climate. While they used a three-level linear model, we extend that methodology to a three-level logistic model for dichotomous item responses. Appendix B provides the details.

Inspection of equation (10) reveals that reliability will be high when (1) the between-NC variance ω_{pp} is large relative to the within-NC variance τ_{pp}; (2) when the number of items in scale n_k is large; (3) when the number of face-blocks sampled, J_k, is large; and (4) when the typical probability of finding an aspect of disorder in a given face-block—that is μ_{ijk}—is near .50, at which point w_k achieves its maximum.

Face-block Reliability. It may be desirable to measure disorder at a lower level of geographic analysis, indeed, at the face-block level. Such measures could be assigned to individuals in a longitudinal study—for example, by geocoding their addresses. Reliability at the face-block level is given by

$$\lambda_{pjk} = \frac{\omega_{pp} + \tau_{pp}}{\omega_{pp} + \tau_{pp} + \dfrac{1}{n_{jk} w_{jk}}} \tag{11}$$

and will depend heavily on the number of items and the value of w_{jk},[4] the average of $\mu_{ijk}(1 - \mu_{ijk})$ within face-block jk. Here n_{jk} is the number of items assessed in that face-block.

---

[4]Equation (11) gives an internal consistency measure for discriminating among face-blocks in different NCs. An internal consistency measure for discriminating among face-blocks within the same NC is

$$\lambda_{\text{within } pjk} = \frac{\tau_{pp}}{\tau_{pp} + \dfrac{1}{n_{jk} w_{jk}}}.$$

Interscale Correlation. Of obvious interest is the correlation between physical and social disorder. This correlation can be estimated at the NC or face-block level. At the NC level, we have

$$\text{Corr}(\beta_{pk}, \beta_{sk}) = \frac{\omega_{ps}}{(\omega_{pp} + \omega_{ss})^{1/2}} \qquad (12)$$

while at the face-block level we have

$$\text{Corr}(\pi_{pjk}, \pi_{sjk}) = \frac{\tau_{ps} + \omega_{ps}}{[(\tau_{pp} + \omega_{pp}) * (\tau_{ss} + \omega_{ss})]^{1/2}} \ . \qquad (13)$$

We illustrate application of these ideas in the next section.

5. RESULTS

Tables 3–6 provide the model fitting results. The two scales behave quite differently, as expected.

5.1. *Item Severity*

In Table 3 items with negative coefficients have low probabilities of occurrence and thus are rarer and, presumably, more "difficult" or "severe" than are items with positive coefficients. Thus, in the physical disorder scale, the presence of cigarettes or cigars and garbage on the street or sidewalk, along with the presence of empty beer bottles, are comparatively less severe than the presence of gang graffiti, abandoned cars, condoms, or drug paraphernalia (needles and syringes). Thus item severity conforms to intuitive expectations. The exception is political graffiti, which is exceptionally rare yet not generally regarded as especially severe. A nice feature of the physical disorder scale is that the item severities vary substantially, a feature of a "well-behaved" scale.

In contrast, all of the severities in the social disorder scale are clumped at the severe end except for the item indicating adults loitering or congregating. This pattern reflects the low frequency of the social disorder indicators apparent in Table 2 and discussed earlier. Although the item severities are not well separated, their ordering does correspond to theoretical expectation, with adults loitering and drinking alcohol being less severe than adults fighting, prostitution, or drug sales.

TABLE 3
Model Fitting Results: Item Difficulty at Face-Block Level

Item	Coefficient	SE
Physical Disorder		
Intercept	−2.215	0.225
Cigarettes, cigars on street or gutter	3.456	0.032
Garbage, litter on street or sidewalk	2.431	0.031
Empty beer bottles visible in street	1.126	0.032
Tagging graffiti	0.338	0.036
Graffiti painted over	(0)	(reference item)
Gang graffiti	−0.667	0.043
Abandoned cars	−1.297	0.046
Condoms on sidewalk	−2.569	0.071
Needles/syringes on sidewalk	−2.893	0.082
Political message graffiti	−5.028	0.269
Social Disorder		
Intercept	−7.017	(0.153)
Adults loitering or congregating	3.884	(0.227)
People drinking alcohol	0.590	(0.280)
Peer group, gang indicators present	(0)	(reference item)
People intoxicated	−0.106	(0.325)
Adults fighting or hostilely arguing	−0.512	(0.366)
Prostitutes on street	−0.599	(0.376)
People selling drugs	−0.696	(0.388)

5.2. Scale Construction

The item maps are displayed graphically in Figures 2 and 3. The horizontal axis gives scale scores and the vertical axis gives the frequency of NC's. The figures include the list of items that compose the scale; distances between items represent differences in item difficulty. Note the spread of item difficulties in the case of physical disorder (Figure 2) and the clumping in the case of social disorder (Figure 3). NC scale scores are in the same metric as are item severities, and the figure suggests that these are nearly unimodal and symmetric in distribution. Note that this "nice distribution" is defined on the logit scale on which the NC scores are measured. Indeed, the construction of such a scale is a key goal of the item response analysis. Differences between NCs in their disorder scores can be interpreted unambiguously as expected differences in the log-odds of finding disorder on a typical item in the scale. The resulting scale is thus mean-

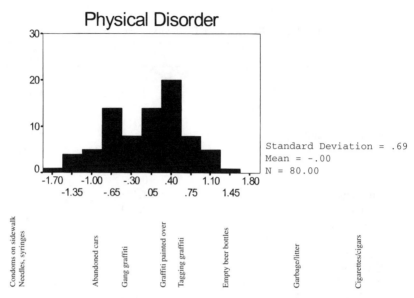

FIGURE 2. Item map for physical disorder.

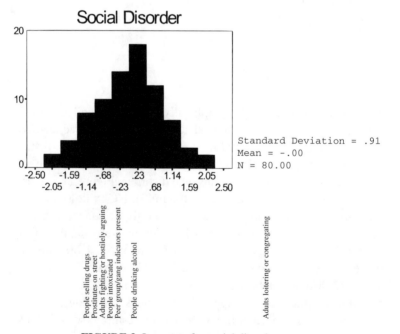

FIGURE 3. Item map for social disorder.

ingfully interpretable and arguably a linear (interval) scale appropriate for analysis via standard linear models (Rasch 1980; Wright and Masters 1982; Lord 1980).

5.3. *Time of Day*

Table 4 provides estimates of the effects of time of day. One would expect social interactions in public view to occur with relatively little frequency early in the morning and more frequently later on. This would presumably be true of those social interactions indicative of disorder as well, and that is what the results show. Note that there is a near linear positive trend in time for social disorder with coefficients of (-0.766, -0.715, -0.363, -0.057, -0.134, and 0.000) as the day progresses. No such trend is apparent in the case of physical disorder. All other model estimates are adjusted for any time-of-day effects.

5.4. *Variance-Covariance Components and Related Quantities*: *Physical Disorders*

Estimation of the variance-covariance components (Table 5) provides the necessary data to compute useful indicators of data quality (Table 6). For

TABLE 4
Model Fitting Results: Time-of-Day Effects at NC Level (N = 80)

Item	Coefficient	SE
Physical Disorder		
7:00–8:59	0.213	0.043
9:00–10:59	0.036	0.031
11:00–12:59	0.057	0.036
1:00–2:59	0.073	0.040
3:00–4:59	0.020	0.033
5:00–6:59	(0)	(reference time)
Social Disorder		
7:00–8:59	−0.766	0.180
9:00–10:59	−0.715	0.115
11:00–12:59	−0.363	0.137
1:00–2:59	−0.057	0.129
3:00–4:59	−0.134	0.107
5:00–6:59	(0)	(reference time)

TABLE 5
Model Fitting Results: Variance-Covariance Components

	Variance-Covariance Component	Estimate	SE
(a) Between face-blocks within NCs	Variance of physical disorder	0.734	0.019
	Variance of social disorder[a]	—	—
	Covariance[b]	—	—
(b) Between NCs	Variance of physical disorder	0.475	0.076
	Variance of social disorder	0.981	0.184
	Covariance	0.394	0.096

[a,b]Variance and covariance were constrained to zero.

physical disorder, the estimated variance between face-blocks is 0.734, while the estimated variance between NCs is 0.475. Thus the estimated ICC for physical disorder (see equation (9) and note 3) is 0.475/(0.475 + 0.734) = 0.39. Thus about 39 percent of the variation in the physical disorder of face-blocks is estimated to be between NCs. This fact, when combined with the typical frequency of "yes" responses (Table 2) and the large number of face-blocks per NC (equation 10), yields a high average reliability of 0.98 (Table 6) at the NC level. Thus the data enable us to distinguish among NCs with high reliability. The reliability for distinguishing among face-blocks within NCs is estimated to be much lower, at 0.36. This reflects the dependence of the reliability at the face-block level on the number of items. More items would be required to increase this reliability.

TABLE 6
Some Measurement Properties

Property	Physical Disorder	Social Disorder
Intra-NC correlations	.39	—
Between NC reliability (average)	.98	.84
Between face-block reliability (average)	.36	—

Level	Correlation
Inter-scale Correlation at NC Level	.58

5.5. *Variance-Covariance Components and Related Quantities*: *Social Disorder*

The social disorder scale behaves quite differently. The point estimate of the variance within NCs for social disorder is zero. This result does not imply that face-blocks within NCs are homogeneous. Rather, the result appears to reflect the extreme rarity of "yes" responses of most social disorder items (Table 2). The data simply are too sparse at the face-block level to facilitate stable estimation of variance between face-blocks within NCs. Yet the variation between NCs is quite substantial ($\hat{\omega}_{ss} = 0.981$), leading to a respectable NC-level reliability estimate of 0.84. Although the frequency of indicators of social disorder is rare at the face-block level, when we aggregate over the many face-blocks within an NC, we are able to achieve a respectable between-NC reliability.

5.6. *Implications for Research Design*

Applying the logic of generalizability analysis, we can use our data to inform the design of new research. Figure 4 plots the expected NC-level reliability of the two scales as a function of the number of face-blocks

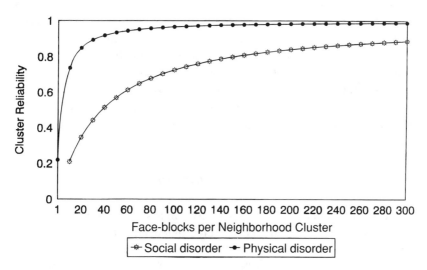

FIGURE 4. NC reliability as a function of face-blocks sampled (holding constant the number of items).

sampled. For physical disorder, there appears to be little point in sampling more than 80 to 100 face-blocks per NC if the sole aim is to obtain reasonable NC reliability. The same is not true for social disorder. More face-blocks are required for adequate reliability in measuring social disorder (as compared to physical disorder).

Physical disorder results provide good news for the next analyses of the PHDCN data. It is clear that physical disorder can be reliably measured at much lower levels of aggregation than the NC. Thus it is feasible to construct physical disorder measures at the level of the block group or census tract,[5] creating a measure that is more proximal geographically to the longitudinal cohort subjects of PHDCN than is the NC. Our results are less encouraging about the measurement of social disorder at lower levels of aggregation because of the low frequency of "yes" responses on most social disorder items.

5.7. Dimensionality

The correlation between physical disorder and social disorder is estimated to be .58 (Table 6). This is the estimated correlation of the two latent variables and is therefore automatically adjusted for measurement error in each. The implication is that physical and social disorder as conceived here are quite strongly related, although not so strongly as to be viewed as a single dimension. There is reason to pursue sound measures of each construct separately. This aspect of the analysis has parallels with confirmatory factor analysis. Here we have hypothesized multiple indicators for each of two traits. The data suggest that the two traits are highly related, but not entirely confounded. In a typical confirmatory factor analysis, factor loadings would vary while the variance of latent traits would be constrained. Here we impose equal loadings while allowing latent trait variances to vary.

5.8. Convergent and Divergent Validity

Key tests of validity of measurement involve assessing correlations with theoretically related constructs measured independently. Convergent va-

---

[5]Indeed, subsequent analysis showed that the reliabilities of the physical disorder at the census tract level were nearly identical to those at the level of the NC even though there are two to three tracts per NC.

lidity implies that theoretically linked measures ought to correlate highly. Divergent validity implies that correlations should be smaller with variables that are not clearly linked theoretically. Table 7 gives some evidence about physical and social disorder.

Observed physical disorder is correlated highly with those constructs measured in both the community survey (described earlier) and independent sources (census data, official police records) most theoretically linked to it. Thus we see that a substantial correlation of $r = .71$ emerges with perceptions of social disorder as measured in the community survey. SSO physical disorder also has a moderately strong correlation with the survey measures of social cohesion and social control ($r = -.62$ and $r = -.55$, respectively), in the direction expected. Further tests not shown indicate that physical disorder also correlates less strongly with those survey-derived constructs for which it has a weaker theoretical connection (e.g., anonymity, intergenerational ties, organizational density).

Turning next to construct validation with other independent sources, physical disorder is strongly related to census measures of concentrated poverty ($r = .64$), and less strongly with residential stability ($r = -.25$) and immigrant concentration ($r = .36$; see Sampson et al. 1997 for further details of these census-based factors). As expected, the observed physical disorder is significantly higher in neighborhoods characterized by poverty and instability, and in areas undergoing ethnic transition. Furthermore,

TABLE 7

Correlations of Systematic Social Observation Scales with Theoretically Related Variables from the U.S. Census and Community Survey

	SSO: Physical Disorder	Social Disorder
I. Community Survey		
Social disorder	.71	.65
Social cohesion	-.62	-.55
Social control	-.55	-.56
II. U.S. Census		
Concentrated poverty	.64	.54
Residential stability	-.25	-.34
Immigrant concentration	.36	.21
III. Violence and Crime		
Perceived violence	.54	.59
Crime victimization	.32	.33

physical disorder measured in the SSO is positively and significantly correlated with survey perceptions of violence ($r = .54$) and aggregated reports of victimization ($r = .32$). These patterns conform to extant theory on urban disorder and crime (Skogan 1990; Taylor et al. 1985; Sampson and Groves 1989; Taub et al. 1984).

A similar pattern of correlations appears with respect to social disorder. In some cases the magnitude of correlations is a bit smaller than those involving physical disorder, which may reflect the less sanguine behavior of the social disorder scale. Nonetheless, the SSO measure of social disorder has quite robust relationships with theoretically linked constructs—again whether derived from the neighborhood survey or census. Taken together, then, the multiple sources of data provide independent evidence of both the convergent and divergent validity of SSO measures of disorder.

6. FINAL REMARKS

As interest in the social sciences turns increasingly to the integration of individual, family, and neighborhood processes, a potential mismatch arises in the quality of measures. Standing behind individual measurement are decades of psychometric research, producing measures that often have excellent statistical properties. In contrast, much less is known about measures of ecological settings such as neighborhoods and schools, and the methodology needed to evaluate these measures is in its infancy. The aim of this paper has been to move toward a science of ecological assessment by integrating and adapting tools from psychometrics to improve the quality of "ecometric" measures. We have used systematic social observation (Reiss 1971; 1975) linked to neighborhood surveys as a case study in this effort. The SSO is an especially important case, given the potential utility of videotaping as an observational strategy in the study of neighborhoods and other collectivities.

The two measures selected—physical and social disorder—behaved sufficiently differently statistically to be useful in clarifying how ideas from item response modeling, generalizability theory, and confirmatory factor analysis can be integrated to better understand the process of measuring ecological units. In the future, we plan to construct additional scales from the systematic social observation data, including land use, housing quality, traffic, advertising of tobacco and alcohol, recreational opportunities, and type of commercial district. The approaches described here can be used to evaluate the quality of measures and to build improved scales for use in the study of neighborhoods and human development. A crucial question is the causal link between crime and disorder, which is being addressed elsewhere (Sampson and Raudenbush forthcoming).

While our ecometric analysis borrows from standard psychometric techniques, it also integrates and otherwise extends them. Thus our random effects item response model is embedded in a three-level hierarchical regression model, enabling estimation of time-of-day effects and of variability within and between face-blocks. In this way, the item response analysis is formally incorporated into a generalizability analysis. Moreover, at the second level (between face-blocks) and third level (between NCs), we estimate the variance and covariance of the two latent variables (physical and social disorder), thus constructing a simple but multilevel confirmatory factor analysis. The resulting three-level hierarchical logistic regression model allows for randomly missing data at the level of items and uses all available information, even from those face-blocks having zero incidence on all disorder indicators.

The logic of ecological assessment and resulting multilevel error structure will generally prescribe such combinations and extensions of standard psychometric techniques. Thus a natural model for survey-based measures of settings (neighborhoods or schools) would have an ordinal response model at level 1 (between items within respondents) and would add two higher levels of variation: between respondents within settings and between settings. Such a model would be a three-level ordinal regression model.

Another extension to the approach sketched here would be to take into account spatial autocorrelation. In this paper, neighborhood clusters have been treated as independent.[6] Ongoing work will build spatial associations into the models presented here. We expect information about spatial dependence to reduce standard errors of measurement, possibly substantially, and to make it possible to obtain reasonable measures of neighborhood ecology even for persons residing in areas sparsely assessed by direct observation. In the meantime, the results of the present analysis suggest that the survey and SSO approaches have considerable promise for the reliable and valid assessment of neighborhood-level social processes.

[6]This assumption is not entirely implausible in the case of the SSO, which involves a probability sample of 80 NCs from among 343 NCs in Chicago. Many of the sample NCs are not contiguous to other sample NCs. Nevertheless, a more complete treatment would model spatial dependence between NCs.

APPENDIX A

Estimation by Penalized Quasi-likelihood "PQL" has several advantages. First, computations are fast, an important consideration for the data in this article, with 23,816 level-2 units and over 300,000 level-1 responses. Second, convergence is remarkably reliable, even when the probability of success is close to zero (Yang 1998). Third, the methodology is currently widely accessible.[7] However, Breslow and Lin (1995) have found that PQL can produce variance components estimates that are substantially negatively biased when the true variance component is large. PQL is based on a linearization of the model—that is, a Taylor-series expansion of μ_{ijk} in equation (6) around the approximate posterior modes of the random effects. An alternative approach, which Breslow and Clayton (1993) have termed MQL, expands μ_{ijk} around 0—that is, in a MacLaurin series for the random effects, produces even greater bias (see Rodriguez and Goldman 1995). The asymptotic bias is eliminated when the model is estimated by maximum likelihood (ML) or by Bayesian methods. These approaches, however, require difficult integrations: the random effects must be integrated to evaluate the likelihood. Hedeker and Gibbons (1994) developed excellent approximations to ML estimates in the case of two levels by using Gauss-Hermite quadrature for numerical integration. Gibbons and Hedeker (1997) extended this approach to three-level models with a single random effect at level 3. Raudenbush and Yang (1998) developed a high-order LaPlace approximation to the integral that produced results comparable to those with quadrature based on 20-30 quadrature points (generally regarded as a large number of points and therefore yielding a good approximation to the likelihood). The LaPlace approach is computationally remarkably efficient. These results are based on Yang's (1998) dissertation. Bayesian estimation can be implemented by the Gibbs sampler (Zeger and Karim 1991) and is implemented in the most recent version of MLWiN (Goldstein et al.1998). The Bayesian approach provides perhaps the most elegant solution, in that all inferences fully take into account the uncertainty about the variance components. However, this solution appears infeasible computationally given the size of the data set at hand and the complexity of the model.

To conduct an analysis of the sensitivity of results arising from bias associated with PQL, we settled on the higher-order LaPlace strategy. The

[7]For example, programs HLM, MLWin (Goldstein et al. 1998), and Proc Mixed (Littel et al. 1996) provide PQL or closely related estimation algorithms.

general theory, with application to binary response data, is described in detail by Raudenbush and Yang (1998). The task is first to integrate the random effects from the joint density of the data and random effects, in effect, a binomial-normal mixture. The integrand is represented by a sixth-order Taylor series expansion around the maximizer of this joint density. The integral then can be seen as equivalent to the expectation taken over a multivariate normal distribution of the third-order and higher-order terms. It is therefore possible to evaluate the integral and maximize it using a Fisher-scoring algorithm.

A comparison of results from PQL and the sixth-order LaPlace ("LaPlace 6"), yielded the results shown in Table A.1.

We conclude from these results that estimates of item difficulty and time-of-day effects are essentially insensitive to choice of estimation procedure. (Note that the magnitudes of the estimated time-of-day effects are a bit larger under LaPlace 6, as expected given the bias toward zero of PQL estimates.) Inferences about the ecometric properties of the physical disorder scale are also insensitive (ICC of 0.39 versus 0.32 for LaPlace 6, reliability of 0.98 for both PQL and LaPlace 6). And the interscale correlation estimates are similar, 0.58 versus 0.52. Inferences about ecometric properties of the social disorder scale are more sensitive (reliability of 0.84 for PQL versus 0.70 for LaPlace 6). LaPlace standard errors are generally somewhat smaller for physical disorder items and larger for social disorder items than are the corresponding PQL standard errors. While we are cautiously optimistic that PQL will produce reasonable inferences about ecometric properties, we expect that much better approximations to likelihood-based inference will rapidly become available to researchers over the next couple of years. We recommend use of these better approximations as they become available.[8]

APPENDIX B

To construct the reliability of NC measures, suppose we conceive the level-1 model (equation 3) as a generalized linear model. In matrix notation, we have

$$\eta_{jk} = D_{jk}\pi_{jk} + X_{jk}\alpha \ , \tag{B1}$$

---

[8]The LaPlace 6 algorithm used in computing this sensitivity analysis is available upon request from the first author (rauden@umich.edu).

TABLE A.1
Sensitivity Analysis Based on Alternative Estimation Approach

	PQL Point Estimates (standard errors)	LaPlace 6 Point Estimates (standard errors)
Item Difficulties: Physical Disorder		
Intercept	−2.215	−2.044
	(0.225)	(0.313)
Cigarettes, cigars	3.456	3.689
	(0.032)	(0.018)
Garbage, litter	2.431	2.541
	(0.031)	(0.015)
Empty beer bottles	1.126	1.097
	(0.032)	(0.014)
Tagging graffiti	0.338	0.432
	(0.036)	(0.020)
Gang graffiti	−0.667	−0.663
	(0.043)	(0.022)
Abandoned cars	−1.297	−1.346
	(0.046)	(0.024)
Condoms	−2.569	−2.816
	(0.071)	(0.053)
Needles/syringes	−2.893	−3.028
	(0.082)	(0.076)
Political graffiti	−5.028	−4.823
	(0.269)	(0.299)
Item Difficulties: Social Disorder		
Intercept	−7.017	−7.156
	(0.153)	(0.124)
Adults loitering	3.884	3.968
	(0.227)	(0.272)
People drinking alcohol	0.590	0.996
	(0.280)	(0.382)
People intoxicated	−0.106	0.386
	(0.325)	(0.392)
Adults fighting, arguing	−0.512	0.147
	(0.366)	(0.527)
Prostitutes	−0.599	0.126
	(0.376)	(0.400)
Selling drugs	−0.696	−0.106
	(0.388)	(0.505)
Time of Day: Physical Disorder		
7:00–8:59	0.213	0.298
	(0.043)	(0.032)

(*Table continues*)

TABLE A.1
Continued.

	PQL Point Estimates (standard errors)	LaPlace 6 Point Estimates (standard errors)
Time of Day: Physical Disorder (Continued)		
9:00–10:59	0.036	0.082
	(0.031)	(0.019)
11:00–12:59	0.057	0.055
	(0.036)	(0.021)
1:00–2:59	0.073	0.141
	(0.040)	(0.025)
3:00–4:59	0.020	0.039
	(0.033)	(0.020)
Time of Day: Social Disorder		
7:00–8:59	−0.766	−1.066
	(0.180)	(0.173)
9:00–10:59	−0.715	−0.923
	(0.115)	(0.091)
11:00–12:59	−0.363	−0.314
	(0.137)	(0.116)
1:00–2:59	−0.057	−0.091
	(0.129)	(0.110)
3:00–4:59	−0.134	−0.121
	(0.107)	(0.101)
Variance-Covariance Components		
$\hat{\tau}_{pp}$	0.734	1.070
$\hat{\tau}_{ss}$	0	0
$\hat{\tau}_{ps}$	0	0
$\hat{\omega}_{pp}$	0.475	0.500
$\hat{\omega}_{ss}$	0.981	0.515
$\hat{\omega}_{ps}$	0.394	0.266
Corr (β_s, β_p)	0.58	0.52
ICC physical	0.39	0.32
NC Reliab physical	0.98	0.98
NC Reliab social	0.84	0.70

where η_{jk} is the n_{jk} by 1 vector consisting of elements η_{ijk}, D_{jk} is an n_{jk} by 2 matrix of indicators (the first column for physical disorder, the second column for social disorder), π_{jk} is a 2 by 1 vector of coefficients; X_{jk} is the n_{jk} by 15 matrix of dummy variables for items; and α is the 15 by 1 vector of item difficulties (assumed equal across all NCs and assumed known). Then, applying maximum-likelihood estimation via iteratively reweighted least squares, we find the approximate variance-covariance matrix of estimates $\hat{\pi}_{jk}$ (McCullagh and Nelder 1989:119, eq. 4.18) to be

$$V_{jk} = \text{Var}(\hat{\pi}_{jk}) = (D_{jk}^T W_{jk} D_{jk})^{-1} \ , \tag{B2}$$

where W_{jk} is a diagonal n_{jk} by n_{jk} matrix with entries $\mu_{ijk}(1 - \mu_{ijk})$. Given the structure of D_{jk} and the diagonal nature of W_{jk}, it is easy to see that V_{jk} is a 2 by 2 matrix with diagonal entries $1/(n_{pjk}w_{pjk})$ and $1/(n_{sjk}w_{sjk})$, with n_{pjk} being the number of physical disorder items assessed in face-block jk, n_{sjk} being the number of social disorder items in that face-block, w_{pjk} the average value of $\mu_{ijk}(1 - \mu_{ijk})$ for the physical disorder items in face-block jk and w_{sjk} the average value of $\mu_{ijk}(1 - \mu_{ijk})$ for social disorder items. Next, we reformulate equation (4) as

$$\hat{\pi}_{jk} = \beta_k + T_{jk}\theta + u_{jk} + (\hat{\pi}_{jk} - \pi_{jk}) \ , \tag{B3}$$

where $\beta_k = (\beta_{pk}, \beta_{sk})^T$, $u_{jk} = (u_{pjk}, u_{sjk})^T$, T_{jk} is a 2 by 10 matrix of time-of-day indicators, and θ is a 10 by 1 vector of time-of-day effects, assumed known. Here $u_{jk} \sim N(0, \tau)$. Generalized least squares estimation of β_k then yields the variance-covariance matrix

$$\text{Var}(\hat{\beta}_k) = \left[\sum_{j=1}^{J_k} (\tau + V_{jk})^{-1} \right]^{-1} \ .$$

When $V_{jk} = V_k$ for all j, we have

$$\text{Var}(\hat{\beta}_k) = J^{-1}(\tau + V_k)$$

with the first diagonal equal to the sum of the second and third terms of the denominator of equation (10). That equation thus represents an approximation that will be accurate when $V_{jk} = V_k$ for all j. Our results, however, are based on the estimated generalized least squares estimates for each NC, not on this approximation. The approximation is primarily useful in revealing the structure of measurement error in the three-level setting.

REFERENCES

Brennan, R., and M. Kane. 1979. "Generalizability Theory: A Review." Pp. 33–51 in *New Directions for Testing and Measurement: Methodological Developments* edited by R. Traub. San Francisco, CA: Jossey-Bass.

Breslow, N., and D. G. Clayton. 1993. "Approximate Inference in Generalized Linear Mixed Models." *Journal of the American Statistical Association* 88:9–25.

Breslow, N. E. and X. Lin. 1995. "Bias Correction in Generalized Linear Mixed Models with a Single Component of Dispersion." *Biometrika* 82:81–91.

Brooks-Gunn, Jeanne, Greg Duncan, and Lawrence Aber, eds. 1997. *Consequences of Growing up Poor*, Vol. 1. New York: Russell Sage Foundation.

Bryk, A., S. Raudenbush, R. Congdon, and M. Seltzer. 1996. *HLM: Hierarchical Linear and Nonlinear Modeling with the HLM/2L and HLM/3L Programs*. Chicago, IL: Scientific Software International.

Carter, Woody, Jody Dougherty, and Karen Grigorian. 1996. "Videotaping Neighborhoods." National Opinion Research Center, University of Chicago, Working Paper.

Cook, T., S. Shagle, and Degirmencioglu. 1997. "Capturing Social Process for Testing Mediational Models of Neighborhood Effects." Pp. 94–119 in *Neighborhood Poverty: Policy Implications in Studying Neighborhoods*, Vol. 2, edited by J. Brooks-Gunn, G. J. Duncan, and L. Aber. New York: Russell Sage Foundation.

Covington, J., and R. B. Taylor. 1991. "Fear of Crime in Urban Residential Neighborhoods: Implications of Between- and Within-Neighborhood Sources for Current Models." *The Sociological Quarterly* 32:231–49.

Cronbach, L., G. Gleser, N. Harinder, and N. Rajaratnam. 1972. *The Dependability of Behavioral Measurements: Theory of Generalizability for Scores and Profiles*. New York: Wiley.

Duncan, Greg, and Stephen Raudenbush. 1997. "Getting Context Right in Quantitative Studies of Child Development." Presented at the conference, "Research Ideas and Data Needs for Studying the Well-being of Children and Families," October.

Elliott, Delbert, William Julius Wilson, David Huizinga, Robert J. Sampson, Amanda Elliott, and Bruce Rankin. 1996. "Effects of Neighborhood Disadvantage on Adolescent Development." *Journal of Research in Crime and Delinquency* 33:389–426.

Gibbons, Robert D., and Donald Hedeker. 1997. "Random Effects Probit and Logistic Regression Models for Three-Level Data." *Biometrics* 53:1527–37.

Goldstein, Harvey, Jon Rashbash, Ian Plewis, David Draper, William Browne, Min Yan, Geoff Woodhouse, and Michael Healy. 1998. *A User's Guide to MLwiN*. London: University of London, Institute of Education.

Hedeker, D., and R. D. Gibbons. 1994. "A Random Effects Ordinal Regression Model for Multilevel Analysis." *Biometrics* 50:933–44.

Joreskog, K., and D. Sorbom. 1988. *LISREL 7: A Guide to the Program and Applications*. Chicago, IL: Statistical Package for the Social Sciences.

Littel, R. C., G. A. Millilen, W. W. Strong, and R. D. Wolfinger. 1996. *SAS System for Mixed Models*. Cary, NC: SAS Institute.

Lord, F. M. 1980. *Applications of Item Response Theory to Practical Testing Problems*. Hillsdale, NJ: Lawrence Erlbaum.

Mayer, Susan E., and Christopher Jencks. 1989. "Growing up in Poor Neighborhoods: How Much Does It Matter? *Science* 243:1441–45.

McCullagh, P., and J. A. Nelder. 1989. *Generalized Linear Models*, 2d ed. London: Chapman and Hall.

Muthen, B. 1991. "Multilevel Factor Analysis of Class and Student Achievement Components. *Journal of Educational Measurement* 28:338–54.

———. 1997. "Longitudinal and Multilevel Modeling: Latent Variable Modeling of Longitudinal and Multilevel Data." Pp. 453–80 in *Sociological Methodology 1997*, edited by Adrian Raftery. Cambridge, MA: Blackwell Publishers.

National Opinion Research Center (NORC). 1995. PHDCN Project 4709. Systematic Social Observation Coding Manual, June 1995. NORC/University of Chicago.

Pallas, A. 1988. "School Climate in American High Schools." *Teachers College Record* 89:541–53.

Rasch, G. 1980. *Probabilistic Models for Some Intelligence and Attainment Tests.* Chicago, IL: University of Chicago.

Raudenbush, S. W. 1995. "Hierarchical Linear Models to Study the Effects of Social Context on Development." Pp. 165–201 in *The Analysis of Change,* edited by J. Gottman. Hillsdale, NJ: Lawrence Erlbaum.

Raudenbush, S., and R. J. Sampson. Forthcoming. "Assessing Direct and Indirect Associations in Multilevel Designs with Latent Variables." *Sociological Methods and Research.*

Raudenbush, S., B. Rowan, and S. Kang. 1991. "A Multilevel, Multivariate Model for Studying School Climate in Secondary Schools with Estimation via the EM Algorithm. *Journal of Educational Statistics* 16:295–330.

Raudenbush, S. W., and Meng-Li Yang. 1998. "Maximum Likelihood for Hierarchical Models via High-Order, Multivariate LaPlace Approximation." Paper submitted to the *Journal of Computational and Graphical Statistics.*

Reiss, A. J., Jr., 1971. "Systematic Observations of Natural Social Phenomena." Pp. 3–33 in *Sociological Methodology 1971,* edited by H. Costner. San Francisco: Jossey-Bass.

———. 1975. "Systematic Observation Surveys of Natural Social Phenomena." Pp. 132–50 in *Perspectives on Attitude Assessment: Surveys and their Alternatives.* NTIS.

Rodriguez, G., and N. Goldman. 1995. "An Assessment of Estimation Procedures for Multilevel Models with Binary Responses." *Journal of The Royal Statistical Society, Series A* 56:73–89.

Sampson, R., and W. Groves. 1989. "Community Structure and Crime: Testing Social-Disorganization Theory." *American Journal of Sociology* 94:774–802.

Sampson, R., and S. Raudenbush. (Forthcoming). "Systematic Social Observations of Public Spaces: A New Look at Neighborhood Disorder." To appear in *American Journal of Sociology.*

Sampson, R., S. Raudenbush, and F. Earls. 1997. "Neighborhoods and Violent Crime: A Multilevel Study of Collective Efficacy." *Science* 277:918–24.

Sirotnik, K. 1980. "Psychometric Implications of the Unit-of-Analysis Problem (with Examples from the Measurement of Organizational Climate)." *Journal of Educational Measurement* 17:245–82.

Skogan, W. 1990. *Disorder and Decline: Crime and the Spiral of Decay in American Neighborhoods.* Berkeley: University of California Press.

Taub, Richard, D. Garth Taylor, and Jan Dunham. 1984. *Paths of Neighborhood Change: Race and Crime in Urban America.* Chicago: University of Chicago Press.

Taylor, R. B., S. D. Gottfredson, and S. Brower. 1984. "Block Crime and Fear: Defensible Space, Local Social Ties, and Territorial Functioning." *Journal of Research in Crime and Delinquency* 21:303–31.

Taylor, R. B., S. Shumaker, and S. D. Gottfredson. 1985. "Neighborhood-Level Links Between Physical Features and Local Sentiments: Deterioration, Fear of Crime, and Confidence." *Journal of Architectural Planning and Research* 21:261–75.

Wright, B., and G. Masters. 1982. *Rating Scale Analysis: Rasch Measurement*. Chicago, IL: MESA Press.

Wright, B., and M. Stone. 1979. *Best Test Design: Rasch Measurement*. Chicago, IL: MESA Press.

Yang, Meng-Li. 1998. "Increasing the Efficiency in Estimating Multilevel Bernoulli Models." Ph. D. dissertation, Michigan State University, East Lansing.

Zeger, S. L., and M. R. Karim. 1991. "Generalized Linear Models with Random Effects: A Gibbs Sampling Approach." *Journal of the American Statistical Association* 86:79–86.

𝕩 2 𝕩

SIMULATING THE MICRO-MACRO LINK: NEW APPROACHES TO AN OLD PROBLEM AND AN APPLICATION TO MILITARY COUPS

Nicole J. Saam*

The central issue of this paper is that one can develop emergent macro-dynamics from micro agent models and that the resulting models fall very much in the complexity-chaos line of the development of theory. The core theoretical contribution is a presentation of a clear, sensical, and potentially very powerful architecture for developing algorithms for the embedding of levels—the so-called master equation approach—and its comparison with alternative architectures. Finally, to illustrate the strategy and to demonstrate that the approach produces interesting and useful results, we give an application: a multilevel simulation model of military coups d'état, which is tested using data from Thailand between 1932 and 1992.

In the last decade many advances have been made in the analysis of multilevel systems. Multilevel analysis methods (Hox and Kreft 1994; DiPrete and Forristal 1994) introduced a powerful new approach for analyzing relationships between several observed levels, and modeling and simulation approaches have addressed the construction of multilevel sociological theories (Markovsky 1987). Research in the mathematical theory of nonlinear dynamical systems has produced some new algo-

This paper was significantly improved by the comments of Josef Brüderl, Randall Collins, and Klaus G. Troitzsch. I would also like to thank the anonymous reviewers for their stimulating observations on earlier drafts.
*University of Munich, Germany

rithms that are capable of modeling multilevel systems. One major problem in the application of these algorithms in the social sciences, however, is the respecification of their variables and operations in sociological terms. For example, aggregation is a typical operation in equations. The formal use of aggregations in algorithms need not imply aggregation as an operation or mechanism in the model social system. This problem is not familiar to the physicists who were the first to suggest the application of these algorithms in the social sciences (e.g., Weidlich and Haag 1983, 1988; Weidlich 1991).

This paper presents one of these algorithms as a new approach to the micro-macro link: the so-called master equation.[1] We attempt a sociological respecification of this clear, sensical, and potentially very powerful multilevel algorithm and compare it with other formal approaches to the micro-macro problem. From our modeling and simulation approach, we expect the following contributions to research in the micro-macro link: By "doing theory" (Hanneman 1988:10; Collins 1988:516), computer simulations foster micro-macro theory development; we construct, state, and analyze a sociologically respecified version of the master equation. Simulation reveals the dynamic character of the micro-macro problem: We show how the individuals on the micro level produce outcomes on the macro level that influence the individual's actions during the next time step. The obtained dynamic pattern on the macro level shows an enormous variety resembling historical pathways, and falls in the complexity-chaos line of theory development. Simulations reformulate the question of emergence in more specific and empirically relevant terms (Conte and Gilbert 1995:2). In the simulation model we develop emergent macrodynamics from the behavior of the micro agents. We are able to specify what kind of emergent effects may or may not be produced by simulations. Simulations expose micro-macro theories to thorough tests: An application of this is a multilevel simulation model of military coups d'état, which is tested using empirical data from Thailand between 1932 and 1992. In sum, it is the objective of this paper to demonstrate the facilities that multilevel simulation has to offer to advance micro-macro theories.

---

[1]This term was introduced by German physicists. In a socio-historical context, it evokes several negative associations: the master-slave relationship and suppression of men and women; in a mathematical context, it suggests the dominance of the master equation on slave equations; at this point I can only regret the insensitive choice of wording; I shall go on using this term only to make clear that the algorithm has been developed by others. I welcome suggestions to rename the algorithm.

    Section 1 works out preconditions for micro-macro simulation. Section 2 presents the master equation approach and compares its aggregation approach with other formal models of attitude formation and the sociological notions of the aggregation approach to those of other formalized multi-level models. Section 3 outlines an application of the master equation that exemplifies micro-macro theory construction by way of computer simulation. We present a multilevel model of military coups d'état, which was tested using data from Thailand between 1932 and 1992. With reference to this application, Section 4 discusses the contribution that our simulation approach can make to the advancement of micro-macro sociological theory in general.

1. INTRODUCTION

1.1. *The Micro-Macro Problem*

It is the main task of sociology to explain how social behavior and society are socially determined. Whether we try to explain marriages, military coups d'état, or the results of the last national election, we will always have to refer to collective phenomena and to individuals. Collective phenomena such as norms, the distribution of power, or public opinion are essential to the explanation of the behavior of bride and bridegroom, military officers, or voters, just as individual behavior explains the existence and shape of norms, power distributions, and election results. What seems so obvious is by no means uncontroversial among sociologists. It is not uncommon to explain increasing divorce rates by the growing individualization of Western societies, military coups by the lack of political institutionalization, and election outcomes by declining economic growth rates. However, as only individuals are able to marry each other, stage a coup, or go to the polls, sooner or later any debate shifts to the relation between both levels. Micro and macro level are identified and, depending on the theoretical position of the disputants, the micro-macro problem is outlined. The basic problem is to explain how individuals affect collectivities and how collectivities affect individuals over time. We cannot go into detail here. The reader may refer to Wiley (1988) for a short overview of the micro-macro problem in social theory; to Collins (1988:375–410), who briefly compares the positions of Coleman and Berger and Luckmann, among others; to Collins (1981), Cicourel (1981), Callon and Latour (1981), Giddens (1984), Archer (1988), and Turner (1988), who have presented micro-macro theories; and to Huber (1991) and Alexander et al. (1987), who have assembled the major participants in the present discussion. Not surprisingly, there is no consensus on a definition of micro and macro phenomena and on the connecting link between micro and macro: Alexander and Giesen (1987:14) outline five major approaches to the micro-macro relation:

1. Rational, purposeful individuals create society through contingent acts of freedom.
2. Interpretive individuals create society through contingent acts of freedom.
3. Socialized individuals recreate society as a collective force through contingent acts of freedom.
4. Socialized individuals reproduce society by translating the existing social environment into the microrealm.
5. Rational, purposeful individuals acquiesce to society because they are forced to by external, social control.

Münch and Smelser (1987:376–85) have found five modes of moving from the micro to the macro: mere aggregation (neoclassical economics, Durkheim), the combination of microinteractions with other factors (a more complicated version of aggregation, Coleman, Weber), externalization (Freud), repeated actions creating, sustaining, or reproducing the macro (Schegloff, Garfinkel, Blumer, Berger and Luckmann, Boudon), and conformity (role theory, Parsons). They distinguish two modes moving from the macro to the micro: (1) internalization (Parsons, Giesen, Schegloff), and (2) the macro setting limits, conceiving macro phenomena as limiting frames of reference that set the agenda for microprocesses (Marx, Dahrendorf, Durkheim, Hegel, Habermas, Alexander).

In sum, the state of the art is quite controversial. Simulation may therefore be a new approach to the advancement theory development.

1.2. The Micro-Macro Problem of Computer Simulations

What does the state of the art in micro-macro theories mean for micro-macro algorithms? It must not be the algorithm or the simulation language that decides about the micro or macro unit or solves the dilemmas of any of the aforementioned sociologists—for example, how to attain the level of macro phenomena from the analysis of situations of action (individualistic approaches), how to demonstrate the relevance of macro phenomena for individual action, or how to sustain their propositions on the macro level by reference to the actions of individuals and groups (macroscopic approaches). If we succeed, Alexander and Giesen's vision (1987:37) become true: "Only by establishing a radically different theoretical starting point can a genuinely inclusive micro-macro link be made. This inclusive model would not simply combine two or three of the theoretical options in an ad hoc manner. Rather, it would provide a systematic model in which all five of the options are included as analytical dimensions of empirical reality as such." If our algorithms and simulation languages do not (yet) fulfill this precondition, it is at least compelling to make explicit those theoretical options that they rely on.

Obviously, apart from all differences in the assignment of micro and macro phenomena, the micro-macro problem has the following formal structure: There are elements (e.g., individuals, interactions, situations, institutions) that are supposed to constitute a micro level. We shall call them micro units here. There are also elements of another type (e.g., populations, organizations, a situational flux, society) that are supposed to be constitutive parts of a macro level. Most important, we do have many more micro units on the micro level than macro units on the macro level. And there are four kinds of relations between these elements: (1) micro-micro, (2) micro-macro, (3) macro-macro, and (4) macro-micro. Due to the difference in numbers, we may have hundreds or thousands or even more of these relations. Micro and macro should be taken as relative poles of a two-dimensional continuum: we may find even more micro or macro phenomena depending on our statement of a problem. Whenever we enter a more fundamental micro level, we find numerous micro units related to each (new) macro unit. A multilevel simulation language therefore has to specify at least micro units, macro units, and interactions between the micro and the macro level and vice versa.

Until recently, the necessity to model dozens or even hundreds of elements including their interactions set a serious obstacle to the realization of micro-macro simulations: In comparison to macro models (modeling macro-macro relations only) as well as micro models (modeling micro-micro relations and some very few micro-macro relations) whose computational realizations represent no particular challenge, tremendous additional complexity is introduced. The number of elements and equations is multiplied by the number of micro units, each micro unit demanding its own equations of possible micro-micro, micro-macro, and macro-micro relations. The computational power needed is increased enormously. Program models involve great expense and become unintelligible. This may be called the micro-macro problem of computer simulations. Due to this problem, simulationists up to the late 1980s renounced multilevel simulation in favor of macro simulation of abstract variables, or micro simulations of small numbers of micro units (e.g., Hanneman, Collins, and Mordt 1995:13).

Meanwhile, multilevel simulation (Troitzsch 1996) is supported by the software packages MIMOSE (Möhring 1996, 1990; Möhring, Strotmann, and Flache 1994) and SOAR (Laird et al. 1987). Blackboard and object-oriented languages offer features that support micro-macro simulation. Neither the software packages nor the artificial intelligence approach (Cohen 1986; Masuch and LaPotin 1989; Carley 1991a, 1992; Harrison and Carrol 1991),[2] the Distributed Artificial Intelligence approach (e.g., Carley et al. 1992; Gilbert and Doran 1994; Conte and Gilbert 1995), or other multilevel approaches (Flache and Macy 1996; Kaufer and Carley 1993) operate with a joint multilevel algorithm.

2. SIMULATING THE MICRO-MACRO LINK

2.1. *The Master Equation: A Micro-Macro Algorithm*[3]

The master equation approach originates with statistical physicists. In ferromagnetism, fluid dynamics, and laser theory, physicists deal with phenomena that are in some respect isomorphic to the micro-macro link in the social sciences: They deal with systems of many particles and certain characteristics: (1) they display an ordered state or sequence of states that is approached from some combinations of initial and boundary conditions; (2) the ordered state results from the interactions of the system's components, not from external influence; and (3) the ordered state is reached spontaneously (Roth 1986:153). These are the characteristics of self-organizing processes. That theories of self-organization—e.g., synergetics (Haken 1978, 1983)—should be able to contribute to a specification of the micro-macro link is explicitly recognized by its natural science proponents. The point they all emphasize is that self-organization produces qual-

---

[2]Some simulations have examined multilevel systems by means of artificial intelligence without explicitly acknowledging this fact, e.g. Markovsky 1987.
[3]See footnote 1.

ities at the macro level of the systems considered that cannot be derived from, or explained by, reference to the measurable properties of the elements (see Haken 1978:3). This judgment is also held by numerous social scientists (e.g., Mayntz 1990:45–47).

The master equation approach has been elaborated as a model of attitude formation in social systems (Weidlich and Haag 1983). In comparison with the dominant information-processing model the master equation approach represents a shift toward a more functionally based view of attitude formation and change (see Pratkanis, Breekler, and Greenwald 1989). Attitudes are related to behavior; recent developments in attitude theory and the attitude-behavior relationship are reviewed and discussed by Heil (1996), McBroom and Reed (1992), Bagozzi (1992), and Pestello and Pestello (1991).

The master equation describes the dynamics of a multilevel system: The model building process starts at the (micro) level of the individual. Take the simpler case of two attitudes: It is assumed that individuals have an attitude i or j and can change their attitudes with a certain probability. The probability for individuals to change from attitude j to i is p_{ji}, the transition probability. The probability of changing one's attitude depends on a flexibility parameter ny, indicating the general inclination to do so, and on the difference between the utility u of attitude j compared with i:

$$p_{ji} = ny * \exp(u_j - u_i) \ . \tag{1}$$

The utility function u may be specified as a dynamic utility function. As a result, individuals change their attitudes due to expected utility gains and their general flexibility. Aggregation of the individual's transition probabilities leads to the transition probabilities of the configuration:

$$w_{ji} = n_i * p_{ji} \quad \text{and} \quad w_{ij} = n_j * p_{ij} \tag{2}$$

respectively. The so-called socio-configuration $\underline{n} = (n_i, n_j)$ is a macro variable, which describes the distribution of attitudes within a system. $P(\underline{n}, t)$ indicates the probability of finding socio-configuration $\underline{n}$ realized at time t. The master equation describes the dynamics of the system—the temporal evolution of the probability distribution of the attitudes in the socio-configuration:

$$\frac{dP(\underline{n}, t)}{dt} = \sum_{\substack{j, i \\ j \neq i}} [w_{ij}(\underline{n}_{ij})P(\underline{n}_{ij}, t) - w_{ji}(\underline{n})P(\underline{n}, t)] \tag{3}$$

The master equation is a simple and—from the sociological point of view—empty balance algorithm: The first term in brackets represents the influx, the second one the outflow. For each application, the master equation has to be elaborated—that is, social contents have to be incorporated. It is not elaborated a priori for special kinds of social applications. The environment in which the individuals interact may be represented by parameters or variables whose behavior is described by dynamical equations of any kind (together called *trend configuration*). The utility functions of the individuals can depend on these parameters or variables. As a result, the utility gains change because of changes in the environment. A concise description of the model building process is given in Weidlich 1994, and more extensively in Weidlich (1991:146ff.). Applications are to be found in Weidlich and Haag 1983, 1988.

2.2. Aggregation Approach I: Comparison with Other Formal Models of Attitude Formation

As stated above, in sociology the master equation has been elaborated as a model of attitude formation. In order to point out its formal characteristics we compare it with other formal models of attitude formation. To different degrees, they have been developed with reference to substantial theories of attitude formation and the emergence of public opinion (e.g., Moscovici 1963; Converse 1964; Ajzen and Fishbein 1980; Noelle-Neumann 1984; Crespi 1988; Iyengar and McGuire 1992).

In attitude formation, one may distinguish between models of direct and indirect interactions between individuals, and a discrete or continuous attitude space. The resulting types of aggregation are not yet systematically classified, although one may distinguish at least between simple, structural, and network aggregation approaches:

Indirect interaction of individuals, discrete attitudes. An example of this type is the master equation approach as introduced in the previous section. Individual interactions are not direct but communicated by the media, formally represented by the mean field. Attitudes are discrete.
Indirect interaction of individuals, continuous attitudes. In this case, individual interactions are not direct but communicated by the media. However, attitudes are continuous. An example is given by Troitzsch (1990), who models political attitude change in Germany. Each person's displacement is visualized in a two-dimensional attitude space representing a "left-right"–

dimension and a dimension of political satisfaction and dissatisfaction. The individuals are endowed with the ability to move in a potential—the "aggregate" of the model individuals—which arises automatically from the sheer existence of these individuals.

Direct interaction of individuals, discrete attitudes. (1) *Pair interactions*. Helbing (1992a) has introduced a mathematical model for attitude formation by pair interactions. He obtains Boltzmann-like equations. Three types of attitude formation can be formalized by this model: (a) through some kind of avoidance behavior, (b) through a readiness for compromise, and (c) through persuasion. The behavior of pedestrians has become the paradigmatic application of this type of model (Helbing 1992b). (2) *Networks*. If interactions are influenced by geographical locations or social positions, they may be modeled using network models—for example, cellular automata. The neighborhood concept of cellular automata allows for the specification of different kinds of interactions between individuals who are located close to each other. Even indirect knowledge of others' behavior is conceivable through direct interactions with neighbors who have slightly different individuals in their neighborhood. It was Couclelis (1985) who introduced cellular worlds as a framework for modeling micro-macro dynamics. Nowak, Szamrej, and Latané (1990), Nowak and Latané (1994), and Nowak and Lewenstein (1996) have used this approach to model public opinion formation.

Direct interaction of individuals, continuous attitudes. (1) *Pair interactions*. Helbing (1993, sect. 4.6, 1994) has extended his model of pair interactions to the case of continuous attitudes. Through Taylerapproximation, he obtains Boltzmann-Fokker-Planck equations. (2) *Networks*. As far as the author knows, this approach has not yet been realized.

*2.3. Aggregation Approach II: Comparison with the Sociological Notions
of Other Formalized Multilevel Models*

Are there sociological notions that underly the aggregation approach as modeled in the master equation? To answer this question, we compare the master equation approach to another formalized multilevel model, the constructural model. The basic model of constructuralism, a structural theory of diffusion, was developed by Carley (1990, 1991b). Kaufer and Carley (1993) have presented an extended version of the theory and an application. There are several formal differences between both models that are not of interest here.

The Master Equation Approach. The general sociological notions that underly the master equation approach are that people behave according to their attitudes and their opinions. If they change their attitudes, they consequently change their behavior (micro units, micro variables). The probability of an attitude change is assumed to be the same for all individuals belonging to one population and depends on the attitude distribution among all relevant persons, the preferences given by the utility functions, and the general inclination to a change of mind. The environment in which the individuals interact may be represented by parameters or variables (macro units, macro variables). The environment variables depend on each other (macro-macro interaction) and on individual behavior (micro-macro interaction). The individuals' utilities depend on the environment parameters or variables (macro-micro interaction). As a result, individuals may change their attitudes due to a change in the environment, and the environment may change due to individual behavior.

The Constructural Model. The general sociological notions that underly the constructural model are that individuals have knowledge and that they can acquire new information. Individuals can interact with each other and there is some probability that they will do so. The probability of individual *i* interacting with *j* depends on *i*'s relative cognitive similarity to *j* (micro units, micro variables). Actually, *i* interacts with *j* if his probability of doing so is high and if *j* is available. Once all individuals have paired up, the partners can communicate pieces of information to each other (micro-micro interaction). The environment in which the individuals interact is represented as social structure—the distribution of interaction probabilities across the population—and as culture—the distribution of information across the population (macro units, macro variables). In response to communication (the individuals having acquired new pieces of information), the culture changes (micro-macro interaction). In response to the new culture, the individuals change their interaction probabilities (macro-micro interaction). This leads in turn to a new social structure (micro-macro interaction).

In a comparison of both multilevel models, each may be related to a set of sociological or sociocognitive theories, but neither gives a sociological (not a formal) explanation of its aggregation approach. Therefore, some suggestions follow showing what direction the search for a sociological explanation might take:

The constructural model. Here, where the macro level is represented as matrices, there is only a minimal kind of aggregation. What we perceive on the macro level—the culture and the social structure matrix—are not really aggregate variables but rather systematically listed values of micro variables. This implies that there is not really a macro "entity," as if individuals were to speak to a dozen friends, inquire about their attitudes toward a certain political party, store these different pieces of information, and act accordingly.

The master equation approach. Compared with the latter approach, we have a stronger kind of aggregation here: What we perceive on the macro level, the socio-configuration, and the trend configuration, are aggregate variables. The values of the micro variables have been aggregated into a new single value; there may even be a kind of weighing or combination of the values of micro variables and other macro variables that result in final values for socio- and trend configuration. This implies that there is rather a macro "entity," as if individuals hear from the media that the unemployment rate is 8.2 percent, and act accordingly.

Looking again at Section 1.1 reveals that there is a significant gap between multilevel modeling in sociology and sociological multilevel theorizing. None of the theories provides an operational model of the dynamics whereby individuals create macro level structures through micro level actions that is sufficiently detailed to permit formal analysis. None of the models provides a sociologically founded explanation of its aggregation method. The crucial point is whether or not we will be able to close this gap. One possibility is to test the application of multilevel models founded in sociological theory that are detailed enough to allow for empirical testing. The following section outlines such an application.

3. APPLICATION: MILITARY COUPS IN THAILAND

3.1. *The Micro-Macro Problem of Coup Theory*

Only a few years after the former colonies of the United Kingdom and France had become independent states, the number of military coups d'état increased enormously, generating an impact on sociological investigations of such events. The development of coup theory proceeded in two ways: (1) single case studies and theory development (Huntington 1957, 1968,

1991, and Finer 1962, 1976 being the first and most influential theoreticians), and (2) comparative cross-national statistical research (e.g., Jackman et al. 1986; O'Kane 1987, 1993; Johnson, Slater, and McGowan 1984; McGowan and Johnson 1984; Jenkins and Kposowa 1990, 1992; Kposowa and Jenkins 1993; see also the review in Saam 1995:72–74). Both groups of scientists referred to the others' work. Coup theory was conceptualized as a macro theory, the incidence of military coups d'état being explained by social structural conditions such as a low degree of political institutionalization, political participation, and social mobilization as well as a low level of economic development and ethnic heterogeneity.

These (conventional) social structural theories of military intervention in politics cannot explain the micro-macro problem of military intervention, nor can they explain the dynamics of military intervention:

1.   Coups don't just happen; coups are created by people. More exactly, they are created by members of national elites. Implicitly, all prevailing social structural approaches must assume that these social structural conditions, in some way or other, influence the behavior of national elites. Most of the existing macro theories have not been wrong, but they cover only the macro level of this phenomenon. This may be called the micro-macro problem of coup theory. In order to contribute to the solution of this problem, we introduce the individual into the theory of military intervention in politics.

2.   We assume that interactions between the macro and micro level of those political systems characterized by military interventions lead to self-organization phenomena which may produce different modes of long-term behavior in the political systems. Unlike prevailing social structural theories of military intervention in politics,[4] our model explains why some countries experience one military coup, others several; why some coups are followed by decades of military rule, others by short periods with democratic interludes; why each country seems to follow its own pattern of political dynamics.

3.2. The Multilevel Model of Military Intervention in Politics

This section describes our multilevel model of military interventions in politics in which individuals interact through the master equation in a sys-

---

[4]We exclude Huntington from this group because he actually has developed a dynamic theory.

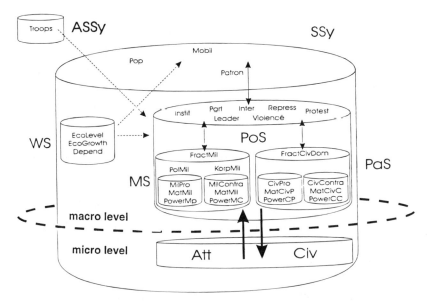

Macro variables: political power of collective actors (PowerMP, PowerMC, PowerCP, Power CC); resources of collective actors (MatMil, MatCivP, MatCivC); number of individual members to collective actors (MilPro, MilContra, CivPro, CivContra); political institutionalization (Instit); political protest (Protest); political violence (Violence); political repression (Repress); political leadership (Leader); political participation (Part); military intervention in politics (Inter); political dominance (Dom); fractionalization of the military (FractMil); political centrality of the military (PolMil); corporate interest of the military (KorpMil); social mobilization (Mobil); population size (Pop); patron-client relations (Patron); level of economic development (EcoLevel); economic growth (EcoGrowth); economic dependence (Depend); and presence of foreign troops (Troops).
Systems and subsystems: Social System (SSy); Economic System (WS); Political system (PoS); Military System (MS); Party system (PaS); Other Social Systems (ASSy).
Micro variables: attitude on democratization (Att); Identity (Civ).
Note: For the sake of clarity we have not used arrows to represent all the relations between variables. Dashed-line arrows start from exogenous variables; solid-line arrows start from endogenous variables.

FIGURE 1. The multilevel model of military intervention in politics.

tem dynamics-like environment realized in MIMOSE.[5] Model individuals are allowed for power maximization and/or maximization of political goals. A graphic representation of the model is given in Figure 1 and explained below.

[5]MIMOSE is referenced in Section 1.2.

We assume:

1. *Micro level*: Coups are staged by members of the national political elite whose members have attitudes and act according to these attitudes. At the micro level, all individuals belong to one population, the national political elite. This population is divided into the four analytic groups shown in Figure 1:[6] military men who either favor or oppose democracy (MilPro, MilContra), and civilians (CivPro, CivContra). Each individual can change his or her attitude. Additionally, we assume birth-death processes within the political elite: elite members may join or be removed from the political elite through power struggle, age, death, etc. Both attitude change and birth-death processes are modeled by the same kind of transition functions as they are used in the master equation approach. The master equation approach has been chosen because it supports modeling the attitude-behavior relationship. Therefore, the competitive information-processing model of attitude formation and change has not been chosen.

At the micro level, we derive two alternative theories of action from political macro theories: Bureaucracy theory[7] (Riggs 1979, 1981) states that "in a bureaucratic polity, power considerations *precede* all other concerns" (Riggs 1981:167). Patron-client networks are the basis of the social organization of Thai politics; "patron-client clusters are based ultimately on power relations" (Scott 1972:100f). Thus, in a case of bureaucratic polity, elite individuals hold and change their attitudes and act according to changes in the power distribution within the elite. In contrast, the theory of action behind democracy theory (Dahl 1982) states that individuality and diversity of interests underly the concept of man in pluralist democracy theory. According to this, elite individuals' attitudes and actions are produced by their interests. These may be political convictions on tolerable degrees of political institutionalization, political protest, political violence, as well as economic or power considerations.

---

[6]These analytic groups are not groups in the proper sociological sense: they are mere aggregations of individuals who have the same characteristics and hold the same opinion and who therefore behave according to the same rules. In reality, cliques that may be regarded as groups in the proper sociological sense stage coups. To introduce them would imply to introduce a third level, a meso level. To avoid complicating this first multilevel model to be tested empirically, we start with a two-level model (micro and macro) and dispense with a proper meso level.

[7]In Thai political theory this term differs significantly from the Weberian theory on bureaucracy. Also, in Weberian theory, patron-client relations are exactly the opposite of bureaucracy. Here, we rely on the use of the term in Thai political theory.

The algorithm applied on the micro level allows for any combination of variables that underlie both theories of action. The general form of the transition function is as follows:[8]

```
Att : int
    := case Civ of 0
              : case Att_1 of 1
                      : 0 if prob (ProbMilContra)
                        else 1 ;
                    default
                      : 1 if prob (ProbMilPro)
                        else 0 ;
                  end ;
              default
                : case Att_1 of 1
                        : 0 if prob (ProbCivContra)
                          else 1 ;
                      default
                        : 1 if prob (ProbCivPro)
                          else 0 ;
                  end ;
end ;
```

If an elite member is a military man (`civ of 0`) and is in favor of political democratization (`Att of 1`), he will change his opinion (`: 0`) with a certain probability that is given by the transition probability (`ProbMil-Contra`) of his group (`MilPro`). Otherwise he will not change his opinion (`else 1`). If a military man is opposed to democratization (`default`), he will change his opinion (`: 1`) with the probability given by the transition probability (`ProbMilPro`) of his group (`MilContra`). The transition function for civilians follows.

2. *Macro-micro link*: Attitudes and actions of the elite are influenced by the socioeconomic and political environment. The macro-micro link is realized by integrating the socioeconomic and political macro environment variables into transition probabilities.

The probability of an attitude change depends on the following:

---

[8]Given in MIMOSE notation.

The individual's previous attitude
The individual's identity as a military man or as a civilian
The states or state changes of the political, economic, and social system
(`Power, EcoGrow, Repress, Mobil, Instit, Protest`)
The assessment of these by the individual (the assessment criteria themselves depend on the individual's previous attitude and identity)
The general inclination to a change of mind (`ny`)

As a result, we obtain four different transition probabilities, one for each group (`ProbMilPro, ProbMilContra, ProbCivPro, ProbCiv-Contra`). For example, in the case of a military man opposed to democratization, the transition probability of a change of mind in favor of democratization is specified as

```
ProbMilPro
  : real
  := ramp⁹(ny * (pipower * ( ... Power ... )
     + pipol * ( ... Repress, Mobil, Instit,
                 Protest ...)));¹⁰
```

`Pipower` and `pipol` are parameters that indicate the overall influence of power and political aspects on transition probability. The algorithm applied allows for any combination of variables underlying both theories of action.

3. *Macro level*: Admittedly, the dynamics of the macro variables of a socioeconomic and political system—for example, social mobilization, political protest—are a result of the actions of all individuals living in this system. We model them on the macro level only.

At the macro level, we have modeled the socioeconomic and political system of Thailand, the environment of elite individuals. We have used system dynamics-like equations to describe their development.

At the macro level theories of military rule, theories of political stability and of redemocratization have been studied (for references, see Section 3.1). Those variables and hypotheses that proved to be statistically significant in cross-national statistical research have been incorporated into the model. Thus the macro model is theoretically and empirically

---

[9]ramp is a user specified function that restricts the expression that follows to the interval [0,1].
[10]The complete code may be found in Saam (1995:236ff.).

grounded. It is characterized by multiple theory reference. Static hypotheses are transformed into dynamic hypotheses. In our model, military interventions in politics are a result of the power struggle between the four groups (MilPro, MilContra, CivPro, CivContra). Whenever the power value of one military group crosses the power of another, we assume that a coup occurs. Additionally, countercoups can take place within either military actor. The civilian groups cannot stage a military coup d'etat

4. *Micro-macro link*: Elite members can fundamentally influence the dynamics of the socioeconomic and political system.

The micro-macro link is realized by aggregating individual attitudes into the socio-configuration and by using them in the system dynamics-like equations of the socioeconomic and political environment. For example, the number of military men who are opposed to democratization is included in the power equation of the MilContra group, and the number of civilians who are opposed to democratization is included in the political violence equation.

3.3. *An Empirical Example*: *Military Intervention in Thailand*

This multilevel model of military coups d'état was applied to the case of Thailand. Between 1932, when the absolute monarchy was overthrown, and 1992, Thailand underwent 21 military coup d'etats, 13 of them successful. The military ruled 80 percent of this time. This intervention dynamic is later illustrated in Figure 2.[11] The degree of military intervention in politics was operationalized according to Finer's definition (Finer 1962:23) as the degree of the armed forces' constrained substitution of their own policies and/or personnel for those of the recognized civilian authorities.[12] In Figure 2, peaks represent coups d'état of either military group, whereas the horizontal lines represent military or civilian rule. The figure also shows that there have been only four short periods of civilian rule: 1932–1933, 1944–1946, 1973–1976, and 1991–1992. Several times coups were followed by consolidating coups—for example, in 1933, 1948, 1951. Countercoups occur during periods of military rule—for example,

---

[11]Figure 2 is presented below together with Figures 3 and 4 to facilitate comparison between the empirical and simulated time series.

[12]We multiply a four-point ordinary scale of constraint with a four-point scale of degree of substitution. This leads to a five-point scale of military intervention: 1.0 (0.833) coup by military against (in favor of) democratization, 0.677 (0.556) rule by military against (in favor of) democratization, 0.0 rule by civilians.

in 1933, 1949, 1951, 1957, 1958, 1981, 1985—and after successful take-
overs (1933, 1948, 1977). It is the aim of the simulation to reproduce and
explain this pattern of military intervention in Thai politics in retrospective. Prediction is not and cannot be a concern.

The complete multilevel model of military intervention in Thai politics includes all variables described in the previous section. In sum, the
model includes 43 endogenous macro variables (several variables appear
four times; once for each group—for example, the power functions, the
rule functions, the transition functions; 20 variables would remain if they
were counted as one variable), 6 endogenous micro variables, 8 exogenous
macro variables, and 42 parameters. All variables were operationalized.[13]
Empirical data on the political, social, and economic dynamics of Thailand, 1932–1992, were collected for all variables. Where several indicators were chosen to operationalize one variable, a factor analysis was carried
out to calculate the empirical data of this variable.

3.4. Simulation Results

The final formal model proved to be a stochastic, nonlinear dynamic system of differential equations including numerous if-else conditions
and birth-death processes. It cannot be solved analytically.

The results of the simulation are shown in three steps:

1. The kind of results obtained are explained and the methods used for
    parameter calibration, model optimization, and analysis of the results
    are outlined.
2. The results of the base run are described: the simulation that produced
    the best fit between the simulated and the empirical data (called sub-
    type X).
3. All behavioral types that resulted with a certain probability are briefly
    described (called type alpha to epsilon).

Types of Results and Methods.   After model coding, the variables and
parameters were initialized with the empirical 1932 data of Thailand
insofar as available. Simulations were run to calibrate all those parameters that could not be determined empirically. They were grouped into
seven categories of values (veryWeak, weak, moderate, moder-
atelyStrong, strong, veryStrong, extremelyStrong). Sim-

[13]Details may be found in Saam 1995:251–70.

ulations were run repeatedly, varying the value category of a parameter, and/or the numeric representation of that category, until all variables were sensitive to each other and stayed within their defined intervals of minimum and maximum value.

Further simulations were run to optimize the fit between the simulated and the empirical data. The model produces time series of 244 data points for each endogenous variable (quarterly from 1932 to 1992). These simulated time series were compared to the empirical time series by qualitative viewing. During the optimization runs, alternative micro and macro hypotheses were tested to reproduce Thai military intervention dynamics. What we presented in Section 3.2 is the structure of the final model resulting from these simulations.

Thus, the result of each *run* is a set of 43 time series with 244 data points, one time series for each variable. The results of each *initialization* are several sets of 43 time series: due to its stochasticity and nonlinearity, one and the same initialization produces different time series for each variable in consecutive runs differing, all things being equal, only in the initialized value of the random number generator. The time series for each variable and initialization may differ not only quantitatively but also qualitatively. Thus we obtain different long-term behavior modes for each variable and initialization occurring with a certain probability.

Most interestingly, as far as the military intervention variable is concerned, we were able to identify types and subtypes of behavior. These result from self-organization effects within the whole multilevel model. The types were determined by qualitative viewing of the military intervention and underlying power-time series. Their behavioral characteristics were compared[14] and sets of typical behavioral characteristics were grouped and used for classification. The subtype that produced the best fit between the simulated and the empirical data was called subtype X. In sum, including the runs during sensitivity analysis,[15] we have found probabilities of the appearance of (only!) 11 subtypes (subtype A to J, and X) that belong to five types (type alpha to epsilon). There may, of course, be more subtypes and types but, as shown by our experiments, not within a certain interval around the initialization of the base run.

To conceive of the probability distribution of subtypes and types of each initialization, numerous consecutive simulations have to be run, keeping the initialization constant and varying only the random number gen-

---

[14]In Figure 5, we mark several of these behavioral characteristics with arrows.
[15]See Section 3.5.

erator. In the ideal case, this should involve hundreds or thousands of runs depending on the number of types and subtypes. The smaller the number of types, the smaller the number of runs. We were able to run 23 consecutive runs.[16] As a consequence, the observed probabilities are interpreted qualitatively rather than quantitatively (see below).

Subtype X.   Subtype X reproduces the empirical pattern of military interventions in Thai politics most satisfactorily. Figure 3 presents the simulated time series of military interventions in Thai politics of subtype X. A comparison of Figures 2 and 3 shows that the model reproduces the trend quite well: periods of military or civilian rule are shown quite well, even if they are short, whereas single events—for example, single coups d'état—are difficult to reproduce at the right point in time. Thus, type X is accepted as a qualitative reproduction of the empirical dynamic.

As explained in Section 3.2, the coups in our model result from the power struggle between elite groups. Whenever the power value of one military group crosses the power value of another military or civilian group, a coup occurs. In addition, countercoups can take place from within either military group. Therefore the simulated intervention dynamics (Figure 3) are a direct result of the simulated power dynamics (Figure 4). We shall concentrate on two periods of time to show the relation between the simulated power functions, simulated intervention dynamics, and empirical intervention dynamics:

1934–1948. Consider the military who are opposed to democratization: their power (`PowerMilContra`) predominates in the 1930s and early 1940s. The power values of the military and civilians who are in favor of democratization start comparatively low, but increase until 1944. Then both military groups' power collapses, giving the civilians who are in favor of democratization (the Free Thai Movement) a short chance to rule. In our model, as in reality, this change in power was mainly a consequence of World War II. The military's resources declined dramatically as the presence of foreign troops on the national territory reduced their power. Both variables are exogenous and induce an exogenous shock. As the war comes to an end, the exogenous influence ceases, and the military opposed to democratization quickly recover and take power once again. As can be

---

[16]This was a result of software restrictions. Twenty-three consecutive runs proved to be the maximum number of runs that the program was able to calculate. During the twenty-fourth run it would crash.

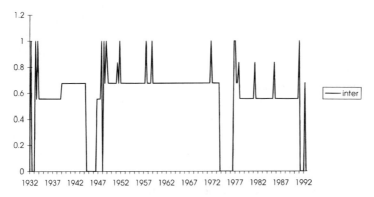

FIGURE 2. The empirical dynamics of military intervention in Thai politics, 1932–1992.

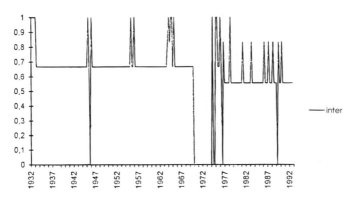

FIGURE 3. The simulated dynamics of military intervention in Thai politics, 1932–1992.

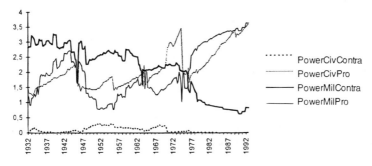

FIGURE 4. The simulated power functions of Thai politics, 1932–1992.

seen from Figure 3, our model produces two military coups: one in 1944 and the other in 1946. The simulated coup of 1944 is an artifact, as can be seen from Figure 2. Marshall Phibun Songkhram resigned "voluntarily" and was not overthrown by a coup. Our model is not able to reproduce this, although it is able to generate resignations generally: When civilians take over power from the military who are opposed to democratization, changes in power occur without coups which may be interpreted as resignation (see Figure 3, 1970). Marshall Phibun's final return to power in 1948 was much more complicated empirically (see Figure 2) than in the simulated reproduction (Figure 3).

1970–1978. Figure 4 illustrates that any successful coup immediately reduces the power of the civilians who are in favor of democratization. After a coup, the political institutionalization decreases, leading to a decrease of the power value of the civilians in favor of democratization. Therefore, although their power value has a tendency to increase, it is not before 1970—empirically 1973—that they cross the power value of the ruling military opposed to democratization, and take power. This time the return to military rule is more complicated in the simulation model than in reality: In 1974 the military opposed to democratization stage an unsuccessful coup in the simulation, which was not perceived empirically. They cannot take over rule immediately because their power value remains lower than the civilians'. Nevertheless, in the model this leads to a significant decrease in the civilians' power, so that six months later the military opposed to democratization stage another coup, this time successfully. In reality, the same group was able to stage a coup in 1976, which was successful immediately. After two years, the military in favor of democratization experience a significant increase in power. They unseat the ruling military— i.e., they stage a coup—and stay in power for more than a decade. Here the simulation model produces an unsuccessful countercoup and three months of civilian rule that was not observed empirically.

Subtype X is a subtype to type delta. Where the base run is concerned, subtype X can be observed in one of 23 runs, and type delta in two of 23 runs. In all other cases other types are observed.[17] In simulations with

[17]We discuss the significance of this probability below. The base run is not the run with the highest probability of subtype X but the run where we discovered subtype X. The probability space of subtype X extends to several parameter spaces; see Section 3.5.

different initializations, the probability of the appearance of subtype X (and type delta) increases or decreases according to changes in values.[18]

Type Alpha to Epsilon.   In sum, the frequency distribution of the base run was type alpha 15, beta 3, gamma 2, delta 2, and epsilon 1 in 23. Figure 5 shows the characteristics of each type: intervention dynamics and dynamics of the underlying struggle for power. The arrows in Figure 5 indicate some of the characteristic behavioral features that were used to identify the types. Two extreme types are identified: *enduring military rule* of the military opposing democratization accompanied by numerous countercoups (*type alpha*) and *successful civilization of politics* (*type beta*).

Type alpha displays how recurrent military coups lead to severe lapses in the power of the democratic civilians. Due to enduring antidemocratic military rule, the antidemocratic civilians experience an unusual increase in power. The dramatic decrease in power of the military group in favor of democratization (arrows) is typical.

After one decade of type beta's history, the democratic military approach the antidemocratic. They assume power after some years of struggle. During the following two decades, some unsuccessful antidemocratic military coups and some democratic countercoups occur. The democratic civilians increase under cover of the pro-democratic military's rule and finally take power (arrows downward). After some years, the democratic military experiences a loss in power (arrows from the right). The result is equilibrium, a stable democratic civilian rule.

By comparison, the *pro-democratic military group* (type gamma) needs three decades to take power. The antidemocratic military group's power does not decrease below a critical threshold. Therefore they are in principle able to stage an unsuccessful coup (arrow from the left); finally, they stage a coup (arrow from the right) after the civilians have ruled for some time (arrows downward). Nevertheless they are only temporarily able to reduce the power of the civilians. They are not able to take power themselves.

Subtype X is a subtype of *type delta*, which was partly (1934–1948, 1970–1978) explained above. Altogether, it shows an early period of civil rule immediately after World War II. As the impulse was coming from outside the system, the antidemocratic military's power is not weakened decisively. After a short period of time, they stage a coup and take over for

---

[18]See Section 3.5.

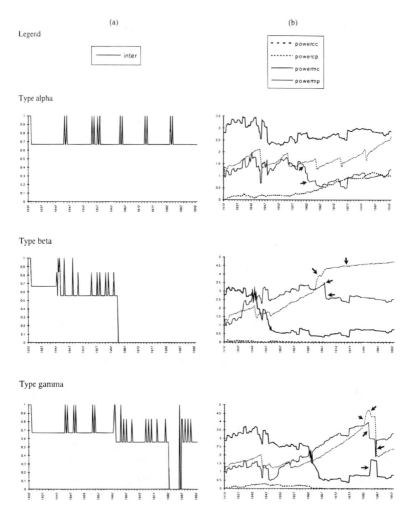

FIGURE 5. Different long-term behavior modes of the Thai military intervention model:
(a) Military intervention in politics (y-axis),* (b) Power Variables (y-axis).†

*y-axis: inter (military intervention in politics); for an explanation, cf.
Figure 4. †y-axis: powercc (power of CivContra), powercp (power of
CivPro), powermc (Power of MilContra), powermp (power of MilPro).

another 25 years. In the sixties they remained the winners in a power struggle between all three strong actors. The democratic civilians recover soon
and the next time—1970 in the model, 1973 in Thailand—they take power
(arrows downward). The antidemocratic military is still very strong whereas

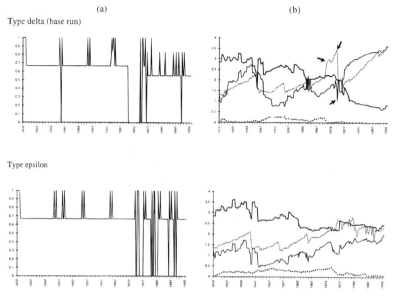

FIGURE 5. Continued.

their democratic counterpart is still quite weak but increases in power. As the power of the antidemocratic military stays above a critical threshold, they are able to stage a successful coup after three years of civilian rule, and they are able to take power. Although the civilians recover quite quickly, the winners in the medium term are the pro-democratic military. They defeat their antidemocratic counterparts and rule for more than a decade. During that time, the latter experience a dramatic loss in power, whereas the power of the democratic civilians continues to increase. They even take power for a short period, but at this time they are still not able to defeat the democratic military.

Type epsilon may be interpreted similarly. Throughout all the work of interpretation, it should not be forgotten that any reduction or increase in the groups' power is induced by changes in the number of their elite members, in resources, in political support, etc. (which are also generated by the simulation model but cannot be displayed here). And again, these changes are partially induced by the elite members' decisions, partially by macro processes. Such decisions, as we know, are induced by changes in the macro variables, such as the groups' power. A closed description of the interrelations between the micro and macro level has been obtained. Strictly speaking, to explain an event, all variables of the model have to be traced back at least one complete time step. Only then can we offer a complete explanation (examples are given in Saam 1995:172ff.).

3.5. *Validation*

There are different methods for validating the results of computer simulations. First, we calculated a goodness-of-fit parameter. Second, we applied two methods of sensitivity analysis.

The goodness-of-fit parameter indicates the number of data points of the simulated time series equal to those of the empirical one (percentage of all data points). To measure this parameter, we used the military intervention time series. As explained in Section 3.3, military intervention was operationalized on a five-point scale: 1.0 (0.833) coup by military against (in favor of) democratization, 0.677 (0.556) rule by military against (in favor of) democratization, 0.0 rule by civilians. Our calculations show that in 68 percent of the data points the simulated time series equals the empirical one. For the time being, we assess 68 percent to be a good value: We do not yet have much experience with empirically tested multilevel models. A value of 68 percent is relatively good in macro modeling even with an ordinary scaled variable. Furthermore, we have increased the complexity of the model essentially by introducing the micro level.

The term sensitivity analysis is generally used to describe a family of methods for altering the input values of the model in various ways. Such analyses are included in the validation step of almost all technical simulations (Law and Kelton 1991:310ff.). Chattoe, Saam, and Möhring (forthcoming) give an overview of current problems in the application of sensitivity analysis to social simulation. For example, the robustness requirement states that we are usually looking for robust solutions, not just the best one. This means that in sensitivity testing small deviations on the input side do not yield large deviations on the output side. In other words, the system behavior is characterized by a fair degree of stability. The robustness request is not supported by the knowledge we have about social reality at present. The nonlinearity paradigm strongly suggests that many social systems have to be regarded as stochastic nonlinear dynamical systems (Albert 1995; Kiel and Elliott 1996; Stewart 1989). We know that small deviations in the input values of these systems typically lead to large deviations in the output values. The request for robustness may therefore reflect an outdated view of the social world. For some kinds of models, it may suffice to redefine the concept of robustness.

Our multilevel model of military coups proved to be this type of stochastic nonlinear dynamical system. As a result of one initialization, we obtain a probability distribution for different types of behavior. An appropriate robustness request to this kind of model asks whether small deviations in the input values lead to large deviations in the probability distribution for these types.

Here, the emphasis is on the results of the sensitivity analysis of the two parameters mentioned above (`pipower`, `pipol`; see Section 3.2) indicating the significance of the theory of action behind bureaucracy theory (in a bureaucratic polity, power considerations precede all other concerns; see Section 3.2) or democracy theory (in a democratic polity, individuals' attitudes and actions are influenced by their interests). In the base run the values of these parameters were : `pipower = 7.0` and `pipol = 0.1`, implying the high importance of the bureaucracy approach and low importance of the democracy approach. Table 1 shows the sensitivity analysis results of varying `piPol`, while keeping all other parameters and variables fixed. We decided to run eight consecutive simulations of each variation. It was known from our model optimization runs that this number of runs would approximately reproduce the overall probability distribution of types. Table 1 shows the increasing probability of type alpha if `pipol` is decreased. Type beta's probability increases continuously with increasing `pipol`. The probability of type delta, which can be said to represent the long-term behavior mode of Thailand, increases at first continuously with increasing `pipol` and then decreases to zero.

We have run numerous sensitivity analyses of this type, varying parameters or the initialized values of variables and evaluating the changed

TABLE 1

Sensitivity Analysis Results (Example: `piPower = 7.0`, `piPol` variated)

	Type alpha	Type beta	Type gamma	Type delta	Type epsilon
`piPol = 0.0`	4	1	1	1	1
`piPol = 0.1`	3	1	1	2	1
`piPol = 0.5`	4	1	1	2	0
`piPol = 1.0`	2	4	0	2	0
`piPol = 3.5`	0	4	1	3	0
`piPol = 7.0`	0	8	0	0	0

probability of each type.[19] The probability space of subtype X/type delta extends to several parameter and variable spaces.

Since only a very limited number of combinations of input values can be checked in this way, this kind of sensitivity analysis generally results in incomplete overviews of the model's implications. Therefore, a semiquantitative sensitivity analysis was carried out in addition in order to cross-validate the results of the conventional sensitivity analysis (results in Saam 1995, 1996).

In sum, the evidence seems to show that our model is valid. The goodness-of-fit parameter is quite satisfactory, the probability distributions are quite robust. Social scientists believe and require that the "window" of reality allowing a certain event or pattern not be too small. The window of subtype X/type delta is quite perceivable and extends to several parameter spaces.

What does all this mean for Thailand and our multilevel model? Due to the complexity of the model and the small number of consecutive runs, we should not take the exact number of types and their frequencies too seriously. Rather, we should interpret them qualitatively. Our model gives some evidence that under those conditions observable in Thailand only a few different types of long-term behavior were probable—for example, the enduring rule of the military opposed to democratization (type alpha), and long-term democratization (type beta). We do not know Thailand's exact position in the parameter space. PiPower and piPol are parameters that have not yet been operationalized or measured empirically. The sensitivity analysis results have shown that there is a changing probability of subtype X/type delta in several parameter spaces. We can now deduce relationships between single parameters and variables and the probability of the types. With regard to long-term democratization (type beta), we can specify those conditions that increase its probability significantly. For instance, if the behavior of the political elite were influenced in a way that power considerations would no longer precede all other concerns and their attitudes and actions would be influenced by their interests, the probability of long-term democratization would increase.[20] Concrete steps in this direction go beyond our simulation approach. They cannot be derived directly. Computer simulations are not creative in this respect. Therefore, we can only speculate about measures of political education,

[19]More results may be found in Saam 1995, 1996.
[20]This is only one of several recommendations that may be derived from the model.

incentives to stay within or sanctions to change political parties. Nevertheless, the simulation results strongly support the argument that the political dynamics can be changed by measures not only on the macro level of the political system but also on the micro level of individual elite behavior. These results may be compared with explanations and recommendations of nonquantitative approaches to politics in Thailand.

3.6. Results for Coup Theory

With regard to coup theory, we have shown that a multilevel model can reproduce the trend of political dynamics in a country that has experienced numerous coups d'état. We have not been successful in reproducing the exact number of coups and the time of occurrence. In comparison with prevailing coup theories, we see at least three advances:

1. The multilevel model of military coups is an advance in theory adequacy because it contributes to the solution of the micro-macro problem of coup theory. The theoretical model combines theories of action and structural theories.

    We can now explain Thai military interventions in politics as a direct result of the power struggle within Thai elites. Elite members are influenced by the sociopolitical conditions they live in, and act and unite in groups. Groups engage in the struggle for political power. Social structural conditions have an influence on the power struggle. The strongest group takes power and influences the sociopolitical system through its political decisions. Conversely, sociopolitical conditions influence the elite members' actions as well as the political actions of all groups. Both levels—micro and macro—and their interdependence are needed to explain military coups in Thailand. For example, experiments (Saam 1995:212–15) have shown that democratization in the 1970s would not have occurred under conditions of stagnating social mobilization (all things being equal).

2. Due to the applied method of computer simulation, the multilevel model is an advance in explicitness and completeness of coup theory, and logical correctness of results.

    The most interesting aspect of this was that theories of political repression, political protest, and political violence had to be incorporated into the model. They have not belonged to the standard repertoire of coup theory up to now, although single case studies often mention occurrences of political repression and the people's reaction to it. Here, we have found some indication that this phenomenon should not be excluded if the dynamics of military coups are to be explained. Another very interesting result was that political fractionalization, which is usually a prominent factor in the incidence of military coups, proved to be negligible.[21]

3. The multilevel model advances the explanatory power of coup theory. Now the dynamics of military coups, military rule, and civilization of politics can be explained. We have demonstrated how individuals on the micro level produce outcomes on the macro level that in turn influence individual actions during the time step that follows. The obtained dynamic pattern on the macro level shows an enormous variety like historical pathways, and falls into the complexity-chaos line of theory development. We can attribute this variety to single parameters, initial conditions of single variables, or characteristics of the model structure.

4. CONCLUSION

What do these results mean for further investigations in the micro-macro link with the help of computer simulations?

The master equation is a potentially very powerful multilevel algorithm. It offers the well-known advantages of formal modeling (Suppes 1968)—for example, revealing the dynamic character of the micro-macro problem, constructing, stating, and analyzing micro-macro theory in both directions, and exposing micro-macro theories to thorough tests. The master equation may be applied to numerous social contexts: whenever individuals unite in groups that influence, and in turn are influenced by, society.

In addition, any multilevel simulation should reflect two factors that indicate the state of the art:

1. At present, there is a distinct gap between multilevel modeling in sociology and sociological multilevel theorizing. None of the theories provides an operational model of the dynamics in which individuals create macro-level structures through micro-level actions that is sufficiently detailed to permit formal analysis. None of the models pro-

---

[21]Additional results on macro theories may be found in Saam 1995.

vides a sociologically founded explanation of its aggregation method. The ability to close this gap will be crucial.

One approach to this problem is to test applications of multilevel models that are founded in sociological theory and that are detailed enough to allow for empirical testing. This was attempted in Section 3.

Another approach is to develop joint concepts. Consider the aggregation concept, for example. In our formal model we use equations. Aggregation is a typical kind of operation in equations. The formal use of aggregations in algorithms need not imply that aggregation is an operation or mechanism in the social system being modeled. In our case, the micro-macro link can be interpreted sociologically as well as a kind of aggregation (individuals unite and form groups). This does not hold for the macro-micro link, which for the program code also appears to be aggregation. Nevertheless, in sociological terms it is the selected cognition of the sociopolitical environment by the individual. Most evidently, therefore, one must not deduce from the formal use of aggregation in the program model that this mechanism is in hand with regard to social reality. It is the close *sociological* investigation of the micro and macro variables that has been used for the formal construction of the micro-macro and macro-micro link of each successful multilevel model which will contribute to the advancement of micro-macro theory development.

2. Related to the micro-macro problem is the concept of emergence. It was John Stuart Mill (1965 [1843]:370) who first described the phenomenon of emergence, although he did not use the term itself. Emergent phenomena appear in aggregate systems, as a consequence of the interaction of the elements. We are not able to deduce or predict them. They represent a new quality, a novelty. Bunge (1979:30) has given an operational definition of emergent phenomena and distinguishes total qualitative novelty, emergent properties, and absolutely emergent properties. We want to add our results to the already published limits that characterize DAI (Distributed Artificial Intelligence) simulation in comparison with sociological approaches to emergent properties (Gilbert 1995) without going into all the existing arguments.[22]

[22]An overview is given in Alexander et al. (1987:19–20, 338–39); different meanings of emergence in current social and computational studies are sketched by Conte and Gilbert 1995:8–12; the relation of emergence and self-organization is discussed in Krohn and Küppers (1992).

We are now able to specify what kind of emergent effects we have (not) produced: In our model the five types of behavior of the intervention variable emerged from the interaction of the micro and the macro level. This is a notion of emergence as preferred by Bunge and found in the natural sciences. To the majority of sociologists, emergence implies the evolution of something that is from a qualitative standpoint completely new—for example, the formation of a group with emergent properties such as overall social identity, common goals, and a division of labor among the group members. These are all emergent properties that our computer simulation cannot reproduce unless they are included in the program model itself. However, they can then no longer be regarded as emergent properties in the proper sociological sense.

REFERENCES

Ajzen, I., and M. Fishbein. 1980. *Understanding Attitudes and Predicting Social Behavior*. Englewood Cliffs, NJ: Prentice-Hall.

Albert, Alain, ed. 1995. *Chaos and Society*. Amsterdam: Presses de l'Université du Québec.

Alexander, Jeffrey C., and B. Giesen. 1987. "From Reduction to Linkage: The Long View of the Micro-Macro Debate." Pp. 1–42 in *The Micro-Macro Link*, edited by Jeffrey C. Alexander et al., Berkeley: University of California Press.

Alexander, Jeffrey C., Bernard Giesen, Richard Münch, and Neil J. Smelser, eds. 1987. *The Micro-Macro Link*. Berkeley: University of California Press.

Archer, M. 1988. *Culture and Agency. The Place of Culture in Social Theory*. London: Cambridge University Press.

Bagozzi, Richard P. 1992. "The Self-Regulation of Attitudes, Intentions, and Behavior." *Social Psychology Quarterly* 55:178–204.

Bunge, Mario. 1979. *Treatise on Basic Philosophy. Vol. 4. Ontology II. A World of Systems*. Dordrecht, Netherlands: Reidel.

Callon, M., and B. Latour. 1981. "Unscrewing the Big Leviathan: How Actors Macro-Structure Reality and How Sociologists Help Them To Do So." Pp. 277–303 in *Advances in Social Theory and Methodology*, edited by K. Knorr-Cetina, and A. Cicourel. London: Routledge and Kegan Paul.

Carley, K. M. 1990. "Group Stability. A Socio-Cognitive Approach." Pp. 1–44 in *Advances in Group Processes*, edited by E. Lawler, B. Markovsky, C. Ridgeway, and H. Walker. Greenwich, CT: JAI.

———. 1991a. "Designing Organizational Structures to Cope with Communication Breakdowns." *Industrial Crisis Quarterly* 5:19–57.

———. 1991b. "A Theory of Group Stability." *American Sociological Review* 5:331–54.

———. 1992. "Organizational Learning and Personnel Turnover." *Organization Science* 3:2–46.

Carley, K. M., J. Kjaer-Hansen, A. Newell, M. Prietula. 1992. "Plural-Soar. A Prolegomenon to Artificial Agents and Organizational Behavior." Pages 87–118 in *Artificial Intelligence in Organization and Management Theory*, edited by M. Masuch and M. Warglien. Amsterdam: North-Holland.

Chattoe, Edmund, Nicole J. Saam, and Michael Möhring. Forthcoming. "Sensitivity Analysis in the Social Sciences: Problems and Prospects." In *Social Science Microsimulation: Tools for Modeling, Parameter Optimization, and Sensitivity Analysis*, edited by G. N. Gilbert, U. Mueller, R. Suleiman, and K. G. Troitzsch. Berlin: Springer.

Cicourel, A. 1981. "Notes on the Integration of Micro- and Macro-Levels of Analysis." Pp. 51–80 in *Advances in Social Theory and Methodology*, edited by K. Knorr-Cetina and A. Cicourel. London: Routledge and Kegan Paul.

Cohen, M. D. 1986. "Artificial Intelligence and the Dynamic Performance of Organizational Designs." Pp. 53–71 in *Ambiguity and Command: Organizational Perspectives on Military Decision Making*, edited by J. G. March and R. Weissinger-Baylon. Marshfield, MA: Pitman.

Collins, Randall. 1981. "Micro-Translations as Theory-Building Strategy." Pp. 81–108 in *Advances in Social Theory and Methodology*, edited by K. Knorr-Cetina and A. Cicourel. London: Routledge and Kegan Paul.

———. 1988. *Theoretical Sociology*. San Diego: Harcourt Brace Jovanovich.

Conte, Rosaria, and Nigel Gilbert. 1995. "Computer Simulation for Social Theory." Pp. 1–15 in *Artificial Societies: The Computer Simulation of Social Life*, edited by Nigel Gilbert and Rosaria Conte. London: UCL Press.

Converse, P. 1964. "The Nature of Belief Systems in Mass Public." Pp. 1–15 in *Ideology and Discontent*, edited by D. E. Apter. New York: Free Press.

Couclelis, H. 1985. "Cellular Worlds: A Framework for Modeling Micro-Macro Dynamics." *Environment and Planning* 17:585–96.

Crespi, I. 1988. *Pre-Election Polling*. New York: Russel Sage Foundation.

Dahl, Robert A. 1982. *Dilemmas of Pluralist Democracy*. New Haven/London: Yale University Press.

DiPrete, Thomas A., and Jerry D. Forristal. 1994. "Multilevel Models: Methods and Substance." *Annual Review of Sociology* 20:331–57.

Finer, Samuel Edward. 1962. *The Man on Horseback: The Role of Military in Politics*. Harmondsworth: Penguin Books.

———. 1976. *The Man on Horseback: The Role of Military in Politics*, 2d ed. Harmondsworth: Penguin Books.

Flache, Andreas, and Michael M. Macy. 1996. "The Weakness of Strong Ties: Collective Action Failure in a Highly Cohesive Group." *Journal of Mathematical Sociology* 21:3–28.

Giddens, A. 1984. *The Constitution of Society: Outline of the Theory of Structuration*. Cambridge, England: Polity Press.

Gilbert, Nigel. 1995. "Emergence in Social Simulation." Pp. 144–56 in *Artificial Societies: The Computer Simulation of Social Life*, edited by Nigel Gilbert and Rosaria Conte. London: UCL Press.

Gilbert, Nigel, and Jim Doran, eds. 1994. *Simulating Societies: The Computer Simulation of Social Phenomena*. London: UCL Press.

Haken, Hermann. 1978. *Synergetics. An Introduction*. Berlin: Springer.

————. 1983. *Advanced Synergetics*. Berlin: Springer.

Hanneman, Robert A. 1988. *Computer Assisted Theory Building: Modeling Dynamic Social Systems*. Newbury Park, CA: Sage.

Hanneman, Robert A., Randall Collins, and Gabriele Mordt. 1995. "Discovering Theory Dynamics by Computer Simulation: Experiments on State Legitimacy and Imperialist Capitalism." *Sociological Methodology* 25:1–46.

Harrison, J. R., and G. R. Carrol. 1991. "Keeping the Faith: A Model of Cultural Transmission in Formal Organizations." *Administration Science Quarterly* 36:552–82.

Heil, John. 1996. "The Propositional Attitudes." *Protosoziologie* 8–9:53–67.

Helbing, Dirk. 1992a. "A Mathematical Model for Attitude Formation by Pair Interactions." *Behavioral Science* 37:190–214.

————. 1992b. "A Fluid-Dynamic Model for the Movement of Pedestrians." *Complex Systems* 6:391–415.

————. 1993. *Stochastische Methoden, nichtlineare Dynamik und quantitative Modelle sozialer Prozesse*. Aachen, Germany: Shaker.

————. 1994. "A Mathematical Model for the Behavior of Individuals in a Social Field." *Journal of Mathematical Sociology* 19:189–219.

Hox, Joop J., and Ita G. G. Kreft. 1994. "Multilevel Analysis Methods." *Sociological Methods and Research* 22:283–99.

Huber, Joan, ed. 1991. *Macro-Micro Linkages in Sociology*. Newbury Park, CA: Sage.

Huntington, Samuel B. 1957. *The Soldier and the State: The Theory and Politics of Civil-Military Relations*. Cambridge, MA: Harvard University Press.

————. 1968. *Political Order in Changing Societies*. New Haven, CT: Yale University Press.

————. 1991. *The Third Wave: Democratization in the Twentieth Century*. Norman: University of Oklahoma Press.

Iyengar, S., and W. J. McGuire, eds. 1992. *Explorations in Political Psychology*. Durham, NC: Duke University Press.

Jackman, Robert W., R. H. T. O'Kane, T. H. Johnson, P. McGowan and R. O. Slater. 1986. "Explaining African Coups d'Etat." *American Political Science Review* 80:225–49.

Jenkins, J. Craig, and Augustine J. Kposowa. 1990. "Explaining Military Coups d'Etat, Black Africa 1957–84." *American Sociological Review* 55:861–75.

————. 1992. "The Political Origins of African Military Coups: Ethnic Competition, Military Centrality, and the Struggle Over the Postcolonial State." *International Studies Quarterly* 36:271–92.

Johnson, Thomas H., Robert O. Slater, and Pat McGowan. 1984. "Explaining African Military Coups d'Etat, 1960–1982." *American Political Science Review* 78:622–40.

Kaufer, David S., and Kathleen M. Carley. 1993. *Communication at a Distance: The Influence of Print on Sociocultural Organization and Change*. Hillsdale, NJ: Lawrence Erlbaum.

Kiel, Douglas L., and Euel Elliott. 1996. *Chaos Theory in the Social Sciences: Foundations and Applications*. Ann Arbor: University of Michigan Press.

Kposowa, Augustine J., and J. Craig Jenkins. 1993. "The Structural Sources of Military Coups in Postcolonial Africa, 1957–1984." *American Journal of Sociology* 99:126–63.

Krohn, Wolfgang, and Günter Küppers. 1992. *Emergenz. Die Entstehung von Ordnung, Organisation und Bedeutung.* Frankfurt/M, Germany: Suhrcamp.

Laird, J., A. Newell, and P. Rosenbloom. 1987. "SOAR: An Architecture for General Intelligence." *Artificial Intelligence* 33:1–64.

Law, A., and W. D. Kelton. 1991. *Simulation Modeling and Analysis,* 2d ed. New York: McGraw-Hill.

Markovsky, Barry. 1987. "Toward Multilevel Sociological Theories: Simulations of Actor and Network Effects." *Sociological Theory* 5:101–17.

Masuch, M., and P. LaPotin. 1989. "Beyond Garbage Cans. An AI Model of Organizational Choice." *Administration Science Quarterly* 34:38–67.

Mayntz, Renate. 1990. "The Influence of Natural Science Theories on Contemporary Social Sciences." Köln: *MPIFG Discussion Paper* 90/7.

McBroom, William H., and Fred W. Reed. 1992. "Toward a Reconceptualization of Attitude-Behavior Consistency." *Social Psychology Quarterly* 55:205–16.

McGowan, Pat, and Thomas H. Johnson. 1984. "African Military Coups d'Etat and Underdevelopment: A Quantitative Historical Analysis." *Journal of Modern African Studies* 22:633–66.

Mill, John Stuart. 1965 (1843). *A System of Logic.* Indianapolis, IN: Bobbs-Merrill.

Möhring, Michael. 1990. "MIMOSE: Eine funktionale Sprache zur Beschreibung und Simulation individuellen Verhaltens in interagierenden Populationen." Ph.D. dissertation, University of Koblenz, Germany.

———. 1996. "Social Science Multilevel Simulation with MIMOSE." Pp. 123–37 in *Social Science Microsimulation,* edited by Klaus G. Troitzsch, Ulrich Mueller, G. Nigel Gilbert, and Jim Doran. Berlin: Springer.

Möhring, M., V. Strotmann, and A. Flache. 1994. "MIMOSE: Eine funktionale Sprache zur Beschreibung und Simulation individuellen Verhaltens in interagierenden Populationen. Einführung in die Modellierung." University of Koblenz, Germany. Unpublished manuscript.

Moscovici, S. 1963. "Attitudes and Opinions." *Annual Review of Psychology* 14:231–60.

Münch, Bernard, and Neil J. Smelser. 1987. "Relating the Micro and Macro." Pp. 356–87 in *The Micro-Macro Link,* edited by Alexander et al. Berkeley: University of California Press.

Noelle-Neumann, E. 1984. *The Spiral of Silence: Public Opinion—Our Social Skin.* Chicago, IL: University of Chicago Press.

Nowak, A., and B. Latané. 1994. "Simulating the Emergence of Social Order from Individual Behavior." Pp. 63–84 in *Simulating Societies: The Computer Simulation of Social Phenomena,* edited by Nigel Gilbert and Jim Doran. London: UCL Press.

Nowak, A., and Macicj Lewenstein. 1996. "Modeling Social Change with Cellular Automata." Pp. 249–85 in *Modeling and Simulation in the Social Sciences from the Philosophy of Science Point of View,* edited by R. Hegselmann, U. Mueller, and K. G. Troitzsch. Dordrecht, Netherlands: Kluwer.

Nowak, A., J. Szamrej, and B. Latané. 1990. "From Private Attitude to Public Opinion: Dynamic Theory of Social Impact." *Psychological Review* 97:362–76.

O'Kane, Rosemary H. T. 1987. *The Likelihood of Coups.* Aldershot: Avebury.

———. 1993. "Coups d'Etat in Africa. A Political Economy Approach." *Journal of Peace Research* 30:251–70.

78 SAAM

Pestello, H. Frances G., and Fred P. Pestello. 1991. "Ignored, Neglected, and Abused: The Behavior Variable in Attitude-Behavior Research." *Symbolic Interaction* 14:341–51.

Pratkanis, A. R., S. J. Breekler, and A. G. Greenwald. 1989. *Attitude Structure and Function.* Hillsdale, NJ: Lawrence Erlbaum.

Riggs, Fred W. 1979. "The Bureaucratic Polity as a Working System." Pp. 356–74 in *Modern Thai Politics: From Village to Nation*, edited by Clark D. Neher. Cambridge, MA: Schenkman.

———. 1981. "Cabinet Ministers and Coup Groups. The Case of Thailand." *International Political Science Review* 2:159–88.

Roth, G. 1986. "Selbstorganisation—Selbsterhaltung—Selbstreferentialität. Prinzipien der Organisation der Lebewesen und ihre Folgen für die Beziehung zwischen Organismus und Umwelt." Pp. 149–80 in *Selbstorganisation. Die Entstehung von Ordnung in Natur und Gesellschaft*, edited by A. Dress, H. Hendrichs, and G. Küppers. Munich, Germany: Piper.

Saam, Nicole J. 1995. *Computergestützte Theoriekonstruktion in den Sozialwissenschaften. Konzeptbasierte Simulation eines theoretischen Modells am Beispiel militärischer Staatsstreiche in Thailand. Unter Anwendung des Mehrebenen-Ansatzes der Synergetik.* San Diego, CA, and Erlangen, Germany: Society for Computer Simulation International.

———. 1996. "Multilevel Modeling with MIMOSE: Experience from a Social Science Application." Pp. 138–54 in *Social Science Microsimulation*, edited by Klaus G. Troitzsch, Ulrich Mueller, G. Nigel Gilbert, and Jim Doran. Berlin, Germany: Springer.

Scott, James C. 1972. "Patron-Client Politics and Political Change in Southeast Asia." *American Political Science Review* 66:91–113.

Stewart, I. 1989. *Does God Play Dice? The Mathematics of Chaos.* Oxford, England: Basil Blackwell.

Suppes, Patrick. 1968. "The Desirability of Formalization in Science." *Journal of Philosophy* 65:24–39.

Troitzsch, Klaus G. 1990. "Self-Organisation in Social Systems." Pp. 353–77 in *Computer Aided Sociological Research*, edited by Johannes Gladitz and Klaus G. Troitzsch. Berlin, Germany: Akademie Verlag.

———. 1996. "Multilevel Simulation." Pp. 107–22 in *Social Science Microsimulation*, edited by Klaus G. Troitzsch, Ulrich Mueller, G. Nigel Gilbert, and Jim Doran. Berlin, Germany: Springer.

Turner, J. H. 1988. *A Theory of Social Interaction.* Stanford, CA: Stanford University Press.

Weidlich, Wolfgang. 1991. "Physics and Social Science: The Approach of Synergetics." *Physics Reports* 204:1–163.

———. 1994. "Synergetic Modeling Concepts for Sociodynamics with Application to Collective Political Opinion Formation." *Journal of Mathematical Sociology* 18:267–91.

Weidlich, Wolfgang, and Günter Haag, eds. 1983. *Concepts and Models of a Quantitative Sociology: The Dynamics of Interacting Populations.* Berlin, Germany: Springer.

————. 1988. *Interregional Migration: Dynamic Theory and Comparative Analysis.* Berlin, Germany: Springer.

Whicker, Marcia, and Lee Sigelman. 1991. *Computer Simulation Applications: An Introduction.* Newbury Park, CA: Sage.

Wiley, Norbert. 1988. "The Micro-Macro Problem in Social Theory." *Sociological Theory* 6:254–61.

Yamaguchi, Kazuo. 1996. "Power in Networks of Substitutable and Complementary Exchange Relations: A Rational-Choice Model and an Analysis of Power Centralization." *American Sociological Review* 61:308–32.

A GOODNESS-OF-FIT TEST FOR THE LATENT CLASS MODEL WHEN EXPECTED FREQUENCIES ARE SMALL

Mark Reiser*
Yiching Lin*

In this paper, a goodness-of-fit test for the latent class model is presented. The test uses only the limited information in the second-order marginal distributions from a set of k dichotomous variables, and it is intended for use when k is large and the sample size, n, is moderate or small. In that situation, a 2^k contingency table formed by the full cross-classification of k variables will be sparse in the sense that a high proportion of cell frequencies will be equal to zero or 1, and the chi-square approximation for traditional goodness-of-fit statistics such as the likelihood ratio will not be valid. The second-order marginal frequencies, which correspond to the bivariate distributions, are rarely sparse even when the joint frequencies have a high proportion of zero cells. Results from Monte Carlo experiments are presented that compare the rates of Type I and Type II errors for the proposed test to the rates for traditional goodness-of-fit tests. Results show that under commonly encountered conditions, a test of fit based on the limited information in the second-order marginals has a Type II error rate that is no higher than the error rate found for full-information test statistics, and that the test statistic given in this paper does not suffer from ill effects of sparseness in the joint frequencies.

The authors would like to thank William W. Eaton, Adrian Raftery, and Lawrence Mayer for helpful suggestions. This research was supported in part by National Institute of Mental Health Grant Number 47447 and in part by a Research Incentive Grant from Arizona State University.
*Arizona State University

1. INTRODUCTION

In this paper, a goodness-of-fit test is presented for the latent class model. The test uses only the limited information[1] in the second-order marginal distributions from a set of k dichotomous variables, and it is intended for use when k is large and the sample size, n, is moderate or small. In that situation, a 2^k contingency table formed by the full cross-classification of k variables will be sparse in the sense that a high proportion of cell frequencies will be equal to zero or 1, and the chi-square approximation for traditional goodness-of-fit statistics such as the likelihood ratio will not be valid. The second-order marginal frequencies, which correspond to the bivariate distributions, are rarely sparse even when the joint frequencies have a high proportion of zero cells. The proposed statistic is for a test of conditional independence in the marginal frequencies of the manifest variables. While the latent class model specifies conditional independence in the joint frequencies, conditional independence in the joint frequencies implies conditional independence in the marginal frequencies. Hence, whenever the test presented in Section 2 indicates that conditional independence does not hold in the marginal frequencies, the hypothesized latent class model can be rejected. The proposed test is similar to one used in factor analysis of dichotomous variables (Christoffersson 1975; Muthen 1978). The statistic proposed in Section 2 could be generalized to test any multinomial model of independence or conditional independence; the results presented here, however, pertain only to the latent class model.

Results from Monte Carlo experiments are presented that compare the rates of Type I and Type II errors for the proposed test to the rates for traditional goodness-of-fit tests. Results show that under commonly encountered conditions, a test of fit based on the limited information in the second-order marginals has a Type II error rate that is no higher than the

---

[1]The term Fisher information is widely used in statistics to refer to the negative expected value of the second derivative of the log-likelihood function. The term "information" is used in a generic sense in the area of factor analysis of categorical variables, where the multinomial distribution is almost always used as the distribution of the cell frequencies. The joint frequencies are the minimal sufficient statistics in most forms of the model. Factor analysis methods that use the joint frequencies for estimation and testing have been referred to as full-information, whereas methods that use univariate and bivariate distributions (i.e., marginal distributions) have been referred to as limited-information (Bock, Gibbons, and Muraki 1988). In this paper, the terms "limited information" and "full information" are used in the same sense as in factor analysis of categorical variables.

error rate found for full-information test statistics, and that the test statistic given in this paper does not suffer from ill effects of sparseness in the joint frequencies. An example that demonstrates the usefulness of the new test is presented in Section 4. The example uses responses to 11 questions regarding anxiety and depression from the National Institute of Mental Health Epidemiological Catchment Area Program. Since conditional independence in the marginal frequencies does not necessarily imply conditional independence in the joint frequencies, some cautions about the use of the test are discussed in Section 5.

1.1. *Latent Class Model*

The latent class model is presented in this section. Suppose that data are available on k manifest variables, or items, for each of n individuals; each variable can take only the values 0 and 1. The probability of the response 1 to the ith item produces manifest variable Y_i. Suppose that the values of the manifest variables are associated with a categorical latent variable X. Then the latent class model is as follows:

$$Y_i | X \sim \text{independent} , \tag{1}$$

with the conditional probability that $Y_i = 1$ for a generic individual at level x of X written as $P(Y_i = 1 | X = x)$ for $i = 1, \ldots, k$. The subscript for individuals is suppressed when no ambiguity occurs. Since

$$P(Y_i = 0 | X = x) = 1 - P(Y_i = 1 | X = x) ,$$

it follows that

$$P(Y_i = y_i | x) = P(Y_i = 1 | x)^{y_i} [1 - P(Y_i = 1 | x)]^{1 - y_i} .$$

Let $Y = (Y_1, Y_2, \ldots, Y_k)$ denote the vector of manifest variables, and let y denote the realization of Y. It is assumed that, *conditional* upon the latent variable, responses to the manifest variables are independent. Thus, for any pattern of responses from a generic individual at level x of X,

$$P(Y = y | x) = \prod_{i=1}^{k} P(Y_i = 1 | x)^{y_i} [1 - P(Y_i = 1 | x)]^{1 - y_i} . \tag{2}$$

There are 2^k possible patterns of responses that represent values that may be taken by Y, and each of these realized values of y can be called a response pattern. Let $s = 1, 2, \ldots, T$, where $T = 2^k$, then s may be used as an index for response patterns, for the probabilities associated with response patterns and for the frequencies associated with response patterns. Finally, the marginal probability that response pattern s will be given by a randomly selected individual is obtained by taking the expected value with respect to the distribution of X in the population:

$$P_s(\mathbf{Y} = \mathbf{y}) = \sum_x P_s(\mathbf{Y} = \mathbf{y} | x) P(X = x) \ , \tag{3}$$

where $P(X = x)$ is the probability that a randomly selected individual is at level x of X. Lazarsfeld (1950) referred to the equations represented by expression (3) as the *accounting equations*.

Let $\mathbf{V}$ denote a multinomial random vector of dimension T for the frequencies associated with the response patterns, and let $\mathbf{n}$ denote the realization of $\mathbf{V}$. n_s is element s of $\mathbf{n}$ and denotes the number of respondents associated with response pattern s. Then the distribution of $\mathbf{V}$ is given by

$$P(\mathbf{V} = \mathbf{n}) = n! \prod_{s=1}^{T} \frac{[P_s(\mathbf{Y} = \mathbf{y})]^{n_s}}{n_s!} \tag{4}$$

where n = total sample size = $\displaystyle\sum_{s=1}^{T} n_s$.

In most applications of the latent class model, the conditional and latent class probabilities in expression (3) are estimated by maximizing the likelihood, using a likelihood function based on the multinomial distribution given in expression (4) and an iterative proportional fitting algorithm, as implemented by Goodman (1974b). Goodman's implementation fits into a larger class of algorithms known as the EM algorithms (Dempster, Laird, and Rubin 1977). The MLLSA program (Clogg 1977) and the ℓEM program (Vermunt 1997) can be used to perform these computations. Clogg and Goodman (1984, 1985) and McCutcheon (1996) present latent class models for comparing populations or groups.

1.2. *Log-Linear Latent Class Model*

The latent class model may also be represented by a log-linear model as given by Haberman (1979). The conditional independence among the manifest variables, Y_i, is expressed in the following model for the log of the joint frequencies for the latent variable X and the Y_i variables:

$$log\ m_{xab...q} = \lambda + \lambda_x^X + \lambda_a^{Y_1} + \lambda_b^{Y_2} + \cdots + \lambda_q^{Y_k} + \lambda_{xa}^{XY_1} + \lambda_{xb}^{XY_2}$$

$$+ \cdots + \lambda_{xq}^{XY_k}\ , \tag{5}$$

where λ = grand mean effect

λ_x^X = first-order effect for latent variable X

$\lambda_c^{Y_i}$ = first-order effect for manifest variable Y_i

$\lambda_{xc}^{XY_i}$ = association effect for X and Y_i,

and where

$$\sum_x \lambda_x^X = \sum_a \lambda_a^{Y_1} = \cdots = \sum_q \lambda_q^{Y_k} = \sum_x \lambda_{xa}^{XY_1} = \sum_a \lambda_{xa}^{XY_1} = \cdots = \sum_x \lambda_{xq}^{XY_k}$$

$$= \sum_q \lambda_{xq}^{XY_k} = 0\ .$$

The parameter λ_x^X is associated with $P(X = x)$. Since the manifest variables, Y_i, are assumed to be dichotomous, each of the subscripts for levels of the Y_i variables—namely, $a, b, \ldots, q$—take on values from the set $\{1,2\}$. Since there are k manifest variables, there are k subscripts in $a, b, \ldots, q$. Other sets of values could also be used for these subscripts, such as $\{0,1\}$. There are T sequences for the values that may be taken on by $a, b, \ldots, q$, and since each sequence corresponds to a pattern of responses to the manifest variables, the subscripts $a, b, \ldots, q$ can be used as an index for response patterns. The subscript s has also been used as an index for response patterns, and there is a one-to-one correspondence between values of $a, b, \ldots, q$ and values of s. Thus $m_{xab...q}$ may be written as m_{xs}. Hagenaars (1993) and Heinen (1996) also discuss the log-linear version of the latent class model.

The expected counts for the joint frequencies under the log-linear model may be expressed as follows:

$$m_{xab...q} = exp(\lambda + \lambda_x^X + \lambda_a^{Y_1} + \lambda_b^{Y_2} + \cdots + \lambda_q^{Y_k} + \lambda_{xa}^{XY_1} + \lambda_{xb}^{XY_2}$$

$$+ \cdots + \lambda_{xq}^{XY_k})\ ,$$

and $$m_{ab...q}^{Y_1 Y_2 \cdots Y_k} = \sum_x m_{xab...q}\ .$$

Since X is a latent variable, the frequencies $n_{xab\cdots q}$ are not directly observable, but the expected counts $m_{xab\cdots q}$ are estimated at each iteration of the procedure for estimating model parameters. Let the elements of the vector $\boldsymbol{\beta}$ consist of the linearly independent λ parameters. The probability that the response pattern s will be given by a randomly selected individual is then

$$\pi_s(\boldsymbol{\beta}) = P_s(Y = \mathbf{y}|\boldsymbol{\beta}) = \frac{m_{ab\cdots q}^{Y_1 Y_2 \cdots Y_k}}{\sum_a \sum_b \cdots \sum_q m_{ab\cdots q}^{Y_1 Y_2 \cdots Y_k}} \ .$$

Maximum-likelihood parameter estimation can be carried out by using a likelihood function based on either the multinomial distribution and the probabilities $\pi_s(\boldsymbol{\beta})$ or on the Poisson distribution for the cell counts. In the multinomial representation, the parameter that relates to total sample size (λ) is not included as an element of $\boldsymbol{\beta}$. Haberman (1979) gives details of both the iterative proportional fitting algorithm and the scoring algorithm as applied to the log-linear version of the latent class model.

The fit of a latent class model is traditionally assessed with a Pearson or likelihood ratio chi-square statistic. These tests will be referred to as full-information tests since they use all of the information in the joint frequencies. In applications of the latent class model, there is often a large number of variables relative to the sample size, resulting in joint frequencies that are sparse. Sparseness may affect the validity of the chi-square distribution as used as an approximation for the distribution of traditional goodness-of-fit statistics (Koehler and Larntz 1980; Simonoff 1986; Haberman 1988a), as discussed below.

1.3. Sparseness

There is a large literature on the topic of sparse frequencies and their effect on goodness-of-fit tests for the multinomial distribution. Throughout this discussion, and in the sections that follow, it is assumed that any zero cells have occurred in a manner that would not prevent the calculation of one or more parameter estimates—i.e., it is assumed that the relevant model is identified. Frequency tables are said to be *sparse* when the ratio of the sample size to the number of cells is relatively small (Agresti and Yang 1987). It is well known that when expected cell frequencies for a frequency table are small, the probability values taken from the chi-square distribution may not be valid for the goodness-of-fit statistics discussed above. There is a lack of universal agreement on what constitutes a small expected frequency. In his very influential paper, Cochran (1954) suggested, like Fisher (1941), that most expected frequencies should be at least five for the use of the Pearson statistic. Cramer (1946) suggested that expected frequencies should be at least 10; Kendall (1952) and Tate and Hyer (1973) have suggested 20. Haberman (1988a) showed that given any minimum expected cell size under the null hypothesis and given any significance level, it is possible to make the power of the Pearson statistic (X^2) arbitrarily close to zero by the selection of a large enough number of cells and suitable cell probabilities for the null and alternative hypotheses.

More recent attempts to deal with the problem of sparseness have used results from Holst (1972) and Morris (1975) to develop a normal approximation for the distributions of the goodness-of-fit statistics. Some authors have found the normal approximation to be useful (Koehler and Larntz 1980; Koehler 1986; Agresti and Yang 1987), but others have not (Berry and Mielke 1988). Zelterman (1987) developed a statistic for large sparse contingency tables, and for which the performance of the normal, as an approximation for the reference distribution, was improved when compared to its performance with the likelihood ratio statistic (G^2) and the Pearson statistic. In general, the required conditions—for example, that the number of cells must increase as the sample size increases—are somewhat restricting for the use of approaches based on normal approximations.

Collins, Fidler, Wugalter, and Long (1993) investigated the performance of the G^2, X^2, as well as the power divergence (PD) statistic (Read and Cressie 1988) specifically for latent class models fit to sparse contingency tables. Their findings are consistent with the results cited above: The mean of the distribution for each of these statistics is farther from the expectation of the chi-square distribution when the average cell expectation is small, when there are more indicator items, and when the model measurement parameters are more extreme. They also found that the mean of the X^2 distribution is generally closer to the expectation of the chi-square distribution than are the means of the other two statistics, but that the standard deviation of the X^2 distribution is considerably larger than that of the other two statistics and larger than the standard deviation of the chi-square distribution. They concluded that "the problems with goodness-of-fit testing for latent class models are extensive."

When sparseness is present in a set of frequencies, informal remedies such as combining cells or adding a small constant such as 0.5 (Goodman 1964) to each cell are sometimes recommended. These remedies may be helpful if only a few cells have low expected counts, but they are not useful if sparseness is severe. Adding a constant such as 0.5 can significantly increase the sample size for a large table, and it smooths the data toward a model where all cells have the same probability. In even moderately sparse tables, adding a small constant often produces a large conservative effect on the outcome of the test of fit (Agresti 1990; Agresti and Yang 1987).

2. A TEST OF FIT

In this section a covariance matrix is obtained for unstandardized residuals. Next, the results for unstandardized residuals are extended to second-order marginals. Finally, the results on residuals are used to obtain a statistic for testing conditional independence in second-order marginals. It is not the purpose of this paper to pursue traditional residual analysis, and the covariance matrix for these residuals is presented only because it will be used in the construction of the test statistic later in this section.

2.1. Residuals

If a model shows a poor fit to a data set, it may be useful to examine residuals for the cells of the multinomial vector of response patterns. There are several approaches to forming residuals, including the unstandardized residual $r_s = \hat{p}_s - \pi_s(\hat{\beta})$, where

$\hat{p}_s = n_s/n$ is element s of $\hat{p}$, the vector of multinomial proportions

$\hat{\beta}$ = parameter vector estimator and

$\pi_s(\hat{\beta})$ = estimated expected proportion for cell s .

Although it has been traditional to examine standardized residuals— i.e., $\sqrt{n}(\pi_s(\hat{\beta}))^{-1/2} r_s$ (Cochran 1954)—when working with models based on the multinomial distribution, the unstandardized residual will be used in the remainder of this paper.

The following result has been obtained by Haberman (1973) as well as Rao (1973). See also Cox (1984) for a review of the results obtained by Haberman and Rao. Under the regularity conditions given by Birch (1964),

$$\sqrt{n}r \xrightarrow{L} N(0, \Omega_r) , \tag{6}$$

where $\Omega_r = D(\boldsymbol{\pi}) - \boldsymbol{\pi}\boldsymbol{\pi}' - G(A'A)^{-1}G'$

$\xrightarrow{L}$ indicates convergence in Law

$\boldsymbol{\pi}(\boldsymbol{\beta})$ = vector of multinomial probabilities as a function of $\boldsymbol{\beta}$

$D(\boldsymbol{\pi})$ = diagonal matrix with (s,s) element equal to $\pi_s(\boldsymbol{\beta})$

$$A = D(\boldsymbol{\pi})^{-1/2}\frac{\partial \boldsymbol{\pi}(\boldsymbol{\beta})}{\partial \boldsymbol{\beta}}, \qquad \text{and}$$

$$G = \frac{\partial \boldsymbol{\pi}(\boldsymbol{\beta})}{\partial \boldsymbol{\beta}}.$$

For the log-linear latent class model,

$$\frac{\partial \boldsymbol{\pi}(\boldsymbol{\beta})}{\partial \boldsymbol{\beta}} = [D(\boldsymbol{\pi}) - \boldsymbol{\pi}\boldsymbol{\pi}']\bar{U},$$

where $\bar{U}$ is a 2^k by g model matrix with full column rank, and where g is the dimension of $\boldsymbol{\beta}$. Let W represent the number of categories for the latent variable X, and let U represent a $W \cdot 2^k$ by g model matrix for $log\, m_{xs}$. $\bar{U}$ is obtained from U by taking the conditional expected value with respect to X over the rows of U. See Haberman (1979) for details.

Cochran (1955) also gave results on asymptotic variances of residuals. The residual divided by its asymptotic variance is sometimes called the adjusted residual (Haberman 1973). Adjusted residuals are often more useful than simple residuals for the purpose of finding the source of poor fit for a model, because the magnitude of the adjusted residual can be assessed in terms of the $N(0,1)$ distribution. In the next section, residuals are considered for second-order marginals.

2.2. Second-Order Marginals

In this section, a covariance matrix is obtained for residuals calculated on the second-order marginals. When the number of manifest variables is large relative to the sample size, sparseness may be present, in which case a test of the model using traditional fit statistics on the T cells of the entire joint distribution may have little or no validity, as discussed in Section 1. In this situation, it may be more useful to assess the fit of the model on the second-order marginal frequencies (i.e., the bivariate distributions of the manifest variables). As discussed earlier, if a latent class model is rejected based on the use of second-order marginals, then it could be concluded that the model does not hold in the joint frequencies either. The second-order marginal frequencies are almost always substantially larger than zero, even with small samples, so a test based on these frequencies would not be expected to suffer from the ill effects of sparseness.

Zeros and 1's can be used to code the levels of the dichotomous response variables. A k-dimensional vector of zeros and 1's, sometimes called a response pattern, can be used to indicate a specific cell from the contingency table formed by the cross-classification of the k response variables. A set of T response patterns can be generated by varying the index of the kth variable most rapidly, the kth-1 variable next, etc. Let w_{is} represent element i of response pattern s, then under the model, the second-order marginal proportion for variables Y_i and Y_j can be defined as

$$P_{ij}(1,1|\boldsymbol{\beta}) = P(Y_i = 1, Y_j = 1|\boldsymbol{\beta}) = \sum_s w_{is} w_{js} \pi_s(\boldsymbol{\beta}) ,$$

and the true second-order marginal proportion is given by

$$P_{ij}(1,1) = P(Y_i = 1, Y_j = 1) = \sum_s w_{is} w_{js} \pi_s .$$

The summation across the frequencies associated with the response patterns to obtain the marginal proportions represents a transformation of the frequencies in the multinomial vector $\boldsymbol{\pi}$, which can be implemented via multiplication by matrix $\mathbf{H}$, where for $j = 1, 2, \ldots k; i = j, j + 1, \ldots k; s = 1, 2, \ldots T$; and $\ell = (j - 1)k + 0.5(j)(j - 1) + i$, element ℓs of $\mathbf{H}$ is given by

$$h_{\ell s} = \begin{cases} 1 & \text{if } w_{is} = w_{js} = 1. \\ 0 & \text{otherwise} \end{cases} .$$

Using matrix $\mathbf{H}$,

$$P_{ij}(1,1|\boldsymbol{\beta}) = P(Y_i = 1, Y_j = 1|\boldsymbol{\beta}) = \mathbf{h}'_\ell \boldsymbol{\pi}(\boldsymbol{\beta}) ,$$

and

$$P_{ij}(1,1) = P(Y_i = 1, Y_j = 1) = \mathbf{h}'_\ell \boldsymbol{\pi} ,$$

where $\mathbf{h}'_\ell$ is row ℓ of matrix $\mathbf{H}$.

Differences associated with the second-order marginals may be defined such that

$$P_{ij}(1,1) - P_{ij}(1,1|\boldsymbol{\beta}) = \delta_{ij} \ .$$

These differences may be placed into the vector $\boldsymbol{\delta}$, where

$$\boldsymbol{\delta} = \mathbf{H}(\boldsymbol{\pi} - \boldsymbol{\pi}(\boldsymbol{\beta})) \ .$$

A simple residual for the second-order marginal may be defined by

$$e_{ij} = \hat{P}_{ij}(1,1) - P_{ij}(1,1|\hat{\boldsymbol{\beta}}) \ ,$$

where

$$P_{ij}(1,1|\hat{\boldsymbol{\beta}}) = P(Y_i = 1, Y_j = 1|\hat{\boldsymbol{\beta}}) = \mathbf{h}'_\ell \boldsymbol{\pi}(\hat{\boldsymbol{\beta}}) \ ,$$

$$\hat{P}_{ij}(1,1) = \hat{P}(Y_i = 1, Y_j = 1) = \mathbf{h}'_\ell \hat{\mathbf{p}}.$$

Theorem 1.

Let $e = \mathbf{H}'\mathbf{r}$ be a vector of residuals on the second-order marginals. Under the regularity conditions given by Birch (1964),

$$\sqrt{n}e \xrightarrow{L} N(0, \boldsymbol{\Omega}_e) \ , \tag{7}$$

where $\boldsymbol{\Omega}_e = \mathbf{H}\boldsymbol{\Omega}_\mathbf{r}\mathbf{H}'$. Because the elements of e are linear combinations of the elements of $\mathbf{r}$, the theorem follows from result 6.a.1(ii) of Rao (1973). ∎

The rank of $\boldsymbol{\Omega}_e$ is generally equal to $\min(2^k - g, 0.5k(k-1))$, where g is the dimension of $\boldsymbol{\beta}$, as defined previously. Let $\boldsymbol{\Sigma}_e$ represent the covariance matrix of e. Then a consistent estimator for this covariance matrix is

$$\hat{\boldsymbol{\Sigma}}_e = n^{-1}\boldsymbol{\Omega}_e \ , \tag{8}$$

evaluated at the maximum likelihood estimates $\hat{\boldsymbol{\pi}}$ and $\hat{\boldsymbol{\beta}}$. In the next section, these results on second-order marginals are used to construct a test of fit for the latent class model.

2.3. The Test of Fit

A method to assess the second-order residuals as a set would test the null hypothesis that the vector of differences, $\boldsymbol{\delta}$, is equal to zero. The Wald statistic

$$X_w^2 = e'\hat{\boldsymbol{\Sigma}}_e^{-1}e \tag{9}$$

may be used for this test. This test will be referred to as a limited-information test since it does not use information from the third- or higher-order marginals.

Since it has already been established that the limiting distribution of e is multivariate normal, and since $\hat{\Sigma}_e$ is converging stochastically to Σ_e, the limiting distribution of X_w^2 as $n \to \infty$ is the chi-square distribution, by Theorem 2.4.5 of Anderson (1984). The degrees of freedom are determined by the rank of Ω_e. Certain configurations of proportions in π may reduce the rank of Ω_e below this stated value. Specifically, whenever parameters for two variables, say Y_i and $Y_{i'}$, are equal—i.e., $\lambda_1^{Y_i} = \lambda_1^{Y_{i'}}$ and $\lambda_{11}^{XY_i} = \lambda_{11}^{XY_{i'}}$—the rank of Ω_e, and thereby the rank of Σ_e, will be reduced by 1. When parameter estimates for two variables are nearly equal in the same way, ill-conditioning may be present in $\hat{\Sigma}_e$.

3. MONTE CARLO SIMULATION

A Monte Carlo simulation was conducted in order to assess the performance of the statistic developed in Section 3. In addition to results for X_w^2, results are given for the likelihood ratio statistic, the Pearson statistic, the FT statistic developed by Freeman and Tukey (1950), and the Power Divergence (PD) statistic. The power-divergence statistic is defined as follows:

$$PD = 2(\gamma(\gamma + 1))^{-1} \sum_s n_s \left((\hat{m}_s^{-1} n_s)^\gamma - 1 \right) .$$

Read and Cressie (1988) have shown that the Pearson, likelihood ratio, and Freeman-Tukey statistics are each a special case of this statistic. The Pearson statistic is obtained when $\gamma = 1$, the likelihood ratio statistic is obtained as the limit when $\gamma \to 0$, and the Freeman-Tukey statistic is obtained when $\gamma = -\frac{1}{2}$. Read and Cressie (1988) have suggested $\gamma = \frac{2}{3}$ as the best choice for the power divergence statistic when it is to be applied to a sparse table, and this value of γ was used to obtain the results reported below for the power divergence statistic.

Tables 1, 2, and 3 contain the results of the simulations. Each column in the tables is based on 1000 samples of size 500, obtained by using the IMSL uniform random number generator. For all simulation results, models were fit using versions of the LAT (Haberman 1979) and NEWTON (Haberman 1988b) programs, modified to produce the statistic presented in Section 2.

For Table 1, data sets were generated from a model that has two latent classes, coded -1 and 1, with $P(X = -1) = P(X = 1) = 0.5$, and

TABLE 1
Latent Class Model Simulation Results for Type I Error (Symmetric)

$\alpha = 0.05$	Number of Manifest Variables = k						
Statistic	4	5	6	7	8	9	10
G^2	0.057	0.069	0.079	0.217	0.355	0.029	0.0
Pearson	0.053	0.057	0.042	0.055	0.044	0.059	0.072
FT	0.060	0.079	0.046	0.0	0.0	0.0	0.0
PD	0.053	0.056	0.042	0.047	0.029	0.0	0.0
X_w^2	0.054	0.057	0.048	0.059	0.056	0.055	0.059
Not converged	0	0	0	0	0	0	0
Sparseness	0.0	0.0005	0.042	0.268	0.574	0.790	0.906
	Rate of Disagreement						
G^2 vs. Pearson	0.006	0.018	0.043	0.162	0.311	0.044	0.072
G^2 vs. FT	0.005	0.012	0.067	0.217	0.355	0.029	0.0
G^2 vs. PD	0.006	0.015	0.039	0.170	0.326	0.029	0.0
G^2 vs. X_w^2	0.013	0.066	0.081	0.200	0.331	0.070	0.059
Pearson vs. FT	0.011	0.028	0.038	0.055	0.044	0.059	0.072
Pearson vs. PD	0.0	0.005	0.004	0.010	0.015	0.059	0.072
Pearson vs. X_w^2	0.007	0.062	0.056	0.082	0.080	0.096	0.113
FT vs. PD	0.011	0.027	0.038	0.047	0.029	0.0	0.0
FT vs. X_w^2	0.018	0.070	0.068	0.059	0.056	0.055	0.059
PD vs. X_w^2	0.007	0.061	0.056	0.074	0.073	0.055	0.059

Note: Each cell entry is based on 1000 samples of size 500. The row labeled "Sparseness" gives the proportion of the $2^k \times 1000$ cells in each column with an observed count of either 0 or 1.

where the degree of association between manifest variables and the latent variable is constant ($\lambda_{11}^{XY_i} = 0.5$). Also, each variable has a marginal probability of 0.5, so the joint probabilities produced by the fully cross-classified contingency table are symmetric. Moving across Table 1 from left to right, the only change in the data for each successive column is that another manifest variable is added, which increases the sparseness of the joint frequencies.

The model that was fit to the data specified two latent classes, so that rejection of the model based on a goodness-of-fit statistic represents a Type I error; the rate of these errors is shown in the top of Table 1. Moving across the columns, sparseness in the data increases from left to right, and at the right of the table, in the columns under nine and ten variables, only the Pearson and X_w^2 statistics have empirical Type I error rates that are close to the nominal rate of $\alpha = 0.05$. Among the other statistics, the likelihood ratio appears to be the most susceptible to the effects of sparseness, followed by the Freeman-Tukey and the power divergence statistics. When interpreting the results from this table, or from Tables 2 and 3, it is important to recognize that as the number of manifest variables increases linearly, the number of cells in the full cross-classification increases geometrically, and the degree of sparseness increases at a super-linear rate.

Table 2 is similar to Table 1, except that the degree of association between the manifest variables and the latent variable was not constant: three different values were used for $\lambda_{11'}^{XY_i}$: 0.371, 0.491, and 0.834. As more manifest variables were added to the data, $\lambda_{11'}^{XY_i}$ values were selected from this set of values on a rotating basis. These parameter values are similar to the values found by Salomaa (1990) in her extensive empirical study of data sets consisting of categorical variables that are multiple indicators used to measure an underlying variable. The marginal probabilities for the

TABLE 2
Latent Class Model Simulation Results for Type I Error (Asymmetric)

$\alpha = 0.05$	Number of Manifest Variables $= k$						
Statistic	4	5	6	7	8	9	10
G^2	0.047	0.062	0.11	0.10	0.016	0.0	0.0
Pearson	0.045	0.052	0.061	0.05	0.095	0.106	0.179
FT	0.052	0.066	0.011	0.0	0.0	0.0	0.0
PD	0.044	0.053	0.052	0.026	0.003	0.0	0.001
X_w^2	0.049	0.047	0.061	0.051	0.051	0.057	0.064
Not converged	5	0	0	1	0	0	7
Sparseness	0.0	0.008	0.146	0.433	0.657	0.808	0.91
Rate of Disagreement							
G^2 vs. Pearson	0.010	0.022	0.063	0.068	0.085	0.106	0.179
G^2 vs. FT	0.005	0.024	0.099	0.100	0.016	0	0
G^2 vs. PD	0.006	0.015	0.058	0.076	0.017	0	0.001
G^2 vs. X_w^2	0.034	0.057	0.105	0.121	0.059	0.057	0.064
Pearson vs. FT	0.015	0.034	0.050	0.050	0.095	0.106	0.179
Pearson vs. PD	0.004	0.007	0.013	0.024	0.092	0.106	0.178
Pearson vs. X_w^2	0.024	0.049	0.084	0.089	0.120	0.147	0.211
FT vs. PD	0.011	0.029	0.041	0.026	0.003	0	0.001
FT vs. X_w^2	0.039	0.067	0.062	0.051	0.051	0.057	0.064
PD vs. X_w^2	0.028	0.048	0.077	0.067	0.054	0.057	0.063

Note: Each cell entry is based on 1000 samples of size 500.

manifest variables are no longer equal to 0.5, and the joint probabilities for the fully cross-classified contingency tables are no longer symmetric. The effect of the asymmetry is to increase the degree of sparseness when compared to Table 1. In Table 2, when the number of manifest variables is eight or greater, only the X_w^2 statistic has an acceptable empirical Type I error rate. Among the results for the other statistics, it is noteworthy that the empirical Type I error rate for the power divergence statistic never exceeds the nominal 0.05 level. The results in Tables 1 and 2 for the Pearson and likelihood ratio statistics are similar to results obtained by Koehler and Larntz (1980) and by Koehler (1986), who found that as sparseness increased, Type I error rates tended to increase and then drop off, but with differences in the performance of the two statistics. As demonstrated by these authors, the increase in cells with observed frequency equal to zero or one accounts for the differences in the behavior of the Pearson and likelihood ratio statistics (G^2) as the number of manifest variables increases. The minimum contribution of a cell with observed count of one is larger for G^2 than for X^2, which would explain the higher empirical rejection rate under G^2 for number of variables equal to five, six, and seven in Table 2, for example.

For number of variables equal to eight or more, cells with observed count equal to zero dominate the G^2 statistic in the following way. The calculation of the value taken on by the likelihood ratio statistic consists of summing contributions from each cell in the table under investigation. The calculation of the contribution from each cell, in turn, requires either the logarithm of, or division by, the observed frequency for that cell. When an observed frequency is zero, the contribution of that cell to the value taken on by the statistic cannot be calculated and is typically defined to be zero. For the Pearson statistic, on the other hand, the contribution of an empty cell is well defined. (Cells with *expected* value equal to zero are problematic for the Pearson statistic.) So, when there are many empty cells, the likelihood ratio statistic may have contributions from less than half of the cells, while the Pearson statistic will have contributions from all or nearly all cells. With so many cells not contributing, the G^2 statistic virtually never rejects H_o, as can be seen in Table 2 for number of variables equal to eight or more.

Table 3 shows simulation results for power against a false null hypothesis. The data for this table were generated by the same method as for Table 2, except a moderate association not accounted for by the latent variable was included for manifest variables 3 and 4. To introduce this moderate association, a second latent variable was added to the model for generating the data sets. The second latent variable has two levels, coded

TABLE 3
Latent Class Model Simulation Results for Power

$\alpha = 0.05$	Number of Manifest Variables = k						
Statistic	4	5	6	7	8	9	10
G^2	0.880	0.83	0.78	0.69	0.23	0.0	0.0
Pearson	0.892	0.83	0.68	0.47	0.33	0.29	0.325
FT	0.878	0.83	0.48	0.0	0.0	0.0	0.0
PD	0.886	0.83	0.67	0.41	0.11	0.0	0.0
X_w^2	0.883	0.9	0.925	0.87	0.84	0.81	0.736
Not converged	5	5	0	0	1	1	8
Sparseness	0.0	0.01	0.13	0.4	0.64	0.81	0.9
	Rate of Disagreement						
G^2 vs. Pearson	0.014	0.027	0.110	0.228	0.166	0.452	0.325
G^2 vs. FT	0.008	0.021	0.306	0.690	0.228	0	0
G^2 vs. PD	0.008	0.020	0.110	0.278	0.132	0.004	0
G^2 vs. X_w^2	0.023	0.110	0.179	0.265	0.633	0.928	0.736
Pearson vs. FT	0.022	0.044	0.228	0.468	0.326	0.452	0.325
Pearson vs. PD	0.006	0.007	0.020	0.062	0.216	0.448	0.325
Pearson vs. X_w^2	0.015	0.106	0.259	0.439	0.565	0.508	0.531
FT vs. PD	0.016	0.039	0.224	0.414	0.110	0.004	0
FT vs. X_w^2	0.031	0.112	0.453	0.871	0.839	0.928	0.736
PD vs. X_w^2	0.015	0.111	0.263	0.481	0.733	0.924	0.736

Note: Each cell entry is based on 1000 samples of size 500.

-1 and 1, with $P(X_2 = -1) = 0.62$ and $P(X_2 = 1) = 0.38$. For the third and fourth manifest variables, $\lambda_{11}^{X_2 Y_3} = \lambda_{11}^{X_2 Y_4} = 0.60$. All other manifest variables have no association with latent variable X_2. Since the model fit to the data specified that all association among the manifest variables should be attributable to one latent variable (X_1), the model is false. Each cell in Table 3 represents a single point on a power curve. The results in the table clearly show the deleterious effects of sparseness on the likelihood ratio, Pearson, Freeman-Tukey, and power divergence statistics. For nine or more variables, only the Pearson and X_w^2 statistics have power greater than the Type I error rate. Power can be directly compared across statistics only when the Type I error rates are equivalent. For the Pearson and X_w^2 statistics, a comparison may be done out to seven variables, where it is apparent that X_w^2 has considerably higher power.

The entries at the bottom of Tables 1, 2, and 3 show rates of disagreement between the tests used in the simulations. To compare the performance of two statistics, let p_{ra} represent the proportion of samples for which the relevant null hypothesis is rejected by using statistic number one, while the null hypothesis for statistic number two is not rejected. In addition, let p_{ar} represent the proportion of samples for which the null hypothesis for statistic number one is not rejected, while the null hypothesis for statistic number two is rejected. The rate of disagreement shown in the tables is equal to $p_{ra} + p_{ar}$. Let p_{r1} represent the proportion of samples for which the null hypothesis was rejected by statistic one, let p_{r2} represent the proportion of samples for which the null hypothesis was rejected by statistic two, and p_{rr} represent the proportion of samples for which the null hypothesis was rejected by both statistics. Then

$$p_{r1} = p_{ra} + p_{rr}$$

$$p_{r2} = p_{ar} + p_{rr} \text{ , and}$$

$$p_{rr} = \tfrac{1}{2}\left(p_{r1} + p_{r2} - (p_{ra} + p_{ar})\right) .$$

For example, to compare the performance of X_w^2 and the likelihood ratio statistic under five manifest variables in Table 3, $p_{r1} = 0.83, p_{r2} = 0.90$, and $p_{rr} = .81$, indicating that X_w^2 and the likelihood statistic both lead to rejecting the specified latent class model in 810 out of 1000 samples. Also the likelihood statistic rejected the null hypothesis of conditional independence in the joint frequencies for 20 samples where X_w^2 did not reject conditional independence in the second-order marginals, X_w^2 rejected the null hypothesis of conditional independence in the second-order marginals for 90 samples where the likelihood ratio statistic did not reject the model of conditional independence in the joint frequencies, and in 75 samples neither statistic led to rejecting the null hypothesis (convergence failed in five samples). As stated previously, conditional independence in the joint frequencies implies conditional independence in the marginal frequencies. In the rates of disagreement shown in Table 3, it can be seen that X_w^2 leads to rejecting the false latent class model in almost all of the samples where the other statistics would lead to rejecting the model, and in addition the false model is rejected in many other samples based on the use of X_w^2.

4. EXAMPLE

Eaton, McCutcheon et al. (1989) studied symptoms of anxiety and depression using data from the Baltimore site of the Epidemiological Catchment Area Program (Eaton et al. 1984; Regier et al. 1984). In their study, exploratory analyses were used to reduce 41 symptoms from the American

Psychiatric Association's *Diagnostic and Statistical Manual III* (DSM-III) down to seven items regarding symptoms of depression and six items regarding symptoms of anxiety and phobia. Although the authors considered a joint model for these 13 symptoms, they did not attempt to develop such a model because they felt that "assessment of fit would be very problematic," due to sparseness in the cross-classifications of the 13 variables; see also Eaton, Dryman et al. (1989).

Here 11 of the symptom variables from Eaton, McCutcheon et al. (1989)—all seven depression symptom variables plus four variables pertaining to phobia symptoms—are used in order to examine the relationship between depression and phobia. The two items that were not used pertained to anxiety that is unrelated to phobias. Some researchers (Sheehan 1982; Goodwin 1983) have suggested that phobia and depression are part of the same progressive disease. In the analysis presented below, latent class models are used to investigate the degree to which the syndromes can be distinguished as well as to determine which symptoms are unique to one syndrome and which overlap the two syndromes.

Although the available sample is fairly large, at 3336, a 2^{11} frequency table has 2048 cells. In this data set, 1826 of these cells have a realized frequency of zero, and only 28 cells have an observed frequency greater than or equal to five, so the table is very sparse. Also, the prevalence rates, which are shown in Table 4, are low for most of the symptoms,

TABLE 4
Symptoms of Anxiety and Depression

Variable	Item	Rate
1	Dysphoria	.012
2	Appetite disturbance	.061
3	Sleep disturbance	.107
4	Psychomotor symptoms	.057
5	Fatigue	.073
6	Concentration disturbance	.052
7	Suicidal symptoms	.024
8	Fright spells	.018
9	Agoraphobia	.071
10	Simple phobia	.193
11	Social phobia	.034

Note: Table entries show the 11 mental health variables used in the example.

TABLE 5
Marginal Frequencies

| | Matrix of Observed First- and Second-Order Frequencies | | | | | | | | | | |
	1	2	3	4	5	6	7	8	9	10	11
1	40										
2	13	203									
3	26	83	358								
4	14	55	89	190							
5	23	60	102	94	245						
6	16	49	75	71	77	173					
7	10	29	42	32	37	36	79				
8	8	20	30	24	23	19	16	61			
9	10	48	72	63	59	52	27	29	236		
10	17	76	121	87	93	57	37	39	177	645	
11	9	32	36	31	30	25	17	17	63	83	113

Note: Table entries are marginal frequencies for the 11 mental health variables.

which results in an asymmetric contingency table. Thus this data set provides a good opportunity to demonstrate the usefulness of the methods developed above for using the second-order marginals to assess models. Second-order marginals for the symptom variables are shown in Table 5, and a description of the symptom variables is given in Appendix 1. More extensive information on the symptom variables is available in Eaton and Bohrnstedt (1989).

A useful model for investigating the relationship between depression and phobias includes two dichotomous latent variables. Latent class models that include several latent variables have been studied by Goodman (1974 a,b) and Haberman (1977). Let X_1 and X_2 represent the latent variables, and Y_1, Y_2, $\cdots$, Y_{11} represent the manifest variables. In this model, depression and phobia are specified as separate but related syndromes with distinct symptoms. Thus an association between X_1 and X_2, $\lambda_{xu}^{X_1 X_2}$, is included in the model, but the manifest depression variables have an association with only X_1 and the manifest phobia variables have an association only with X_2. If the parameter $\lambda_{xu}^{X_1 X_2}$ is not equal to zero, then a person suffering from phobic fears would have a tendency to experience depression that is higher than would be expected by chance, and a depressed person would have a tendency to experience phobic fears that is higher than would be expected by chance. The log-linear version of this model includes 26 parameters:

$$log\, m_{xs} = \lambda + \lambda_x^{X_1} + \lambda_u^{X_2} + \lambda_a^{Y_1} + \lambda_b^{Y_2} + \cdots + \lambda_q^{Y_{11}} + \lambda_{xu}^{X_1 X_2} + \lambda_{xa}^{X_1 Y_1}$$

$$+ \lambda_{xb}^{X_1 Y_2} + \cdots + \lambda_{xc}^{X_1 Y_7} + \lambda_{ud}^{X_2 Y_8} + \lambda_{ue}^{X_2 Y_9} + \cdots + \lambda_{uq}^{X_2 Y_{11}} .$$

where

$$\sum_x \lambda_x^{X_1} = \sum_u \lambda_u^{X_2} = \sum_a \lambda_a^{Y_1} = \cdots = \sum_q \lambda_q^{Y_{11}} = \sum_x \lambda_{xu}^{X_1 X_2} = \sum_u \lambda_{xu}^{X_1 X_2}$$

$$= \sum_x \lambda_{xa}^{X_1 Y_1} = \sum_a \lambda_{xa}^{X_1 Y_1} = \cdots = \sum_u \lambda_{uq}^{X_2 Y_{11}} = \sum_q \lambda_{uq}^{X_2 Y_{11}} = 0 .$$

This model is analogous to the simple-structure model used widely in factor analysis of continuous variables, where each manifest variable is associated with one and only one factor from a set of factors that have a correlation matrix that is not necessarily diagonal. The likelihood ratio statistic for this model has the value 826.20 and Pearson's statistic is 7700.73. It is difficult to determine the appropriate degrees of freedom for these statistics: $2^{11} - 26 = 2022$, but 1826 cells are empty. Given the severe sparseness, there would seem to be little justification for attaching a p-value to these statistics on the basis of a large sample chi-square distribution. The statistic calculated on the second-order marginals has the value 131.61 on 55 degrees of freedom, which would indicate a poor fit to the second-order marginals, and on this result, the model can be rejected.

Because of the poor fit found on the second-order marginals, a second model with 22 association parameters was employed. In this model, which will be called Model 2, $\lambda_{xu}^{X_1 X_2}$ is omitted, but there is a parameter for an association between each manifest variable and each latent variable. Model 2 fits the second-order marginals well, but from the parameter estimates and standard errors, it appears that only one symptom variable, Y_8 (spells of sudden fright), requires an association with both latent variables. Hence a final model, which will be called Model 3, was obtained by adding the parameter $\lambda^{X_1 Y_8}$ to the first model given above. Table 6 shows fit statistics as well as the Bayesian Information Criterion (BIC) for the three models. The BIC was calculated using the approximation given in Raftery (1995). For Model 3, the statistic on the second-order marginals, X_w^2, takes on the value 31.55 on 55 degrees of freedom, indicating a good fit to the second-order marginals. Note that even though this model includes one more parameter than the first model, $\min(\frac{1}{2} k \cdot (k-1), 2^k - g)$ is 55, so the degrees of freedom for the test on

TABLE 6
Fit Statistics

Model	G^2	Number of Parameters	X_w^2	BIC
1	826.20	26	131.61	−15,577.33
2	757.40	36	15.65	−15,565.00
3	795.89	27	31.55	−15,599.53

the second-order marginals are the same as in the test of Model 1. In general, when parameters are added to or deleted from a model, the degrees of freedom for X_w^2 will not change because the number of second order marginals does not change—i.e., $\frac{1}{2}k\cdot(k-1)$ usually determines the degrees of freedom. However, if the number of manifest variables is small relative to the number of model parameters, $2^k - g$ would determine the degrees of freedom, which would then change if parameters are added or deleted from a model. In contrast to the likelihood ratio statistic, the difference in X_w^2 values across nested models cannot be evaluated as a statistic with an approximate chi-square distribution in this application. However, a comparison of the nested models using the likelihood ratio statistic can be valid even if a table is very sparse (Haberman 1977; Agresti and Yang 1987). For Model 3, the likelihood ratio statistic is 795.89, giving a difference from the first model of 30.31 on one degree of freedom ($p < 0.001$). In this case, the comparison of the likelihood ratio statistics indicates an improvement over the original model, which is consistent with the conclusion based on X_w^2. In general, however, the two methods will not necessarily give the same conclusion. Model 3 is not nested within Model 2, because Model 2 does not contain $\lambda_{xu}^{X_1 X_2}$. While both Models 2 and 3 fit well to the second-order marginals, Model 3 is more parsimonious, and the BIC also suggests Model 3 as the better choice. Parameter estimates and standard errors for the final model are shown in Table 7.

Since the model contains two dichotomous latent variables, there is a total of four latent classes: (1) normal, (2) depressed, (3) phobic, and (4) both depressed and phobic. The significant $X_1 X_2$ association parameter indicates that a person with phobic fears will have a tendency to experience depression, and a depressed person will have a tendency to experience phobic fears. The picture that emerges from the model is two

TABLE 7
Parameter Estimates

Variable	λ^{Y_i}	$\lambda^{Y_i X_1}$	$\lambda^{Y_i X_2}$
Y_1	2.440 (0.304)	1.348 (0.315)	0
Y_2	1.083 (0.043)	0.754 (0.046)	0
Y_3	0.689 (0.038)	0.763 (0.039)	0
Y_4	1.196 (0.058)	1.003 (0.061)	0
Y_5	0.987 (0.050)	0.970 (0.052)	0
Y_6	1.250 (0.058)	0.971 (0.061)	0
Y_7	1.755 (0.089)	0.979 (0.015)	0
Y_8	1.723 (0.084)	0.614 (0.116)	0.455 (0.109)
Y_9	1.169 (0.154)	0	1.480 (0.146)
Y_{10}	0.145 (0.056)	0	0.829 (0.054)
Y_{11}	1.560 (0.095)	0	1.114 (0.096)
X_i	λ^{X_1}	λ^{X_2}	$\lambda^{X_1 X_2}$
	-5.208 (0.369)	-1.659 (0.254)	0.652 (0.048)

Note: Table entries show parameter estimates from the model developed for the eleven mental health variables. Estimated asymptotic standard errors are shown in parentheses.

distinct but related syndromes that have spells of sudden fright as a shared symptom—i.e., experiencing panic attacks is a symptom of depression as well as a symptom of phobic fears. Andrade et al. (1994) found that the co-occurrence of panic attacks and major depression over the lifetime was 11 times higher than expected by chance (odds ratio = 11.4). This is essentially the same result as found above, where $\lambda^{X_1 Y_8} > 0$ indicates that the association between panic attacks and depression is greater than what would be expected simply on the basis of panic attacks as a symptom of phobias, and certainly more than what would be expected by chance. In order for panic attacks to be independent of depression, Model 3 would have to be modified so that both $\lambda^{X_1 Y_8}$ and $\lambda^{X_1 X_2}$ would be equal to zero (i.e., dropped from the model). Based on the standard errors in Table 7, it is clear that dropping these two parameters from the model would result in a significantly poorer fit.

5. DISCUSSION

As demonstrated by the example in Section 4 and the simulation results discussed in Section 3, the proposed method of testing a latent class model by

using the information in the second-order marginals can be especially useful when the joint frequencies are sparse. However, some cautionary remarks about the uses of the proposed test are in order. The null hypothesis
for the test presented in Section 2 specifies conditional independence in the
second-order marginals. A test of a latent class model using the traditional
fit statistics is a test of the null hypothesis that conditional independence
holds for the manifest variables in the joint frequencies. Conditional independence in the joint frequencies implies conditional independence in the
marginal frequencies, so if a latent class model is rejected based on use of
the statistic given in Section 2, then it could be concluded that the model does
not hold in the joint frequencies either.

If the null hypothesis of conditional independence in the marginals
is not rejected, however, it does not necessarily follow that the latent class
model fits the joint frequencies well. A model that has a poor fit to the joint
frequencies due to a misspecification regarding a third- or higher-order
association may also show a poor fit to the second-order marginals; on the
other hand, it could fit the second-order marginals well, and the power for
testing the latent class model may be substantially reduced. If a set of
variables contains higher-order effects that are not well represented by the
latent class model, but second-order effects that are well represented by
the model, or no second-order effects at all, then a test of complete conditional independence using the statistic given in Section 2 as a substitute
for a test on the joint frequencies would have power equal only to the Type
I error level. These limitations should always be kept in mind when using
the test given in Section 2. Another circumstance that could lead to a difference between the result from a test on the second-order marginals and
the result from a test on the joint frequencies would be the presence of
confounding among the variables of interest. Depending on the degree of
confounding, a poor fit for a model in the joint frequencies may or may not
be reflected by a poor fit in the second-order marginals.

Confounding and/or higher-order associations are more likely to be
present in some data sets than in others. The example presented in Section
4 demonstrated the latent class model as a measurement model where the
manifest variables are multiple indicators, and the modeling is similar to a
confirmatory factor analysis. An extensive empirical study by Salomaa
(1990) has demonstrated that data sets consisting of categorical variables
that are multiple indicators used to measure an underlying variable contain
little or no information in the third- or higher-order marginals, so it can be
expected that a test based on the statistic given in Section 2 would be a

valid substitute for testing conditional independence among the joint frequencies for that type of data. In other applications where confounding or higher-order interactions are more likely to be encountered—such as latent class transition models (Collins and Wugalter, 1992)—the test given in Section 2 may not be appropriate. It would seem reasonable to reject the model if conditional independence is rejected in either the marginal or joint frequencies. But if the null hypothesis of conditional independence is not rejected in either the joint or second-order marginals, some caution should be taken when interpreting the results in this type of application. If sparseness is not present, the traditional statistics can be relied upon, taking the usual caveats about "accepting" a null hypothesis into account. But if sparseness is present, the test of the model on the joint frequencies most likely suffers from low power, and the test using conditional independence in the marginals as a substitute for conditional independence in the joint frequencies may have low power to detect higher-order interactions or confounding not consistent with the model. In this situation, an investigator may want to pursue other methods for testing the model if higher-order interactions or confounding may be present.

One method that might reduce the risk of accepting a model that does not fit the joint frequencies would be to extend the test developed here to the third-, fourth-, or higher-order marginals. It may be feasible to search for the highest order at which the marginal frequencies are not sparse, and test the model on those marginals. The potential benefit of using higher-order marginals would depend on the nature of the application, as will be discussed below. Even in the absence of higher-order interactions or confounding, the power of such tests of fit may not be the same at different orders of collapsing the joint frequencies, so some comparisons of results using Monte Carlo simulations at different levels of collapsing would be warranted. The method developed here can also be extended readily to polytomous variables.

Some other potential methods with promise are computationally intensive. By using bootstrapping (Efron 1982; Hinkley 1988, 1989) and/or Monte Carlo methods (Besag and Clifford 1991) it might be possible to develop valid inference for test statistics that assess conditional independence in the joint frequencies, even in the presence of sparseness. With these methods, instead of relying on theoretical distributions, resampling would be used to obtain an empirical distribution for the statistic of interest. Whereas bootstrapping uses resampling from the data at hand, Monte

Carlo sampling is done from a hypothetical parent population with known characteristics. Either method results in an empirical distribution function with mean and quantiles that are estimates of the expectation and quantiles of the unknown true distribution for the statistic of interest. For model testing, p-values could be obtained from the empirical distribution. A small demonstration of Monte Carlo sampling used with the latent class model is given in Collins et al. (1993). As mentioned, these methods are computationally intensive in each application, and since software is not readily available, their use can be time consuming. These methods have not been widely used with multinomial models, so simulation studies are needed to determine the adequacy of the tests, particularly in terms of power against a false null hypothesis. A key reference on bootstrapping goodness-of-fit statistics in sparse multinomials is Simonoff (1986), who studied the bootstrap for estimating the variance of asymptotic normal distributions for traditional fit statistics. Simonoff recommends cells of the multinomial distribution, rather than individual observations, as the natural unit for resampling in this context. In this context, he also finds the jackknife superior to the bootstrap for the purpose of estimating the variance of the asymptotic distributions for the goodness-of-fit statistics.

Another possibility for assessing a latent class model directly on the joint frequencies would be to develop exact or approximate ways to calculate Bayes factors, where the Bayes factor in favor of hypothesis H provided by evidence E is the ratio of the final to the initial odds of H, i.e.,

$$\frac{O(H|E)}{O(H)} = \frac{P(H|E)P(\bar{H})}{P(H)P(\bar{H}|E)} \; ,$$

where $\bar{H}$ represents the negation of H. Kass and Raftery (1995) give a review of work on Bayes factors and recommend an interpretation based on twice the natural logarithm of the Bayes factor. If the null hypothesis is placed in the denominator of the Bayes factor, they suggest, for example, a value greater than 20 for twice the log of the Bayes factor constitutes strong or very strong evidence against the null hypothesis. As in most applications of Bayesian methods, selection of prior distributions may be controversial. Also, calculation of Bayes factors may be complex and time consuming. Computer intensive methods are now available for these calculations, and Raftery (1996) discusses Markov chain Monte Carlo methods for hypothesis testing using Bayes factors. Bayes factors are useful for comparing two competing models, and Raftery (1995) recommends the Bayesian Information Criterion (BIC) as a rough approximation to the logarithm of the Bayes factor in such applications. Use of the BIC for choosing among models was demonstrated in the example of Section 4. The main point of the present paper, however, is improving upon a goodness-of-fit test rather than comparing competing models. Some Bayesians (Box 1980; Dempster 1971; Rubin 1984) see a useful role for the frequentist goodness-of-fit tests in calibrating diagnostic checks as part of a search for a better model.

When sparseness is not present, comparisons of results obtained by using the second-order marginals with results based on the joint frequencies can be meaningful. There may be discrepancies between the test results due to higher-order interactions or confounding as discussed above. Random variation may also produce discrepancies. Although conditional independence in the joint frequencies implies conditional independence in the marginals, the rates of disagreement shown in Tables 1 and 2 demonstrate that it is possible for a Type I error to occur in the test on the joint frequencies but not in the test on the second-order marginals, and vice versa. It should be kept in mind, however, that among tests on the joint frequencies, it is also possible to find a Type I error in the X^2 statistic but not in the G^2 statistic, and vice versa, and these differences seem to be unremarkable.

The test of fit on the second-order marginals presented in Section 2 is similar to methods given by Christoffersson (1975) and Muthen (1978) for testing model fit in dichotomous variable factor analysis. Their methods use first- and second-order marginals for both estimation of parameters and test of fit. Reiser (1996) developed a similar statistic for testing goodness of fit with item response models. The test presented in Section 2 uses the same amount of information from dichotomous variables as tetrachoric correlations, which can be obtained from PRELIS and used for modeling in LISREL. The test proposed in Section 2 is also similar to the Cochran-Mantel-Haenszel test (Mantel and Haenszel 1959) in that it uses marginal proportions. However the test proposed here collapses across several dimensions of the observed data table, while the Cochran-Mantel-Haenszel test collapses across only one dimension of a three-way table. Also, the Cochran-Mantel-Haenszel test uses the hypergeometric distribution to obtain the variance of a cell count, while a model-based estimator is used here.

The statistic developed in Section 2 may be used to test any multinomial model of independence or conditional independence, and investigations are currently underway on applications to more general models.

APPENDIX: DEFINITIONS OF SYMPTOM VARIABLES

Y1 Dysphoria: This variable was coded as 1 if a respondent reported feelings of sadness for two years, or if two or more of the following symptoms were reported: thoughts of death, diminished libido, feelings of hopelessness, feeling sad for two weeks, or feelings of worthlessness; otherwise it was coded as 0.

Y2 Appetite: This variable was coded as 1 if a respondent reported lost appetite, lost weight, or increased eating; otherwise it was coded as 0.

Y3 Sleep: This variable was coded as 1 if a respondent reported trouble falling asleep, staying asleep, waking too early, or a period of sleeping too much for at least two weeks; otherwise it was coded as 0.

Y4 Psychomotor: This variable was coded as 1 if a respondent reported either talking or moving slowly or talking and moving all the time for a period of at least two weeks; otherwise it was coded 0.

Y5 Fatigue: This variable was coded as 1 if a respondent reported feeling tired all the time for a period of at least two weeks; otherwise it was coded 0.

Y6 Concentration: This variable was coded as 1 if a respondent reported trouble concentrating, thoughts mixed up, or thinking slower for at least two weeks; otherwise it was coded as 0.

Y7 Suicidal: This variable was coded as 1 if a respondent reported wishing death, thinking of suicide, or attempting suicide.

Y8 Fright: This variable was coded as 1 if a respondent reported spells of sudden fright, or panic attacks; otherwise it was coded as 0.

Y9 Agoraphobia: This variable was coded as 1 if a respondent reported a fear of one or more of the following: crowds, public transportation, being out by his- or herself, being alone, tunnels or bridges; otherwise it was coded as 0.

Y10 Simple Phobia: This variable was coded as 1 if a respondent reported a fear of one or more of the following: heights, closed places, storms, water, insects, or animals; otherwise it was coded as 0.

Y11 Social Phobia: This variable was coded as 1 if a respondent reported a fear of eating in public, speaking in public, or speaking to new people; otherwise it was coded as 0.

REFERENCES

Agresti, Alan. 1990. *Categorical Data Analysis*. New York: Wiley.

Agresti, Alan, and M. C. Yang. 1987. "An Empirical Investigation of Some Effects of Sparseness in Contingency Tables." *Computational Statistics and Data Analysis* 5:9–21.

Anderson, T. W. 1984. *An Introduction to Multivariate Statistical Analysis*, 2d ed. New York: Wiley.

Andrade, Laura, William W. Eaton, and Howard Chilcoat. 1994. "Lifetime Comorbidity of Panic Attacks and Major Depression in a Population-Based Study." *British Journal of Psychiatry* 165:363–69.

Bartholomew, David J. 1987. *Latent Variable Models and Factor Analysis*. New York: Oxford University Press.

Berry, K. J. and P. W. Mielke. 1988. "Monte Carlo Comparisons of the Asymptotic Chi-square and Likelihood-Ratio tests with the Nonasymptotic Chi-square Test for Sparse R × C Tables." *Psychological Bulletin* 2:256–64.

Besag, Julian, and Peter Clifford. 1991. "Sequential Monte Carlo p-values." *Biometrika* 78:301–4.

Birch, M. W. 1964. "A New Proof of the Pearson-Fisher Theorem." *Annals of Mathematical Statistics* 35:818–24.

Bock, R. Darrell, Robert Gibbons, and Eiji Muraki. 1988. "Full-Information Item Factor Analysis." *Applied Psychological Measurement* 12:261–80.

Bock, R. Darrell, and M. Lieberman. 1970. "Fitting a Response Model for n Dichotomously Scored Items." *Psychometrika* 35:179–97.

Box, G. E. P. 1980. "Sampling and Baye's Inference in Scientific Modeling" (with discussion). *Journal of the Royal Statistical Society*, Series A 143:383–430.

Christoffersson, Anders. 1975. "Factor Analysis of Dichotomized Variables." *Psychometrika* 40:5–32.

Clogg, Clifford C. 1977. "Unrestricted and Restricted Maximum Likelihood Latent Structure Analysis: A Manual for Users." Working paper 1977-09. University Park, PA: Population Issues Research Center.

Clogg, Clifford C., and Leo Goodman. 1984. "Latent Structure Analysis of a Set of Multidimensional Contingency Tables." *Journal of the American Statistical Association* 79:762–71.

Clogg, Clifford C., and Leo Goodman. 1985. "Simultaneous Latent Structure Analysis in Several Groups." Pp. 81–110 in *Sociological Methodology 1985*, edited by Nancy B. Tuma. San Francisco: Jossey-Bass.

Cochran, William G. 1954. "Some Methods for Strengthening the Common Chi-square Test." *Biometrical Journal* 10:417–51.

———. 1955. "A Test of a Linear Function of the Deviations Between Observed and Expected Numbers." *Journal of the American Statistical Association* 50:377–97.

Collins, Linda M., P. L. Fidler, S. E. Wugalter, and J. D. Long. 1993. "Goodness-of-Fit Testing for Latent Class Models." *Multivariate Behavioral Research* 28:375–89.

Collins, Linda M., and S. E. Wugalter. 1992. "Latent Class Models for Stage-sequential Dynamic Latent Variables. *Multivariate Behavioral Research* 27:131–57.

Cox, Christopher. 1984. "An Elementary Introduction to Maximum Likelihood Estimation for Multinomial Models: Birch's Theorem and the Delta Method." *The American Statistician* 38:283–287.

Cramer, Harald. 1946. *Mathematical Statistics.* Princeton, NJ: Princeton University Press.

Dempster, A. P. 1971. "Model Searching and Estimation in the Logic of Inference." In *Foundations of Statistical Inference*, edited by V. P. Godambe and D.A. Sprott. Toronto: Holt, Rinehart, and Winston.

Dempster, Arthur P., Nan M. Laird, and Donald B. Rubin. 1977. "Maximum Likelihood from Incomplete Data Via the EM Algorithm" (with discussion). *Journal of the Royal Statistical Society*, Series B 39:1–38.

Eaton, William W., and George Bohrnstedt. 1989. "Introduction: Latent Variable Models for Dichotomous Outcomes." *Sociological Methods and Research* 18:4–17.

Eaton, William W., Amy Dryman, Ann Sorenson, and Allan McCutcheon. 1989. "DSM-III Major Depressive Disorder in the Community: A Latent Class Analysis of Data from the NIMH Epidemiological Catchment Area Program." *British Journal of Psychiatry* 155:48–54.

Eaton, William W., C. E. Holzer, M. V. Korff, J. C. Anthony, J. E. Helzer, L. George, M. A. Burnam, J. H. Boyd, L. G. Kessler, and B. Z. Locke. 1984. "The Design of the Epidemiological Catchment Area Surveys." *Archives of General Psychiatry* 41:942–48.

Eaton, William W., Allan McCutcheon, Amy Dryman, and Ann Sorenson. 1989. "Latent Class Analysis of Anxiety and Depression." *Sociological Methods and Research* 18:104–25.

Efron, Bradley. 1982. *The Jackknife, the Bootstrap, and Other Resampling Plans.* Philadelphia: Society for Industrial and Applied Mathematics.

Fisher, Ronald A. 1941. *Statistical Methods for Research Workers.* Edinburgh: Oliver and Boyd.

Freeman, M. F., and J. Tukey. 1950. "Transformations Related to the Angular and the Square Root." *Annals of Mathematical Statistics* 21:607–11.

Goodman, Leo A. 1964. "Simple Methods for Analyzing Three-Factor Interaction in Contingency Tables." *Journal of the American Statistical Association* 59:319–85.

———. 1974a. "The Analysis of Systems of Qualitative Variables when Some of the Variables Are Unobservable. Part I—A Modified Latent Structure Approach." *American Journal of Sociology* 79:1179–1259.

———. 1974b. "Exploratory Latent Structure Analysis Using Both Identifiable and Unidentifiable Models." *Biometrika* 61:215–31.

Goodwin, Donald W. 1983. *Phobia: The Facts.* New York: Oxford University Press.

Haberman, Shelby J. 1973. "The Analysis of Residuals in Cross-Classified Tables." *Biometrics* 29:205–20.

———. 1977. *The Analysis of Frequency Data.* University of Chicago Press, 1974, Midway Reprint 1977.

———. 1978. *Analysis of Qualitative Data*, Volume 1. New York: Academic Press.

———. 1979. *Analysis of Qualitative Data*, Volume 2. New York: Academic Press.

————. 1988a. "A Warning on the Use of Chi-Squared Statistics with Frequency Tables with Small Expected Cell Counts." *Journal of the American Statistical Association* 85:555–60.

————. 1988b. "A Stabilized Newton-Raphson Algorithm for Log-Linear Models for Frequency Tables Derived by Indirect Observation." Pp. 193–211 in *Sociological Methodology 1988*, edited by Clifford C. Clogg. Washington: The American Sociological Association.

Hagenaars, Jacques A. 1993. *Loglinear Models with Latent Variables*. Newbury Park, CA: Sage.

Heinen, Ton. 1996. *Latent Class and Discrete Latent Trait Models*. Thousand Oaks, CA: Sage.

Hinkley, D. V. 1988. "Bootstrap Methods" (with discussion). *Journal of the Royal Statistical Society Series B* 50:321–37.

————. 1989. "Bootstrap Significance Tests." *Proceedings of the 47th Session of International Statistical Institute*," Paris, 65–74.

Holst, L. 1972. "Asymptotic Normality and Efficiency for Certain Goodness-of-Fit Tests." *Biometrika*, 59:137–45.

Kass, Robert E., and Adrian E. Raftery. 1995. "Bayes Factors." *Journal of the American Statistical Association* 90:377–95.

Kendall, M. G. 1952. *The Advanced Theory of Statistics*. London: Griffin.

Koehler, Kenneth J. 1986. "Goodness-of-Fit Tests for Log-Linear Models in Sparse Contingency Tables." *Journal of the American Statistical Association* 81:483–93.

Koehler, Kenneth J., and Kinley Larntz. 1980. "An Empirical Investigation of Goodness-of-Fit Statistics for Sparse Multinomials." *Journal of the American Statistical Association* 75:336–44.

Lazarsfeld, Paul F. 1950. "The Logical and Mathematical Foundation of Latent Structure Analysis." Pp. 362–412 in S. A. Stouffer et al., *Measurement and Prediction*. Princeton, NJ: Princeton University Press.

Lord, Frederic M. 1980. *Applications of Item Response Theory to Practical Testing Problems*. Hillsdale, NJ: Erlbaum.

Mantel, Nathan, and W. Haenszel. 1959. "Statistical Aspects of the Analysis of Data from Retrospective Studies of Disease." *Journal of the National Cancer Institute* 22:719–48.

McCutcheon, Allan L. 1996. "Multiple Group Association Models with Latent Variables: An Analysis of Secular Trends in Abortion Attitudes, 1972–1988. Pp. 79–111 in *Sociological Methodology 1996*, edited by Adrian Raftery. Cambridge, MA: Blackwell Publishers.

Morris, C. 1975. "Central Limit Theorems for Multinomial Sums." *Annals of Statistics* 3:365–84.

Muthen, Bengt. 1978. "Contributions to Factor Analysis of Dichotomous Variables." *Psychometrika* 43:551–60.

Raftery, Adrian E. 1995. "Bayesian Model Selection in Social Research." Pp. 111–163 in *Sociological Methodology 1995*, edited by Peter V. Marsden. Cambridge, MA: Blackwell Publishers.

————. 1996. "Hypothesis Testing and Model Selection." Pp. 163–87 in *Markov Chain Monte Carlo in Practice*, edited by W. R. Gilks, S. Richardson, and D. J. Spiegelhalter. New York: Chapman Hall.

Rao, C. Radhakrishna. 1973. *Linear Statistical Inference and Its Applications*, 2d ed. New York: Wiley.

Read, Timothy R. C., and Noel A. C. Cressie. 1988. *Goodness-of-Fit Statistics for Discrete Multivariate Data*. New York: Springer-Verlag.

Regier, Darrel A., Jerome K. Myers, Morton Kramer, Lee N. Robins, Dan G. Blazer, Richard L. Hough, William W. Eaton, and Ben Z. Locke. 1984. "The NIMH Epidemiologic Catchment Area Programs." *Archives of General Psychiatry* 41:934–41.

Reiser, Mark. 1996. "Analysis of Residuals for the Multinomial Item Response Model." *Psychometrika* 61:509–28.

Rubin, Donald B. 1984. "Bayesianly Justifiable and Relevant Frequency Calculations for the Applied Statistician." *The Annals of Statistics* 12:1151–72.

Salomaa, Hely. 1990. *Factor Analysis of Dichotomous Data*. Helsinki, Finland: Finnish Statistical Society.

Sheehan, D. 1982. "Current Perspectives in the Treatment of Panic and Phobic Disorders." *Drug Therapy* 12:179–93.

Simonoff, Jeffrey S. 1986. "Jackknifing and Bootstrapping Goodness-of-Fit Statistics in Sparse Multinomials." *Journal of the American Statistical Association* 81:1005–11.

Tate, Merle W., and Leon A. Hyer. 1973. "Inaccuracy of the Chi-Squared Test of Goodness of Fit When Expected Frequencies Are Small." *Journal of the American Statistical Association* 68:836–41.

Vermunt, Jeroen K. 1997. "ℓEM: A general program for the analysis of categorical data." Tilburg, Netherlands: Tilburg University, Department of Methodology.

Zelterman, Daniel. 1987. "Goodness-of-Fit Tests for Large Sparse Multinomial Distributions." *Journal of the American Statistical Association*. 82:624–29.

4

ALGEBRAIC REPRESENTATIONS OF BELIEFS AND ATTITUDES: PARTIAL ORDER MODELS FOR ITEM RESPONSES

James A. Wiley*
John Levi Martin†

A partial order of discrete beliefs based on a generalization of item order in Guttman scaling generates a nonunidimensional collection of latent belief states that can be represented by a distributive lattice. By incorporating misclassification errors under local independence assumptions, the lattice structure is transformed into a latent class model for observed response states. We apply this model to survey responses dealing with government welfare programs and suggest that our approach can retrieve information where unidimensional and multidimensional models do not fit. The concluding section discusses directions for future work.

The authors would like to thank Ronald Breiger, Philip Converse, Robin Hanson, Michael Hout, Hans Schadee, and Samuel Shye for their comments on previous drafts of this paper. We are grateful to Edward Haertel and David Wiley for discussions of related models for item response data. Aaron Cicourel provided an insightful analysis of the text of the survey questions we use to illustrate our approach to the study of survey responses to belief items. Paul Sniderman supplied the data for our example from his 1991 Race and Politics Survey and encouraged us to pursue this line of work. Finally, we wish to thank the reviewers and editors for their helpful comments, critiques, and suggestions. The research reported in this paper was partially supported by funds from the Survey Research Center, University of California, Berkeley. An earlier version was presented at the annual meeting of the American Sociological Association, San Francisco, August 21–25, 1998. The authors can be reached at jwiley@uclink3.berkeley.edu or jlmartin@rci.rutgers.edu.

*University of California, Berkeley (at time of submission); currently at Public Health Institute, Berkeley, CA

†Rutgers University, New Brunswick

Very rarely, however, is there only a single logic operat-
ing in a mind, and even more rarely in a society, which is
essentially a collective and enormously inclusive mind.
The most diverse and mutually contradicting deductions
advance by zigzags, crossing each other, swerving, min-
gling sometimes, then separating once again.

—Gabriel Tarde (1902)

In this paper we develop a representation of the structure of responses to
belief and attitude questions which relies on a discrete and nonunidimensional view of the underlying response process. We shall try to demonstrate that this way of looking at responses tells a different story about the
composition and connections between beliefs and attitudes than do existing methods. Although most discussions of subjective measurement follow tradition in referring to "attitudes," we will generally speak of "beliefs,"
since the former term accentuates the affective component of cognition
and the latter the propositional component. The methods outlined here are
geared more toward the propositional than the affective elements of beliefs.

Our approach is built on a generalization of the item order concept
in Guttman scaling (Guttman 1950). We relax Guttman's strictly ordered
scale model, permitting a *partial order* among beliefs that generates an
algebraic representation of latent belief states in the form of a distributive
lattice. The transition from latent belief states to observed item responses
is implemented in a latent class model that allows for misclassification
errors. This paper deals only with the case in which survey responses are
binary (i.e., where the items are dichotomous or may be considered so),
and hence the response to any item can be interpreted as designating that
the respondent holds or does not hold some belief. Extensions to more
general cases are discussed briefly at the end of the paper.

Section 1 introduces the mathematical apparatus (partial orders and
lattice algebra) that we use to formalize the concept of *belief precedence*
and analyze its consequences, and shows how this strategy can be seen as
a generalization of Guttman's fundamental work on scaling. Section 2 makes
our lattice approach to belief structure operational by building a latent
class model of the relation between observed responses and the unobserved belief states generated by the partial order of relations among beliefs. In Section 3 we use this approach to identify relationships among
beliefs held by white Americans about welfare programs and their recipi-

ents. We conclude in Section 4 by briefly comparing our approach with others that rely on latent trait or latent class concepts, and indicating directions for further research on the algebraic representation of survey responses.[1]

1. ORDERS, PARTIAL ORDERS, AND DISTRIBUTIVE LATTICES

The Guttman theory of scaling is based on the premise that the items have a strict order (we can speak of them as being ranked in terms of how hard it is to give a positive answer to them, or "item difficulty"). All those who answer an item of a certain difficulty positively also answer all items of lesser difficulty positively. Thus the consistent ranking of items produces an equally consistent ranking of respondents. For questionnaire items pertaining to respondents' beliefs, the Guttman assumption of unidimensionality (i.e., all items can be ranked on a single dimension of difficulty) gives us information not only about the relative ordering of persons along this dimension, but also as to how respon-

---

[1]A related algebraic approach was first used in a pioneering study of new developments in educational testing by Haertel and Wiley (1993). Readers may be familiar with some similar algebraic approaches. Galois lattices (Freeman and White 1993; Duquenne 1995) are used to analyze matrices that are a good deal squarer—and smaller—than the large rectangular matrices of many respondents and a few items that characterize survey analysis. A related method is the HICLAS system of De Boeck and Rosenberg (1988). Like the Galois lattice, the HICLAS system retrieves a partial ordering among a set of response categories. The approach outlined here, as demonstrated below, can retrieve such partial orderings, but it can also retrieve more complex structures in the absence of such partial orderings (as shown by Haertel and Wiley).

Our approach is also similar in some respects to the "partial order scalogram analysis by base coordinates" (POSAC) developed by Shye and his colleagues (Shye and Amar 1985; Shye, Elizur, and Hoffman 1994). Their technique begins with a set of profiles (i.e., vectors of ordinally scaled values) that are partially ordered with respect to comparison of their components. But in contrast to our emphasis on the discreteness of the underlying process, POSAC then seeks to embed these profiles in a two-dimensional continuous space that preserves as much of the partial order information as possible. The POSAC approach is different in other respects as well. There is no emphasis on making sure that the profiles form any kind of lattice because there is no motivation for inversion to obtain either a fundamental precedence relation or a set of item requirements. Further, whereas the latent class operationalization of the lattice models we propose leads to the usual goodness-of-fit tests, POSAC models are judged by nonstatistical fitness criteria. Hence while our approach has much in common with other algebraic methods that have aroused great interest in recent years, it is in no way redundant.

dents' beliefs are structured—namely, according to a strict order of precedence. Some beliefs are "impossible" to hold without first holding other ones. We consider this notion of the "precedence" of beliefs to be a fundamental and testable theoretical claim. But seen in this light (seeing items as connected by relations of precedence), the Guttman scale is only one particular set of precedence relations—it gives us information that is equivalent to a finding of deterministic unidimensionality. We can conceive of other possible structures that have deterministic relations of precedence between items but do not imply unidimensionality. Such structures are the partial order models we explore in this paper.

1.1. *The Guttman Scale as an Order*

To generalize from the Guttman scale to the structures we will explore is equivalent to generalizing from an *order* of items to a *partial order*. Let us define a person's belief state as a vector describing which beliefs are held and which are not held. Thus a person who does not hold any of the beliefs in question is in belief state 0000. A person holding only belief A is thus in state 1000, etc. Consider a Guttman scale for four items, A, B, C, and D, consisting of admissible response patterns 0000, 1000, 1100, 1110, and 1111. Looking at these permissible responses in terms of relations of *precedence* between items, we can interpret them as implying that A→B→C→D where → means "precedes" (and we do not explicitly label transitive relations, though A does precede C and D, etc.). Thus one must hold belief A before one holds belief B, B before C, and C before D. The sequence of precedence relations forms a "chain."

Now let us look at another subset of response patterns, one discussed by Goodman (1975): 0000, 1000, 1100, 1010, 1110, 1111. One "non-Guttman" pattern has been added, 1010. As a result, B no longer precedes C, but item A still precedes all the others. Furthermore, B and C both precede D. Goodman discussed this as being a combination of "different types" of people with different scale orderings, but we can also see it as a set of items where some precede others, but other items are "incomparable": we cannot say B is before C or that C is before B on some continuum. Such a set of elements that have both relations that order them in terms of precedence *and* incomparable items is called a *partially ordered set* (or *poset*, for short). The partial order of beliefs implied by these considerations is shown in Figure 1.

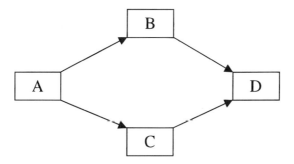

FIGURE 1. Hypothetical belief poset.

The set of all belief states permitted under a system of precedence relations is also a partially ordered set related to (and induced by) the fundamental partial order among beliefs. (In our approach, the belief states are *latent* qualities pertaining to persons; we will later discuss how these translate to manifest "response states.") We can graph these belief states as in Figure 2. The arrows indicate a relation of *immediate precedence*. Various transitive relations of mediated precedence are implied but not shown. For example, 0000 precedes 1100, mediated by 1000.

Although both beliefs and belief states are partially ordered sets, the latter satisfy a stronger set of conditions: the belief states always constitute an algebraic object known as a distributive lattice. The approach we introduce exploits the mathematical connection between the belief poset and the belief state lattice. This connection generates the algorithms that transform theories of belief structure into predictions about response patterns and vice versa.

1.2. Precedence as Constraint

This approach differs from conventional scaling in two obvious ways. First, the underlying elements we wish to measure are assumed to be discrete (one either holds an attitude or belief or one does not) as opposed to continuous. Second, it is assumed that there is a logically *asymmetric* relation between beliefs; one has to hold one belief before another, and the first belief is therefore *necessary but not sufficient* for the other. These assumptions need not be defended as a general way of conceiving of attitudes or beliefs. Rather, they are testable hypotheses that lead to certain models of

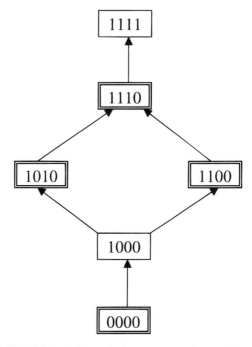

FIGURE 2. Belief state lattice corresponding to Figure 1.

responses. When such a model fits the data, we use the aggregate information of the table to make inferences about possible "ways of believing." More particularly, the rules of precedence are *rules governing the formation of belief states*: Some states are possible, others are not.

Recall that the Guttman scale can be considered a strict order of items imposing an equally strict order as to how one could acquire (or shed) beliefs. This we envisioned as a chain of precedence relations. Consider the opposite case now (aptly termed an "antichain"), in which there are no precedence relations between items. For three dichotomous variables, all eight ($=2^3$) states formed by the cross-classification of these dichotomies are possible, leading to the belief state diagram in Figure 3. In this case, the cube formed by the lines of possible movement makes it clear that this is equivalent to unrestrained choice of belief in a three-dimensional "space" of dichotomies. Each precedence relation between items can be thought of as eliminating some of these lines and therefore as causing a collapse of the structure formed by treating each item as an independent

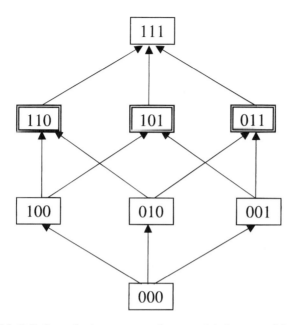

FIGURE 3. Belief state lattice corresponding to antichain poset of three beliefs.

statement of belief. Thus while the lattice approach we will outline is not unidimensional, it is not multidimensional in the conventional sense. We now formalize this approach, using notation summarized in Appendix A. To facilitate the exposition, our discussion is practical and relatively non-technical; formal definitions and related theorems have been placed in Appendix B.

1.3. *The Consequences of Precedence*

Let α_i represent the ith member of a set of M beliefs and let x_i represent the state of α_i. Since we deal here with beliefs having only two states, we let $x_i = 1$ if the belief is held and $x_i = 0$ otherwise. Given a pair of beliefs, α_i and α_j, α_i "precedes" α_j, denoted by $\alpha_i \to \alpha_j$, if $x_i = 0$ implies ($\Rightarrow$) $x_j = 0$. In a fourfold table that cross-classifies the states of two beliefs, precedence shows itself as a null combination, in this case the joint occurrence $x_i = 0$ and $x_j = 1$. The distribution of observations in the non-null (i.e., possible) cells is not constrained in any way by the concept of precedence (see Guttman [1950:70] for a related observation).

Precedence is a *binary relation* between a pair of dichotomous beliefs characterized by

1. Transitivity: $\alpha_i \rightarrow \alpha_j$, $\alpha_j \rightarrow \alpha_k$ implies $\alpha_i \rightarrow \alpha_k$ (since $x_i = 0 \Rightarrow x_j = 0$ and $x_j = 0 \Rightarrow x_k = 0$ implies $x_i = 0 \Rightarrow x_k = 0$);
2. Reflexivity: $\alpha_i \rightarrow \alpha_i$ (since $x_i = 0$ implies itself trivially);
3. Antisymmetry: $\alpha_i \rightarrow \alpha_j$ and $\alpha_j \rightarrow \alpha_i$ implies $\alpha_i = \alpha_j$ ($x_i = 0$ iff $x_j = 0$ is perfect association in the fourfold table, a definition of operationally equivalent beliefs; in all other cases, a pair of beliefs are either incomparable or asymmetrically related).

Let $A = [\alpha_1, \alpha_2, \ldots, \alpha_M]$ be a set of beliefs and assume that either $\alpha_i \rightarrow \alpha_j$ or $\alpha_j \rightarrow \alpha_i$ for *all* pairs i, j. The result is a belief set *ordered* by precedence that is the mathematical equivalent of a perfect Guttman scale. As noted earlier, when some pairs of items are incomparable, the set A is said to be *partially ordered* by precedence. This partial ordering defines A as a *belief poset*.

A belief α_i is said to *immediately precede* a belief α_k if there is no α_j in A such that $\alpha_i \rightarrow \alpha_j$ and $\alpha_j \rightarrow \alpha_k$. Immediacy is always defined in relation to the set A. A belief may be an immediate predecessor in one set and a distant predecessor in another. In an ordered set (i.e., a Guttman scale), a belief has a single immediate predecessor or, if the belief precedes all others, none at all. There is no such restriction in a belief poset.

A partially ordered belief set admits of *multiple immediate precedents* that combine to produce an aggregate precedence relation. Consider, for example, a subset of three beliefs (α_i, α_j, and α_k) such that $\alpha_i \rightarrow \alpha_k$ and $\alpha_j \rightarrow \alpha_k$, and both of these relations are immediate (which implies that α_i and α_j are incomparable). Formally, $x_i = 0 \Rightarrow x_k = 0$ *and* $x_j = 0 \Rightarrow x_k = 0$, so that $x_i = 1$ *and* $x_j = 1$ are jointly necessary conditions for $x_k = 1$. In general, multiple immediate precedents concatenate via "and" operations on the necessary conditions for the preceded belief.

1.4. *From Poset to Lattice and Back Again*

A distribution of precedence relations in a belief poset determines which patterns of belief are admissible and which are not. A theorem of Birkhoff ([1940] 1967:58f.) says that every poset is associated with a unique algebraic structure called a *distributive lattice* (defined in Appendix B, Section 1). Furthermore, every distributive lattice generates a unique poset. Applying that theorem to the present context, we may say that a belief poset—a structural model of how beliefs are asymmetrically connected via relations of necessity—is algebraically equivalent to a set of admissible belief states that, taken together, satisfy the definition of a distributive lattice.

A *belief state* defined with respect to a set of beliefs (i.e., the belief poset) can be represented as a vector $\mathbf{x} = [x_1, x_2, \ldots, x_M]$ where, as before, $x_i = 1$ if the ith belief is held and 0 otherwise. The set of admissible belief states that correspond to a particular poset A is defined as

$$B = [\mathbf{x} | x_i = 0 \Rightarrow x_j = 0 \text{ whenever } \alpha_i \rightarrow \alpha_j \text{ in } A] \ .$$

It can be shown that the set B has the following properties:

1. The belief states $\mathbf{I} = (1,1,\ldots,1)$ and $\varnothing = (0,0,\ldots,0)$ are members of B;
2. B is closed under two binary operations that we may call *union* and *intersection*, defined as follows: the union of two belief states, denoted by $\mathbf{x} \cup \mathbf{y}$, is a belief state $\mathbf{z}$ such that $z_i = 1$ if $x_i = 1$ *or* $y_i = 1$, and $z_i = 0$ otherwise; the intersection of two belief states, denoted $\mathbf{x} \cap \mathbf{y}$, is a belief state $\mathbf{z}$ such that $z_i = 1$ if $x_i = 1$ *and* $y_i = 1$ and $z_i = 0$ otherwise.

Property (1) follows from the fact that $\mathbf{I}$ and $\varnothing$ cannot be ruled out by any distribution of precedence relations in the poset. The closure property means that the result of an intersection or union of two elements of B is also a member of B. Together (1) and (2) ensure that B satisfies the definition of a distributive lattice: a partially ordered set that is closed under binary operations called *meet* and *join* that satisfy a distributive law (Birkhoff [1940] 1967). Given the 0 and 1 coding convention for beliefs we have adopted, the meet and join operations are equivalent to the operations we call intersection and union. Below we show how to go from poset to lattice and back again in easy steps. The identity on which the algorithm is based is proved in Appendix B.

1.4.1. *Poset to Lattice*
All the information necessary to reconstruct the set of admissible belief states (the set B) is contained in the precedence relations which characterize the belief poset. If the poset A is known, the following algorithm will produce B:

1. Suppose A is the belief poset given in Figure 1.

2. Form the matrices **P** and **P*** as follows:

$$
\mathbf{P} = \begin{bmatrix} 1 & 1 & 1 & 1 \\ 0 & 1 & 0 & 1 \\ 0 & 0 & 1 & 1 \\ 0 & 0 & 0 & 1 \end{bmatrix}
\qquad
\mathbf{P^*} = \begin{bmatrix} 0 & 0 & 0 & 0 \\ 1 & 0 & 1 & 0 \\ 1 & 1 & 0 & 0 \\ 1 & 1 & 1 & 0 \end{bmatrix}
$$

3. Find any additional belief states in B, using the intersection operation:

Belief States in B	Sources
(0000), (1010), (1100), (1110)	Rows of **P***, and therefore MIREs represented with double-edged boxes in Figure 2
(1111)	Null and unit states, Ø and **1**, are always in B (the null state may also be included as a row of **P***).
(1000)	Additional belief state obtained by intersection of rows of **P***: (1000)=(1010) ∩ (1100)

4. Hence $B = [(0000), (1000), (1100), (1010), (1110), (1111)]$

FIGURE 4. Obtaining the belief state lattice from the belief poset.

1. Represent the precedence relations in A by an M × M matrix **P** whose elements p_{ij} are defined by $p_{ij} = 1$ if $\alpha_i \to \alpha_j$ and $p_{ij} = 0$ otherwise.
2. Construct the complement of the matrix **P**—that is, the matrix $\mathbf{P^*} = [p_{ij}^*]$ such that $p_{ij}^* = 0$ if $p_{ij} = 1$ and $p_{ij}^* = 1$ if $p_{ij} = 0$.
3. The rows of $\mathbf{P^*}$ represent belief states that belong to the set B. B consists of the rows of $\mathbf{P^*}$, any additional belief states that can be formed as intersections of the rows of $\mathbf{P^*}$, and the unit and null vectors (**I** and Ø). The poset to lattice algorithm is illustrated in Figure 4.

1.4.2. Lattice to Poset

The set B of admissible belief states contains exactly the same information as the belief poset A. If the belief state lattice B is known, the following algorithm will produce A:

1. Define the grade g of any element $\mathbf{x} = \{x_1, x_2 \ldots x_M\}$ as follows:

$$g = \sum_{i=1}^{M} x_i$$

2. A belief state $\mathbf{x}$ of grade g is said to "cover" a belief state $\mathbf{y}$ of grade $g - 1$ iff $y_i = 1 \Rightarrow x_I = 1$. In the terminology of Appendix B, $\mathbf{y}$ is therefore an immediate precedent of $\mathbf{x}$.

3. Analysis is facilitated by the construction of what is called a "Hasse" diagram, in which elements of B are arranged as in our Figures 2 and 3 ordered by grade from the null vector $\varnothing = (0,0,\ldots 0)$ to the unit vector $\mathbf{I} = (1,1,1\ldots 1)$. Any node is connected to those that cover it by an arrow proceeding toward the node of higher grade.

4. Identify each belief state that has only one covering element and stack these row-wise into an $M \times M$ matrix $\mathbf{C}$. Such belief states are called *meet-irreducible elements* or MIREs, and are denoted in our figures by a double-outline box.

5. The *columns* of this matrix $\mathbf{C}$ can be identified with the corresponding belief—i.e., column 1 is associated with the first belief α_1, column 2 with α_2, and so on. The intersections of the column vectors contain information about the precedence relations in A. Let $\mathbf{c}_i$ represent the ith column vector of the matrix $\mathbf{C}$. Reconstruct the precedence relations by using the following rules: (a) for any i and j, $\mathbf{c}_i \cap \mathbf{c}_j = \mathbf{c}_j$ implies $\alpha_i \rightarrow \alpha_j$ and (b) $\mathbf{c}_i \cap \mathbf{c}_j \neq \mathbf{c}_i$ or $\mathbf{c}_j$ implies α_i and α_j are incomparable.

The lattice to poset algorithm, which we refer to as the "inversion" of the lattice, is illustrated in Figure 5.

2. METHODS

2.1. *Finding Plausible Partial Order Models*

We have not yet discussed how the lattice of latent belief states (or equivalently, the partial order of beliefs) is chosen as a model of the latent structure of an observed response distribution. We have tested three ways of deriving such models.

First, it is possible to specify precedence relations based on *a priori* reasoning about the structure of beliefs embedded in survey questions.

1. Assume that B is the belief state lattice in Figure 2.

2. Stack the meet irreducible belief states—those with a single connection to "higher" belief states—to form the matrix $\mathbf{C}$:

$$\mathbf{C} = \begin{bmatrix} 0 & 0 & 0 & 0 \\ 1 & 0 & 1 & 0 \\ 1 & 1 & 0 & 0 \\ 1 & 1 & 1 & 0 \end{bmatrix}$$

3. Use intersections of the columns of $\mathbf{C}$ to recover precedence relations in A.

$c_1 \cap c_2 = c_2$	implies	$A \rightarrow B$,
$c_1 \cap c_3 = c_3$	implies	$A \rightarrow C$,
$c_1 \cap c_4 = c_4$	implies	$A \rightarrow D$,
$c_2 \cap c_3 \neq c_2$ or c_3	implies	B and C are incomparable
$c_2 \cap c_4 = c_4$	implies	$B \rightarrow D$,
$c_3 \cap c_4 = c_4$	implies	$C \rightarrow B$,

4. The recovered poset is:

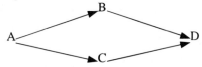

FIGURE 5. Obtaining the belief poset from the belief state lattice.

This requires a careful reading and interpretation of the text of the questions which permits an inference about precedence. In many cases, this inference takes the form of an assertion that belief A is "contained in" belief B, and thus precedes it. For example, in the logic of "social distance scales" (e.g., Bogardus 1925), "willingness to marry a member of group X" would normally imply "accepting a member of group X as a neighbor," if the responses to both items are driven by a simple concept of acceptable intimacy. More complicated structures of precedence arise from multifaceted or multidimensional interpretations and/or constructions of item content.

Second, it is possible to derive a partial order model by inspecting all $M(M-1)/2$ two-way subtables of responses. For example, likely precedence orderings can be identified by calculating measures of fit of each two-way table to the canonical asymmetric Guttman precedence pattern. Such a procedure is used by Mokken (1971) to identify unidimensional structures and can be used for partial order models as well. In our experience, this approach, though plausible, rarely produces the best characterization of response distributions.

Third, we may begin not with the belief poset but with the belief state lattice itself, by taking the most common response patterns in our sample as the kernel from which to build a distributive lattice. By maintaining closure of this set of patterns under union and intersection, which can be accomplished simply by adding any previously omitted states that are the union or intersection of these most frequent states, we ensure that our set of patterns will form a distributive lattice which can be inverted to retrieve a partial order of beliefs. One can easily compare those partial orders that result from the addition of response patterns, using an algorithm authored by Edward Haertel, as one begins from a more restrictive set of most frequent patterns, and successively incorporates less frequent patterns. All of these methods are incorporated in a computer program available from the authors.[2]

2.2. The Latent Class Operationalization

We have outlined the correspondence between a set of precedence relations among beliefs and a set of belief states that form a lattice. Were we able to measure these belief states directly, we would be able to deduce relations of precedence between items without further ado. But instead, as in other cases of the analysis of subjective phenomenon, we expect only a probabilistic relation between our underlying theoretical concepts and the manifest responses. We attempt to measure each of M beliefs with responses to questions that imperfectly record whether the respondent holds or rejects the belief. More specifically, we consider the individual to be in one and only one *latent belief state* at the time of measurement, and assume that the observed response pattern (which we shall call the *manifest response state*) is probabilistically related to the latent states according to traditional concepts of latent class analysis (Lazarsfeld and Henry 1968; Goodman 1974). We can then test whether a hypothesized lattice can explain the observed distribution of responses in an M-way table, given that there is a chance that respondents misclassify themselves with respect to their "true" position. We employ Goodman's version of latent class analy-

---

[2]This program, called ELLA, is available from the authors on request. The closure and inversion routines adapted from those originally authored by Edward Haertel are used by his kind permission.

sis, as he did in his (1975) test of selected latticelike hypotheses, but use a probabilistic model of response error as opposed to Goodman's combination of deterministic latent classes and an inherently unscalable class of random answerers.

The general latent class model consists of two principal elements: (1) a set of mutually exclusive and exhaustive latent classes and proportion of the population falling into each; (2) probabilities of each observed response pattern, given membership in a particular latent class. The latter probabilities are usually specified by a local independence rule that justifies defining the conditional probability of a *response pattern*, given latent class membership, as the product of elementary conditional probabilities pertaining to each observed item response. The probability of an observed response pattern is then composed, in the usual way, as a sum over latent classes of the products of latent class probabilities and conditional probabilities of response patterns given latent class membership.

In our application of the latent class model, the latent classes are the latent belief states—the elements of a distributive lattice of belief states—permitted under a given partial order model of beliefs. Each $\mathbf{x}$ in the lattice represents a latent class whose probability is given by $P[\mathbf{x}]$. (Note that we do not index the latent classes by subscripts since it is understood that $\mathbf{x}$ is an arbitrary element of the lattice and that the sum of the probabilities over the lattice of belief states is 1.) Represent an observed response state by $\mathbf{y} = (y_1, y_2, \ldots, y_M)$, where $y_i = 1$ and $y_i = 0$ are imperfect measures of the corresponding elements $x_i = 1$ and $x_i = 0$ of the latent state. The probability of the observed response state, given the latent belief state, is denoted by $P[\mathbf{y}|\mathbf{x}]$.

We specify $P[\mathbf{y}|\mathbf{x}]$ as a function of simpler probabilities of classification and misclassification as follows. Let $\pi_i = P[y_i = 1|x_i = 1] = P[y_i = 0|x_i = 0]$ be the probability that a response to the ith item correctly represents the ith component of the belief state of the respondent. We assume that this probability is invariant with respect to other latent components of a belief state (i.e., other components of $\mathbf{x}$), and that responses to all items are independent, conditional on the latent belief state (a local independence assumption). (Other specifications of the elementary misclassification probabilities are possible. See, for example, the specifications reviewed in McCutcheon [1987] and given in Proctor's [1970] latent class version of Guttman scaling.) Thus $P[\mathbf{y}|\mathbf{x}]$ can be written as

$$P[\mathbf{y}|\mathbf{x}] = \prod_{i=1}^{M} [\pi_i^{x_i y_i + (1-x_i)(1-y_i)}][(1 - \pi_i)^{(x_i - y_i)^2}]$$

Note that $P[\mathbf{y}|\mathbf{x}]$ is written here as a function of the parameters π_i and the components of $\mathbf{x}$ and $\mathbf{y}$.

The unconditional probability $P[\mathbf{y}]$ is defined as the sum of products of the form $P[\mathbf{y}|\mathbf{x}]\ P[\mathbf{x}]$ over all $\mathbf{x}$ in the lattice. When $\pi_i = \pi$ for all i, $P[\mathbf{y}|\mathbf{x}] = \pi^{M-d}(1 - \pi)^d$, where d is the Hamming distance (Hamming 1950) between the latent belief state $\mathbf{x}$ and the manifest response state $\mathbf{y}$. In this special case, it is clear that the probability of classification "errors"—i.e., differences between latent and observed states—declines as the size of the error (measured by d) increases, so long as probability π of correct classification is greater than .5.

More generally, when the probability of making a response that matches the latent belief is close to 1 for each item, the conditional probability of being in a manifest response state "close" to the latent belief state is high, whereas the probability of being in a manifest state "far" from the latent state is low. If the probabilities of correct classification are substantially less than 1 (significantly closer to .5 than to 1), the model is untenable even if it fits the data, for then there is insufficient evidence that the latent states are determining the manifest responses in a meaningful way.

We use a version of Clifford Clogg's MLLSA program (Clogg 1977; McCutcheon 1987) to fit the latent class models. We generally choose starting values for latent class probabilities based on the observed distribution of those manifest states corresponding directly to the latent belief states and use .90 as our starting value for the probability of correct classification from any latent class. Our modification of the MLLSA program (incorporated in the program referred to in note 2) obtains standard errors of the estimates of the parameters by computing and inverting the information matrix evaluated at the maximum likelihood point (Rao 1965:291–309; Eliason 1993:40). We also check the identifiability of the model by inspecting the column rank of the Jacobian of the transformation from the model parameters to the response state probabilities for plausible values of the parameters. The incorporation of the standard LCA routine in our program facilitates the fitting of the models discussed in this paper; more complex models with different types of error structures may be fit with Jeroen Vermunt's (1997) ℓEM program.

3. AN EXAMPLE USING QUESTIONS ABOUT WELFARE

For an illustration, we take five items from the 1991 Race and Politics Survey (Sniderman, Tetlock, and Piazza 1991:123ff.) regarding attitudes toward welfare. The sample consists of 982 white respondents who agreed to fill out a self-administered questionnaire during a national telephone interview survey and actually returned a completed questionnaire. The response rate for the self-administered part of the survey protocol is estimated at 61.7 percent of those who initially agreed to participate.

The items were as follows:

A. "When people can't support themselves, the government should help by giving them money to meet their basic needs."
B. "Most people on welfare would rather be working than taking money from the government."
C. "The high cost of welfare puts too big a burden on the average taxpayer."
D. "Most people on welfare could get by without it if they really tried."
E. "Most of the money we pay for welfare goes to the bureaucrats instead of going to people who need help."

We have collapsed an original four-point response ("strongly agree," "somewhat agree," "somewhat disagree," "strongly disagree") into agree/disagree; items A and B were then coded agree = 1, disagree = 0; the others were coded agree = 0, disagree = 1. Missing data accounted for only about 1 percent of the responses on each item. To determine whether or not our dichotomization of the four response categories is appropriate, we used Goodman's (1981:644) test of the collapsibility of columns and rows in a symmetric table—i.e., the difference between the independence model under the uncollapsed and collapsed versions of the table, which is equivalent to the sum of the quasi-independence tests of uniformity for the collapsed rows and columns.[3] The chi-squared test of the null hypothesis of no loss of information is nonsignificant in this case, indicating that the collapsing is acceptable. Recoded data for 982 white respondents who answered all five questions are given in Table 1.

We will discuss only one model fully in this example, though we make comparisons to other pertinent models. In comparing models, we use the criterion of Raftery's (1985, 1994) BIC, equal to L^2-(df)ln(N), with L^2 representing the model likelihood-ratio chi-square, df the degrees

---

[3]While this test is equivalent to that which would result from a set of nested tests of the loss of fit due to the combination of categories within a wide class of association models (e.g., see Breiger 1994), it does not have such a relation to all latent class models. We use this test as a reasonable convention for the purposes of illustration; in the conclusion, we discuss possible extensions to polychotomous data, and there propose more rigorous tests.

TABLE 1
Response Data Used for Analysis of Welfare Items

A	B	C	D	E	Frequency
0	0	0	0	0	65
0	0	0	0	1	37
0	0	0	1	0	10
0	0	0	1	1	10
0	0	1	0	0	0
0	0	1	0	1	1
0	0	1	1	0	0
0	0	1	1	1	3
0	1	0	0	0	44
0	1	0	0	1	10
0	1	0	1	0	16
0	1	0	1	1	4
0	1	1	0	0	0
0	1	1	0	1	1
0	1	1	1	0	4
0	1	1	1	1	1
1	0	0	0	0	139
1	0	0	0	1	53
1	0	0	1	0	37
1	0	0	1	1	29
1	0	1	0	0	9
1	0	1	0	1	7
1	0	1	1	0	8
1	0	1	1	1	9
1	1	0	0	0	121
1	1	0	0	1	50
1	1	0	1	0	111
1	1	0	1	1	73
1	1	1	0	0	11
1	1	1	0	1	14
1	1	1	1	0	62
1	1	1	1	1	43

Source: From Sniderman et al. (1991).

of freedom of the model, and N the sample size. (Table 2 contains a list of models and their BICs.) Raftery (1994) contends that BIC, based on Bayesian principles, is more likely to successfully select correct models given noisy data than will conventional tests of significance. We adopt the BIC statistic as our criterion because it is applicable in all cases in which the

TABLE 2
List of Models for Sniderman Data

Model	Likelihood-Ratio Chi-Square	df	BIC
Saturated	0.00	0	0.00
Independence	323.74	26	+144.61
Log-linear Rasch	122.77	22	−28.80
Guttman scale/latent class	73.10	21	−71.58
Lattice model	38.31	19	−92.59
Pairwise interactions	29.09	16	−81.14
Response consistency	20.84	14	−75.61

classical likelihood ratio test is applicable, and it can be used to compare non-nested models. The saturated model has a BIC of 0; a BIC below 0 is preferred to the saturated model (even if the chi-square is significant), and the model with the lowest BIC is considered to be the best choice for representing the observed data. We note that the BIC criterion prefers parsimonious models within a set of equally well-fitting models.

Using this criterion, we first note that the items are not independent—the independence model has a BIC much higher than 0, and so must be rejected. But neither are the items unidimensional. The Rasch model does not fit well, though the BIC is negative (note that a Guttman scale operationalized in the same latent class approach that we use for the lattice model fits better). The items, therefore, do not measure the "same thing" in a conventional sense.

As we see in Table 2, the lowest BIC is found in a lattice model; indeed, while this model is not accepted by the classical criterion, according to the Bayesian criterion it is the best model of any kind that we have examined for these data. Two other substantively interesting loglinear models—one that includes only marginal and pairwise interactions and one that adds terms for the $\emptyset$ and $\mathbf{I}$ cells (i.e., Duncan's [1985] response consistency model)—are also presented in Table 2. Note that the response consistency model fits better than the alternatives under a significance criterion (the test statistic generates $p > .05$ with 14 degrees of freedom), but not by a BIC criterion.

Our particular lattice model was tested on *a priori* grounds, based on our reading of the items and construction of the belief poset. In this model, the first and second items both precede the fourth, which in turn

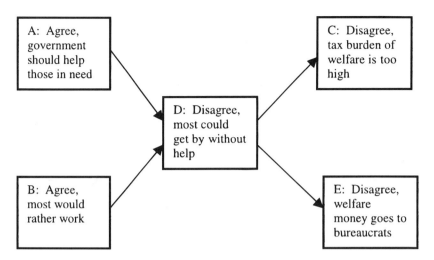

FIGURE 6. A poset model for welfare beliefs from Sniderman et al. (1991).

precedes the third and fifth (see Figure 6). This leads to a belief state lattice presented in Figure 7 (the nodes are given heuristic labels to facilitate interpretation). This model claims that the observed distribution of respondents in the 32 manifest response states actually comes from only eight underlying belief states.

Such a model, whatever the degree of fit, cannot be considered an explanation if—as can be the case—most of the variation is opportunistically accounted for as "misclassification." We therefore insist that such misclassification must be theoretically interpretable as response error stemming from misunderstood questions, and hence a property of the *item*, not of the model. Thus in addition to constraining every item to have only one misclassification pattern, the same in every latent state, we also compare these parameters across slightly different models (adding or dropping a few precedence relations). When there is little variation in misclassification parameters across models (as was the case with these data), we are encouraged to believe that these parameters do reflect aspects of the items themselves. In addition, we inspect the magnitude and order of these misclassification parameters. We consider probabilities of correct classifications of under .75 suspect; more importantly, we believe that the degree of misclassification should be related to factors that are known to produce variations in survey responses, such as interviewer effects or cognitive

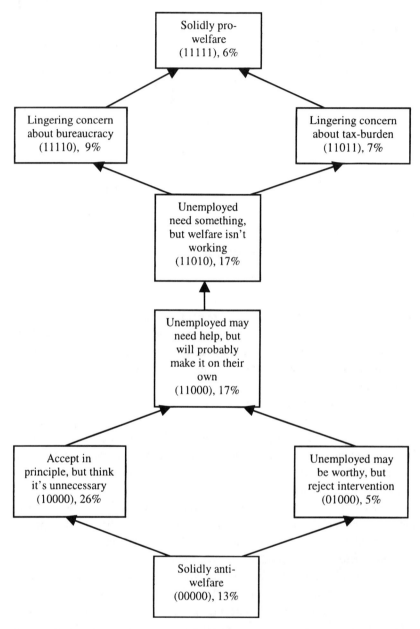

FIGURE 7. Belief state lattice corresponding to the poset model of welfare beliefs in Figure 7.

TABLE 3
Estimated Probabilities of Correct Classification

Item	Statement Structure	Probability of Correct Response
A	When X, Y	.951
B	Most X prefer Y to Z	.838
C	X harms Y	.971
D	Most X could Y if Z	.833
E	Most X goes to Y and not Z	.703

complexity. In this case (see Table 3), we find that the items with apparently greater cognitive complexity have greater probabilities of misclassification. Items (A and C), involving only two simply connected concepts, both have very high probabilities of correct classification. Those items that connect three elements and involve a judgment of quantity (i.e., use word "most") (B and D) have markedly increased noise. Finally, the item with the greatest probability of misclassification error (E) contains at least three elements ("money we pay for welfare," "bureaucrats," and "people who need help") and involves both a quantity judgment ("most") and a form of negation ("instead of").

The model itself tells us something interesting about how the respondents understand the moral logic of welfare. Items A and B precede D; in other words, in order for someone to hold that people on welfare cannot get by without it, they need also to believe that the government *should* give such aid and that people would rather work than accept it. Clearly, this precedence ordering is not deducible on the basis of formal logic, by which one might expect that the belief that people can't get by without welfare (disagree on D) would precede believing that the government should provide it (agree on A). It is similarly unclear on purely logical grounds why one must believe that people on welfare would rather work if they could (agree on B) would precede D. Nevertheless, we can envision an *order in the arguments for and against welfare* according to which respondents must first hold *both* that such assistance is *abstractly* good (agree on A) and that those qualifying for it are *morally fit* recipients (agree on B), before they concede the *necessity* of welfare (disagree on D). This belief in the *necessity* of welfare is then a prerequisite for believing in the efficiency and acceptability of the existing costs of welfare (disagree on C and E).

This may seem to be a logical reversal, but it seems sociologically quite plausible. Thus people can accept the necessity of welfare (disagree on D) without believing that its costs as currently implemented are bearable (i.e., agree on C and E). Indeed, 17 percent of respondents are estimated to come from this category, as opposed to 6 percent holding that the costs are bearable *and* that the money goes to the people who need help (disagree on C and E).

4. DISCUSSION

4.1. *Choices in the Representation of Item Responses Associated with Beliefs*

The model of item responses we propose is clearly one derived from deliberate choices concerning the representation of belief states and their observed manifestations in responses to survey questions. These are as follows: (1) to represent the fundamental unobservables as discrete states, as opposed to continuous traits; (2) to emphasize asymmetric as opposed to symmetric connections between beliefs; (3) to allow for solutions not organized by the concept of dimensionality, as opposed to requiring either unidimensionality or a multidimensionality with fewer dimensions than items; and (4) to assume that the stochastic component of the model comes from error in the measuring instruments, as opposed to originating in an intrinsically aleatory response process in the respondents.

We make no claim that these choices are optimal in all circumstances—indeed, we shall suggest that they may not always be appropriate. Nevertheless, we believe that our approach provides a new foundation for research on the structure of beliefs and of questionnaire items, especially in cases where available methods (for example, forms of unidimensional latent trait theory such as the Rasch model and its derivatives [see Rasch 1966; Duncan 1984a, 1984b, 1984c; Andrich 1988; Fischer and Molenaar 1995]) fail to fit response patterns. In other words, there may be times when valuable information is contained in a set of items that fail the criteria of fundamental measurement.

Finally, we would add that these representational choices can be considered to be a strong theory of the processes of believing and responding, one that is unlikely to be applicable in all situations. We do not see this as a drawback. Our goals in the formulation of theoretically restrictive models must include a substantive—and predictive—understanding of the social circumstances in which one or another will prove valid. Comparisons of similar models to different sets of data may suggest what conditions lead one choice of representation to be more useful than another, and comparison of different models to the same data over time (see Hout 1995) may suggest what conditions lead to a transformation in belief, not simply in quantity, but in quality (see Latane and Nowak 1994).

4.2. *Directions for Further Research*

We conclude by discussing several directions that future work may take. These pertain largely to possible improvements in the specification of both latent and observed distributions. First, it is known that the distinction between discrete and continuous representations is not always rigid. This point was demonstrated by Haertel's (1990) comparison between Bock and Lieberman's 2PN (normal ogive) latent trait model and Goodman-Clogg type latent class models, which showed not only that both representations yielded similar fits and interpretations of the data but also that it was possible to approximate the parameters of one type of model in terms of those of the other, despite there being no direct correspondence. Lindsay, Clogg, and Grego (1991) demonstrate that even assuming a Rasch-type response process, there is no way to adjudicate between a model postulating a continuous latent trait and one with more than half as many discrete latent classes as there are items. Since with proper specification, a continuous two-parameter IRT response process will, as the item discrimination parameter tends toward infinity, turn into a discrete threshold function (for example, see Birnbaum 1968), it might be asked whether the models here are compatible with an IRT specification, in which a high (but not infinite) discrimination parameter would explain both the concentration of responses "on" the lattice and the presence of responses "off" the lattice.

Our preliminary investigations suggest that such an approach is not likely to be productive. The structure of lattice models, which are neither unidimensional nor fully multidimensional, leads to a proliferation of traits and hence unidentifiable models. But it may be possible to extend some of the principles of such limited multidimensionality to more general response processes, which may be treatable within an IRT framework.

Second, it should be noted that our current implementation makes no restrictions as to the distribution of persons across the latent classes on the lattice. While this is not intrinsically unreasonable, there may be more restrictive models that make substantive claims about this distribution. Consider, for example, the following restriction, which can be called a "poset conditional independence model." For any belief α_i in a poset A consisting of M beliefs, let $J_i = \{ \forall\, j \,|\, \alpha_j \to \alpha_i \}$. Poset conditional independence can then be defined as the condition that the probability of holding belief α_i, given that one holds all preceding beliefs α_j ($j \in J_i$), is independent of the probability of holding any belief α_k, $k \notin J_i$; $i \notin J_k$. Thus in addition to the constraint imposed by precedence (the probability of holding belief α_i when one does not hold some α_j, $j \in J_i$ is zero), we add that the probability of holding belief α_i when one does hold all such α_j is some β_i. This then leads to a multiplicative form for latent class probabilities in terms of a set of M item probability parameters, and a more restrictive model.[4] Other possible restrictions on the latent distribution may be worth examination.

Third, our presentation has been restricted to the case where both the latent beliefs and the manifest responses are dichotomous. This restriction is not necessary. Either the manifest responses or the latent beliefs may be ordered polychotomies, though such an extension may produce complications in the analysis and interpretation of models. Most tractable is the case in which the latent beliefs are dichotomous but respondents are presented with ordered categories. Here, suitable parameterization can link a distributive lattice of latent beliefs to a standard latent class analysis (though it may be necessary to take individual "response styles" such as extremism versus centertropism into account in addition to item-based misclassification). The case in which the latent beliefs are themselves ordered polychotomies is more complex. (For simplicity's sake, we assume that the latent beliefs have the same polychotomous structure as the response categories.) Such beliefs may be incorporated in the partial order models by being transformed into a set of dichotomous "indicator beliefs" that combine to form a chain.

Table 4, for example, shows a representation of four ordered responses in terms of three dichotomous indicator variables, each indicating a transition from a lower category to a higher. Hence if we let α_1 represent the belief indexed by x_i ($i = 1$ to 3), then the coding in Table 4 is equivalent to the precedence order $x_1 \to x_2 \to x_3$, a chain poset of discretized "stages of belief." All that is required in building lattice models that include ordered categories is the imposition of a coding scheme that constrains the

---

[4]This restriction is incorporated into the program that we distribute.

TABLE 4
Coding Ordered Categories to Fit a Chain Poset

Response Categories	x_1	x_2	x_3
Strongly disagree	0	0	0
Somewhat disagree	1	0	0
Somewhat agree	1	1	0
Strongly agree	1	1	1

relevant elements of the belief poset to form a chain. Two tetrachotomies, α_1 and α_2, parameterized respectively as $\{x_1, x_2, x_3\}$ and $\{y_1, y_2, y_3\}$, can have a large number of possible precedence relations between them, as long as they do not violate the chain poset of either tetrachotomy. Figure 8 displays two possible relations between such ordered categories. The first is quite complex, not allowing us to assign unambiguous precedence to either α_1 or α_2, since before one can go from "disagree strongly" to "disagree" on α_2, one must first make this transition on α_1. But before one can switch from "disagree" to "agree" on α_1, one must have made the aforementioned transition on α_2. Once one has switched from "disagree" to "agree" on α_1, one may switch from "agree" to "strongly agree" on α_2. This then allows for a similar transition on α_1.

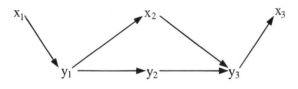

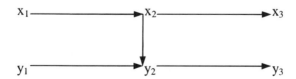

FIGURE 8. Two possible relations between ordered categories.

The second possible relation displayed is much simpler. There is only one connection between the two tetrachotomies—namely, that before one switches from disagree to agree on α_2, one must switch from disagree to agree on α_1. It will be seen that this formulation is equivalent to dichotomizing both tetrachotomies, and letting $\alpha_1 \rightarrow \alpha_2$. Our dichotomization of the data used in Section 3 may then be also seen as the imposition of such a precedence structure between the two tetrachotomies, with additional constraints on the item misclassification parameters. It should be noted that the transformation of the tetrachotomy into three dummy variables rules out certain types of misclassification but not others, and accordingly the misclassification probabilities are not independent across a set of indicator variables. It should be also noted that this poses complications for the specification of misclassification probabilities within a latent class framework.

Finally, the partial order models outlined here may be seen as a special case of models introduced in test theory by Haertel and Wiley (1993). These more general models may also be of utility in sociological investigations. We hope to make this clear in work that will follow.

APPENDIX A: NOTATION

SYMBOL	DEFINITION
$\rightarrow$	A BINARY RELATION OF PRECEDENCE BETWEEN TWO BELIEFS
A_I	THE I^{TH} BELIEF IN A POSET $A = [\alpha_1, \alpha_2, \ldots, \alpha_M]$ of M distinct beliefs that is partially ordered under a precedence relation
x_i	The state of the ith belief where $x_i = 1$ if the belief is held and $x_i = 0$ otherwise
$x_i = 0 \Rightarrow x_j = 0$	If $x_i = 0$, then $x_j = 0$; this relation implies that α_i precedes α_j
$\mathbf{x} = [x_1, x_2, \ldots, x_M]$	An arbitrary belief state
$\mathbf{I} = [1, 1, \ldots, 1]$	The unit belief state
$\emptyset = [0, 0, \ldots, 0]$	The null belief state
B	The set of admissible belief states; a distributive lattice we call the belief state lattice
$\cap$	Intersection, binary operation on a pair of belief states
$\cup$	Union, binary operation on a pair of belief states
$\mathbf{P} = [p_{ij}]$	An M by M matrix of precedence relations; $p_{ij} = 1$ iff $\alpha_i \rightarrow \alpha_j$ and 0 otherwise
$\mathbf{P}^* = [p_{ij}^*]$	The matrix complement of $\mathbf{P}$, with rows $\mathbf{p}_i^*$
$\mathbf{C} = [c_{ij}]$	M by M matrix constructed by stacking the M meet-irreducible elements of B; these elements are represented in the Hasse diagram of B as belief states from which a single arrow emerges

$\mathbf{y} = [y_1, y_2, \ldots, y_M]$ An arbitrary manifest response pattern; $y_i = 1$ for a positive response to an item and 0 otherwise

$P[\mathbf{y}|\mathbf{x}]$ The conditional probability of a manifest response pattern $\mathbf{y}$ for a person in belief state $\mathbf{x}$; under local independence in a latent class formulation, this probability is the product of item-specific conditional probabilities

$P[\mathbf{x}]$ Probability of observing a person in belief state $\mathbf{x}$ under random sampling from the population of interest

APPENDIX B: THEOREMS ON POSETS AND LATTICES

This appendix is intended as a commentary on the mathematical properties of posets and lattices used to formulate the models of belief structure presented in the text. The notation used here follows Appendix A. We begin with an abstract definition of a lattice and of the distributive property of lattices, and then show that the unique set of belief states consistent with given precedence relations does indeed satisfy the defining properties of a distributive lattice. We demonstrate that the poset-to-lattice algorithm described in the text and shown in Figure 4 follows from the general theory of representation for distributive lattices. Finally, we present proof that the belief state lattice can be inverted to obtain the unique belief poset according to the algorithm of Figure 5.

B.1. General Definition of a Lattice

Consider a poset A, consisting of elements α, β, δ, etc., together with a binary relation that is transitive, reflexive, and antisymmetric, denoted by "$\leq$". The "lower bound" of a pair of elements, α and β, in A is an element δ, such that $\delta \leq \alpha$ and $\delta \leq \beta$. Similarly, the "upper bound" of a pair of elements, α and β, in A is an element δ, such that $\alpha \leq \delta$ and $\beta \leq \delta$. The "greatest lower bound" or "meet" of any two elements α and β in A is a unique element γ in A such that $\gamma \leq \alpha$ and $\gamma \leq \beta$ and there is no δ in A such that $\gamma \leq \delta \leq \alpha$ and $\gamma \leq \delta \leq \beta$. The meet operation maps each pair of elements in A into a unique element in A and is signified by the symbol $\wedge$; the definition above says that $\gamma = \alpha \wedge \beta$. Similarly, the "least upper bound" or "join" of any two elements, α and β, in A, represented by $\alpha \vee \beta$, is a unique element γ in A such that $\alpha \leq \gamma$ and $\beta \leq \gamma$, and there is no δ in A such that $\alpha \leq \delta \leq \gamma$ and $\beta \leq \delta \leq \gamma$. Thus $\gamma = \alpha \vee \beta$: γ is the join of α and β. A lattice is then a poset that is closed under the binary operations of meet and join; that is, for any two elements α and β in A, $\alpha \vee \beta \in A$ and $\alpha \wedge \beta \in A$.

A lattice is "distributive" if for any three elements α, β, and γ in A, $\alpha \wedge (\beta \vee \gamma) = (\alpha \wedge \beta) \vee (\alpha \wedge \gamma)$ and $\alpha \vee (\beta \wedge \gamma) = (\alpha \vee \beta) \wedge (\alpha \vee \gamma)$.

B.2. Definitions of Binary Relations and Operations in Belief and Belief State Posets

In most treatments of lattice algebra, the generic binary relation that induces a partial order is denoted by "$\leq$". This symbol has a specific meaning in the posets of beliefs and belief states that are the subject of this paper. For a belief poset, $\alpha \leq \beta$ means either that belief α precedes belief β (i.e., $\alpha \rightarrow \beta$) or that the two beliefs are equivalent. For a poset of belief states, $\mathbf{x} \leq \mathbf{y}$ means that x_i is less than or equal to y_i for all i. Obviously, the interpretation of $\leq$ establishes the meaning of the binary operations of meet and join.

For posets of belief states represented by vectors of 1s and 0s, the union of two belief states, denoted by $\mathbf{x} \cup \mathbf{y}$, is defined as a belief state $\mathbf{z}$ where $z_i = 1$ if $x_i = 1$ *or* $y_i = 1$, and $z_i = 0$ otherwise. The intersection of two belief states, denoted $\mathbf{x} \cap \mathbf{y}$, is a belief state $\mathbf{z}$ such that $z_i = 1$ if $x_i = 1$ *and* $y_i = 1$ and $z_i = 0$ otherwise. The following theorem is stated here without proof (available from the authors), which is trivial.

Theorem 1: Assume that the belief states are represented by vectors of 1s and 0s. Then for any pair of belief states $\mathbf{x}$ and $\mathbf{y}$ in a poset of belief states, $\mathbf{x} \cap \mathbf{y} = \mathbf{x} \wedge \mathbf{y}$ whenever both the meet of $\mathbf{x}$ and $\mathbf{y}$ and their intersection are contained in the poset. Similarly, $\mathbf{x} \cup \mathbf{y} = \mathbf{x} \vee \mathbf{y}$ whenever both the join and the union of $\mathbf{x}$ and $\mathbf{y}$ are contained in the poset. By theorem 1, establishing closure under both union and intersection determines a poset to be a distributive lattice.

B.3. The Belief State Lattice Induced by a Partial Order of Beliefs

The algorithms connecting sets of beliefs and belief states depend on the fundamental fact that a belief poset induces a belief state lattice with the distributive property. The general theorem is stated and proved in Birkhoff ([1940] 1967). Here we give a proof consistent with our representation of belief states as vectors of 1s and 0s.

Theorem 2: Given a belief poset A with precedence relation $\rightarrow$, the set of admissible belief states $B = [\mathbf{x} | x_i = 0 \Rightarrow x_j = 0$ whenever $\alpha_i \rightarrow \alpha_j$ in $A]$ is a distributive lattice.

Proof: B consists of all belief states not explicitly excluded by precedence relations in A. Since precedence relations in A translate into restrictions of the form $x_i = 0 \Rightarrow x_j = 0$ and its contrapositive $x_j = 1 \Rightarrow x_i = 1$, it is clear the universal upper and lower bounds $\mathbf{I} = (1,1,\ldots,1)$ and $\varnothing = (0,0,\ldots 0)$ are not excluded and are thus contained in B. Now suppose that $\mathbf{x}$ and $\mathbf{y}$ are members of B. If $\alpha_i \rightarrow \alpha_j$ in A, the component pairs (x_i,x_j) and (y_i,y_j) can only take on values $(0,0)$, $(1,0)$, or $(1,1)$. Note that there are thus no two component pairs of these three possible values whose intersection or union is $(0,1)$. Under the definition of intersection, then, the component pairs of $\mathbf{z} = \mathbf{x} \cap \mathbf{y}$ must obey the same restriction, and thus $\mathbf{z}$ is contained in B. By a similar argument, the components of the union $\mathbf{w} = \mathbf{x} \cup \mathbf{y}$ must obey the same precedence restrictions as those imposed on $\mathbf{x}$ and $\mathbf{y}$ and thus $\mathbf{w}$ is contained in B. Given theorem 1, closure under union and intersection implies that the poset of belief states B is a lattice.

The distributive property can be confirmed by examining each of a small number of possibilities. To prove that $\mathbf{x} \cap (\mathbf{y} \cup \mathbf{z}) = (\mathbf{x} \cap \mathbf{y}) \cup (\mathbf{x} \cap \mathbf{z})$, we need to show that the ith components on each side of the equation are equal. For example, if $x_i = 0$, $y_i = 1$, and $z_i = 1$, then $\{\mathbf{x} \cap (\mathbf{y} \cup \mathbf{z})\}_i = \{(\mathbf{x} \cap \mathbf{y}) \cup (\mathbf{x} \cap \mathbf{z})\}_i = 0$. Since there are only eight combinations of 1s and 0s, it is easy to show that equality holds in all cases. We omit this proof via direct enumeration (available upon request) for purposes of space. The equality $\mathbf{x} \cup (\mathbf{y} \cap \mathbf{x}) = (\mathbf{x} \cup \mathbf{y}) \cap (\mathbf{x} \cup \mathbf{z})$ can be demonstrated in a similar way.

B.4. *From Poset to Distributive Lattice*

A theorem of Birkhoff says that every element of a distributive lattice can be represented uniquely and irredundantly as the meet (and in our case equivalently the intersection) of elements in a special subset of elements in the lattice called meet-irreducible (Birkhoff [1940] 1967:58–59). An element $\mathbf{z}$ is meet-irreducible if $\mathbf{z} = \mathbf{x} \cap \mathbf{y}$ implies that either $\mathbf{x} = \mathbf{z}$ or $\mathbf{y} = \mathbf{z}$. The universal upper-bound $\mathbf{I}$ may be considered trivially meet-irreducible because $\mathbf{I} = \mathbf{x} \cap \mathbf{y}$ implies $\mathbf{x} = \mathbf{I}$ and $\mathbf{y} = \mathbf{I}$. The poset to lattice algorithm given in the text and in Figure 4 relies on Birkhoff's representation theorem. In order to justify our use of Birkhoff's result, we need to prove the following theorem:

Theorem 3: Let $\mathbf{P}$ be the M×M matrix representation of the precedence relations that characterize a belief poset A. The rows of the complement of $\mathbf{P}$, denoted by $\mathbf{P}^*$, are the nontrivial meet-irreducible elements of B.

Proof: $\mathbf{P}$ *and* $\mathbf{P}^*$ are defined in the text of the paper. Let $\mathbf{p}_i^*$ be the M-tuple $(p_{i1}^*, p_{i2}^*, \ldots, p_{iM}^*)$ formed from the elements of the ith row of $\mathbf{P}^*$. First we show (1) that each $\mathbf{p}_i^*$ is an element of B, and then (2) that each $\mathbf{p}_i^*$ is meet-irreducible. (1) Since $p_{ii}^* = 0$ for all i and $p_{ij}^* = 0$ iff $\alpha_i \rightarrow \alpha_j$, it follows that $p_{ii}^* = 0 \Rightarrow p_{ij}^* = 0$ for all j such that $\alpha_i \rightarrow \alpha_j$. For j such that $\alpha_j \rightarrow \alpha_i$, $p_{ij}^* = 1$ and $p_{ii}^* = 0$, which is consistent with the definition of B. Thus $\mathbf{p}_i^* \in B$ for all i. (2) For any i, and distinct elements $\mathbf{x}$ and $\mathbf{y}$ in B, suppose that $\mathbf{p}_i^* = \mathbf{x} \cap \mathbf{y}$. Let J_1 be the set of indices j for which $p_{ij}^* = 0$ and let J_2 be the set of indices j for which $p_{ij}^* = 1$. For $j \in J_2$, $p_{ij}^* = x_j = y_j = 1$ by the definition of intersection. Now for $j \in J_1$, $\alpha_i \rightarrow \alpha_j$ (since by definition of J_1 $p_{ij}^* = 0$ and hence $p_{ij} = 1$) and thus $z_i = 0$ implies $z_j = 0$ for any $\mathbf{z}$ in B. Since $p_{ii}^* = 0$, it must be true that either $x_i = 0$ or $y_i = 0$, by the definition of intersection. If $x_i = 0$, then $x_j = 0$ for all j in J_1 in which case $\mathbf{p}_i^* = \mathbf{x}$. If $y_i = 0$, then $y_j = 0$ for all j in J_1 and $\mathbf{p}_i^* = \mathbf{y}$. Thus $\mathbf{p}_i^*$ is meet-irreducible in B.

It can be shown that the $\mathbf{p}_i^*$ (plus $\mathbf{I}$) are the only meet-irreducible elements of B and that each element of B can be *uniquely* represented as a meet of meet-irreducible elements. We will be content here to prove a weaker result, namely:

Theorem 4: Each element of B can be represented as a meet (intersection) of a subset of the $\mathbf{p}_i^*$.

Proof: We shall prove this theorem by construction. Let $\mathbf{x} \neq \mathbf{I}$ be a belief state in B. Let J_x be the set of indices i such that $x_i = 0$. Then represent $\mathbf{x}$ by

$$\mathbf{x} = \cap \mathbf{p}_i^*$$

$$i \in J_x$$

We first establish that this intersection leads to a 0 for every index $i \in J_x$ and then that the intersection leads to a 1 for every index $i \notin J_x$, thus proving the identity. For $i \in J_x$, $x_i = 0$ and the ith element of the intersection is 0 by construction since $p_{ii}^* = 0$ for all i. (In other words, by selecting for our intersection those rows corresponding to indices of $\mathbf{x}$ that have 0s, we guarantee a 0 for each x_i, $i \in J_x$; see Figure 4 for an illustration.) For $i \in J_x$ and $j \notin J_x$, $x_i = 0$ and $x_j = 1$. Then it must be true that $\alpha_i \rightarrow \alpha_j$ for no

$i \in J_x$ and $j \notin J_x$. Then $p_{ij} = 0$, which implies $p^*_{ij} = 1$ for this case. Consequently, for $j \notin J_x$, the jth element of the intersection must equal 1.

Theorems 3 and 4 show that the poset to lattice algorithm presented in the text always recovers the complete belief state lattice.

B.5. Lattice to Poset

It is possible to work the algorithm of the preceding section in reverse to retrieve the belief poset from a distributive lattice of belief states—i.e., locate the meet-irreducible elements, stack them in just the right order, and take the complement of the resulting matrix to get the precedence relations among the beliefs. This method performs well for small posets but can become maddeningly confusing in large ones. We present here a theorem that justifies the algorithm suggested in the text. Note that this algorithm does not require any ordering of the meet-irreducible elements.

Theorem 5: α_i precedes α_j in A if and only if there is no row vector $\mathbf{p}^*_k$ ($k = 1,\ldots,M$) such that $p^*_{ki} = 0$ and $p^*_{kj} = 1$. We note that the falsity of this latter condition is established if and only if the product $p^*_{ki}p^*_{kj} = p^*_{kj}$ for each k, which is equivalent to the assertion (used in the algorithm of Figure 5) that the intersection of the ith and j^{th} column vectors of $\mathbf{P}^*$ equals the jth column vector, if and only if $\alpha_i \rightarrow \alpha_j$ in A.

Proof: We will prove this theorem in two parts, first demonstrating the sufficiency, and second the necessity, of the relation between precedence in A and the contents of $\mathbf{P}^*$.

a.   Suppose $\alpha_i \rightarrow \alpha_j$ in A. Then $p_{ij} = 1$ and $p_{ji} = 0$ in $\mathbf{P}$. Since $p_{ii} = 1$ and $p_{jj} = 1$ by reflexivity, we have the following results for the ith and j^{th} components of $\mathbf{p}^*_i$ and $\mathbf{p}^*_j$: $p^*_{ii} = 0$, $p^*_{ij} = 0$ and $p^*_{ji} = 1$, $p^*_{jj} = 0$. For any $k \neq i$, $k \neq j$, p_{ki} and p_{kj} (and hence p^*_{ki} and p^*_{kj}) take on only those values that are consistent with the possible relations between α_k, α_i, and α_j. By hypothesis, $\alpha_i \rightarrow \alpha_j$, so for any α_k there are just five possibilities for the precedence structure of the sub-poset consisting of α_k, α_i, and α_j—namely, (i) $\alpha_k \rightarrow \alpha_i \rightarrow \alpha_j$, (ii) $\alpha_i \rightarrow \alpha_j$, $\alpha_i \rightarrow \alpha_k$, (iii) $\alpha_i \rightarrow \alpha_j \rightarrow \alpha_k$, (iv) $\alpha_i \rightarrow \alpha_k \rightarrow \alpha_j$, and (v) $\alpha_i \rightarrow \alpha_j$, α_k disconnected. Each possibility constrains the values of p^*_{ki} and p^*_{kj} such that $p^*_{ki} = 0$ and $p^*_{kj} = 1$ for no k, as confirmed by direct inspection. Thus $\alpha_i \rightarrow \alpha_j$ is sufficient for $p^*_{ki} = 0$ and $p^*_{kj} = 1$ for no $\mathbf{p}^*_k$.

b. To prove necessity, we need to establish the following: If there exists no $\mathbf{p}_k^*$ such that $p_{ki}^* = 0$ and $p_{kj}^* = 1$ $(k = 1,\ldots,M)$, then $\alpha_i \to \alpha_j$ in A. Let $S =$ "there is no $\mathbf{p}_k^*$ such that $p_{ki}^* = 0$ and $p_{kj}^* = 1$" and let $T =$ "$\alpha_i \to \alpha_j$ in A." We shall show that S implies T by proving the contrapositive statement, not-T implies not-S. Assume not-T—i.e., that α_i does not precede α_j in A. Then either (i) α_i and α_j are incomparable in A, or (ii) $\alpha_j \to \alpha_i$ in A. Consider the first case. If α_i and α_j are incomparable in A, then $p_{ij} = 0$ and $p_{ii} = 1$. Whence $p_{ii}^* = 0$ and $p_{ij}^* = 1$ and the statement not-S holds, where the $\mathbf{p}_k^*$ in question happens to be $\mathbf{p}_i^*$. For case (ii) $\alpha_j \to \alpha_i$ in A implies that $p_{ij} = 0$ (the precedence relation is antisymmetric), and since $p_{ii} = 1$, we have once again $p_{ii}^* = 0$ and $p_{ij}^* = 1$—i.e., not-S is true, with $\mathbf{p}_k^* = \mathbf{p}_i^*$. Thus not-T implies not-S and therefore S implies T, proving necessity.

REFERENCES

Andrich, David. 1988. "Rasch Models for Measurement." Series: *Quantitative Applications in the Social Sciences*, No. 68. Newbury Park: Sage Publications.

Birkhoff, Garrett. [1940] 1967. *Lattice Theory*, Vol. 25, Providence, RI: American Mathematical Society, Colloquium Publications.

Birnbaum, Allan. 1968. "Some Latent Trait Models and Their Use in Inferring an Examinee's Ability." Pp 397–479 in *Statistical Theories of Mental Test Scores*, edited by Frederic M. Lord and Melvin R. Novick. Reading, MA: Addison-Wesley.

Bogardus, E. S. 1925. "Measuring Social Distance." *Journal of Applied Sociology* 9:299–308.

Breiger, Ronald L. 1994. "Dual Aggregation on the Basis of Relational Homogeneity." Presented at the International Social Networks Conference, February 17–20, New Orleans.

Clogg, Clifford. 1977. "Unrestricted and Restricted Maximum Likelihood Latent Structure Analysis: A Manual For Users." Working Paper 1977-09. University Park, PA: Population Issues Research Office.

De Boeck, Paul, and Seymour Rosenberg. 1988. "Hierarchical Classes: Model and Data Analysis." *Psychometrika* 53:361–82.

Duncan, Otis D. 1984a. *Notes on Social Measurement*. New York: Russell Sage Foundation.

———. 1984b. "Measurement and Structure." Pp. 179–229 in *Surveying Subjective Phenomena*, Vol. 1, edited by Charles F. Turner and Elizabeth Martin. New York: Russell Sage Foundation.

———. 1984c. "Rasch Measurement in Survey Research: Further Examples and Discussion." Pp. 367–404 in *Surveying Subjective Phenomena*, Vol. 2, edited by Charles F. Turner and Elizabeth Martin. New York: Russell Sage Foundation.

———. 1985. "Indicators of Sex Typing: Traditional and Egalitarian, Situational and Ideological Responses." *American Journal of Sociology* 85:251–60.

Duquenne, Vincent. 1995. "Models of Possessions and Lattice Analysis." *Social Networks* 34:253–67.

Eliason, Scott. 1993. *Maximum Likelihood Estimation: Logic and Practice.* Vol. 96, *Quantitative Applications in the Social Sciences.* Thousand Oaks, CA: Sage.

Fischer, G. H., and I. V. Molenaar, eds. 1995. *Rasch Models: Foundations, Recent Developments, and Applications.* New York: Springer-Verlag.

Freeman, Linton C., and Douglas R. White. 1993. "Using Galois Lattices to Represent Network Data." Pp. 127–146 in *Sociological Methodology,* Vol. 23, edited by Peter V. Marsden. Cambridge, MA: Blackwell Publishers.

Goodman, Leo A. 1974. "The Analysis of Systems of Qualitative Variables When Some of the Variables are Unobservable. Part 1: A Modified Latent Structure Approach," *American Journal of Sociology* 79, reprinted in *Analyzing Qualitative/ Categorical Data,* edited by Jay Magdison. Cambridge, MA: Abt Books, 1978.

———. 1975. "A New Model for Scaling Response Patterns." *Journal of the American Statistical Association* 70, reprinted in *Analyzing Qualitative/Categorical Data,* edited by Jay Magdison. Cambridge, MA: Abt Books, 1978.

———. 1981. "Criteria for Determining Whether Certain Categories in a Cross-Classification Table Should Be Combined, with Special Reference to Occupational Categories in an Occupational Mobility Table." *American Journal of Sociology* 87:612–50.

Guttman, Louis. 1950. "The Basis for Scalogram Analysis." Pp. 60–90 in *Measurement and Prediction, Studies in Social Psychology in World War II,* Vol. 4, edited by Samuel A. Stouffer et al. Princeton, NJ: Princeton University Press.

Haertel, Edward H. 1990. "Continuous and Discrete Latent Structure Models for Item Response Data." *Psychometrika* 55:477–494.

Haertel, Edward H., and David E. Wiley. 1993. "Representations of Ability Structures: Implications for Testing," Pp. 359–84 in *Test Theory for a New Generation of Tests,* edited by Norman Frederiksen, Robert Mislevy, and Isaac Bejar. Hillsdale, NJ: Lawrence Erlbaum.

Hamming, R. W. 1950. "Error Detection and Error Correcting Codes." *Bell System Technical Journal* 29: 147–60.

Hout, Michael. 1995. "Abortion Politics in the United States, 1972–1994: From Single Issue to Ideology." Presented at the annual meeting of the American Sociological Association, Washington.

Latane, Bibb, and Andrezj Nowak. 1994. "Attitudes as Catastrophes: From Dimensions to Categories with Increasing Involvement." Pp. 219–49 in *Dynamical Systems in Social Psychology,* edited by R. R. Vallacher and Andrezj Nowak. New York: Academic Press.

Lazarsfeld, Paul F., and Neil W. Henry. 1968. *Latent Structure Analysis.* Boston: Houghton-Mifflin.

Lindsay, Bruce, Clifford C. Clogg, and John Grego. 1991. "Semiparametric Estimation in the Rasch Model and Related Exponential Response Models, Including a Simple Latent Class Model for Item Analysis." *Journal of the American Statistical Association* 86:96–107.

McCutcheon, Allan L. 1987. *Latent Class Analysis.* Newbury Park, CA: Sage.

Mokken, R. J. 1971. *A Theory and Procedure of Scale Analysis.* The Hague, Netherlands: Mouton.

Proctor, C. H. 1970. "A Probabilistic Formulation and Statistical Analysis of Guttman Scaling." *Psychometrika* 35:73–78.

Raftery, Adrian. 1985. "A Note on Bayes Factors for Log-Linear Contingency Table Models with Vague Prior Information." *Journal of the Royal Statistical Society*, Series B 48:249–250.

———. 1994. "Bayesian Model Selection in Sociology." Working Paper No. 94-12, Center for Studies in Demography and Ecology, University of Washington.

Rao, C. Radhakrishna. 1965. *Linear Statistical Inference and Its Applications*. New York: Wiley.

Rasch, Georg. 1966. "An Individualistic Approach to Item Analysis." Pp 89–107 in *Readings in Mathematical Social Science*, edited by Paul F. Lazarsfeld and Neil W. Henry. Cambridge, MA: MIT Press.

Shye, Samuel, and Reuven Amar. 1985. "Partial-Order Scalogram Analysis by Base Coordinates and Lattice Mapping of the Items by Their Scalogram Roles." Pp. 277–98 in *Facet Theory: Approaches to Social Research*, edited by David Cantor. New York: Springer-Verlag.

Shye, Samuel, Dov Elizur, and Michael Hoffman. 1994. *Introduction to Facet Theory*, Vol. 35, *Applied Research Methods Series*. Thousand Oaks, CA: Sage.

Sniderman, Paul M., Philip E. Tetlock, and Thomas Piazza. 1991. *Race and Politics Survey Codebook*. Berkeley, CA: Survey Research Center.

Vermunt, Jeroen K. 1997. *ℓ*EM: A General Program for the Analysis of Categorical Data [computer program], Tilburg University, Tilburg, Netherlands.

❦5❧

AN EXTENDED STUDY INTO THE RELATIONSHIP BETWEEN CORRESPONDENCE ANALYSIS AND LATENT CLASS ANALYSIS

Peter G.M. van der Heijden*
Zvi Gilula†
L. Andries van der Ark‡

Researchers dealing with frequency data today can choose from a vast range of methods, descriptive and inferential. Two such well-known and useful methods are correspondence analysis and latent class analysis. Although these two methods were initially used for different research objectives, they are mathematically related to each other. Relations between these methods, however, have only been reported in the literature regarding the bivariate case. In this paper, we extend the study of such relations to the multivariate case. In particular the multivariate X latent class model is shown to imply the (relatively new) joint multivariate correspondence model with $X - 1$ positive eigenvalues. Such relations allow the underlying methods to be treated as variants of the same conceptual idea, providing some new meaningful aspects, which may help researchers better interpret the findings of their investigation.

1. INTRODUCTION

Researchers in many disciplines, particularly in the behavioral, marketing, and medical sciences, frequently encounter the need to analyze multivar-

*Utrecht University
†Hebrew University of Jerusalem
‡Tilburg University

iate relationships among variables that are nonquantitative (categorical). The abundance of categorical data analytic methods available today to such researchers is impressive. In the last 15 years, efforts have been made to study the possible relationships between such methods. The aim of such efforts is basically a desire to derive a common conceptual frame within which many of these methods can be unified. The advantage of having a unified frame is to provide additional insight into the interpretation of empirical findings. In this paper we show that two well-known methods for analyzing multivariate categorical variables, *correspondence analysis* (CA) and *latent class analysis* (LCA) share a common methodological frame, which is detailed later.

A major problem concerning categorical variables is the lack of a natural scale. Scaling categorical variables has been a scientific challenge for many years, as is evident from the wealth of literature on this subject. The common frame for most scaling methods is known today as *optimal scaling*. Nishisato (1980) and Gifi (1990) provide an introduction to these methods, and a recent state-of-the-art review of the unified frame for scaling methods is found in Michailidis and de Leeuw (1998). CA is a very familiar representative of the optimal scaling family. Officially introduced as a descriptive method by the French school of data analysis founded by Benzécri (Benzécri et al. 1973), CA has become one of the leading data-descriptive methods. Many widely used computer routines and software packages contain such analysis. Most of the marketing research courses in business schools contain CA in their curriculum. A good account of CA is given by Greenacre (1984). Goodman (1985) and Gilula and Haberman (1986, 1988) report the derivation of the relevant theory making CA a family of estimable and statistically testable models.

LCA was officially started by Lazarsfeld (1950) as a method of indirectly measuring unobservable variables, called *latent* variables. Starting from the conjecture that latent variables are highly correlated with certain measurable variables (called *manifest* variables), the latent class theory provides tools of measuring the latent variables through certain patterns of association between the manifest variables. A comprehensive introduction to this analysis is given by Lazarsfeld and Henry (1968), and inferential aspects of it are developed by Goodman (1974a,b), Gilula (1979) and Clogg (1981) among others.

In the bivariate case, both CA and LCA utilize the matrix form of the joint distribution of the manifest variables, and both methods use optimization criteria based on reduced rank joint distributions. It is therefore natural that relations between these two methods were subject to wide investigation (e.g., Gilula 1983, 1984; Goodman, 1985, 1987; de Leeuw and van der Heijden, 1991).

Multivariate versions of both CA and LCA have been developed. In particular *multiple* correspondence analysis (MCA) has become quite popular. Greenacre (1988) has developed a finer multivariate version of CA called *joint* correspondence analysis (JCA), and showed some advantages of JCA over MCA.

The association between multivariate LCA and JCA has not been investigated yet. This is the concern of this paper. In particular we show that latent class models having X latent classes imply joint correspondence models with $X - 1$ positive eigenvalues. We discuss ways of rescaling parameters of LCA models, graphical representations that are implied from such rescaling, and compare these graphical displays with those of JCA. The findings of this study together with their interpretation provide the already popular CA with added interpretative benefit, and applicability. Although this is *not* another review paper comparing the two underlying methods, we first start with the well-known bivariate case for expository purposes. We then report the main result, and exemplify its importance by analyzing two empirical data sets.

2. THE BIVARIATE CASE

In this section we will first define simple CA and LCA for two-way contingency tables. Then we will describe the relation, reviewing the results summarized by de Leeuw and van der Heijden (1991).

2.1. *Simple Correspondence Analysis*

We start with simple CA of an $I \times J$ probability matrix $\mathbf{\Pi}$, with a row variable A with I categories indexed by i and a column variable B with and J categories indexed by j. The elements are π_{ij} $(i = 1, \ldots, I; j = 1, \ldots, J)$, where $\pi_{ij} \geq 0$ and $\sum_i \sum_j \pi_{ij} = 1$. We denote the margins by $\sum_j \pi_{ij} = \pi_{i+}$ and $\sum_i \pi_{ij} = \pi_{+j}$. The decomposition by CA has the following form:

$$\pi_{ij} = \pi_{i+} \pi_{+j} \left(1 + \sum_{m=1}^{M-1} \lambda_m \rho_{im} \gamma_{jm} \right) , \qquad (1)$$

with $M \leq \min(I, J)$. Model (1) is restricted by

$$\lambda_m > 0 \ ,$$

$$\sum_i \pi_{i+} \rho_{im} = \sum_j \pi_{+j} \gamma_{jm} = 0 \ ,$$

$$\sum_i \pi_{i+} \rho_{im} \rho_{im'} = \sum_j \pi_{+j} \gamma_{jm} \gamma_{jm'} = \delta^{mm'} \ , \tag{2}$$

where $\delta^{mm'}$ is Kronecker delta. Greenacre (1988) discusses three interpretations of CA. We discuss here briefly the interpretation of CA as a model providing a reduced rank decomposition of a probability matrix. The other two interpretations focus on CA as a tool that provides graphic representations of a probability matrix (see Benzécri et al. 1973; Gifi 1990; Goodman 1991; Gower and Hand 1996), and on the interpretation on CA as a tool for canonical correlation analysis of categorical data (see Kendall and Stuart 1979). For more details and other interpretations, we refer to overviews such as those by Nishisato (1980), Greenacre (1984), and Gifi (1990).

The interpretation that focuses on the reduced rank emphasizes that (1) gives a reduced rank decomposition of Π, in the sense that model (1) defines a matrix of rank M. When $M = \min(I, J)$, then Π has full rank, and the model is saturated. When $M = 1$, (1) is the independence model. Assume that Π has rank M, where $M \leq \min(I, J)$. Then Π can always be decomposed by CA using $M - 1$ sets of parameters indexed by m, $m = 1, \ldots, M - 1$. (For a proof, see de Leeuw and van der Heijden 1991.)

This reduced rank decomposition is closely related to the well-known Pearson chi-square statistic X^2 for testing independence in a two-way contingency table. The relation between (1) and X^2 is through the parameters λ_m in the following way:

$$\sum_{i=1}^{I} \sum_{j=1}^{J} (\pi_{ij} - \pi_{i+} \pi_{+j})^2 \Big/ \pi_{i+} \pi_{+j} = \sum_{m=1}^{M-1} \lambda_m^2 \ . \tag{3}$$

Now consider a two-way contingency table $\mathbf{N}$ with elements n_{ij}, where $n = \sum_i \sum_j n_{ij}$. We derive relative frequencies p_{ij} by $p_{ij} = n_{ij}/n$. The marginal relative frequencies are denoted as p_{i+} and p_{+j}, respectively. The relative frequencies form a probability matrix that can be decomposed with (1). Notice that estimates of expected probabilities under independence are equal to $p_{i+} p_{+j}$, and therefore the left side of equation (3) is then equal to the coefficient of contingency, which is equal to X^2/n. The quantity $\sum_m^{M-1} \lambda_m^2$ is called the total inertia of a matrix. Equation (3) shows that (1) provides a decomposition of the total inertia into $M-1$ dimensions.

Model (1) is usually estimated by weighted least squares using a generalized singular value decomposition (for example, see Greenacre 1984), where the parameters λ_m are the singular values. Computer programs are widely available, for example, in software packages such as SPSS, SAS, and BMDP. More recently maximum-likelihood estimation procedures have become available (see Goodman 1985; Gilula and Haberman 1986).

2.2. The Bivariate Latent Class Model

The latent class model (LCM) assumes the existence of a categorical latent variable, Z, having categories indexed by x, $x = 1,\ldots,X$. This latent variable explains the relation between manifest categorical variables in the sense that, given the category of the latent variable, the manifest variables are independent. For the bivariate case, the model for the two-way probability matrix $\mathbf{\Pi}$ is

$$\pi_{ij} = \sum_{x=1}^{X} \pi_x^Z \pi_{ix}^{\bar{A}Z} \pi_{jx}^{\bar{B}Z} \tag{4}$$

with all parameters nonnegative and

$$\sum_{x=1}^{X} \pi_x^Z = 1, \sum_{i=1}^{I} \pi_{ix}^{\bar{A}Z} = 1, \sum_{j=1}^{J} \pi_{jx}^{\bar{B}Z} = 1 \ .$$

Here π_x^Z is the class size—i.e., the probability that an observation falls in latent class x, and $\pi_{ix}^{\bar{A}Z}$ (or $\pi_{jx}^{\bar{B}Z}$) are conditional probabilities indicating the probability of falling in category i (or j) given that the observation falls into latent class x.

Just like CA, model (4) can also be interpreted as a reduced rank decomposition of a probability matrix. Model (4) defines a matrix of rank X. When $X = \min(I,J)$, the matrix $\mathbf{\Pi}$ is of full rank, and the model is saturated. When $X = 1$, (4) reduces to the independence model. When $1 < X < \min(I,J)$, (4) defines a matrix having a reduced rank.

In the bivariate case the LCM can be rewritten as

$$\pi_{ij}/\pi_{i+} = \sum_{x=1}^{X} \pi_{ix}^{A\bar{Z}} \pi_{jx}^{\bar{B}Z} \tag{5}$$

where

$$
\pi_{ix}^{A\bar{Z}} = \frac{\pi_x^Z \pi_{ix}^{\bar{A}Z}}{\displaystyle\sum_{x=1}^{X} \pi_x^Z \pi_{ix}^{\bar{A}Z}} = \frac{\pi_x^Z \pi_{ix}^{\bar{A}Z}}{\pi_{i+}}
\tag{6}
$$

(Goodman 1974a), which is also known in the social sciences as the latent budget model (for an overview, see van der Heijden, Mooijaart and de Leeuw 1992; van der Ark 1999) and in geology as the end member model (Renner 1993).

The LCM is usually estimated by maximum likelihood (cf. Goodman 1974a).

2.3. Relations

We will first show how models (1) and (4) are related (cf. Gilula 1979, 1983; de Leeuw and van der Heijden 1991; van der Ark, van der Heijden and Sikkel 1999). Then we will discuss the implications for data analysis.

First we note that both models provide rank decompositions of the matrix Π. We also note that the rank decomposition is provided in the LCM by nonnegative parameters, whereas the parameters in CA are both positive and negative.

Let the rank of a matrix Π be denoted by R. We already noted that a matrix of rank R can always be decomposed by CA with $M = R$. In terms of the rank of a matrix Π we have the following four situations.

1. When $R = 1$, the matrix Π can be decomposed by CA with $M = 1$ and by LCA with $X = 1$, since then both CA as well as LCA are equivalent to the independence model.
2. When $R = \min(I, J)$, the matrix Π can always be decomposed both by CA with $M = R$ as well as by LCA with $X = R$, since both models are equivalent to the saturated model.
3. When $1 < R < \min(I, J)$, the matrix Π can always be decomposed by CA with $M = R$ but not always by LCA with $X = R$, since the decomposition provided by LCA is less general than that of CA because of the nonnegativity restrictions on the parameters. It follows that, if LCA of rank $X = R$ is true (i.e., a matrix Π can be decomposed by LCA with $1 < X < \min(I, J)$ latent classes), then CA of rank $M = R$ is

true (i.e., a matrix $\mathbf{\Pi}$ can also be decomposed by CA with $M = R$), but the reverse does not hold. There are, therefore, matrices of reduced rank R that can be decomposed by CA with $M = R$ but not by LCA with $X = R$. It follows that the models are not equivalent.

4. When $R = 2$, CA implies the LCM (see de Leeuw and van der Heijden 1991, for a proof). Therefore, for rank 2 the models are equivalent.

For data analytic situations, this implies that if both models are estimated using the same criterion—for example, maximum likelihood—then the fitted values (estimates of expected probabilities) of CA are equal to those of LCA if $M = X = 2$. If $2 < X < \min(I, J)$ it often turns out that fitted values of both models are the same, but this is not necessarily the case. (For more details see van der Ark et al. 1999.)

Assume for the moment a matrix for which the fitted values of CA are equal to those of LCA. Then the CA-parameters are related to the LCA-parameters. This relation is most clearly seen from the LCA parameters rescaled as in equation (6). First a set of rescaled parameters $\pi_{ix}^{A\bar{Z}}$ is obtained from the original parameters $\pi_{ix}^{\bar{A}Z}$, and in a comparable way a set of rescaled parameters $\pi_{jx}^{B\bar{Z}}$ is obtained from the original parameters $\pi_{jx}^{\bar{B}Z}$. Using $\pi_{ix}^{\bar{A}Z} = \pi_{i+}\pi_{ix}^{A\bar{Z}}(\pi_x^Z)^{-1}$ from equation (6), we can now rewrite the LCA model in (4) as

$$\pi_{ij} = \sum_{x=1}^{X} \pi_x^Z \pi_{ix}^{\bar{A}Z} \pi_{jx}^{\bar{B}Z} = \pi_{i+}\pi_{+j} \sum_{x=1}^{X} \pi_{ix}^{A\bar{Z}} \pi_{jx}^{B\bar{Z}}(\pi_x^Z)^{-1} \qquad (7)$$

Comparing (6) with (1) makes the relation between the rescaled LCA parameters and the CA parameters evident:

$$\left(1 + \sum_{m=1}^{R-1} \lambda_m \rho_{im} \gamma_{jm}\right) = \sum_{x=1}^{R} \pi_{ix}^{A\bar{Z}} \pi_{jx}^{B\bar{Z}}(\pi_x^Z)^{-1} . \qquad (8)$$

This shows that, if we collect the CA parameters ρ_{im} in a $I \times R$ matrix $\mathbf{P}$ where the first column is a unit vector, and γ_{jm} in a $J \times R$ matrix $\mathbf{\Gamma}$ where the first column is a unit vector (the unit vector corresponds to the '1' in [1]), and if we collect the rescaled LCA parameters $\pi_{ix}^{A\bar{Z}}$ in a $I \times R$ matrix $\mathbf{\Pi}_i$ and the rescaled LCA parameters $\pi_{jx}^{B\bar{Z}}$ in a $J \times R$ matrix $\mathbf{\Pi}_j$, then

$$\mathbf{P} = \mathbf{\Pi}_i \mathbf{S} \qquad (9)$$

and

$$\Gamma = \Pi_j T, \tag{10}$$

where S and T are $R \times R$ transformation matrices. This shows that linear combinations of the rescaled LCA parameters lead to the CA parameters and the other way around. But we repeat that equation (8) is correct only if for some matrix the fitted values of CA are equal to the fitted values of LCA.

Of course, this result becomes more interesting if the rescaled parameters $\pi_{ix}^{A\bar{Z}}$ and $\pi_{jx}^{B\bar{Z}}$ give us any insight into the latent class model (4). Fortunately they do, as we will explain now. The presentation of the latent class model in (4) is only one way to represent the latent class model, and there exist alternatives. A well-known alternative representation of the latent class model is as a loglinear model for the manifest variables A and B and the latent variable Z. In this presentation the latent variable Z is related to variable A and to variable B, and A and B are not directly related: conditional on X, the variables A and B are independent. Let us define the probabilities in this joint table of variables A, B and X as π_{ijx}. Collapsibility rules from loglinear analysis (see Fienberg 1980) show that, under conditional independence, the dependence between X and A in the three-variable probabilities π_{ijx} is equal to the dependence between X and A in the marginal probabilities π_{i+x}. Dependence can be studied by making a comparison with independence. Probability theory tells us that there are three ways to define independence for elements such as π_{i+x} (cf. Mood Graybill and Boes 1974:40). The first is $\pi_{i++} \pi_{++x}$, and these can be compared with dependence in π_{i+x}. The second way is $\pi_{i+x}/\pi_{++x} = \pi_{i++}$, and dependence can be easily studied by comparing conditional probabilities π_{i+x}/π_{++x} with the marginal probabilities π_{i++}. This is the usual way to study the latent class model, since $\pi_{i+x}/\pi_{++x} = \pi_{ix}^{AZ}$. The third way is $\pi_{i+x}/\pi_{i++} = \pi_{++x}$, and now dependence can be easily studied by comparing conditional probabilities π_{i+x}/π_{i++} with the marginal probabilities π_{++x}. This is the alternative way to study the latent class model proposed here, because $\pi_{i+x}/\pi_{i++} = \pi_{ix}^{A\bar{Z}}$. Basically, insight in the LCA model is obtained since parameter $\pi_{ix}^{A\bar{Z}}$ can be interpreted as the mass of category i falling in class x.

We emphasize here that the strength of the relationship between the latent variable and the manifest variable is equally strong, whether we use the original or the rescaled parameters. In other words, if we consider rows i and i', and x and x', then the odds ratio based on four original parameters is equal to the odds ratio based on four rescaled parameters: $\pi_{ix}^{\bar{A}Z} \pi_{i'x'}^{\bar{A}Z} / \pi_{ix'}^{\bar{A}Z} \pi_{x'i}^{\bar{A}Z} = \pi_{ix}^{A\bar{Z}} \pi_{i'x'}^{A\bar{Z}} / \pi_{ix'}^{A\bar{Z}} \pi_{i'x}^{A\bar{Z}}$. (This can be easily checked by rewriting these parameters into elements such as π_{i+x}/π_{i++} and π_{i+x}/π_{++x}.)

Now that we have shown that it can also be useful to interpret LCA by means of the rescaled parameters $\pi_{ix}^{A\bar{Z}}$ and $\pi_{jx}^{B\bar{Z}}$, we will now discuss graphic representations that can be made from them (for details, see van der Ark and van der Heijden 1998). If $X = 2$, then the I categories can be displayed on a line of a two-dimensional space by using the new parameters $\pi_{i1}^{A\bar{Z}}$ (or, equivalently, $\pi_{i2}^{A\bar{Z}}$); if $X = 3$, they can be displayed in two-dimensional subspace of a three-dimensional space, in a so-called ternary diagram, and so on. (A similar interpretation holds for the parameters $\pi_{jx}^{B\bar{Z}}$.) In Sections 2.4 and 3.5 we will give examples of such graphs.

From the relation of the rescaled parameters $\pi_{ix}^{A\bar{Z}}$ and $\pi_{jx}^{B\bar{Z}}$ with the CA parameters, it will be clear that these graphic LCA-representations are very similar to the graphic CA-representation, since the parameters can be obtained from each other by linear transformations. In conclusion, if the fitted values of CA and LCA are equal, the graphical representation of CA for the row parameters can be perfectly matched with the graphical representation of LCA for the row parameters, and similarly for the column. We will illustrate this in the next section.

2.4. Example

As an example, we reanalyze the data collected by Srole et al. (1962) (see Table 1). The data are a cross-classification of 1660 adults in Manhattan, obtained from a sample of midtown residents aged 20–59, according to their parental socioeconomic status (SES), with categories 1 = high, ...,

TABLE 1
Midtown Manhattan Data

	1 = A	2 = B	3 = C	4 = D	5 = E	6 = F	Total
1 Well	64	57	57	72	36	21	307
2 Mild	94	94	105	141	97	71	602
3 Moderate	58	54	65	77	54	54	362
4 Impaired	46	40	60	94	78	71	389
Total	262	245	287	384	265	217	1660

6 = low, and mental health status with categories "well," "mild" (mild symptom formation), "moderate" (moderate symptom formation), "impaired." They have been studied previously with CA and LCA by Goodman (1987), among others, and many details can be found there. We have the following aims. First, we will illustrate that the fit of simple CA and LCA is identical. Second, we show that the interpretation of rescaled LCA parameters $\pi_{ix}^{A\bar{Z}}$ and $\pi_{jx}^{B\bar{Z}}$ gives a very similar insight into the latent class model as the interpretation of the original LCA parameters π_{ix}^{AZ} and π_{jx}^{BZ}. Third, we will illustrate the rescaled LCA parameter estimates by a graphic representation. And fourth, we will show the similarity of such a graph with a CA graph.

A first remark is that the results in Section 2.3 hold for probability matrices of an exact rank R. Here we have an observed data matrix, and we can apply the results of Section 2.3 by fitting models to the observed data matrix, so that the fitted values of these models form matrices that have an exact rank R. However, if we want to compare the results from analyses of simple CA and LCA, both models should be fit with the same fitting criterion in order to obtain identical fitted values. Therefore, we fit both models with maximum likelihood. When we fit simple CA with a single dimension (i.e., model [1] with rank $R = M = 2$) the likelihood ratio chi-square equals $G^2 = 2.73$, with 8 degrees of freedom. For rank $R = X = 2$, LCA is equivalent to CA, and LCA with two latent classes has an identical fit. The results in Section 2.3 show that, for rank $R = 2$, this is always the case.

In Table 2 we give the parameter estimates of simple CA and LCA. In column 1 we find the parameter estimates for simple CA. In columns 2 and 3 we find the parameter estimates for LCA. In column 4 and 5 the rescaled parameter estimates are given. Using the interpretation of the simple CA parameters from the perspective of canonical correlation analysis of categorical variables, the CA parameter estimates show optimal category quantifications that lead to a maximized correlation of .163. The quantifications show that this positive correlation is attained by giving positive quantifications for a better mental health and a better parental socioeconomic status, and negative quantifications for a worse mental health and a worse parental socioeconomic status.

Another useful way to interpret the parameter estimates becomes evident when we rewrite (1) as

$$\frac{\pi_{ij}}{\pi_{i+}\pi_{+j}} - 1 = \frac{\pi_{ij} - \pi_{i+}\pi_{+j}}{\pi_{i+}\pi_{+j}} = \left(\sum_{m=1}^{M-1} \lambda_m \rho_{im} \gamma_{jm} \right) . \qquad (11)$$

TABLE 2

Maximum-Likelihood Parameter Estimates for Srole Data. CA with One Dimension (Column 1), for LCA with 2 Latent Classes (Columns 2 and 3), and Rescaled Parameter Estimates for LCA (Columns 4 and 5)

	CA	LCA		LCA	
	$\hat{\rho}_{i1}$	$\hat{\pi}_{i1}^{\bar{A}Z}$	$\hat{\pi}_{i2}^{\bar{A}Z}$	$\hat{\pi}_{i1}^{A\bar{Z}}$	$\hat{\pi}_{i2}^{A\bar{Z}}$
Well	−1.60	.39	.00	1.00	.00
Mild	−.19	.41	.32	.54	.46
Moderate	.09	.21	.23	.45	.55
Impaired	1.48	.00	.45	.00	1.00
	$\hat{\gamma}_{j1}$	$\hat{\pi}_{j1}^{\bar{B}Z}$	$\hat{\pi}_{j2}^{\bar{B}Z}$	$\hat{\pi}_{j1}^{B\bar{Z}}$	$\hat{\pi}_{j2}^{B\bar{Z}}$
A	−1.09	.20	.12	.62	.38
B	−1.17	.19	.11	.63	.37
C	−.37	.19	.16	.53	.47
D	.05	.23	.23	.47	.53
E	1.01	.12	.20	.35	.65
F	1.80	.07	.19	.25	.75
	$\hat{\lambda}_1$	$\hat{\pi}_1^Z$	$\hat{\pi}_2^Z$	$\hat{\pi}_1^Z$	$\hat{\pi}_2^Z$
	.163	.48	.52	.48	.52

For this example, where $M = 2$, (11) shows that the product of the parameters $\lambda_1 \rho_{i1} \gamma_{j1}$ decomposes the departure from independence (i.e., $\pi_{ij} - \pi_{i+} \pi_{+j}$ scaled by the expected probability under independence). From Table 2 we can then see from the signs of the parameter estimates that rows $i = 1,2$ are positively related to columns $j = 1,2,3$, and rows $i = 3,4$ are positively related to columns $j = 4,5,6$ (i.e., the departure from independence is positive), and for the other cells there are negative relations. For cell $(i,j) = (1,1)$, the scaled departure from independence is $1.60 \times 1.09 \times .163 = .28$.

Next to these two interpretations for CA parameters many others exist, but it is beyond the scope of this paper to discuss these here. Instead we refer to Greenacre (1984), Goodman (1987, 1991), Gifi (1990), and Gower and Hand (1996), and we go on with the interpretation of the LCA solution.

For LCA of a two-way matrix, the parameters are unidentified, and in column 2 and 3 of Table 2 we have chosen solution H5 from Table 6 in Goodman (1987). For more details on this identification problem, we refer to Gilula (1979, 1983, 1984) and Goodman (1987); van der Ark, van der Heijden and Sikkel (1999) discuss the identification for the equivalent LBA model (5), and van der Ark (1999) discusses the relation between

both identification problems, and the solutions proposed by Gilula, Goodman and van der Ark, van der Heijden and Sikkel. Column 2 of Table 2
shows that, given that someone is in latent class 1, his probabilities are
relatively high to have a better mental health (the probability to fall in
levels 1 and 2 add up to .80) and his probabilities are relatively high to have
a better parental socioeconomic status (the probability to fall in levels 1, 2,
and 3 add up to .58). In latent class 2 the probabilities are relatively high to
have a worse mental health (levels 3 and 4 add up to .68), and his probabilities are relatively high to have a worse parental socioeconomic status
(the probability to fall in levels 4, 5, and 6 add up to .62). This led Goodman (1987) to interpret the first latent class as the class for those individuals who are favorably endowed (.48 of the individuals are estimated to
fall in this class), and the second latent class as the class for those individuals who are unfavorably endowed (.52 of the individuals are estimated to
fall in this class).

We now interpret the rescaled LCA parameter estimates in columns
4 and 5 of Table 2. This is most simple by comparing the estimates of the
parameters $\pi_{ix}^{A\bar{Z}}$ and $\pi_{jx}^{B\bar{Z}}$ with the estimates of the latent class sizes π_x^Z (see
Section 2.3 for a theoretical justification). The estimate of latent class size
1 is .48 and that of latent class 2 is .52. Columns 4 and 5 show that, given
that one belongs to the "well" mental health status, the probability to fall in
class 1 is 1.00 and the probability to fall in class 2 is .00. This shows that
being in the category "well" is closely related to the first latent class because 1.00 is much larger than .48, so knowledge about this particular row
category increases the probability to fall in class 1 enormously. This relation is reversed for the "impaired" mental health status, showing that having impaired mental health is closely related to falling in the second latent
class. There is a weaker relation for the intermediate categories showing
that individuals having mental health status 2 fall in class 1 a bit more than
average (the average being the estimate for class size, .48), and individuals
having mental health status 3 fall in class 2 a bit more than average (the
average being the estimate .52). For parental socioeconomic status we find
a rather strong relation between levels 1 and 2 and the first latent class
(estimates .61 and .61 being much higher than the average .48) and a strong
relation of levels 5 and 6 with latent class 2 (estimates .64 and .75 compared with .52). This shows, first, that an interpretation of the rescaled
LCA parameter estimates also leads to an interpretation of the latent classes
in terms of (un)favorable endowment, and second, that the rescaled parameter estimates in columns 4 and 5 are related to the latent classes in the
same way as the original parameter estimates in columns 2 and 3.

What remains is to show the similarity of a graph of the CA parameter estimates with a graph of the rescaled LCA parameter estimates in columns 4 and 5. We can compare the graph of the CA row parameters with the graph of the LCA row parameters, and we can compare the graph of the CA column parameters with the graph of the LCA column parameters. For simple CA, there are various ways to make these graphs (for example, see Goodman 1987, 1991), and we choose to make a graph using $\hat{\rho}_{i1}$ as coordinates for the rows and of $\hat{\gamma}_{j1}$ as coordinates for the columns. We will use the parameter estimates in column 5 as coordinates for the LCA graph (see Figure 1)—i.e., we make a graph for the second latent class. It will be clear from the graphs that the relative distances between points on a CA line are equal to the relative distances between points on an LCA line. This is due to (9) and (10)—i.e., if we compare, for example, the distance between rows 1 and 2 with the distance between rows 3 and 4, both for CA as well as for LCA, the ratio of their differences is $(1.60 - .19)/(-.09 - -1.48) = (1.00 - .54)/(.46 - .00)$. In both types of graphs there is a point of reference, which is 0.0 in the CA graphs and $\hat{\pi}_2^X = .52$ in the LCA graphs. In CA this point represents the point for the estimates of marginal probabilities— for example, in the CA row graph it represents the vector of the estimated

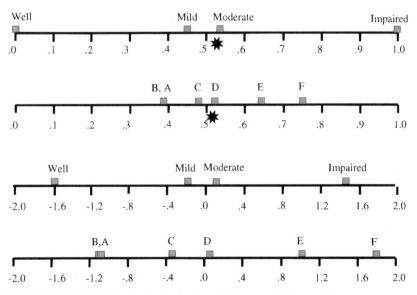

FIGURE 1. Graphic display for Srole data (1) the rescaled latent class parameter estimates with two latent classes (column 5 of Table 2) in line 1 and 2, and (2) the CA estimates (column 1 of Table 2) in line 3 and 4.

column probabilities $\hat{\pi}_{+j}$ (this is the weighted mean of all row vectors with fitted values). By comparing the CA row graph with the CA column graph, this point of reference is helpful because it shows that, for example, mental health status 4 goes together more often than average (i.e., the marginal probabilities) with levels 4, 5, and 6 of parental socioeconomic status. Similarly, in the LCA graphs the point with coordinate .52 is helpful because it shows that mental health status 4 is positively related with latent class 2, and similarly for parental socioeconomic status 4, 5, and 6. A difference between the CA and the LCA graphs is that the LCA graphs have interpretable endpoints—namely, 0.0 and 1.0. These are absent in CA. But on the whole the similarities between the graphs of CA and LCA are large.

Concluding, we have seen an illustration that simple CA and LCA are closely related. This does not mean that it does not matter which model is chosen when analyzing a contingency table. A proper choice depends on the question asked about the data. If the question is formulated in terms of a categorical latent variable explaining the interaction of the two manifest variables, LCA is the model of choice. For CA, there is more than one interpretation, but if, for example, the question is framed in terms of a maximized correlation between the categorical row and column variable, then simple CA should be the model of choice. However, it is clear that both models focus on the same aspects in the data (namely, a factorization of the relation between the variables) and therefore that the interpretations of both models are far from unrelated.

3. THE MULTIVARIATE CASE

In Section 2 we discussed the relation between CA and LCA for two-way tables. We will now discuss this relation when the number of variables is greater than two. Usually CA is then generalized into either multiple correspondence analysis (MCA) or joint correspondence analysis (JCA), and LCA is extended by including one extra set of parameters for each extra variable.

To keep the exposition simple, we will discuss the relation between the models for the situation of three variables. The relation for more than three variables is identical to the relation for three variables. We switch from probabilities π_{ij} to π_{ijk}, where k ($k = 1, \ldots, K$) indexes the level of the third variable, C.

3.1. *Multiple Correspondence Analysis*

MCA can be introduced in many ways (for example, see Tenenhaus and Young 1985; Gifi 1990). For the purpose of this paper, where we want to compare MCA and JCA with LCA, it is easiest if we introduce MCA using the so-called Burt matrix.

The Burt matrix is a matrix of order $(I + J + K) \times (I + J + K)$ and is a concatenation of matrices consisting of the bivariate margins π_{ij+}, π_{i+k} and π_{+jk}, and diagonal matrices consisting of the univariate margins of π_{ijk} (see Figure 2). The generalization of the Burt matrix to more than three variables, and its decomposition, is straightforward: for each additional variable, the relevant bivariate and diagonal univariate matrices are concatenated to the Burt matrix in Figure 2.

It is a well-known result from the CA literature that MCA is equivalent to simple CA applied to the Burt matrix. Simple CA of the Burt matrix leads to the simultaneous decomposition of each of the sub matrices of the Burt matrix. Thus the three bivariate margins in the Burt matrix are decomposed as follows:

$$\pi_{ij+} = \pi_{i++}\pi_{+j+}\left(1 + \sum_{m=1}^{M-1} \phi_m \eta_{im} \upsilon_{jm}\right), \tag{12}$$

$$\pi_{i+k} = \pi_{i++}\pi_{++k}\left(1 + \sum_{m=1}^{M-1} \phi_m \eta_{im} \omega_{km}\right), \tag{13}$$

π_{1++}	0	$\cdots$	0	π_{11+}	$\cdots$	π_{1j+}	$\cdots$	π_{1J+}	π_{1+1}	$\cdots$	π_{1+k}	$\cdots$	π_{1+K}
0			:	:		:		:	:		:		:
0		π_{i++}	0	π_{i1+}	$\cdots$	π_{ij+}	$\cdots$	π_{iJ+}	π_{i+1}	$\cdots$	π_{i+k}	$\cdots$	π_{i+K}
:			:	:		:		:	:		:		:
0	$\cdots$	0	π_{I++}	π_{I1+}	$\cdots$	π_{Ij+}	$\cdots$	π_{IJ+}	π_{I+1}	$\cdots$	π_{I+k}	$\cdots$	π_{I+K}
π_{11+}	$\cdots$	π_{i1+}	$\cdots$	π_{I1+}	π_{+1+}	0	$\cdots$	0	π_{+11}	$\cdots$	π_{+1k}	$\cdots$	π_{+1K}
:		:		:	:			:	:		:		:
π_{1j+}	$\cdots$	π_{ij+}	$\cdots$	π_{Ij+}	0		π_{+j+}		0	π_{+j1}	$\cdots$	π_{+jk}	$\cdots$	π_{+jK}
:		:		:	:			:	:		:		:
π_{1J+}	$\cdots$	π_{iJ+}	$\cdots$	π_{IJ+}	0	$\cdots$	0	π_{+J+}	π_{+J1}	$\cdots$	π_{+Jk}	$\cdots$	π_{+JK}
π_{1+1}	$\cdots$	π_{i+1}	$\cdots$	π_{I+1}	π_{+11}	$\cdots$	π_{+j1}	$\cdots$	π_{+J1}	π_{++1}	0	$\cdots$	0
:		:		:	:		:		:	:			:
π_{1+k}	$\cdots$	π_{i+k}	$\cdots$	π_{I+k}	π_{+1k}	$\cdots$	π_{+jk}	$\cdots$	π_{+Jk}	0		π_{++k}		0
:		:		:	:		:		:	:			:
π_{1+K}	$\cdots$	π_{i+K}	$\cdots$	π_{I+K}	π_{+1K}	$\cdots$	π_{+jK}	$\cdots$	π_{+JK}	0	$\cdots$	0	π_{++K}

FIGURE 2. Burt matrix.

and

$$\pi_{+jk} = \pi_{+j+}\,\pi_{++k}\left(1 + \sum_{m=1}^{M-1} \phi_m v_{jm}\omega_{km}\right) \tag{14}$$

where

$$\lambda_m > 0 \;,$$

$$\sum_i \pi_{++i}\eta_{im} = \sum_j \pi_{+j+}v_{jm} = \sum_k \pi_{++k}\omega_{km} = 0 \;,$$

$$\sum_i \pi_{++i}\eta_{im}\eta_{im'} + \sum_j \pi_{+j+}v_{jm}v_{jm'} + \sum_k \pi_{++k}\omega_{km}\omega_{km'} = \delta^{mm'} \;. \tag{15}$$

The simultaneity of the three decompositions reveals itself by the fact that the parameters ϕ_m are found in both (12) and (13) as well as in (14), that the parameters η_{im} in (12) are also found in (13), that the parameters v_{jm} in (12) are also found in (14), and, lastly, that the parameters ω_{km} in (13) are also found in (14). Because of the way the Burt matrix is built up, its maximal rank is $1 + (I-1) + (J-1) + (K-1)$. The above three decompositions show that, when M is chosen such that attention is restricted to the first few sets (indexed by m) of parameters of the solution, the three observed bivariate margins are simultaneously approximated by matrices of rank M. MCA is computed using a singular value decomposition, and due to the properties of the singular value decomposition, the rank M approximation of the complete Burt matrix is optimal in a least squares sense.

One way to motivate MCA is as a generalization of principal component analysis (PCA) to nominal variables. This is similar to the interpretation of simple CA as a generalization of correlation analysis to nominal variables: There the parameters ρ_{i1} and γ_{j1} could be interpreted as quantifications of the categories that yield a maximal correlation between the quantified row and column variable. In MCA the generalization of PCA is as follows: if the parameters η_{i1}, v_{j1}, and ω_{k1} are used as quantifications of the categories, then a 3×3 correlation matrix can be derived that has the property that the first eigenvalue is maximized (this property of MCA also holds for larger numbers of variables). We refer to van de Geer (1993) for a discussion of the second and higher dimensional interpretation of MCA seen from the perspective of PCA of nominal variables.

The final observation to be made about this perspective is that it explains why interest goes out to bivariate margins, which may come as a surprise to those researchers who are less familiar with MCA but more familiar with modeling approaches that model the multivariate frequencies. A justification for modeling bivariate margins is that, if correlations are an appropriate way to model the interaction between variables, only the second order moments in the data are needed. Using this interpretation of MCA the model is often used for the analysis of a large number of variables, often having a large number of categories. Sparseness of data then plays a relatively minor role irrespective of the number of variables, because the cells of the bivariate margins are usually reasonably filled.

Multidimensional graphic representations play an important role in the interpretation of MCA. The categories of the distinct variables can be represented in a space of dimension $M - 1$ with coordinates $(\eta_{im} \phi_m^{1/2})$ for the categories of variable A, $(v_{jm} \phi_m^{1/2})$ for the categories of variable B, and $(\omega_{k1} \phi_m^{1/2})$ for the categories of variable C. Thus, if we consider category i of variable A and category j of variable B, for example, their inner product in $M - 1$-dimensional space is equal to $(\pi_{ij+} - \pi_{i++} \pi_{+j+})/\pi_{i++} \pi_{+j+}$ (compare [12]). If $(\pi_{ij+} - \pi_{i++} \pi_{+j+})/\pi_{i++} \pi_{+j+} > 0$, then these two categories will have an angle with the origin less than 90 degrees. Thus we can see from the multidimensional representation that π_{ij+} is greater than $\pi_{i++} \pi_{+j+}$—in other words, that i and j are positively related; given a certain angle, the further i and j are away from the origin, the greater this departure will be. If the angle is greater than 90 degrees, $(\pi_{ij+} - \pi_{i++} \pi_{+j+})/\pi_{i++} \pi_{+j+} < 0$, so i and j are negatively related. And if they form a right angle, $\pi_{ij+} = \pi_{i++} \pi_{+j+}$, so i and j are unrelated. So inner products between categories of different variables give a clear and interpretable relation between the graph and the data. Now consider two categories of the same variable, say category i and i' of variable A. In the Burt matrix the element where i and i' cross equals zero. The result is that, in full-dimensional space, the inner product should equal $(0 - \pi_{i++} \pi_{i'++})/\pi_{i++} \pi_{i'++} = -1$, so category i and i' have an angle that is greater than 90 degrees. Here the inner products between the categories of the same variable give a clear relation between the graph and the data, but it does not show an aspect of the data we are interested in.

We conclude that, in going from simple CA to MCA, distinct interpretations of simple CA can be generalized to the MCA setting. We have seen that this is successful for the principal component analysis interpretation, and there are more interpretations that can be applied successfully that we have not discussed here (for example, see Tenenhaus and Young [1985] for an interpretation of MCA as generalized canonical correlation analysis, and Gifi [1990] for an interpretation of MCA as homogeneity analysis). The inner product interpretation is less useful: This last interpretation showed that the inertias in each of the subtables of the Burt matrix are decomposed (compare Section 2.1). For the subtables with bivariate margins, this is a useful property of MCA, since it shows how the bivariate margins depart from marginal independence. For the diagonal matrices with univariate margins, this interpretation is not very insightful, because we are not interested in these particular inner products, and yet they can have a large impact on the full-dimensional solution. This does not imply that this effect will always be clearly visible on the first few dimensions, to which attention is usually restricted in MCA, but it is clear that the inner products for the univariate margins play a role, and for this purpose an alternative is proposed for MCA, which is called JCA. This alternative will be discussed in Section 3.2.

Before we discuss JCA, we pay some attention to individual response patterns. An individual response pattern consists of one category of every variable, and for each dimension m each response pattern is quantified separately by averaging the quantifications of the categories it has. So, if a particular response pattern consists of categories i of variable A, j of variable B, and k of variable C, the quantification for dimension m is

$$x_{(ijk)m} = (\eta_{im} + v_{jm} + \omega_{km})/3\sigma_m \ , \tag{16}$$

where σ_m is chosen such that the weighted variance of $\sum_{m=1} \pi_{ijk} x_{(ijk)m}^2 = 1$. Due to restrictions (15) $\sum_{m=1} \pi_{ijk} x_{(ijk)m} = 0$.

3.2. Joint Correspondence Analysis

We have just seen that the interpretation of MCA from the perspective of decomposition of inertia is only partly successful. This is used as a starting point for the proposal of a different generalization of simple CA to the multivariate case. This generalization is called joint correspondence analysis (JCA; Greenacre 1988).

In JCA the rank of the approximation has to be fixed at a prespecified $m^* = M$. Then a rank-m^* approximation is obtained that is optimal in a generalized least squares sense for the bivariate margins in the Burt matrix only. So, just as in MCA this results in the simultaneous decompositions (12), (13), and (14). However, where in MCA the rank-m^* approximation is also optimal for the diagonal matrices with univariate margins, in JCA the rank-m^* approximation is optimal only for the bivariate margins. In other words, where MCA decomposes the total inertia of the complete Burt matrix, JCA concentrates on the total inertia of each of the off-diagonal submatrices only.

Greenacre (1988) and Boik (1996) point out and discuss an analogy between MCA and principal component analysis of a correlation matrix, where both the diagonal and the off-diagonal elements are approximated by a matrix of lower rank, and an analogy between JCA and factor analysis, where the approximation holds only for the off-diagonal elements of the correlation matrix. More details and examples can be found in a series of papers by Greenacre—for example, Greenacre (1988, 1990, 1991, 1994)—in Gower and Hand (1996), and in Boik (1996).

These papers also explain how JCA can be estimated by performing MCA iteratively by updating the diagonal submatrices after each iteration. Let the prefixed rank be m^*. Let $d_{ii'}^{(q)}$ be the updated element using the parameter estimates found in iteration $q - 1$ for categories i and i'. In the first step, when $q = 1$, $d_{ii'}^{(1)} = 0$. After the first step, when MCA is performed for the first time, $d_{ii'}^{(2)}$ is obtained as $d_{ii'}^{(2)} = \pi_{i++} \pi_{i'++} (1 + \sum_{m=1}^{m^*-1} \phi_m^{(1)} \eta_{im}^{(1)} \eta_{i'm}^{(1)})$, where the superscripts (1) indicate that these estimates are found by doing a generalized singular value decomposition on the Burt matrix with modified marginal elements in step 1. In general,

$$d_{ii'}^{(q+1)} = \pi_{i++} \pi_{i'++} \left(1 + \sum_{m=1}^{m^*-1} \phi_m^{(q)} \eta_{im}^{(q)} \eta_{i'm}^{(q)} \right) , \qquad (17)$$

and this procedure is iterated until convergence. Boik (1996) has recently proposed a more efficient algorithm for JCA.

In JCA graphic displays are made in the same way as in MCA. So in a rank-m^* JCA, a $m^* - 1$-dimensional graphic display can be made using coordinates $(\eta_{im} \phi_m^{1/2})$ for the categories of variable A, $(v_{jm} \phi_m^{1/2})$ for the categories of variable B, and $(\omega_{k1} \phi_m^{1/2})$ for the categories of variable C. This $m^* - 1$-dimensional display can be interpreted using inner products for the bivariate margins of the Burt matrix, where it should be noted that the inner products are not equal to the bivariate marginal probabilities, but approximate them, unless $m^* = (I - 1) + (J - 1) + (K - 1)$. The quality of the approximation can be expressed in terms of percentage of inertia displayed by the $m^* - 1$-dimensional solution. In general, compared to MCA of the Burt matrix, the percentage of inertia displayed is dramatically higher in JCA because the diagonal submatrices of the Burt matrix are not approximated. For more details, we refer to Gower and Hand (1996: chs. 4 and 10).

We conclude by mentioning that in JCA quantifications of individual response patterns are obtained in the same way as in MCA.

3.3. *The Multivariate Latent Class Model*

Moving from the bivariate case to the multivariate case, the latent class
model is extended in a straightforward way by including an extra set of
parameters for each additional variable. For the trivariate case, LCA is
written as

$$\pi_{ijk} = \sum_{x=1}^{X} \pi_x^Z \pi_{ix}^{\bar{A}Z} \pi_{jx}^{\bar{B}Z} \pi_{kx}^{\bar{C}Z} \tag{18}$$

with restrictions

$$\sum_{x=1}^{X} \pi_x^Z = 1, \sum_{i=1}^{I} \pi_{ix}^{\bar{A}Z} = 1, \sum_{j=1}^{J} \pi_{jx}^{\bar{B}Z} = 1, \sum_{k=1}^{K} \pi_{kx}^{\bar{C}Z} = 1 \ .$$

Just as we did for the two-variable case discussed in Sections 2.3
and 2.4, we propose to rescale the parameters $\pi_{ix}^{\bar{A}Z}$, $\pi_{jx}^{\bar{B}Z}$, and $\pi_{kx}^{\bar{C}Z}$ into
parameters $\pi_{ix}^{A\bar{Z}}$, $\pi_{jx}^{B\bar{Z}}$, and $\pi_{kx}^{C\bar{Z}}$. For the parameter $\pi_{ix}^{A\bar{Z}}$, the way to obtain
such a rescaled parameter $\pi_{ix}^{A\bar{Z}}$ is shown in (6). We showed there that the
rescaled parameters give us an alternative insight into the latent class model,
and we showed that these rescaled parameters could be used to make graphic
representations. We refer to Section 2.3 for a detailed discussion of these
issues. In Section 2.4 we illustrated that these rescaled parameters led to
basically the same interpretation of the latent class model as the original
parameters.

In multivariate LCA it is possible to obtain probabilities that a particular individual response pattern (i, j, k) is falling in latent class x by

$$\pi_{ijkx}^{ABC\bar{Z}} = \pi_x^Z \pi_{ix}^{\bar{A}Z} \pi_{jx}^{\bar{B}Z} \pi_{kx}^{\bar{C}Z} / \pi_{ijk} \tag{19}$$

using (18). These probabilities can be used to classify individual response
patterns as belonging to latent classes. They can also be used to make a
graphic display, following the principles discussed in Section 2.3.

3.4. *Relations*

The relation between LCA and MCA and JCA becomes simple when we
add up π_{ijk} in (18) over k, j, and i respectively. We then get the three
equations

$$\pi_{ij+} = \sum_{x=1}^{X} \pi_x^Z \pi_{ix}^{\bar{A}Z} \pi_{jx}^{\bar{B}Z} , \tag{20}$$

$$\pi_{i+k} = \sum_{x=1}^{X} \pi_x^Z \pi_{ix}^{\bar{A}Z} \pi_{kx}^{\bar{C}Z} , \tag{21}$$

and

$$\pi_{+jk} = \sum_{x=1}^{X} \pi_x^Z \pi_{jx}^{\bar{B}Z} \pi_{kx}^{\bar{C}Z} . \tag{22}$$

What this shows is that LCA implies that the three two-way matrices with bivariate margins have reduced rank X, and that equations (20) to (22) have parameters in common, showing that they should be considered simultaneously.

This is the key to our comparison of MCA and JCA with LCA. If we compare equation (12) with (20), (13) with (21), and (14) with (22), we can interpret the relation in a way similar to what we did for simple CA and LCA of two-way matrices in Section 2. For example, if we compare equation (12) with (20), we can conclude from the results of Section 2 that if the decomposition (20) is true (the bivariate margin has rank X), then the decomposition (12) with $X = M$ is true. It follows that if LCA with X latent classes is true, then the decompositions of the margins defined in (20), (21), and (22) with X latent classes are simultaneously true, and then the decompositions (12), (13), and (14) with $M = X$ are also simultaneously true.

In Section 3.1 we saw that an important distinction between MCA and JCA was that MCA is defined in terms of both the decompositions of the bivariate margins as defined in (12), (13), and (14), as well as the decomposition of the diagonal matrices with univariate margins. On the other hand, JCA is defined solely in terms of the decomposition of the bivariate margins (12), (13), and (14). An important result of this paper now follows directly: LCA with X latent classes implies JCA with $m^* = X$.

For two-way matrices, we saw in Section 2 that there was also a reverse relation for rank 2. However, it is evident that the reverse relation does not hold, because a set of lower rank two-way margins (JCA) does not have clear implications for a higher-way table (LCA).

The precise relation between LCA and JCA does not hold for LCA and MCA due to the fact that the decomposition of MCA is also defined in terms of the univariate margins.

For the bivariate case we saw in Section 2.3 that, if LCA is true, the LCA parameters can be transformed into CA parameters and the other way around. This result also holds for the multivariate case, as we will see here. To show this, consider equations (20), (21), and (22). In Section 2.3 we have shown that the original parameters π_{ix}^{AZ}, π_{jx}^{BZ}, and π_{kx}^{CZ} can be re-scaled into parameters $\pi_{ix}^{A\bar{Z}}$, $\pi_{jx}^{B\bar{Z}}$, and $\pi_{kx}^{C\bar{Z}}$ using equation (6) for variable A and similar equations for variable B and C. These rescaled parameters can be used to rewrite equations (20), (21), and (22) into

$$\pi_{ij+} = \sum_{x=1}^{X} \pi_x^Z \pi_{ix}^{\bar{A}Z} \pi_{jx}^{\bar{B}Z} = \pi_{i++} \pi_{+j+} \sum_{x=1}^{X} \pi_{ix}^{A\bar{Z}} \pi_{jx}^{B\bar{Z}} (\pi_x^Z)^{-1} \, , \qquad (23)$$

$$\pi_{i+k} = \sum_{x=1}^{X} \pi_x^Z \pi_{ix}^{\bar{A}Z} \pi_{kx}^{\bar{C}Z} = \pi_{i++} \pi_{++k} \sum_{x=1}^{X} \pi_{ix}^{A\bar{Z}} \pi_{kx}^{C\bar{Z}} (\pi_x^Z)^{-1} \, , \qquad (24)$$

and

$$\pi_{+jk} = \sum_{x=1}^{X} \pi_x^Z \pi_{jx}^{\bar{B}Z} \pi_{kx}^{\bar{C}Z} = \pi_{+j+} \pi_{++k} \sum_{x=1}^{X} \pi_{jx}^{B\bar{Z}} \pi_{kx}^{C\bar{Z}} (\pi_x^Z)^{-1} \, , \qquad (25)$$

(compare [7]). Assume now that the LCA model with X latent classes is true. Then, if we compare Equation (23) to (12), (24) to (13), and (25) to (14), we find the following relation between the rescaled LCA parameters and the CA parameters:

$$\left(1 + \sum_{m=1}^{R-1} \phi_m \eta_{im} \upsilon_{jm} \right) = \sum_{x=1}^{R} \pi_{ix}^{A\bar{Z}} \pi_{jx}^{B\bar{Z}} (\pi_x^Z)^{-1} \, , \qquad (26)$$

$$\left(1 + \sum_{m=1}^{R-1} \phi_m \eta_{im} \omega_{km} \right) = \sum_{x=1}^{R} \pi_{ix}^{A\bar{Z}} \pi_{kx}^{C\bar{Z}} (\pi_x^Z)^{-1} \, , \qquad (27)$$

and

$$\left(1 + \sum_{m=1}^{R-1} \phi_m \upsilon_{jm} \omega_{km} \right) = \sum_{x=1}^{R} \pi_{jx}^{B\bar{Z}} \pi_{kx}^{C\bar{Z}} (\pi_x^Z)^{-1} \, . \qquad (28)$$

(compare [8]). As in Section 2.3, collect the LCA-parameters $\pi_{ix}^{A\bar{Z}}$ in a $I \times R$ matrix $\mathbf{\Pi}_i$, $\pi_{jx}^{B\bar{Z}}$ in a $J \times R$ matrix $\mathbf{\Pi}_j$, and $\pi_{kx}^{C\bar{Z}}$ in a $K \times R$ matrix $\mathbf{\Pi}_k$; and collect the CA-parameters η_{im} in a $I \times R$ matrix $\mathbf{H}$, υ_{jm} in a $J \times R$ matrix $\mathbf{Y}$, and ω_{km} in a $K \times R$ matrix $\mathbf{\Omega}$, where the first columns of $\mathbf{H}$, $\mathbf{Y}$, and $\mathbf{\Omega}$ are unit vectors. Then equation (26) shows that $\mathbf{H} = \mathbf{\Pi}_i \mathbf{U}$, (27) shows that $\mathbf{Y} = \mathbf{\Pi}_j \mathbf{U}$, and (28) shows that $\mathbf{\Omega} = \mathbf{\Pi}_k \mathbf{U}$, where $\mathbf{U}$ is a $R \times R$ transformation matrix. This shows that, if the LCA model is true, linear combinations of the rescaled LCA parameters lead to JCA parameters.

The relations just shown are interesting, because they give more insight into JCA for those who are accustomed to LCA, and vice versa. This is particularly interesting because the two tools for data analysis stem from distinct schools: LCA stems from the more traditional school of statistical modeling, where concepts like maximum likelihood and model fit are important; JCA stems from a school of exploratory data analysis, where models are fitted by least squares and interpreting graphical displays are central. This is of theoretical interest. This close relation does not lead to a preference of one model over the other, as we already argued at the end of Section 2.4. Both LCA as well as JCA give answers to different questions, and depending on the question that is asked about the data, a researcher could choose one of those models. The interesting point is that JCA focuses on the bivariate margins, and that the decompositions used in JCA are closely related to bivariate decompositions that are fitted as byproducts of the fitting of multivariate frequencies.

The relations also lead to the following practical implication, that will be illustrated in the next section. First, in the analysis of a set of data it is possible to do an LCA with R latent classes, and then this analysis can be illustrated by a JCA-graph of dimensionality $R - 1$. This JCA graph should then be obtained from a JCA on the fitted values found in LCA. The JCA-graph can then be supplemented with points for the R latent classes as well as with the point for the class sizes. The interpretation of the JCA graph can be both in terms of inner products, which is the interpretation discussed in Section 3.2, as well as in terms of the rescaled LCA-parameters. An example will be shown in the next section.

A last point to be discussed is how the representations of the response patterns are related. These representations are not as closely related as the parameters of LCA and JCA. The reason can be seen by comparing (16) with (19). This shows that in JCA the response patterns are quantified by a linear operation on the category parameters, whereas in LCA the response patterns are quantified by a multiplicative operation on the category parameters (rescaling the category parameters does not change this). Interestingly, a linear operation on the rescaled LCA-parameters would make them very similar to the quantification found for JCA in (16). For latent class m and response pattern (i, j, k) this linear operation would be

$(\pi_{ix}^{A\bar{Z}} + \pi_{jx}^{B\bar{Z}} + \pi_{kx}^{C\bar{Z}})/3$, which could be interpreted as an average conditional probability. It is not clear to us yet how useful this measure is over the usual measure (19) and we leave this as a topic for further study.

3.5. *Examples*

We will now illustrate our results by two examples. The data in the first example, shown in Table 3, were analyzed earlier with LCA by McCutcheon (1987).

There are four items on political campaign participation from the 1980 National Election Study: whether a respondent (1) voted in the election, (2) tried to influence people, (3) attended any political meetings, and (4) worked for one of the parties or candidates. For more details, see McCutcheon (1987). McCutcheon tried out a series of models for scale construction. Here we perform only an ordinary LCA. We will fit a latent class model with $X = 2$ latent classes, and first interpret the original LCA parameters. Then we will show that the rescaled LCA parameters lead to the same interpretation of the latent class model. Subsequently the rescaled LCA parameters are displayed in a one-dimensional graph. A JCA is performed on the fitted values found under LCA, and we show that this leads to a JCA graph that is very similar to the LCA graph. This JCA of fitted values is compared with a JCA and an MCA of the data.

The latent class model does not fit adequately because $G^2 = 41.6$ (df is 7). We have intentionally chosen this nonfitting example because it makes the comparison between the JCA performed on the fitted values

TABLE 3
McCutcheon Data, Four Dichotomous Items

			Vote	
Work	Attend	Influence	Yes	No
Yes	Yes	Yes	27	0
		No	2	0
	No	Yes	16	0
		No	4	1
No	Yes	Yes	40	3
		No	32	2
	No	Yes	339	83
		No	543	310

under LCA with the JCA on the data interesting: if the model would have fit the data, then the fitted values would be approximately equal to the data, and those two JCAs would necessarily lead to approximately the same solutions. Now we can see to what extend these JCAs differ.

The original parameter estimates for a solution with $X = 2$ latent classes are in columns 1 and 2 of Table 4. In the first latent class ($x = 1$), the probabilities to work, attend, influence, and vote are much lower than in latent class 2 (.002, .022, .297, and .675 respectively, as compared with .274, .452, .822, and 1.000), so that we interpret the first latent class as the class of nonactive people and the second class as the class of active people. These conditional probabilities also show that, in both classes, the probabilities to work, attend, influence, and vote are increasing in the same order.

We will now show that the rescaled parameter estimates will lead to the same interpretation of the latent classes. In column 3 (and 4) we find the estimated probabilities to fall in latent class 1 (and 2), given the response to a specific category. Given that someone works for a candidate, the estimated probability to fall in latent class 1 is .039 (and for latent class 2 it is .961), and given that one does not work for a candidate, the probability to fall in latent class 1 is .906 (and for latent class 2 it is .094). In Section 2.3 it has been shown that these estimates are to be compared with the class size estimates of .875 and .125. This shows that the parameter estimate for "yes" on working is very high indeed in class 2 (.961 respondents who have answered "yes" compared with .125 overall). Comparable interpretations for the parameter estimates of the other variables lead to the

TABLE 4
Parameter Estimates for Latent Class Analysis with Two Latent Classes

		Original Parameters		Rescaled Parameters	
		$x = 1$	$x = 2$	$x = 1$	$x = 2$
Work	Yes	.002	.274	.039	.961
	No	.998	.726	.906	.094
Attend	Yes	.022	.452	.253	.747
	No	.978	.547	.926	.074
Influence	Yes	.297	.822	.717	.283
	No	.703	.178	.965	.035
Vote	Yes	.675	1.000	.825	.175
	No	.325	.000	1.000	.000
Class size		.875	.125	.875	.125

172

VAN DER HEIJDEN, GILULA, AND VAN DER ARK

interpretation of the first latent class as the class for nonactive people and the second class as the class of active people. Notice that the voting "yes" category is not very indicative of being in the active class, because the estimate of .175 is not much higher than the overall class size of .125. We conclude that the interpretation of the original LCA parameters leads to the same conclusion as the rescaled parameters. Notice that the rescaled parameter estimates are also ordered from work to vote, for the "yes" categories (in class 2 .961, .747, .283, and .175) as well as for the "no" categories (.094, .074, .035, and .000).

In the upper line of Figure 3, we find a graph of the rescaled LCA parameter estimates for class 2. On the left we find the "no" categories, having low probabilities, and more to the right we find the "yes" categories, having higher probabilities. The graph should be interpreted in terms of the coordinates of the points, which are the rescaled parameter estimates that we have just interpreted without having a graph. The usefulness of this graph should be that it helps in finding the same interpretation more quickly, or that it illustrates the interpretation found. It is possible to relate the parameter estimates in this graph to the bivariate margins of the fitted values, using equations like (23), but this is not easy because of the number

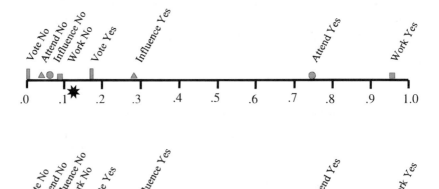

FIGURE 3. Graphic display for McCutcheon data in Table 3 (1) rescaled latent class parameter estimates with two latent classes (column 4 of Table 4) in line 1, and (2) the JCA estimates (column 1 of Table 6) in line 2.

TABLE 5
Burt Matrix Derived from Parameter Estimates of Latent Class Analysis
with Two Latent Classes

.03566	.00000	.01553	.02013	.02857	.00709	.03521	.00045
.00000	.96434	.06008	.90426	.33377	.63057	.68019	.28414
.01553	.06008	.07561	.00000	.05208	.02352	.06939	.00622
.02013	.90426	.00000	.92439	.31026	.61414	.64602	.27838
.02857	.33377	.05208	.31026	.36234	.00000	.27788	.08446
.00709	.63057	.02352	.61414	.00000	.63766	.43753	.20013
.03521	.68019	.06939	.64602	.27788	.43753	.71541	.00000
.00045	.28414	.00622	.27838	.08446	.20013	.00000	.28459

of operations involved. We come back to a further interpretation of this graph after we have discussed the JCA graph of the fitted values of LCA.

In Table 5 the Burt matrix derived from the fitted values under LCA is given. In Table 6, first column, we provide the estimates obtained by JCA of this table. Since the Burt matrix in Table 5 has rank 2, JCA with one dimension provides a perfect fit of the solution. The estimates are displayed in a graph shown in the lower line of Figure 3. We have multiplied the estimates in the first column with $\phi_1^{1/2}$ so that we can relate the inner products of the coordinates of the points using equa-

TABLE 6
Parameter Estimates for Joint CA of LCA Estimates (Column 1), for JCA of Observed
Data (Column 2), and MCA of Observed Data (Column 3)

		JCA of LCA	JCA of Data	MCA of Data
Work	Yes	5.989	6.381	5.824
	No	−.222	−.236	−.215
Attend	Yes	4.456	4.372	3.948
	No	−.365	−.358	−.323
Influence	Yes	1.134	1.017	1.237
	No	−.644	−.578	−.703
Vote	Yes	.356	.370	.489
	No	−.895	−.929	−1.229
	$\hat{\phi}$	.1783	.2213	.4034
	prop.	1.0000	.8796	.4034

tions like (12) (see Section 3.1 for details). For example, for this four-variable example the bivariate margin of the first two variables is π_{ij++}, and equations such as (12), (13), and (14) show that the coordinates of the points for the first two variables are related to the data (here: the fitted values of LCA) by $(\pi_{ij++} - \pi_{i+++}\pi_{+j++})/\pi_{i+++}\pi_{+j++} = (\eta_{i1}\phi_1^{1/2})(v_{j1}\phi_1^{1/2})$. For example, for the categories work-yes, attend-yes $(\eta_{i1}\phi_1^{1/2})(v_{j1}\phi_1^{1/2}) = .1783 \times (5.989 \times 4.456) = 4.752$, and this is equal to $(\pi_{ij++} - \pi_{i+++}\pi_{+j++})/\pi_{i+++}\pi_{+j++} = (.01553 - .03566 \times .07561)/.03566 \times .07561 = 4.752$. As discussed in Section 3.1, when the inner products are positive, then $\pi_{ij++} > \pi_{i+++}\pi_{+j++}$; when they are negative, then $\pi_{ij++} < \pi_{i+++}\pi_{+j++}$. It follows that points are positively related in the bivariate margins to points on the same side of the origin, and points are negatively related to points on the opposite side of the origin. This shows that in the bivariate margins, all the yes-categories are positively related, and all the no-categories are positively related, and every yes-category is negatively related to every no-category.

Due to the fact that the Burt matrix analyzed by JCA consisted of the fitted values from JCA, the relative distances between the categories in the JCA graph are identical to the relative distances between the categories in the LCA graph. But this also means that some properties derived from the inner product interpretation of the JCA graph also hold for the LCA graph. In particular, where we concluded for JCA that points on one side of the origin are positively related in the bivariate margins and points on opposite sides of the origin are negatively related in the bivariate margins, we can now conclude for the LCA graph that points on one side of the class size point (indicated with a star in Figure 3) are positively related in the bivariate margins and points on opposite sides of the class size points are negatively related. Thus the straightforward aspects of the interpretation of both graphs can supplement each other. The coordinates of the JCA plot are more easily related to the bivariate margins using an inner product interpretation; yet their precise values are more difficult to interpret. For the LCA graph, it is the other way around: here the precise values are easily interpreted, since they are conditional probabilities; yet these conditional probabilities are more difficult to relate to the bivariate margins of the fitted values.

We now discuss the JCA of the observed Burt matrix and compare it with the JCA of the Burt matrix with fitted LCA values. In the observed Burt matrix most relations between the yes-yes and the no-no combinations are a bit stronger than in the Burt matrix with fitted LCA values, in particular between the variables Influence and Vote, where the departure is

.023. The total inertia for the observed Burt matrix is higher (.2515, whereas it is .1783 for the Burt matrix with fitted values), of which .2213/.2515 = 87.96 percent displayed. The parameter estimates are given in column 2 of Table 6. Apart from the larger first eigenvalue (.2213 compared with .1783), that reflects the stronger association between the yes-yes and the no-no combinations, no interpretable differences can be found between the JCA of the fitted LCA values and the JCA of the data.

In column 3 of Table 6 we find the scores obtained with MCA of the Burt matrix from the observed data (eigenvalues are .4034, .2391, .2004, and .1570). The total inertia is much higher, due to the fact that the inertia of the diagonal submatrices is now also decomposed. Yet the estimates for the categories in the MCA solution are rather similar to the estimates of the two JCA solutions.

We conclude that the estimates of the three solutions are similar, and this is remarkable, because the fit of LCA was not very good; yet the maximum likelihood approximation provided by LCA to the bivariate margins is very similar to the least-squares approximation to the bivariate margins provided by JCA and MCA.

This similarity is not found in the second example, also taken from McCutcheon (1987). Table 7 shows the observed frequencies for four categorical variables from the 1982 General Social Survey. Two are white

TABLE 7
Cross-tabulation of Observed Variables for White Respondents
of 1982 General Social Survey

Purpose	Accuracy	Understanding	Interested	Cooperative	Impatient/ Hostile
Good	Mostly true	Good	419	35	2
		Fair, poor	71	25	5
	Not true	Good	270	25	4
		Fair, poor	42	16	5
Depends	Mostly true	Good	23	4	1
		Fair, poor	6	2	0
	Not true	Good	43	9	2
		Fair, poor	9	3	2
Waste	Mostly true	Good	26	3	0
		Fair, poor	1	2	0
	Not true	Good	85	23	6
		Fair, poor	13	12	8

respondents' evaluations of surveys and two are interviewers' evaluations of these respondents.

The first variable asks about the perceived purpose of surveys, the second about the accuracy of survey results, the third about the perceived cooperation of the respondent in the survey and the fourth about the perceived understanding (for more details, see McCutcheon 1987). LCA with $X = 3$ latent classes has an acceptable fit ($G^2 = 21.89$, df is 16). The parameter estimates are presented in the first three columns of Table 8.

McCutcheon (1987) interprets the first latent class as the class of "ideal respondents," because they often find the purpose of surveys "good" (estimated probability is .888), the results are "mostly true" (.613), they always have a "good" understanding (1.000), and their cooperation is almost always "interested" (.943); the third class has "skeptics," they often answer that surveys are a "waste" of time (.633), the results are often found "not true" (.969), but they are often found "interested" (.641) and have often a "good" understanding (.753). The second class is interpreted as the class for "believers": they often answer that the purpose is "good" (.910), and that the results are "mostly true" (.648), their cooperation is often "interested" (.688) but their understanding is "fair/poor" (.686).

In columns 4, 5, and 6 of Table 8, we find the rescaled parameter estimates. These lead to the same interpretation of the latent classes. To

TABLE 8

Parameter Estimates for Latent Class Analysis with Three Latent Classes. First Three Columns Give Original Parameter Estimates, and Columns 4 to 6 Give Rescaled Parameter Estimates Discussed in Section 2.2

		$x = 1$	$x = 2$	$x = 3$	$x = 1$	$x = 2$	$x = 3$
Purpose	Good	.888	.912	.143	.721	.247	.032
	Depends	.053	.072	.225	.382	.171	.447
	Waste	.059	.017	.633	.245	.023	.732
Accuracy	Mostly true	.613	.648	.031	.732	.258	.010
	Not true	.387	.352	.969	.500	.152	.348
Understanding	Good	1.000	.313	.753	.761	.079	.159
	Fair, poor	.000	.687	.247	.000	.770	.230
Cooperation	Interested	.943	.690	.641	.698	.170	.132
	Cooperative	.057	.255	.256	.267	.400	.333
	Impatient/ hostile	.000	.055	.103	.000	.391	.609
Class Size		.621	.207	.172	.621	.207	.172

find the correct interpretation, we have to compare these conditional probabilities with the class sizes (see Section 2.3). This shows that given that the purpose is judged as "good," respondents fall more than average in latent class 1 (estimated probability .721 compared with the average—i.e. class size estimate, .621), similarly for accuracy "mostly true" (.732), "good" understanding (.761), and "interested" cooperation (.698). This leads again to the labeling of the first latent class as "ideal respondents." For the second latent class, the following categories have higher estimated probabilities than the average—i.e., the class size estimate, .207: "good" purpose (.247), accuracy "mostly true" (.258), "fair, poor" understanding (.770), cooperation "cooperative" (.400), and "impatient/hostile" (.391). This leads again to the labeling of the second latent class as "believers." For the third latent class, the categories "depends" and "waste" of Purpose, "not true" of Accuracy, "fair, poor" of Understanding and "cooperative" and "impatient/hostile" are larger than the class size estimate; this leads again to the interpretation of class 3 as a class of "skeptics."

Figure 4 gives a graphic display of the rescaled parameter estimates in columns 4, 5, and 6 of Table 8. We could graph them as points in a three-dimensional space, but because these rescaled estimates add up to 1 for each category, they are all lying in a two-dimensional subspace of this three-dimensional space; and because the estimates are all nonnegative, they fall in a triangle. Such a triangle is called a ternary diagram. The top of the triangle is the point with coordinates (1,0,0), and this shows that it is the point for latent class 1 (i.e., there the mass is falling completely in class 1); the bottom-right point has coordinates (0,1,0) and it is the point for latent class 2; the bottom-left point has coordinates (0,0,1) and it is the point for latent class 3. As an example of a point in the triangle, we will discuss the coordinates of the point for the class sizes, which has coordinates (.621, .207 and .172) (see Table 8). We use the edge of the triangle going from bottom left (first coordinate is zero) to the top (first coordinate is one) as the coordinate axis for the first latent class. From point .621, a dotted line is found going from the first coordinate axis to the right. We use the edge going from the top to bottom-right as the coordinate axis for the second latent class. From point .207, a dotted line is going parallel to coordinate axis 1, and the edge going from the bottom-right to the bottom-left is the coordinate axis for the third latent class. At point .172, a dotted line is going parallel to the second coordinate axis. The three dotted lines meet in the point for class size.

We have already interpreted the rescaled parameter estimates, and Figure 4 is simply a graph of these estimates. We will now show how the

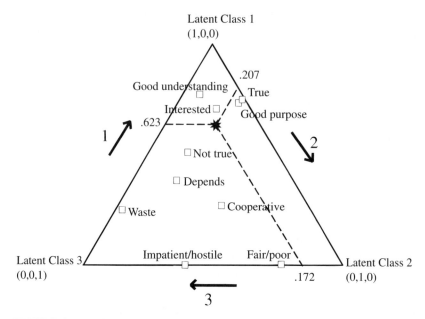

FIGURE 4. Graphic display of the rescaled estimates of the latent class model with three latent classes (columns 4, 5, and 6 of Table 8).

interpretation made of the rescaled parameter estimates can also be obtained from the graph. In our interpretation of the rescaled parameter estimates, the first latent class was characterized by relatively higher estimates for "good" purpose, "good" understanding, mostly "true" accuracy, and "interested" cooperation, and points for these categories are all in-between the point for the class sizes and the point for the first latent class (the top corner of the triangle). The second latent class was characterized by "good" purpose and "mostly true" (but their estimates of .247 and .258 are only marginally higher than the average .207), "fair, poor" understanding and "cooperative" cooperation; this is also revealed by Figure 4. The third latent class was characterized by "waste" and "depends," by purpose "not true," marginally by "fair/poor" and "cooperative," but particularly by "impatient/hostile." These characterizations are all rather clear from Figure 4, and this figure can give support in the interpretation and presentation of the results of the LCA.

In Table 9 we give the Burt matrix derived from the fitted values of LCA. Table 10 gives in the first two columns the estimates for JCA of

TABLE 9
Burt Matrix Derived from Parameter Estimates of Latent Class Analysis
with Three Latent Classes

.765	.000	.000	.461	.304	.629	.136	.666	.086	.013
.000	.087	.000	.031	.055	.067	.020	.066	.016	.005
.000	.000	.149	.028	.121	.120	.029	.107	.031	.011
.461	.031	.028	.520	.000	.427	.093	.455	.057	.008
.304	.055	.121	.000	.480	.389	.091	.384	.075	.017
.629	.067	.120	.427	.389	.815	.000	.713	.085	.017
.136	.020	.029	.093	.091	.000	.185	.125	.047	.012
.666	.066	.107	.455	.384	.713	.125	.839	.000	.000
.086	.016	.031	.057	.075	.085	.047	.000	.132	.000
.013	.005	.011	.008	.021	.017	.012	.000	.000	.029

Table 9 (eigenvalues are .1970 and .1329, and the other eigenvalues are equal to zero). Notice that 100 percent of the inertia is displayed in two dimensions, and this follows directly from the result that LCA of three latent classes implies JCA with two dimensions.

In Figure 5 we find the JCA graph of the fitted LCA values. As in the first example in this section, we have scaled the parameter estimates in such a way that we can interpret inner products between the categories. For example, the category "waste" has coordinates $(1.346, -.631)$ and the category "impatient/hostile" has coordinates $(1.346, .284)$ (these coordinates are found by multiplying parameter estimates for "waste" and "impatient/hostile" in the first two columns of Table 10 with the estimates $\hat{\phi}_m^{1/2}$). The inner product between these points is $(1.346 \times 1.346 + (-.631) \times .284) = 1.633$, and this is equal to $[.011 - (.149 \times .029)]/ (.149 \times .029)$ (see Table 9). This means that when we consider the "waste" and "impatient/hostile" in the bivariate margins for the variables "purpose" and "cooperation," the difference between the LCA-estimates and marginal independence (i.e., $[.011 - (.149 \times .029)]$) is 1.633 times as large as the estimate under marginal independence $(.149 \times .029)$, so there is a strong positive dependence between "waste" and "impatient/hostile."

By a linear transformation, the first and second dimension of the configuration of points in Figure 5 one could obtain precisely the configuration of points in the ternary diagram in Figure 4. Graphically, this linear transformation is equivalent to rotating and stretching the three axes of the triangle in Figure 4.

TABLE 10
Parameter Estimates for JCA of LCA Estimates (Columns 1 and 2), for JCA of Observed Data (Columns 3 and 4), and MCA of Observed Data (Columns 5 and 6)

		LCA		JCA		MCA	
		$m = 1$	$m = 2$	$m = 1$	$m = 2$	$m = 1$	$m = 2$
Purpose	Good	-.772	.393	-.066	-.863	-.613	.385
	Depends	1.600	-.495	.167	1.658	1.222	-.577
	Waste	3.032	-1.730	.240	3.468	2.437	-1.644
Accuracy	Mostly true	-.882	.486	-.069	-.983	-.996	.878
	Not true	.955	-.526	.075	1.065	1.079	-.951
Understanding	Good	-.339	-.817	-.935	.110	-.327	-.642
	Fair, poor	1.497	3.608	4.126	-.488	1.444	2.834
Cooperation	Interested	-.322	-.200	-.147	-.216	-.434	-.392
	Cooperative	1.372	1.099	.643	.843	1.769	2.103
	Impatient/hostile	3.033	.778	1.328	2.396	4.463	1.727
$\hat{\phi}_m$		.1970	.1329	.4231	.1920	.3709	.2858
Proportion		.5972	.4028	.6787	.3080	.2473	.1906

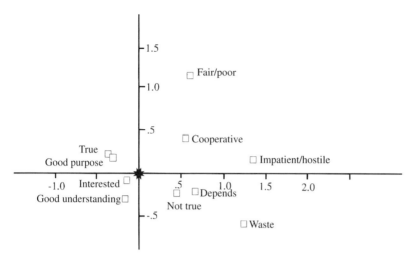

FIGURE 5. Graphic display of two principal axes of JCA (columns 1 and 2 of Table 10).

For the first example in this section, we concluded that the graphic LCA in Figure 4 and the graphic JCA representation in Figure 5 each have their strong points: the JCA graph is rather easily interpreted in terms of inner products, and the LCA graph is interpreted rather easily by its coordinates that are conditional probabilities. This conclusion also holds for the second example. In Figure 6 we combine the two advantages by adding to the JCA graph the three points for the latent classes. It should be noticed that through this joint representation the origin in the JCA solution coincides with the point for latent class size, so this point now has a double interpretation.

Examples such as Figure 6 can very well supplement an LCA. In Figure 6 the rescaled LCA parameter estimates are displayed graphically, and this can be helpful in the interpretation of the latent classes. The JCA interpretation relates inner products between the coordinates to bivariate margins of the fitted values. Thus JCA shows how LCA explains the dependence in the bivariate margins by assuming a latent variable.

We now compare the estimates for the JCA of the fitted values with the estimates of JCA and MCA of the observed data. (Eigenvalues are .4231, .1920, .0056, and .0026 for JCA, and the first two dimensions display 98.48 percent of the inertia; eigenvalues are .3709, .2858, .2505, .2486,

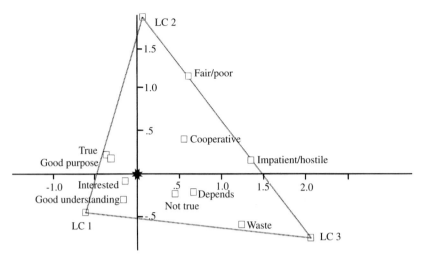

FIGURE 6. Graphic display combining aspects of Figure 4 (triangle) and Figure 5.

.1806, and .1636 for MCA, and the first two dimensions display 43.97 percent of the total inertia.) We can thus conclude that we have here an example that the adequate maximum likelihood approximation provided by LCA to the bivariate margins is similar to the least-squares approximation to the bivariate margins provided by MCA but rather different from the least-squares approximation provided by JCA. The reason is that the approximation provided for the diagonal matrix of the third variable has negative elements (cf. Boik 1996, who uses the parallel between JCA and factor analysis by calling this a Heywood case). This makes it possible for the JCA of the data to find much higher inertias than in the JCA of the fitted LCA values by using rather different parameter estimates.

4. CONCLUSIONS AND DISCUSSION

We have seen that LCA and JCA are closely related models, and their similarity makes it possible to use the same type of graphical representations of the parameters in both models. The relation just shown between LCA and JCA is remarkable, because both models have very different interpretations. First, LCA uses a latent variable, whereas JCA does not. Second, the latent variable in LCA is categorical and finds X classes of objects, whereas JCA finds $M = X - 1$ quantifications of each of the objects; in other words, in LCA the objects differ in a discrete way, whereas in JCA the objects differ in a quantitative way.

There are a few points that deserve further study, and we will discuss them shortly.

A first point deals with representations of individual response patterns. At the end of Section 3.4, we concluded that the representations used for LCA and JCA are not closely related, but we also proposed a different representation for LCA that was closely related to the representation of JCA. Further study should lead to an answer to the question of what the properties are of this different representation, and in what circumstances it is useful.

A second point for further study has to do with the comparison between the JCA of fitted values from LCA, the JCA of the observed data, and the MCA of the observed data. A central question to be asked is under what circumstances these three analyses are similar or dissimilar. For the first example, we found a remarkable resemblance between the estimates for the categories for all three analyses, although the fitted values from JCA differed significantly from the observed data. In the second example, the LCA model fitted well, and therefore we expected resemblance of the JCA of fitted values from LCA and the JCA of the observed data. However, due to negative elements in the JCA of the observed data the solutions differed considerably. Similarly, when can we expect JCA of the observed data and MCA of the observed data to be similar or dissimilar? This seems to be an open question.

And last, of natural interest is to extend JCA to a full multivariate model, so that it starts off from multivariate probabilities instead of from the bivariate marginal probabilities. This could possibly lead to an even greater similarity between JCA and LCA than we have found thus far. In particular a referee suggested the following trivariate JCA model, which indeed has a great appeal:

$$\pi_{ijk} = \pi_{i++}\pi_{+j+}\pi_{++k}\left(1 + \sum_{m=1} \phi_m \eta_{im} \upsilon_{jm} \eta_{km}\right) . \tag{29}$$

Such models however go beyond the scope of the current paper, which compares models for distributions that have canonical forms. As is well known, joint distributions of three or more variables do not have a canonical representation but bivariate distributions do. A canonical form is a saturated model for a joint distribution of a given dimension, and in our study represents a hierarchy of models starting from full independence (for the lowest possible dimension) on the one end, up to the saturated model for that given dimension on the other end. One very important aspect of a canonical form is that it decomposes the association into orthogonal components, and each component accounts for part of the association. In that respect each component must include an interpretable measure of association between the underlying variables. In bivariate forms we have ϕ_m as a correlation measure between the two variables. All CA models contain correlation measures. In model (29) the parameter does not have such an interpretation. Gilula (1986) deals with some of these aspects, where a variety of trivariate models based on two-dimensional association is proposed. Gilula and Haberman (1988) also use bivariate CA representations for multivariate prediction problems. Also it was illustrated by Gilula (1984) that comparing latent class models with CA models in terms of reparameterization is far more complex in the multivariate case than in the bivariate case. For all these reasons, we do not consider model (29) in this paper, but we intend to investigate in the near future models such as model (29) which could add more insight into the analysis of multivariate categorical variables.

REFERENCES

Benzécri, J.-P. et al. 1973. *L'Analyse des Données. L'Analyse de Correspondence.* Paris: Dunod.

Boik, R. J. 1996. "An Efficient Algorithm for Joint Correspondence Analysis." *Psychometrika* 61:255–69.

Clogg, C. C. 1981. "Latent Structure Models of Mobility." *American Journal of Sociology* 86:836–68.

de Leeuw, J., and P. G. M. van der Heijden. 1991. "Reduced Rank Models for Contingency Tables." *Biometrika* 78:229–32.

Fienberg, S. E. 1990. *The Analysis of Cross-classified Categorical Data.* Cambridge, MA: MIT Press.

Gifi, A. 1990. *Non-linear Multivariate Analysis.* New York: Academic Press.

Gilula, Z. 1979. "Singular Value Decomposition of Probability Matrices: Probabilistic Aspects of Latent Dichotomous Variables." *Biometrika* 66:339–44.

———. 1983. "Latent Conditional Independence in Two-way Contingency Tables: A Diagnostic Approach." *British Journal of Mathematical and Statistical Psychology* 36:114–22.

———. 1984. "On Some Similarities Between Canonical Correlation Models and Latent Class Models for Two-way Contingency Tables." *Biometrika* 71:523–29.

———. 1986. "Grouping and Association in Contingency Tables: An Exploratory Canonical Correlation Approach." *Journal of the American Statistical Association* 81:773–79.

Gilula, Z., and S. J. Haberman. 1986. "Canonical Analysis of Contingency Tables by Maximum Likelihood." *Journal of the American Statistical Association* 81:780–88.

———. 1988. "The Analysis of Multivariate Contingency Tables by Restricted Canonical and Restricted Association Models." *Journal of the American Statistical Association* 83:760–71.

Goodman, L. A. 1974a. "Exploratory Latent Structure Analysis Using Both Identifiable and Unidentifiable Models." *Biometrika* 61:215–31.

———. 1974b. "The Analysis of Systems of Qualitative Variables When Some of the Variables Are Unobservable. *I*. A Modified Latent Structure Approach." *American Journal of Sociology* 79:1179–259.

———. 1985. "The Analysis of Cross-classified Data Having Ordered and/or Unordered Categories: Association Models, Correlation Models, and Asymmetry Models for Contingency Tables with or Without Missing Entries." *The Annals of Statistics* 13:10–69.

———. 1987. "New Methods for Analyzing the Intrinsic Character of Qualitative Variables Using Cross-classified Data." *American Journal of Sociology* 93:529–83.

———. 1991. "Measures, Models, and Graphical Displays in the Analysis of Cross-classified Data." *Journal of the American Statistical Association* 86:1085–138.

Gower, J. C., and D. J. Hand. 1996. *Biplots*. London: Chapman and Hall.

Greenacre, M. J. 1984. *Theory and Applications of Correspondence Analysis*. London: Academic Press.

———. 1988. "Correspondence Analysis of Multivariate Categorical Data by Weighted Least-squares." *Biometrika* 75:457–67.

———. 1990. "Some Limitations of Multiple Correspondence Analysis." *Computational Statistics Quarterly* 3:249–56.

———. 1991. "Interpreting Multiple Correspondence Analysis." *Applied Stochastic Models and Data Analysis* 7:195–210.

———. 1994. "Multiple and Joint Correspondence Analysis." Pp. 141–61 in *Correspondence Analysis in the Social Sciences: Recent Developments and Applications*, edited by M. Greenacre and J. Blasius. London: Academic Press.

Kendall, M. G., and A. Stuart. 1979. *The Advanced Theory of Statistics*, Vol. 2, 4th ed. New York: Hafner.

Lazarsfeld, P. F. 1950. "The Logical and Mathematical Foundations of Latent Structure Analysis." Pp. 362–412 in *Measurement and Prediction*, edited by S. A. Stouffer et al. Princeton, NJ: Princeton University Press.

Lazarsfeld, P. F., and N. W. Henry. 1968. *Latent Structure Analysis*. New York: Houghton Mifflin.

McCutcheon, A. L. 1987. *Latent Class Analysis. Series: Quantitative Applications in the Social Sciences, 64*. London: Sage.

Michailides, G., and J. de Leeuw. 1998. "The Gifi Sytem for Nonlinear Multivariate Analysis." *Statistical Science* 13(4):307–36.

Mood, A. M., R. A. Graybill, and D. C. Boes. 1974. *Introduction to the Theory of Statistics*, 3rd ed. London: MacGraw-Hill.

Nishisato, S. 1980. *Analysis of Categorical Data: Dual Scaling and Its Applications*. Toronto: University of Toronto Press.

Renner, R. M. 1993. "The Resolution of a Compositional Data Set into Mixtures of

Fixed Source Compositions." *Applied Statistics, Journal of the Royal Statistical Society Series C*, 42, no. 4, 615–31.

Srole, L., T. S. Langner, S. T. Michael, M. K. Opler, and T. A. C. Rennie. 1962. *The Midtown Manhattan Study*. New York: McGraw-Hill.

Tenenhaus, M., and F. W. Young. 1985. "An Analysis and Synthesis of Multiple Correspondence Analysis, Optimal Scaling, Dual Scaling, Homogeneity Analysis, and Other Methods for Quantifying Categorical Multivariate Data." *Psychometrika* 50:91–119.

van de Geer, J. P. 1993. *Multivariate Analysis of Categorical Data*. (2 vols.) Sage: Newbury Park.

van der Ark, L. A. 1999. "Contributions to Latent Budget Analysis; A Tool for the Analysis of Compositional Data." Leiden, Netherlands: DSWO Press.

van der Ark, L. A., and P. G. M. van der Heijden. 1998. "Graphical Display of Latent Budget Analysis and Latent Class Analysis, with Special Reference to Correspondence Analysis." Pp 489–509 in *Visualization of Categorical Data*, edited by J. Blasius, and M. Greenacre. San Diego: Academic Press.

van der Ark, L. A., P. G. M. van der Heijden, and D. Sikkel. (1999). "On the Geometry and Identifiability in the Latent Budget Model." *Journal of Classification* 16:117–37.

van der Heijden, P. G. M., A. Mooijaart, and J. de Leeuw. 1992. "Constrained Latent Budget Analysis." Pp. 279–320 in *Sociological Methodology 1992*, Cambridge, MA: Blackwell Publishers.

6

A GENERAL CLASS OF NONPARAMETRIC MODELS FOR ORDINAL CATEGORICAL DATA

Jeroen K. Vermunt*

This paper presents a general class of models for ordinal categorical data that can be specified by means of linear and/or log-linear equality and/or inequality restrictions on the (conditional) probabilities of a multiway contingency table. Some special cases are models with ordered local odds ratios, models with ordered cumulative response probabilities, order-restricted row association and column association models, and models for stochastically ordered marginal distributions. A simple unidimensional Newton algorithm is proposed for obtaining the restricted maximum-likelihood estimates. In situations in which there is some kind of missing data, this algorithm can be implemented in the M step of an EM algorithm. Computation of p-values of testing statistics is performed by means of parametric bootstrapping.

1. INTRODUCTION

Although the variables and the relationships that are studied in the social sciences are often of an ordinal nature, truly ordinal models are rarely used. Researchers confronted with ordinal data generally use nominal, interval, or quasi-ordinal methods. When using nominal analyses methods, such as standard hierarchical log-linear models, the ordinal variables are treated as nominal variables, which means that the information on the or-

For helpful comments, I am grateful to Jacques Hagenaars, the editors, and two anonymous reviewers. This research was supported by the WORC Research Program on "Analysis of Social Change." The author can be reached at j.k.vermunt@kub.nl.
*Tilburg University, The Netherlands

der of their categories is ignored. Interval analyses are based on assigning scores to the categories of the ordinal variables, as in linear-by-linear association models (Goodman 1979; Haberman 1979). The assumption of known category scores implies that the ordinal variables are actually treated as interval level variables. And finally, quasi-ordinal analyses involve estimating category scores for the ordinal variables, such as in log bi-linear association and correspondence models (Goodman 1979, 1986; Clogg 1982; Gilula and Haberman 1988; Clogg and Shihadeh 1994). Although the latter type of methods yields easily interpretable results when the estimated scores have the assumed order, there is no guarantee that the estimated ordering of the categories will be the expected one.

This paper follows a different modeling strategy for ordinal categorical variables. A nonparametric approach is presented which is based on imposing linear or log-linear inequality restrictions on (conditional) probabilities. This approach is truly ordinal in the sense that the estimated probabilities satisfy the specified order restrictions without the necessity of assuming the variables to be measured on interval level. Although not very well-known among social scientists, linear and log-linear inequality restrictions have been advocated by several authors for the specification of relationships between ordinal categorical variables (Grove 1980; Agresti and Chuang 1986; Agresti, Chuang, and Kezouh 1987; Dykstra and Lemke 1988; Robertson, Wright, and Dykstra 1988; Croon 1990, 1991; Ritov and Gilula 1993; Agresti and Coull 1996; Evans, Gilula, Guttman, and Swartz 1997; Hoijtink and Molenaar 1997).

The general form in which the inequality restrictions are presented in this paper makes it possible to formulate nonparametric variants of log-linear models for cell probabilities, of logit models, and of linear models for cumulative and mean responses. It is also shown that the combination of inequality restrictions with equality restrictions makes it possible to specify hybrid models having both parametric and nonparametric features. An example is a row association model with ordered row scores.

Estimation of the order-restricted probabilities is performed by means of maximum likelihood using the method of activated constraints. A simple unidimensional Newton procedure for solving the corresponding Lagrange likelihood equations is presented. It is also demonstrated that the same procedure can be used in conjunction with the EM algorithm, which makes it possible to apply the proposed inequality restrictions in situations in which some of the variables are partially or completely missing (latent). In addition, attention is paid to likelihood-ratio tests based on asymptotic distribution functions and bootstrapping.

First, a small empirical example is presented to illustrate the differences between parametric and nonparametric analyses of ordinal categorical data. Then, the general class of restrictions yielding the ordinal models of interest is described. Next, attention is paid to maximum likelihood estimation with and without missing data and to model testing. And finally, the use of the proposed ordinal models is exemplified by means of a number of empirical examples.

2. AN EXAMPLE

This section illustrates the possible benefits of using nonparametric models for ordinal data by means of a small example. The example concerns the analysis of the two-way cross-classification reported in Table 1. This table, which is taken from Clogg's 1982 paper on ordinal log-linear models, describes the relationship between number of siblings (S) and happiness (H). The original table is a three-way cross-classification of the ordinal variables years of schooling, number of siblings, and happiness. For this example, the original table is collapsed over education yielding the 5-by-3 table formed by S and H, in which S serves as row variable and H as column variable.

The use of parametric or nonparametric ordinal approaches to the analysis of categorical data makes, of course, sense only if there is some reason to assume that the relationship between the variables of interest is of an ordinal nature. Let us assume that we want to test whether there is a positive relationship between number of siblings and happiness, or, worded differently, whether individuals having more siblings are happier than individuals having fewer siblings.

TABLE 1
Cross-Classification of Number of Siblings and Happiness: Observed Frequencies

Number of Siblings (S)	Happiness (H)		
	Not Too Happy	Pretty Happy	Very Happy
0–1	99	155	19
2–3	153	238	43
4–5	115	163	40
6–7	63	133	32
8 +	99	118	47

Source: From Clogg (1982), table 2.

One way of defining such a positive relationship is on the basis of the cumulative conditional responses on happiness given the number of siblings that a person has. In that case, we treat happiness as the dependent variable and number of siblings as the independent. Let $\pi_{h|s}$ denote the conditional probability that $H = h$ given that $S = s$. In addition, let $F_{h|s}$ denote the cumulative conditional probability that $H \leq h$ given that $S = s$, which is defined as

$$F_{h|s} = \sum_{p=1}^{h} \pi_{p|s} .$$

A positive relationship between S and H implies that

$$F_{h|s} \geq F_{h|s+1} , \tag{1}$$

or that the cumulative conditional probability that $H = h$ decreases or remains equal as S increases. We may also say that the cumulative probabilities are monotonically nonincreasing. Note that even if this assumption holds for the population, as a result of sampling error, this may not hold for the data. Table 2 reports the cumulative conditional probabilities calculated from the observed cell entries reported in Table 1. As can be seen, there are several order violations in the data.

Another way of defining a positive relationship is on the basis of the local odds ratios. Let π_{sh} denote the probability that $H = h$ and $S = s$. In addition, let θ_{sh} denote a local odds ratio, which is defined as

$$\theta_{sh} = \frac{\pi_{sh}\,\pi_{s+1h+1}}{\pi_{sh+1}\,\pi_{s+1h}} .$$

TABLE 2
Cross-Classification of Number of Siblings and Happiness:
Observed and Estimated Cumulative Probabilities

Number of Siblings (S)	Happiness (H)		
	Not Too Happy	Pretty Happy	Very Happy
0–1	0.363/0.363	0.930/0.930	1.000/1.000
2–3	0.353/0.356	0.901/0.912	1.000/1.000
4–5	0.362/0.356	0.874/0.873	1.000/1.000
6–7	0.276/0.329	0.860/0.870	1.000/1.000
8 +	0.375/0.329	0.822/0.809	1.000/1.000

TABLE 3
Cross-Classification of Number of Siblings and Happiness:
Observed and Estimated Odds Ratios

Number of Siblings (S)	Happiness (H)	
	Not Too Happy/Pretty Happy	Pretty Happy/Very Happy
0–1/2–3	0.994/1.000	1.474/1.471
2–3/4–5	0.911/1.000	1.358/1.308
4–5/6–7	1.489/1.023	0.980/1.125
6–7/8 +	0.565/1.000	1.655/1.327

Using this measure, a positive relationship involves

$$\theta_{sh} \geq 1 \ , \tag{2}$$

or that each local odds ratio in the two-way table is larger than or equal to 1. As can be seen from Table 3, the pattern of observed odds ratios is not in agreement with the definition of a positive relationship since some of them are smaller than 1.

The fact that the data are not fully in agreement with the assumption of an ordinal relationship may be the result of sampling error. One way of testing whether the observed order violations are the result of sampling error is by using some kind of parametric model to impose restrictions on the cumulative conditional probabilities or the local odds ratios.

Table 4 reports the test results for the estimated parametric models. As can be seen, the independence model does not fit the data ($L_{A.1}^2 = 26.27, df = 8, p < .01$), which indicates that there is an association between H and S. The next model (A.2) is a logit model for the cumulative response probabilities—that is,

$$\ln \frac{F_{h|s}}{1 - F_{h|s}} = \alpha_h + \beta_s \ .$$

It should be noted that this parametric model fulfils the conditions specified in equation (1) only if $\beta_s \geq \beta_{s+1}$. The model could be characterized as ordinal-nominal because it treats the dependent variable as ordinal and the independent as nominal. The cumulative logit model does not fit the data:

TABLE 4
Test Results for the Four Examples

Model	L^2 value	df [a]	p value[b]
A. Ordinal association models			
1. Independence	26.27	8	.00
2. Cumulative logit	18.52	4	.00
3. Row-column association	7.33	3	.06
4. Row association	17.52	4	.00
5. Column association	8.36	6	.21
6. Uniform association	20.21	7	.01
7. Nonincreasing $F_{h\mid s}$	5.50	0 + 2	.10
8. Nonnegative $\log \theta_{sh}$	8.32	0 + 3	.04
9. Ordered row-column association	8.36	3 + 1	.08
10. Ordered row association	18.60	4 + 1	.00
11. Ordered column association	8.84	6 + 1	.22
B. Ordinal regression models			
1. No three-variable interaction	24.88	24	.41
2. Only effect of S	53.42	30	.01
3. Only effect of E	39.62	32	.17
4. 1 + uniform associations	54.58	36	.02
5. 1 + order-restricted local odds ratios	35.30	24 + 6	.23
C. Marginal models with missing data			
1. Marginal homogeneity	22.36	3	.00
2. Nondecreasing marginals	3.17	0 + 1	.07
3. Linearly changing marginals	13.73	2	.00
D. Ordinal latent class models			
1. Unrestricted four-class model	15.11	24	.92
2. Uniform associations	115.79	48	.00
3. Column associations	105.86	42	.00
4. Nonincreasing cumulative probabilities	15.55	24 + 2	.96
5. Nonnegative local log odds ratios	39.20	24 + 16	.34

[a]The reported number of degrees of freedom for the order-restricted models is the df of the model without constraints plus the number of activated constraints.

[b]The p values of the models with inequality constraints are estimated on the basis of 1000 bootstrap samples. The standard errors of these estimates are less than .01 for $p \leq .11$ and $p \geq .89$, and at most .02 for other p values.

$L^2_{A.2} = 18.52, df = 4, p = .00$. Apparently, its underlying assumption of proportional odds does not hold for this data set. In addition, the estimated β_s's are out of order, which also means that the assumption of monotonically nonincreasing $F_{h\mid s}$'s is not satisfied.

A parametric model that can be used to restrict local odds ratios is the row-column (RC) association model (Goodman 1979; Clogg 1982) which is defined by

$$\ln \pi_{sh} = u + u_s^S + u_h^H + \nu_s^S \nu_h^H .$$

Here, ν_s^S and ν_h^H are unknown "scores" for the levels of S and H. The RC model satisfies the conditions described in equation (2) if $\nu_s^S \leq \nu_{s+1}^S$ and $\nu_h^H \leq \nu_{h+1}^H$—that is, if the row and column scores are monotonically non-decreasing. Because the RC model does not restrict the row and column scores to be ordered, it can be labeled as nominal-nominal, or quasi ordinal. The RC model fits the data quite well: $L_{A.3}^2 = 7.33, df = 3, p = .06$. There is a problem however: both the row and the columns scores are out of order. More precisely, the order of the scores for rows 3 and 4 and for columns 1 and 2 is incorrect.

One way to prevent the occurrence of solutions that are out of order is to assign *a priori* scores to the levels of S and H. Note that this amounts to assuming that the variable concerned is of interval measurement level. Although for simplicity of exposition here I will work only with equal-interval scores, any set of scores that is in agreement with the assumed order may be used. Three restricted variants of the above RC model can be obtained, depending on whether we use *a priori* (equal-interval) scores for the column variable (H), the row variable (S), or both. The resulting models can be classified as row (R), column (C), and uniform (U) association, respectively. They can also be labeled as nominal-interval, interval-nominal, and interval-interval.

The test results reported in Table 4 show that the R model does not fit the data ($L_{A.4}^2 = 17.52, df = 4, p < .01$), which indicates that H may not be treated as an interval level variable. In addition, the estimated scores for S are not ordered: the score for row 4 is slightly higher than for row 5. The C model fits very well ($L_{A.5}^2 = 8.36, df = 6, p = .21$), but again the category scores, in this case for $H = 1$ and $H = 2$, have an incorrect order. The uniform association model (Model A.6) does not fit the data at all ($L_{A.6}^2 = 20.21, df = 7, p = .01$), which indicates that the assumption that H and S are interval level variables is too strong. Nevertheless, the uniform association parameter is significant and has the "expected" positive sign.

The above parametric ordinal approach illustrates that on the one hand the specified models make too strong assumptions, such as proportional odds or constant local odds ratios. On the other hand, they may not be restrictive enough in the sense that they do not force the solution to be ordered in one of the ways defined above. This is the main reason for proposing a nonparametric approach for the kinds of problems we are dealing with here.

The next two models reported in Table 4 are nonparametric. More precisely, Model A.7 is defined by the inequality restrictions described in equation (1) and Model A.8 by the restrictions described in equation (2). The model obtained by imposing inequality restrictions on the cumulative conditional probabilities fits quite well: $L^2_{A.7} = 5.50, p \approx .10$. The fit of the model restricting the local odds ratios to be at least 1 is somewhat worse: $L^2_{A.8} = 8.32, p \approx .04.$[1]

The estimated cumulative probabilities for Model A.7 and the estimated odds ratios for Model A.8 are reported in Tables 2 and 3, respectively. These "parameter" estimates show very well the nature of an order-restricted maximum likelihood (ML) solution: as long as an order restriction is not violated, nothing happens, but if an order is violated, the corresponding estimate gets a boundary value. In the current situation, this involves equating adjacent cumulative conditional probabilities or equating local odds ratios to 1. It should be noted that although such a procedure seems to be simple to implement, it cannot always be determined from that data which restrictions have to be imposed. This can be seen from the ML solution for Model A.8, which contains 3 odds ratios equal to 1, while in the observed table there were 4 odds ratios smaller than 1.

A disadvantage of using the nonparametric approach is that there are no real parameters to report. The interpretation of the results has to be based on the fit statistics and on the estimated values of the probabilities or the functions of probabilities for which order restrictions were specified: in the above examples, these were the cumulative probabilities and the local odds ratios. To deal with this problem, we will also present models that combine parametric and nonparametric features, such as row association models with order-restricted row scores.

Another disadvantage of using nonparametric models is that estimation and testing are much more complicated than they are for parametric models. One of the objectives of this paper is to show that a quite general class of nonparametric models can be estimated with a very simple

---

[1]As is explained in Section 5, the p-values for the order-restricted models are estimated by means of bootstrapping. The reported p-values are point estimates based on 1000 bootstrap samples. The number of degrees of freedom is not defined in models with inequality constraints.

algorithm. In addition, the availability of fast computers makes it feasible to have goodness-of-fit testing and computation of standard errors of the relevant measures, such as local odds ratios and cumulative probabilities using computationally intensive resampling methods.

3. A GENERAL CLASS OF (IN)EQUALITY RESTRICTIONS

This section discusses linear and log-linear restrictions on (conditional) probabilities that can be used for specifying ordinal models for categorical data. Although the specification of ordinal models is based on imposing inequality constraints, we also discuss equality constraints of the same form. This is because of didactic reasons—equality constraints are some-what easier to understand and most inequality constraints are variants or extensions of the simpler equality constraints—and because in some sit-uations it may be relevant to combine the two types of restrictions. For each of the four types of constraints—linear equalities, linear inequalities, log-linear equalities, and log-linear inequalities—a number of possible applications is presented.

Let n_{ij} denote an observed cell count in an I-by-J table, where i serves as an index for the (possibly composite, possibly degenerate) inde-pendent variable X and j for the (possibly composite) dependent variable Y. For example, Y might be a bivariate random vector (Y_1, Y_2), in which case $j = (j_1, j_2)$ would index the possible level combinations of Y_1 and Y_2. In situations in which no distinction is made between dependent and in-dependent variables, X has only one level, which makes the index i redun-dant. The conditional probability that $Y = j$ given that $X = i$ is denoted by $\pi_{j|i}$.

3.1. *Linear Equality Restrictions*

The first type of restrictions are linear equality restrictions on the (condi-tional) probabilities $\pi_{j|i}$. The pth restriction of this form is defined by

$$\sum_{ij} z_{1ijp} \pi_{j|i} - c_{1p} = 0 \ . \tag{3}$$

As can be seen, a linear combination of $\pi_{j|i}$'s defined by the z_{1ijp}'s minus some constant c_{1p} is postulated to be equal to zero. In most situations, c_{1p} will be 0. It should be noted that we have in fact a linear model for (conditional) probabilities that is well-known from the GSK framework (Grizzle, Starmer, and Koch 1969).

These linear equality restrictions can be used to test several types of assumptions on the relationships between categorical variables. Some examples are independence, equal means, conditional independence, marginal homogeneity, equal marginal means, and symmetry.

Suppose that we are studying the relationship between two categorical variables A and B, with category indexes a and b, respectively. Using the above linear equality restrictions, independence between A and B can be specified as

$$\pi_{a|b} - \pi_{a|b+1} = 0 \ .$$

Let $F_{a|b}$ denote that (cumulative) probability that $A \leq a$, given $B = b$: $F_{a|b} = \sum_{p=1}^{a} \pi_{p|b}$. An alternative formulation of the independence assumption is in terms of these cumulative probabilities:

$$F_{a|b} - F_{a|b+1} = \sum_{p=1}^{a} \pi_{p|b} - \sum_{p=1}^{a} \pi_{p|b+1} = 0 \ .$$

Although working with cumulative probabilities seems to be unnecessarily complicated, it will prove very useful in the context of inequality restrictions.

A less restrictive assumption than independence, which makes sense only if A is an interval level variable, is that the mean of A is the same for each category of B. Using ν_a^A as category scores for A, such an assumption can be formulated as

$$\mu_b^A - \mu_{b+1}^A = \sum_a \nu_a^A \pi_{a|b} - \sum_a \nu_a^A \pi_{a|b+1} = 0 \ ,$$

where μ_b^A is the mean of A for $B = b$.

The generalization of the independence assumption to a multivariate context yields the conditional independence assumption. Suppose that A and B are independent of one another within the levels of a third variable C with index c. Such a conditional independence model can be specified as

$$\pi_{a|bc} - \pi_{a|b+1c} = 0 \ .$$

Of course, as in the bivariate case, we may also specify this hypothesis using the cumulative probabilities $F_{a|bc}$.

Rather than testing assumptions on the level of conditional probabilities as in the above examples, it is also possible to formulate hypotheses that have to be specified in the form of linear restrictions on the joint probability distribution of a set of categorical variables. An example is the marginal homogeneity assumption for a two-way square table formed by the variables A and B, which can be defined as:

$$\pi_{a.} - \pi_{.a} = \sum_b \pi_{ab} - \sum_b \pi_{ba} = 0 \ .$$

Here, π_{ab} denotes the probability that $A = a$ and $B = b$, and a dot indicates that the corresponding probability is obtained by summation over the subscript concerned. For instance, $\pi_{a.} = \sum_b \pi_{ab}$.

Let $F_{a.}$ denote the cumulative marginal probability that $A \leq a$: $F_{a.} = \sum_{p=1}^{a} \sum_b \pi_{pb}$. In a similar way, we can define the cumulative marginal probability that $B \leq b$, $F_{.b}$. The marginal homogeneity model can also be specified in the form of constraints on these cumulative marginal probabilities—that is,

$$F_{a.} - F_{.a} = \sum_{p=1}^{a} \sum_b \pi_{pb} - \sum_{p=1}^{a} \sum_b \pi_{bp} = 0 \ . \tag{4}$$

Another marginal hypothesis, which may be relevant in situations in which A and B are interval level categorical variables, is the assumption of equal marginal means for A and B (for an example, see Haber and Brown 1986). This is obtained by

$$\mu^A - \mu^B = \sum_a \sum_b \nu_a^A \pi_{ab} - \sum_a \sum_b \nu_b^B \pi_{ab} = 0 \ , \tag{5}$$

where the ν's denote category scores assigned to the levels of A and B.

Another interesting model for squared tables is the well-known symmetry model. Using linear equality restrictions, such a model can be specified as

$$\pi_{ab} - \pi_{ba} = 0 \ . \tag{6}$$

It should be noted that the independence, conditional independence, and symmetry models can also be formulated as log-linear models. The other examples of linear restrictions cannot be specified as standard log-linear models.

3.2. Linear Inequality Restrictions

The linear inequality restrictions of interest are of the form

$$\sum_{ij} z_{2ijq} \pi_{j|i} - c_{2q} \geq 0 \; . \tag{7}$$

Here, the z_{2ijq} are used to define the qth linear combination of probabilities $\pi_{j|i}$. This linear combination minus a constant (c_{2q}) is assumed to be at least 0. Restrictions of this form can be used to specify ordered variants of the equality restrictions discussed above, such as ordered conditional distributions, ordered conditional means, and ordered marginal distributions.

Rather than assuming independence between A and B, it is possible to postulate a positive relationship. This can be specified in the form of monotonically nonincreasing cumulative conditional probabilities

$$F_{a|b} - F_{a|b+1} = \sum_{p=1}^{a} \pi_{p|b} - \sum_{p=1}^{a} \pi_{p|b+1} \geq 0 \; . \tag{8}$$

It should be noted that this formulation of a positive relationship, which has been used by several authors (for instance, see Grove 1980; Croon 1990; Evans et al. 1997), yields an asymmetrical ordinal hypothesis. The same type of assumption but with B dependent yields a different model. In other words, stochastically ordered $F_{a|b}$'s do not imply stochastically ordered $F_{b|a}$'s.

Linear inequalities can also be used to specify hypotheses about the conditional relationship between A and B, given an individual's score on a third variable C. Suppose that A and B are positively related given $C = c$. This can be specified as follows:

$$F_{a|bc} - F_{a|b+1c} = \sum_{p=1}^{a} \pi_{p|bc} - \sum_{p=1}^{a} \pi_{p|b+1c} \geq 0 \; ,$$

in other words, in the form of monotonically nonincreasing cumulative probabilities. If C is also ordinal, we may also wish to assume that

$$F_{a|bc} - F_{a|bc+1} = \sum_{p=1}^{a} \pi_{p|bc} - \sum_{p=1}^{a} \pi_{p|bc+1} \geq 0 \; .$$

This model, in which the cumulative distribution of A is assumed to be stochastically ordered in two directions, was described by Robertson, Wright, and Dykstra (1988:32–33).

An ordinal variant of the marginal homogeneity model (see equation 4) is obtained by assuming that the cumulative marginal probabilities for A ($F_{a.}$) are at least as large as those of B ($F_{.a}$):

$$F_{a.} - F_{.a} = \sum_{p=1}^{a} \sum_{b} \pi_{pb} - \sum_{p=1}^{a} \sum_{b} \pi_{bp} \geq 0 \ .$$

This model of stochastically ordered cumulative marginal distributions was described by Robertson, Wright, and Dykstra (1988:290–92). In a similar way, we could formulate order-restricted variants of the equal marginal means model described in equation (5) and the symmetry model described in equation (6) by replacing the "=" sign by a "≥" sign.

3.3. Log-Linear Equality Restrictions

The rth log-linear equality restriction on the probabilities $\pi_{j|i}$ is defined as

$$\sum_{ij} z_{3ijr} \ln \pi_{j|i} - c_{3r} = 0 \ , \tag{9}$$

where the z_{3ijr} define the rth linear combination of logs of cell probabilities, which minus a constant (c_{3r}) is postulated to be equal to zero. Restrictions of this form can be used to specify any kind of log-linear model, such as independence, row association, linear-by-linear association, conditional independence, and no-three-variable interaction models. In addition, the term c_{3r} makes it possible to impose fixed-value restrictions on the log-linear parameters. It should be noted that this is actually the orthogonal complement notation of the standard log-linear model. Such a reformulation is also used by Lang and Agresti (1994) and Bergsma (1997) for specifying extended log-linear models. This orthogonal complement formulation is very appealing in many situations because, as is demonstrated below, assumptions about relationships between variables are specified directly in terms of restrictions on (local) odds ratios.

Let θ_{ab} denote a local odds ratio in the two-way table formed by the variables A and B. It is defined as

$$\theta_{ab} = \frac{\pi_{ab}\,\pi_{a+1b+1}}{\pi_{ab+1}\,\pi_{a+1b}} \ .$$

In an independence model, it is assumed that each θ_{ab} equals 1, or, equivalently, that each $\ln \theta_{ab}$ equals zero. Using the above log-linear equality restrictions, such a model can be specified as

$$\ln \theta_{ab} = \ln \pi_{ab} - \ln \pi_{ab+1} - \ln \pi_{a+1b} + \ln \pi_{a+1b+1} = 0 \ .$$

In a similar way, other types of nonsaturated log-linear models can be defined for the same two-way table. A row association model, for example, assumes that the local odds ratios are independent of the columns. This can be specified as

$$\ln \theta_{ab} - \ln \theta_{ab+1} = \ln \pi_{ab} - 2 \ln \pi_{ab+1} - \ln \pi_{a+1b} + 2 \ln \pi_{a+1b+1}$$

$$+ \ln \pi_{ab+2} - \ln \pi_{a+1b+2} = 0 \ . \tag{10}$$

Note that this is a standard row association model with equal-interval scores for the levels of the column variable. However, it is also possible to use other scoring schemes for the column variable. The general row association model specified in the form of log-linear restrictions on θ_{ab} (and on π_{ab}) is

$$\frac{\ln \theta_{ab}}{v_{b+1}^B - v_b^B} - \frac{\ln \theta_{ab+1}}{v_{b+2}^B - v_{b+1}^B} = 0 \ , \tag{11}$$

where v_b^B denotes the score assigned to level b of B. As can be seen, the logs of local odds ratio are weighted by the inverse of the distance between the corresponding column scores. In a similar way, it is possible to specify column association models and linear-by-linear association with any type of category scoring.

To illustrate the use of the constant c_{3r}, it is also possible to test the assumption that the local odds ratios are equal to a specific value. By

$$\ln \theta_{ab} - c = \ln \pi_{ab} - \ln \pi_{ab+1} - \ln \pi_{a+1b} + \ln \pi_{a+1b+1} - c = 0 \ ,$$

we obtain a uniform association model in which the local odds ratios are fixed to be equal to $\exp(c)$.

As in the case of linear restrictions, it is also possible to constrain the relationships between more than two variables. For instance, restrictions of independence, row association, column association, linear-by-linear association, and fixed uniform association could be applied conditionally on C. Such restricted conditional association models can be specified by replacing π_{ab} by π_{abc} or $\pi_{ab|c}$ in the corresponding log-linear restrictions.

Another interesting assumption in a three-way table is the no-three-variable interaction model, which implies that the local odds ratios are independent of the third variable. This can be specified as follows:

$$\ln \theta_{ab|c} - \ln \theta_{ab|c+1} = \ln \pi_{abc} - \ln \pi_{ab+1c} - \ln \pi_{a+1bc} + \ln \pi_{a+1b+1c}$$

$$- \ln \pi_{abc+1} + \ln \pi_{ab+1c+1} + \ln \pi_{a+1bc+1}$$

$$+ \ln \pi_{a+1b+1c+1} = 0 \ .$$

Here, $\theta_{ab|c}$ denotes a conditional local odds ratio for variables A and B within level c of variable C. The specification of log-linear models using these types of contrasts of log odds ratios can easily be generalized to higher-way tables.

3.4. Log-Linear Inequality Restrictions

The fourth and last type of restriction presented here are log-linear inequality restrictions. The sth restriction of this form is

$$\sum_{ij} z_{4ijs} \ln \pi_{j|i} - c_{4s} \geq 0 \ . \tag{12}$$

Log-linear inequality restrictions can be used to specify ordinal variants of the log-linear models discussed above. We may, for instance, define models with a positive bivariate relationship in the form of nonnegative local log odds ratios, row or column association models with monotonically nondecreasing scores, or models assuming a bivariate association to be stronger for one group than for another.

With the linear inequality restrictions, a postulated positive relationship between two ordinal variables was defined in the form of nonincreasing cumulative conditional probabilities (see equation 8). A natural definition of a positive relationship between A and B in log-linear terms is that all local odds ratios are at least 1 (Dykstra and Lemke 1988). This yields the following set of log-linear inequality restrictions on the θ_{ab}'s or the π_{ab}'s:

$$\ln \theta_{ab} = \ln \pi_{ab} - \ln \pi_{ab+1} - \ln \pi_{a+1b} + \ln \pi_{a+1b+1} \geq 0 \ . \tag{13}$$

It should be noted that, contrary to the definition in terms of cumulative conditional probabilities, this definition of a positive relationship is a symmetric one since reversing A and B yields the same model.

A positive association could also be specified by means of a row association model with monotonically nondecreasing row scores (see Agresti, Chuang, and Kezouh 1987). Such a model, which assumes that the column variable is an interval level variable and that the row variable is ordinal, can be specified by combining the restriction of column independent local odds ratios (equation 10) with the restriction of nonnegative local log odds ratios (equation 13). The more general order-restricted row association proposed by Agresti, Chuang, and Kezouh (1987) is obtained by using equation (11) instead of (10). In a similar way, we can specify ordered variants of the column and linear-by-linear association models.

Unfortunately, the log-linear inequality restrictions cannot be used to define row-column association models with ordered row and column scores as proposed by Ritov and Gilula (1991) since these models are not log-linear but log-bilinear (see also Vermunt 1998). The log-linear inequality restrictions can, however, be used to specify correspondence or correlation models with ordered row and column scores. As was demonstrated by Ritov and Gilula (1993), this can be accomplished by specifying the row-column correlation model as a latent class model with log-linear inequality restrictions of the form described in equation (13).

As in the case of log-linear equality restrictions, the above examples of log-linear inequality restrictions can also be used in a multivariate setting. We may, for instance, assume a positive association, a row association with ordered scores, or a correlation model with ordered scores for A and B within levels of a third variable, say C. An example is the binary logit model with ordered-restricted parameters for one of the two regressors proposed by Agresti and Coull (1996).

Another interesting ordinal hypothesis for a three-way table is that a bivariate relationship is stronger in one subgroup than in another. Suppose that we assume a nonnegative association between A and B within levels of C. In addition, we want the association to increase with C. The latter assumption can be specified by the following additional set of log-linear constraints on the conditional local odds ratio:

$$\ln \theta_{ab|c+1} - \ln \theta_{ab|c} = -\ln \pi_{abc+1} + \ln \pi_{ab+1c+1} + \ln \pi_{a+1bc+1}$$
$$- \ln \pi_{a+1b+1c+1} + \ln \pi_{abc} - \ln \pi_{ab+1c}$$
$$- \ln \pi_{a+1bc} + \ln \pi_{a+1b+1c} \geq 0 \ .$$

Note that this set of order restrictions concerns the three-variable interaction term between A, B, and C.

4. MAXIMUM-LIKELIHOOD ESTIMATION

Maximum-likelihood estimation of cell probabilities under ordinal restrictions is an optimization problem under inequality constraints. One of the methods for solving such a problem is the Lagrangian method with activated constraints (see Gill and Murray 1974; Gill, Murray, and Wright 1981). The Lagrangian method, which is well-known in maximum-likelihood estimation with equality constraints, involves augmenting the object function to be maximized with one Lagrange term for each of the constraints. If a constraint has the form of an inequality constraint, the corresponding equality constraint is activated or deactivated during the optimization process, depending on whether the corresponding inequality constraint is violated or not. Appendix A describes some of the basic principles of optimization under equality and inequality constraints.

Assuming a (product-)multinomial sampling scheme, maximum-likelihood estimation of the $\pi_{j|i}$ parameters under the restrictions described in equations (3), (7), (9), and (12) involves finding the saddle point of the following (Lagrange) function

$$\mathcal{L} = \sum_{ij} n_{ij} \ln \pi_{j|i} + \sum_i \alpha_i \left(\sum_j \pi_{j|i} - 1 \right)$$

$$+ \sum_p \beta_{1p} \left(\sum_{ij} z_{1ijp} \pi_{j|i} - c_{1p} \right) + \sum_q \beta_{2q} \left(\sum_{ij} z_{2ijq} \pi_{j|i} - c_{2q} \right) \quad (14)$$

$$+ \sum_r \beta_{3r} \left(\sum_{ij} z_{3ijr} \ln \pi_{j|i} - c_{3r} \right) + \sum_s \beta_{4s} \left(\sum_{ij} z_{4ijs} \ln \pi_{j|i} - c_{4s} \right) ,$$

with

$$\beta_{2q} \geq 0$$

$$\beta_{4s} \geq 0 ,$$

where the α and the β parameters are Lagrange multipliers. As can be seen, the first term at the right-hand side of equation (14) is the well-known kernel of the (product-)multinomial log-likelihood function. The second component specifies a set of Lagrange terms which guarantee that the probabilities $\pi_{j|i}$ sum to 1 within each level of the independent variable X. The other four terms belong to the linear equality, linear inequality, log-linear equality, and log-linear inequality restrictions, respectively.

Because the second and the fourth set of constraints are inequality constraints, the β_{2q} and β_{4s} parameters must be greater than or equal to zero, which implies that the corresponding equality constraints are only activated if the inequality constraints concerned are violated. More precisely, an active constraint corresponds with a β_{2q} or β_{4s}, which is larger than 0, while an inactive constraint corresponds with a β_{2q} or β_{4s}, which equals 0.

Taking the first derivative with respect to $\pi_{j|i}$ and setting the result equal to zero yields the following expression for the ML estimate of $\pi_{j|i}$:

$$\pi_{j|i} = \frac{n_{ij} + \sum_r z_{3ijr}\beta_{3r} + \sum_s z_{4ijs}\beta_{4s}}{-\alpha_i - \sum_p z_{1ijp}\beta_{1p} - \sum_q z_{2ijq}\beta_{2q}} . \tag{15}$$

Thus, given the Lagrange multipliers, there is a closed form solution for the $\pi_{j|i}$'s. What is needed is a method for finding the Lagrange multipliers. This can, for instance, be accomplished by means of the unidimensional Newton method. This method involves updating one parameter at a time, fixing all the other parameters at their current values.[2] For α_i, a unidimensional Newton update is of the form

$$\alpha_i' = \alpha_i - step \; \frac{\sum_j \pi_{j|i} - 1}{\sum_j \pi_{j|i} \Big/ \left(-\alpha_i - \sum_p z_{1ijp}\beta_{1p} - \sum_q z_{2ijq}\beta_{2q} \right)} , \tag{16}$$

for β_{1p},

$$\beta_{1p}' = \beta_{1p} - step \; \frac{\sum_{ij} z_{1ijp}\pi_{j|i} - c_{1p}}{\sum_{ij} z_{1ijp}^2 \pi_{j|i} \Big/ \left(-\alpha_i - \sum_p z_{1ijp}\beta_{1p} - \sum_q z_{2ijq}\beta_{2q} \right)} ,$$

$$\tag{17}$$

[2]Vermunt (1997:312–15) applied unidimensional Newton for a similar problem—that is, for the estimation of (conditional) probabilities under simple equality and fixed-value restrictions.

and for β_{3r},

$$\beta'_{3r} = \beta_{3r} - step \; \frac{\sum\limits_{ij} z_{3ijr} \ln \pi_{j|i} - c_{3r}}{\sum\limits_{ij} z^2_{3ijr} \Big/ \left(n_{ij} + \sum\limits_{r} z_{3ijr} \beta_{3r} + \sum\limits_{s} z_{4ijs} \beta_{4s}\right)} . \tag{18}$$

In each of these updating equations, the numerator is the function that must become zero and the denominator its first derivative with respect to the parameter concerned.

The updating equations for β_{2q} and β_{4s} have the same form as for β_{1p} and β_{3r}, respectively. As already indicated above, the Lagrange parameters pertaining to the inequality restrictions must be greater than or equal to zero, which implies that β'_{2q} and β'_{4s} must be set equal to zero if they become negative. This amounts to not activating or deactivating the equality constraint corresponding to an inequality constraint.

With *step* it is possible to change the step size of the adjustments. This may be necessary if $\pi_{j|i}$ takes on an inadmissible value, or, more precisely, a value smaller than zero. In addition, *step* may be used to start with somewhat smaller step sizes in the first iterations.

The exact iteration scheme is as follows:

1. Set $\alpha_i = -n_{i\cdot}$, $\beta_{1p} = \beta_{2q} = \beta_{3r} = \beta_{4s} = 0$, and *step* $= 1/4$, and compute $\pi_{j|i}$'s using equation (15).
2. Save current α's, β's, and $\pi_{j|i}$'s.
3. For each Lagrange parameter,
   a. update parameter using equation (16), (17), or (18).
   b. if smaller than 0, set parameter equal to 0 (only for β_{2q} and β_{4s}).
   c. compute new $\pi_{j|i}$'s using equation (15).
   d. if one or more $\pi_{j|i} < 0$: half *step*, restore saved α, β's, and $\pi_{j|i}$'s from 2, and restart with 3(a).
4. If no convergence is reached, double *step* if *step* < 1 and restart with 2—that is, go to next iteration.

As can be seen from step 1, the starting values for $\pi_{j|i}$ are $n_{ij}/n_{i\cdot}$—that is, the unrestricted observed probability of $Y = j$ given $X = i$. Step 3(b) shows how the algorithm deals with inequality constraints: If an update of β_{2q} or β_{4s} yields a value smaller than zero, the parameter concerned is set to zero. In this way, an inactive constraint may remain inactive or an active constraint may become inactive, depending on whether its previous value was zero or positive. An inactive inequality constraint is activated if the value of the corresponding Lagrange multiplier changes from zero into a positive value. The convergence mentioned in step 4 can be defined either in terms of a maximum change of the Lagrange parameters or a minimum change of the log-likelihood function.

The above unidimensional Newton method will converge to the ML solution if the restrictions do not contradict one another, if all observed cell entries are larger than zero, and if the model does not combine linear with log-linear restrictions.

The first condition states that the algorithm will not converge if contradictory restrictions, such as $a = 0$, $b = 3$, and $a \geq b$, are imposed. This is, of course, not specific for the current algorithm. It should be noted that contrary to multidimensional methods like Newton-Raphson and Fisher-scoring, the unidimensional method does not have problems with redundant restrictions such as $a \geq b$, $b \geq c$, and $a \geq c$.

The problem associated with the second condition is well-known in the analysis of categorical data and is therefore not specific for this algorithm. As in standard log-linear models, some parameters may be undefined because some observed cells are equal to zero. A simple way to overcome this problem is to add a small number to each cell entry. To solve the numerical problems associated with zero cells, a very small number, say 10^{-10}, already suffices.[3]

A third problem is that the algorithm may fail to converge to the ML solution if a model combines linear and log-linear restrictions. This problem was noted by Bergsma (1998) in the context of the algorithm proposed by Haber and Brown (1986) for log-linear models with linear (equality) restrictions on the expected cell entries. Haber and Brown proposed an algorithm in which first the log-linear parameters and then the parameters associated with the linear restrictions are updated at each iteration cycle. Bergsma showed that their proof of convergence contains an incorrect assumption—namely, that the term belonging to the linear part of the model, the denominator of equation (15), is positive for each cell entry. In the ML solution, both the numerator and denominator may be negative for some cells. A problem arises, however, because an algorithm that does not simultaneously update the terms belonging to the linear and to the log-linear

---

[3]Adding somewhat larger numbers to the observed cell entries can very well be defended from a Bayesian point of view (Clogg and Eliason 1987). With an informative (Dirichlet) prior, the estimated cell entries can, for instance, be smoothed to the independence model. For an excellent overview of this topic, see Schafer(1997).

restrictions may not converge because of the requisite that the probabilities should remain positive after each update. The results by Haber and Brown hold asymptotically, which means that if the model holds and the sample size is large enough this problem will not occur. Thus, in practice, this problem is more likely to occur if the model of interest fits badly or if the sample size is small.

Bergsma (1998) proposed estimating models that combine linear and log-linear equality restrictions with a Fisher-scoring algorithm developed for the estimation of extended log-linear models (Lang and Agresti 1994; Bergsma 1997). This multidimensional saddle point method for finding ML estimates under a general class of equality constraints can easily be modified into an activate set procedure to allow for inequalities (see Appendix A). Another advantage of applying this more advanced method is that an even more general class of inequality constraints can be formulated, such as log-linear inequality restrictions on marginal probabilities. This may, for instance, yield a nonparametric variant of the cumulative logit model. Nevertheless, the procedure described above remains very attractive because of its simplicity. It can easily be implemented using macro languages of packages as SAS, GLIM, and S-plus. For the examples presented in the next section, we used both the simple unidimensional Newton algorithm and an adaptation of Bergsma's (1997) algorithm to inequalities. In all estimated models, both procedures yielded the same results.

Robertson, Wright, and Dykstra (1988, chap. 1) described an alternative procedure for obtaining order-restricted maximum-likelihood estimates. They showed that some order-restricted maximum-likelihood problems can be transformed into isotonic regression problems. One of the algorithms they proposed for solving these isotonic regression problems is the pooling adjacent violators algorithm (PAVA), which is a simple IPF-like algorithm that can be used to solve models with simple order restrictions. Another method for finding ML estimates under equality and inequality constraints is to transform the constrained ML estimation problem into a quadratic programming problem (for instance, see Fahrmeir and Klinger 1994 and Schoenberg 1997).

4.1. *Latent Variables and Other Types of Missing Data*

The proposed nonparametric ordinal modeling approach can also be applied in situations in which there is some type of missing data, such as in latent class models and in models for panel data subject to partial nonresponse. However, to be able to deal with missing data, we have to adapt the estimation algorithm described in Section 4.

The simplest option is to use the EM algorithm (Dempster, Laird, and Rubin 1977). The main advantage of using this iterative method is that it is obtained with minor modifications of the estimation procedure for complete data. In the E step of the EM algorithm, we estimate the complete data on the basis of the incomplete data and the current parameter estimates. The M step of the algorithm involves estimating the model parameters as if all data were observed. Croon (1990), for instance, implemented (PAVA) in the M step of the version of the EM algorithm that he used for estimating his ordinal latent class model. Here, we will use an EM algorithm which implements the simple unidimensional Newton method in the M step. Appendix B discusses the EM algorithm for a marginal model with partially missing data and for an order-restricted latent class model.

5. MODEL TESTING

Suppose that H_1 denotes the hypothesized order-restricted model, H_0 is a more restrictive alternative obtained by transforming the inequality restrictions into equality restrictions, and H_2 is a less restrictive alternative that is obtained by omitting the inequality restrictions. This could, for instance, be non-negative local odds-ratios (H_1), independence (H_0), and the saturated model (H_2). The two tests of interest are between H_0 and H_1 and between H_1 and H_2. Such tests can be performed using standard likelihood-ratio statistics. The corresponding statistics, $L^2_{1|0}$ and $L^2_{2|1}$, are defined as

$$L^2_{1|0} = 2 \sum_{ij} n_{ij} \ln \left(\frac{\hat{\pi}_{j|i(1)}}{\hat{\pi}_{j|i(0)}} \right)$$

$$L^2_{2|1} = 2 \sum_{ij} n_{ij} \ln \left(\frac{\hat{\pi}_{j|i(2)}}{\hat{\pi}_{j|i(1)}} \right),$$

where $\hat{\pi}_{j|i(0)}$, $\hat{\pi}_{j|i(1)}$, and $\hat{\pi}_{j|i(2)}$ denote the estimated probabilities under H_0, H_1, and H_2, respectively.

A complication in using these test statistics is, however, that they are not asymptotically χ^2 distributed. Wollan (1985) has shown that the above two test statistics follow chi-bar-squared distributions, which are weighted sums of chi-squared distributions, when H_0 holds (see Robertson, Wright, and Dykstra, 1988:321).

Let l_{max} denote the number of inequality constraints, or the maximum number of activated constraints, and df_0 the number of degrees of freedom under H_0. The p-values for $L^2_{1|0}$ and $L^2_{2|1}$ are approximated as follows

$$P(L^2_{1|0} \geq c) \approx \sum_{l=0}^{l_{max}} P(l)P(\chi^2_{(df_0-l)} \geq c)$$

$$P(L^2_{2|1} \geq c) \approx \sum_{l=0}^{l_{max}} P(l)P(\chi^2_{(l)} \geq c) \quad,$$

that is, as the sum over all the possible numbers of active constraints of the probability of the corresponding number of constraints times the asymptotic p-value concerned.

A problem is encountered however, when computing the $P(l)$'s, which depend on the maximum number of constraints, a vector of weights $\mathbf{w}$—in our case the observed frequencies—and the type of order restrictions that is used. For simple order restrictions, the $P(l)$'s can be computed analytically up to $l_{max} = 5$. Robertson, Wright, and Dykstra (1988) reported $P(l)$ tables for $1 \leq l_{max} \leq 19$, assuming uniform weights $\mathbf{w}$ and simple order restrictions. Simulation studies by Grove (1980) and Robertson, Wright, and Dykstra (1988) showed that the uniform weights assumption does not seriously distort the results when testing whether multinomials are stochastically ordered.

Rather than combining asymptotic results with an approximation of the $P(l)$'s, it is also possible to determine the p-values for the test statistics using parametric bootstrapping methods, which are also known as Monte Carlo studies. This very simple method, which is based on an empirical reconstruction of the sampling distributions of the test statistics, is the one followed here. Ritov and Gilula (1993) proposed such a procedure in ML correspondence analysis with ordered category scores. Schoenberg (1997) advocated using bootstrap testing methods in a general class of constrained maximum-likelihood problems. Langeheine, Pannekoek, and Van de Pol (1996) proposed using bootstrapping in categorical data analysis for dealing with sparse tables, which is another situation in which we cannot rely on asymptotic theory for the test statistics. Agresti and Coull (1996) used Monte Carlo studies in combination with exact tests to determine the goodness-of-fit of order-restricted binary logit models that were estimated with a small sample.

In the $L^2_{1|0}$ case, T frequency tables with the same number of observations as the original observed table are simulated from the estimated probabilities under H_0. For each of these tables, we estimate the models defined by H_0 and H_1 and compute the value of $L^2_{1|0}$. This yields an empirical approximation of the distribution of $L^2_{1|0}$. The estimated p-value is the proportion of simulated tables with an $L^2_{1|0}$ at least as large as for the original table. The standard error of the estimated p-value equals $\sqrt{p(1-p)/T}$. The bootstrap procedure for $L^2_{2|1}$ differs only from the above one in that frequency tables have to be simulated from the estimated probabilities of the order-restricted maximum-likelihood solution—that is, H_1.[4]

A simulation study by Ritov and Gilula (1993) showed that parametric bootstrapping yields reliable results when applied in order-restricted correlation models, which are special cases of the models presented in this paper. To further assess the performance of bootstrapping, the examples for which Grove (1980) and Robertson, Wright, and Dykstra (1988:234–39) reported multinomial likelihood-ratio tests based on asymptotic chi-bar-squared distribution were replicated. For these examples, the bootstrapped p-values were very close to the reported asymptotic p-values. It should be noted that although bootstrapping seems to work well in these situations, it is not clear at all how the method performs when applied to sparse tables.

6. EXAMPLES

This section discusses four situations in which the nonparametric ordinal models presented in this paper may be useful. The first example is a continuation of the bivariate example presented in Section 2. The second example illustrates the use of inequality restrictions in logit regression models for ordinal dependent and independent variables. The third example focuses on marginal models for longitudinal data subject to partial nonresponse. The last example deals with latent class models for ordinal items.

6.1. Association Between Two Ordinal Variables

In Section 2, some parametric and nonparametric models were presented for the 5-by-3 cross-classification of number of siblings (S) and happiness

---

[4]As was noted by one of the reviewers, in the $L^2_{2|1}$ case, the bootstrap is not estimating the p-value corresponding to the chi-bar-squared distribution. The chi-bar-squared approximation of $P(L^2_{2|1} \geq c)$ requires that H_0 holds, which means that it yields what could be called the least favorable p-value. On the other hand, the empirical bootstrap approximation of the distribution of $L^2_{2|1}$ holds under H_1, which is more in agreement with standard tests.

(H) reported in Table 1. More precisely, we specified independence (A.1), cumulative logit (A.2), row-column association (A.3), row association (A.4), column association (A.5), and uniform association (A.6) models, as well as a model assuming nonincreasing cumulative probabilities (A.7) and a model assuming local odds ratios of at least 1 (A.8).

The models presented so far for this two-way table are either parametric or nonparametric. There is, however, another interesting class of models for this type of data—that is, models that combine parametric with nonparametric features, such as order-restricted variants of the row-column, row, and column association models. According to the assumed measurement level of the row and the column variables, these three models could be labeled as ordinal-ordinal, ordinal-interval, and interval-ordinal, respectively.

The order-restricted RC model fits the data quite well:[5] $L^2_{A.9} = 8.36$, $p \approx .08$. While in the unrestricted RC model, the scores for rows 3 and 4 and for columns 1 and 2 were out of order. In the order-restricted ML solution, only one equality restriction is imposed: the score for column 1 is equated to the score for column 2. This demonstrates again that it is dangerous to specify ordinal models by *post hoc* equality constraints.

Since the unrestricted row association model (A.4) fits badly, it is not surprising that the order-restricted R model fits very badly too ($L^2_{A.10} = 18.60, p \approx .00$). In the ML solution for this model, the estimated scores for rows 5 and 6 are equated. On the other hand, the ordinal C model fits very well ($L^2_{A.11} = 8.84, p \approx .22$). The ML solution for this model contains one activated constraint: the parameters belonging to the first two columns are equated.

On the basis of these results, it can be concluded that the relationship between number of siblings and happiness can be described by means of a (partially) nonparametric ordinal model. The two nonparametric models, as well as the order-restricted RC and C models, fit the data quite well. The most parsimonious model that fits the data is the order-restricted C model. This indicates that the row variable, number of siblings (S), may be treated as an interval level variable with equal-interval scored categories, while the column variable, happiness (H), should be treated as an ordinal.

---

[5]It should be noted that this model cannot be specified with the linear or loglinear constraints presented in this paper. It was estimated with a modified version of the PAVA-like procedure proposed by Ritov and Gilula (1991) which is described in detail in an accompanying paper (Vermunt 1998).

6.3. *Logit Regression Models for Ordinal Variables*

This example uses the data reported in Clogg (1982, table 2). The table concerns a 4-by-5-by-3 cross-classification of the ordinal variables years of schooling (Y), number of siblings (S), and happiness (H).[6] We treat happiness (H) as a dependent variable and years of schooling (Y) and number of siblings (S) as independent variables. In fact, we are interested in modeling the probability that $H = h$ given that $Y = y$ and $S = s$, denoted by $\pi_{h|ys}$. With this example we want to illustrate the use of order restrictions in the context of a logit model with ordinal dependent and independent variables.

The test results for the estimated logit models are reported in Table 4. A standard multinomial logit analysis treating each of the three variables as nominal shows that the three-variable interaction is not significant $(L^2_{B.1} = 24.88, df = 24, p = .41)$. In addition, the test results for Models B.2 and B.3 indicate that both independent variables have a significant effect on happiness.

The usual way of dealing with the fact that Y, S, and H are ordinal variables within the framework of logit analysis is the assignment of *a priori* scores to the levels of Y, S, and H. This yields linear-by-linear (partial) associations, or, in the case equal-interval scoring, uniform associations for the YH and SH interactions. Note that such an approach actually assumes that we are dealing with interval level variables. The model that further restricts Model B.1 by assuming uniform two-way interactions does not fit at all: $L^2_{B.4} = 54.58, df = 36, p = .02$.

An alternative way of specifying an ordinal logit model is by means of inequality restrictions on the conditional local odd ratios—that is, $\theta_{hy|s} \leq 1$ and $\theta_{hs|y} \geq 1$. This is a way of formulating that Y has a negative effect on H within each level of S and that S has a positive effect on H within each level of Y. If we also want to exclude the three-variable interaction term, we need the additional constraint $\theta_{hy|s} = \theta_{hy|s+1}$. The model, which combines these log-linear equality and inequality constraints, fits well $(L^2_{B.5} = 35.30, p \approx .35)$. The conclusion could be that the partial effects of Y and S on H are ordinal and equal across levels of the other explanatory variable.

---

[6]The original table in Clogg (1982) is a 3-by-4-by-5 table. For convenience here, another order between the variables is used.

6.3. *Marginal Models for Partially Missing Longitudinal Data*

This example illustrates the use of marginal models with linear (in)equality constraints in the context of longitudinal data. In addition, it demonstrates the possibility to deal with partially missing data. The data, which are taken from the 1986-1987 SIPP panel, concern measurements of a person's employment status at four time points, where each time point is separated by three months.[7] Employment status is classified into two categories: employed and not employed. A complication in the analysis of this data is that for many subjects in the sample there is missing information. More precisely, for 28 percent of the 6754 cases, information on the employment status is missing for one or more time points. In addition, except for observing only the first and the last time point, all possible missing data patterns are present in the sample. The nonzero observed frequencies are reported in Table 5.

We are interested in studying the trend in the employment rate over the four periods. Suppose that because of macroeconomic conditions one expects a monotonically increasing employment rate during the observation period. As will be shown below, the data are not fully in agreement with such a trend, which may, however, be the result of sampling error.

Since this paper does not deal with missing data mechanisms, we will just assume an ignorable, missing at random (MAR), missing data mechanism (Little and Rubin 1987). For the partially observed SIPP data, four marginal models were estimated: a saturated, a marginal homogeneity, a nondecreasing marginal, and a linearly changing marginal model. The test results are presented in Table 4.

According to the saturated model, which of course fits perfectly, the estimated marginal probabilities of being employed at each of the four time points are .587, .607, .599, and .605, respectively. This indicates that there is a small increase in the number of employed individuals during the observation period. The increase is, however, not monotonic. The marginal homogeneity model tests whether the observed differences between the time points are significant. The bad fit of this model ($L_{C.1}^2 = 22.36$, $df = 3$, $p < .01$) shows that this is the case. The third model assumes that the marginal probability of being employed is nondecreasing between con-

---

[7]For more information about this data set, see Vermunt (1997:216 and 286–87). Here, we use only the information on the first four of the six panel waves.

TABLE 5
Observed Response Patterns with Frequencies from SIPP Panel

Pattern	Frequency	Pattern	Frequency	Pattern	Frequency
1 1 1 1	2447	1 1 1 2	114	1 1 2 1	75
1 1 2 2	79	1 2 1 1	87	1 2 1 2	9
1 2 2 1	22	1 2 2 2	84	2 1 1 1	147
2 1 1 2	31	2 1 2 1	41	2 1 2 2	80
2 2 1 1	103	2 2 1 2	36	2 2 2 1	61
2 2 2 2	1450	1 1 1 0	106	1 1 2 0	9
1 2 1 0	8	1 2 2 0	5	2 1 1 0	8
2 1 2 0	5	2 2 1 0	3	2 2 2 0	75
1 1 0 1	38	1 1 0 2	3	1 2 0 1	5
1 2 0 2	3	2 1 0 1	4	2 2 0 1	7
2 2 0 2	23	1 1 0 0	103	1 2 0 0	15
2 1 0 0	24	2 2 0 0	99	1 0 1 1	14
1 0 1 2	4	1 0 2 1	1	1 0 2 2	1
2 0 1 1	3	2 0 2 1	1	2 0 2 2	18
1 0 1 0	5	2 0 2 0	7	1 0 0 0	183
2 0 0 0	155	0 1 1 1	70	0 1 2 1	7
0 1 2 2	7	0 2 1 1	8	0 2 1 2	7
0 2 2 1	2	0 2 2 2	40	0 1 1 0	19
0 1 2 0	3	0 2 1 0	3	0 2 2 0	13
0 1 0 1	3	0 1 0 0	39	0 2 0 0	28
0 0 1 1	65	0 0 1 2	2	0 0 2 1	17
0 0 2 2	56	0 0 1 0	26	0 0 2 0	16
0 0 0 1	89	0 0 0 2	64	0 0 0 0	369

Note: 0 = missing; 1 = employed; 2 = not employed.

secutive time points. This model, which has one activated constraint, fits quite well ($L^2_{C.2} = 3.17, p \approx 07$). As might be expected on the basis of the marginal distribution from the saturated model, the inequality constraint concerning the second and third time point is activated, which means that in the ML solution the marginal distributions of these time points are equated. And finally, a model was estimated with a linear change in the number of employed. As can be seen, this model is too restrictive: $L^2_{C.3} = 13.73, df = 2, p < .01$.

6.4. *Latent Class Models for Ordinal Items*

The last example illustrates the use of the nonparametric approach in the context of latent class models for ordinal items. For this purpose, we use a

4-by-4-by-4 cross-tabulation of three extrinsic job satisfaction items used by Shockey (1988) in a paper on latent class analysis (see also Hagenaars 1998). The three ordinal items measure an individual's satisfaction with job security (S), pay (P), and fringe benefits (B). The levels of the items are (1) not at all true, (2) a little true, (3), somewhat true, and (4) very true. The latent variable will be denoted by W.

For the three-way classification, different types of latent class models are specified, each having the general form

$$\pi_{wspb} = \pi_w \pi_{s|w} \pi_{p|w} \pi_{b|w} \; . \tag{19}$$

The models, which are all four class models, differ with respect to the restrictions that are imposed on the conditional response probabilities $\pi_{s|w}$, $\pi_{p|w}$, and $\pi_{b|w}$. The test results are reported in Table 4.

As reported by Shockey (1988), the unrestricted latent class model with four latent classes fits the job satisfaction data very well: $L_{D.1}^2 = 15.11$, $df = 24$, $p = .92$. When using such a standard latent class model, there is, however, no guarantee that the latent classes are ordered. By ordered, we mean that the higher the latent class the more satisfied one becomes with each of the job items. In this context, it also means that the latent variable is unidimensional. The linear and log-linear equality and inequality constraints proposed in this paper can be used to impose such an ordinal structure on the relationships between the latent variable and the indicators. More precisely, they can be used to further restrict the conditional response probabilities $\pi_{s|w}$, $\pi_{p|w}$, and $\pi_{b|w}$.

The most restricted model that is used is a four-class model in which the WS, WP, and WB interactions are assumed to be uniform. This model does not provide a good description of the data: $L_{D.2}^2 = 115.79$, $df = 48$, $p < .01$. A less restrictive model is obtained by using column associations for the WS, WP, and WB interactions, with the items as column variables. This means that the latent variable is treated as interval level and the items as nominal. Although the category scores for each of the indicators have the expected order, the model fits badly: $L_{D.3}^2 = 105.86$, $df = 42$, $p < .01$.

It is also possible to use the nonparametric ordinal specifications in the context of latent class analysis. One interesting type of assumption is that each of the cumulative response probabilities, $F_{s|w}$, $F_{p|w}$, and $F_{b|w}$, is stochastically ordered, which means that they have to be restricted as described in equation (8). This yields the ordinal latent class model proposed by Croon (1990). Another option is to use log-linear inequality constraints on the local odds ratios θ_{ws}, θ_{wp}, and θ_{wb} (see equation 13). The former specifications yield a well-fitting model ($L^2_{D.4} = 15.55$, $p \approx .96$). Actually, the unrestricted four-class model was already very close to this solution. This can be seen from the fact that the L^2 values of the nominal and the ordinal model are almost identical and, in addition, that only 2 of the 36 inequality constraints need to be activated in the ordinal model. Although the four-class model with nonnegative local log-odds ratios does not perform as well as the other ordinal model, it also fits the data quite well: $L^2_{D.5} = 39.20$, $p \approx .34$. The ML solution for this ordinal latent class model contains 16 activated constraints, which means that 16 estimated local odds ratios are equal to one.

Table 6 reports the estimated latent class probabilities π_w, as well as the estimated cumulative conditional probabilities according to Model D.4. As can be seen, the restriction imposed is that the probability that an individual selects a particular item category or lower decreases or remains equal as w increases. This is one way of expressing a positive relationship

TABLE 6
Parameter Estimates for Model D.4
(Order-Restricted Latent Class Model)

	$W = 1$	$W = 2$	$W = 3$	$W = 4$
π_w	0.16	0.17	0.37	0.30
$F_{b\mid w}$	$S = 1$	$S = 2$	$S = 3$	$S = 4$
$W = 1$	0.61	*0.76	0.95	1.00
$W = 2$	0.16	*0.76	0.94	1.00
$W = 3$	0.03	0.17	0.85	1.00
$W = 4$	0.03	0.09	0.34	1.00
$F_{c\mid w}$	$P = 1$	$P = 2$	$P = 3$	$P = 4$
$W = 1$	0.45	0.62	0.86	1.00
$W = 2$	*0.04	0.46	0.81	1.00
$W = 3$	*0.04	0.13	0.70	1.00
$W = 4$	0.02	0.08	0.18	1.00
$F_{b\mid w}$	$B = 1$	$B = 2$	$B = 3$	$B = 4$
$W = 1$	0.75	0.87	0.98	1.00
$W = 2$	0.22	0.70	0.95	1.00
$W = 3$	0.08	0.22	0.79	1.00
$W = 4$	0.02	0.03	0.19	1.00

Note: A '*' indicates an activated constraint.

between the latent variable and the items. Only two inequality constraints are activated in the reported ML solution.

This example showed that nonparametric ordinal restrictions may yield well-fitting and easy to interpret latent class models. The log-linear latent class models with uniform and column association structures were much too restrictive, while the results obtained by unrestricted latent class analyses may be difficult to interpret.

7. DISCUSSION

This paper described a general nonparametric approach for dealing with ordinal categorical data, which is based on specifying linear or log-linear inequality constraints on (conditional) probabilities. Several types of ordinal models can be defined with the proposed inequality constraints. In addition, inequality constraints can be combined with equality constraints, which makes it possible to define models that combine nonparametric with parametric features, such as order-restricted row association models, ordinal row-column correlation models, and ordinal regression models in which higher-order interaction terms are omitted.

A simple estimation method was proposed that performs very well in most situations. Implementation of this unidimensional Newton method in the M step of the EM algorithm makes it possible to use the ordinal restrictions when there is partially missing data or when the model contains one or more latent variables. The difficulties associated with goodness-of-fit testing in models with inequality constraints were overcome by using bootstrap or Monte Carlo methods rather than relying on asymptotic distribution functions. The proposed estimation algorithm and testing procedure perform well in the analysis of tables that are not too sparse.

The examples showed that in most situations truly ordinal models fit much better than models in which *a priori* scores are assigned to the categories of the ordinal variables. In addition, these ordinal models do not have the interpretation problems associated with quasi-ordinal models, in which estimated category scores may be out of order.

A possible extension of the approach proposed here is the application of inequality constraints in extended log-linear models (Lang and Agresti 1994; Bergsma 1997). This would yield new types of ordinal models, such as cumulative logit models for ordinal independent variables, ordinal models for global odds ratios, and ordinal models for a general class of association measures. For this purpose, the saddle point algorithm proposed by Bergsma (1997), which is a generalization of the algorithm proposed by Lang and Agresti (1994), should be transformed into an active set method.

Another interesting direction for future research is the use of Bayesian approaches for estimating parameters and assessing fit of nonparametric ordinal models for categorical data. Some work has already been done on this subject by Agresti and Chuang (1986); Evans et al. (1997); Hoijtink and Molenaar (1997); McDonald and Prevost (1997).

APPENDIX A: OPTIMIZATION UNDER (IN)EQUALITY CONSTRAINTS

Suppose we have to find the value of a set of parameters γ that maximizes a function $f(\gamma)$ under the following r equality constraints:

$$h_1(\gamma) = 0, h_2(\gamma) = 0, \ldots, h_r(\gamma) = 0 . \tag{20}$$

This is a standard constraint optimization problem that can be solved by finding the saddle point of the Lagrange function

$$k(\gamma, \lambda) = f(\gamma) + \sum_{i=1}^{r} \lambda_i h_i(\gamma) , \tag{21}$$

where the λ_i's are called Lagrange parameters. This objective function contains, besides the γ parameters of interest, a set of parameters corresponding to the constraints. It should be noted that the saddle point of $k(\gamma, \lambda)$ is the maximum of $f(\gamma)$ under the above equality constraints.

The saddle point of the Lagrange function is the point in the parameter space at which the first derivatives to all parameters are equal to zero, in this case,

$$\frac{\partial k(\gamma, \lambda)}{\partial \gamma_j} = \frac{\partial f(\gamma)}{\partial \gamma_j} + \sum_{i=0}^{r} \lambda_i \frac{\partial h_i(\gamma)}{\partial \gamma_j} = 0 \tag{22}$$

$$\frac{\partial k(\gamma, \lambda)}{\partial \lambda_i} = h_i(\gamma) = 0 . \tag{23}$$

As can be seen, the second set of conditions corresponds to the constraints that we want to impose. The first set is the modification of the standard condition $\partial f(\gamma)/\partial \gamma_j = 0$ resulting from the imposed constraints. The solution to these equations can be found using standard algorithms, such as Fisher scoring, Newton-Raphson, or unidimensional Newton.

When some of the constraints have the form of inequalities, $h_i(\gamma) \geq 0$, the situation is slightly different. In that case, we have to formulate the additional condition that $\lambda_i \geq 0$. Actually, this condition guarantees that the constraint $h_i(\gamma) = 0$ is imposed only if the unrestricted $h_i(\gamma)$ is smaller than 0. In other words, the inequality restriction concerned is activated, which means that the corresponding equality restriction is imposed only if it is violated.

In optimization under inequality constraints, one may also refer to the Kuhn-Tucker conditions. These state that an optimum of $f(\gamma)$ under the inequality constraints $h_i(\gamma) \geq 0$ satisfies the following four conditions:

1. $h_i(\gamma) \geq 0$
2. $(\partial f(\gamma)/\partial \gamma_j) + \sum_{i=0}^{r} \lambda_i(\partial h_i(\gamma)/\partial \gamma_j) = 0$
3. $\lambda_i \geq 0$
4. $\lambda_i h_i(\gamma) = 0.$

The first condition states that inequality restrictions should be fulfilled. The second corresponds to setting the first derivative of the Lagrange function to zero for all γ_j's. The third is the above-mentioned condition with respect to the sign of the Lagrange parameters. The fourth condition is automatically fulfilled because, depending on whether a constraint is inactive or active, either λ_i or $h_i(\gamma)$ will be equal to zero.

As in the case of equalities, standard algorithms can be used for finding the optimum of $f(\gamma)$ under the specified inequality constraints. The only necessary modification is that at each iteration cycle it must be checked which inequalities should be activated and which should be deactivated. This is exactly what is done by so-called active set methods. A possible implementation is the following. Start with all λ_i's equal to zero. Each iteration cycle consists of two steps: (1) determine the active set of constraints, and (2) update the γ_j's, as well as the λ_i's belonging to the active set of constraints. Step 1 involves deactivating the constraints that are no longer necessary, which correspond with λ_i's smaller than zero, and activating constraints that are violated, which correspond with gradients indicating that the λ_i's will become larger than zero. Note that we are in fact checking the first and third Kuhn-Tucker conditions.[8]

---

[8]McDonald and Diamond (1983) gave an overview of methods that can be used to determine the active set in the estimation on generalized linear models with linear inequality constraints.

APPENDIX B: THE EM ALGORITHM FOR MODELS WITH (IN)EQUALITY CONSTRAINTS

The linear and log-linear (in)equality constraints described in this paper can also be applied when there are missing data or latent variables. This can be accomplished by implementing the active set variant of the unidimensional Newton method in an EM algorithm.

In the E step of the EM algorithm, we have to calculate the expectation of the complete data, given the observed data and the current parameter estimates. The M step involves estimating the "parameters" of interest, treating the expectation of the observed data as if it were the observed data. This means that a single M step has the same form as ML estimation with fully observed data. The EM algorithm cycles between the E step and the M step until convergence.

Suppose we are interested in the estimation of a model with stochastically ordered marginal distributions for three-wave panel data. The variable of interest at the three points in time is denoted by A, B, and C. What we are interested in is obtaining estimates for the probabilities π_{abc} under the linear inequality constraint $F_{a..} \geq F_{.a.} \geq F_{..a}$. Suppose that respondents may have missing values on B, on C, or on both B and C. In other words, there is a subgroup for which we observe A, B, and C, a subgroup for which we observe A and B, a subgroup for which we observe A and C, and a subgroup for which we observe A. The cell entries in the frequency tables for these four subgroups are denoted by n_{abc}, n_{ab}, n_{ac}, and n_a, respectively.

The E step of the tth iteration cycle involves computing the expected value of the complete data, $\hat{n}_{abc}$, in the following way:

$$\hat{n}_{abc}^{(t)} = n_{abc} + n_{ab}\,\hat{\pi}_{c|ab}^{(t-1)} + n_{ac}\,\hat{\pi}_{b|ac}^{(t-1)} + n_a\,\hat{\pi}_{bc|a}^{(t-1)} \ . \tag{24}$$

Note that the $\hat{\pi}$'s are computed from the estimated probabilities from the previous iteration $(t-1)$. In the M step, new $\hat{\pi}_{abc}^{(t)}$ are obtained with the active set method described in Section 4 using $\hat{n}_{abc}^{(t)}$ as observed frequencies.

Another example of the implementation of the EM algorithm concerns an order-restricted latent class model. Suppose we have a latent class model with a single latent variable X and three indicators A, B, and C. The model has the form

$$\pi_{xabc} = \pi_x\,\pi_{a|x}\,\pi_{b|x}\,\pi_{c|x} \ , \tag{25}$$

in which the probabilities $\pi_{a|x}$, $\pi_{b|x}$, and $\pi_{c|x}$ are assumed to fulfil some kind of order restriction—for instance, that all local odds are at least 1.

The E step of tth EM cycle involves obtaining the expectation of the complete data, $\hat{n}_{xabc}^{(t)}$, by

$$\hat{n}_{xabc}^{(t)} = n_{abc} \, \hat{\pi}_{x|abc}^{(t-1)} \; . \tag{26}$$

In the M step, new order-restricted estimates $\hat{\pi}_{a|x}^{(t)}$, $\hat{\pi}_{b|x}^{(t)}$, and $\hat{\pi}_{c|x}^{(t)}$ can be obtained by using $\hat{n}_{xa..}^{(t)}$, $\hat{n}_{x.b.}^{(t)}$, and $\hat{n}_{x..c}^{(t)}$ as data in the standard restricted ML procedure described in Section 4.

REFERENCES

Agresti, A., and C. Chuang. 1986. "Bayesian and Maximum Likelihood Approaches to Order Restricted Inference for Models from Ordinal Categorical Data." Pp. 6–27 in *Advances in Ordered Statistical Inference*, edited by R. Dykstra and T. Robertson. Berlin: Springer-Verlag.

Agresti, A., C. Chuang, and A. Kezouh. 1987. "Order-Restricted Score Parameters in Association Models for Contingency Tables." *Journal of the American Statistical Association* 82:619–23.

Agresti, A., and B. A. Coull. 1996. "Order-Restricted Tests for Stratified Comparisons of Binomial Proportions. *Biometrics* 52:1103–11.

Bergsma, W. P. 1997. *Marginal Models for Categorical Data*. Tilburg, Netherlands: Tilburg University Press.

———. 1998. *A Note on Maximum Likelihood Methods for Log-Linear Models When Expected Cell Frequencies Are Subject to Linear Constraints*. Research note, Tilburg University.

Clogg, C. C. 1982. "Some Models for the Analysis of Association in Multi-way Cross-classifications Having Ordered Categories." *Journal of the American Statistical Association* 77:803–15.

Clogg, C. C., and S. R. Eliason. 1987. "Some Common Problems in Log-Linear Analysis." *Sociological Methods and Research* 16:8–14.

Clogg, C. C., and E. S. Shihadeh. 1994. *Statistical Models for Ordinal Data*. Thousand Oaks, CA: Sage.

Croon, M. A. 1990. "Latent Class Analysis with Ordered Latent Classes." *British Journal of Mathematical and Statistical Psychology* 43:171–92.

———. 1991. "Investigating Mokken Scalability of Dichotomous Items by Means of Ordinal Latent Class Analysis." *British Journal of Mathematical and Statistical Psychology* 44:315–31.

De Leeuw, J., and P. G. M. Van der Heijden. 1991. "Reduced Rank Models for Contingency Tables." *Biometrika* 8:229–32.

Dempster, A. P., N. M. Laird, and D. B. Rubin. 1977. "Maximum Likelihood Estimation from Incomplete Data via the EM Algorithm (with discussion). *Journal of the Royal Statistical Society*, ser. B, 39:1–38.

Dykstra, R. L., and J. H. Lemke. 1988. "Duality of I Projections and Maximum-Likelihood Estimation for Log-Linear Models under Cone Constraints." *Journal of the American Statistical Association* 83:546–54.

Evans, M., Z. Gilula, I. Guttman, and T. Swartz. 1997. "Bayesian Analysis of Stochastically Ordered Distributions of Categorical Variables." *Journal of the American Statistical Association* 92:208–14.

Fahrmeir, L., and J. Klinger. 1994. "Estimating and Testing Generalized Linear Models Under Inequality Restrictions." *Statistical Papers* 35:211–29.

Gill, P. E., and W. Murray. 1974. *Numerical Methods for Constrained Optimization.* London: Academic Press.

Gill, P. E., W. Murray, and M. H. Wright. 1981. *Practical Optimization.* London: Academic Press.

Gilula, Z., and S. J. Haberman. 1988. "The Analysis of Contingency Tables by Restricted Canonical and Restricted Association Models." *Journal of the American Statistical Association* 83:760–71.

Goodman, L. A. 1979. "Simple Models for the Analysis of Association in Cross-Classifications Having Ordered Categories." *Journal of the American Statistical Association* 74:537–52.

———. 1986. "Some Useful Extensions of the Usual Correspondence Analysis Approach and the Usual Log-Linear Approach in the Analysis of Contingency Tables." *International Statistical Review* 54:243–309.

Grizzle, J. E., C. F. Starmer, and G. G. Koch. 1969. "Analysis of Categorical Data by Linear Models." *Biometrics* 25:489–504.

Grove, D. M. 1980. "A Test of Independence Against a Class of Ordered Alternatives in a 2 × C Contingency Table." *Journal of the American Statistical Association* 75:454–59.

Haber, M., and M. B. Brown. 1986. "Maximum Likelihood Methods for Log-Linear Models When Expected Frequencies Are Subject to Linear Constraints." *Journal of the American Statistical Association* 81:477–82.

Haberman, S. J. 1979. *Analysis of Qualitative Data.* Vol. 2, *New Developments.* New York: Academic Press.

Hagenaars, J. A. 1998. "Categorical Causal Modeling: Directed Log-Linear Models with Latent Variables." *Sociological Methods and Research* 23:436–86.

Hoijtink, H., and I. W. Molenaar. 1997. "A Multidimensional Item Response Model: Constrained Latent Class Analysis Using the Gibbs Sampler and Posterior Predictives." *Psychometrika* 62:171–90.

Lang, J. B., and A. Agresti. 1994. "Simultaneously Modeling Joint and Marginal Distributions of Multivariate Categorical Responses." *Journal of the American Statistical Association* 89:625–32.

Langeheine, R., J. Pannekoek, and F. Van de Pol. 1996. "Bootstrapping Goodness-of-Fit Measures in Categorical Data Analysis." *Sociological Methods and Research* 24:492–516.

Little, R. J., and D. B. Rubin. 1987. *Statistical Analysis with Missing Data.* New York: Wiley.

McDonald, J. W., and I. Diamond. 1983. "Fitting Generalised Linear Models with Linear Inequality Parameter Constraints." *Glim Newsletter* (June 1983):29–36.

McDonald, J. W., and A. T. Prevost. 1997. "The Fitting of Parameter-Constrained Demographic Models." *Mathematical Computation and Modelling* 26:79–88.

Ritov, Y., and Z. Gilula. 1991. "The Order-Restricted RC Model for Ordered Contingency Tables: Estimation and Testing for Fit." *The Annals of Statistics* 19:2090–101.

———. 1993. "Analysis of Contingency Tables by Correspondence Models Subject to Order Constraints." *Journal of the American Statistical Association* 88:1380–87.

Robertson, T., F. T. Wright, and R. L. Dykstra. 1988. *Order Restricted Statistical Inference.* Chichester, England: Wiley.

Schafer, J. L. 1997. *Analysis of Incomplete Multivariate Data.* London: Chapman and Hall.

Schoenberg, R. 1997. "CML: Constrained Maximum-Likelihood Estimation." *The Sociological Methodologist* (Spring 1997):1–8.

Shockey, J. 1988. "Latent Class Analysis: An Introduction to Discrete Data Models with Unobserved Variables." In *Common Problems in Quantitative Research,* edited by J. S. Long. Newbury Park, CA: Sage.

Vermunt, J. K. 1997. *Log-linear Models for Event Histories.* Thousand Oaks: Sage.

———. 1998. *RC Association Models with Ordered Row and Column Scores: Estimation and Testing.* Paper presented at the annual conference of the Society for Multivariate Analysis in the Behavioral Sciences, Leuven, Belgium, July 13–15, 1998.

Wollan, P. C. 1985. "Estimation and Hypothesis Testing Under Inequality Constraints." Ph.D. dissertation, University of Iowa.

⚜ 7 ⚜

TESTING TRANSITIVITY IN DIGRAPHS

Martin Karlberg *

The problem of testing the transitivity of a relationship observed in a digraph, taking as many nontransitivity related irregularities as possible into account, is studied. Two test quantities are used: (1) the proportion of transitive triples out of all nonvacuously transitive triples, and (2) the density difference (the difference between mean local transitivity density and overall edge density). The null distribution used is the rather complex uniform distribution on digraphs conditional on the indegrees and outdegrees. A simulation study is made in order to estimate critical values of the tests for different significance levels. When all vertices have the same indegree and outdegree, the occurrence of transitive triples is rather infrequent in most conditional uniform graphs; this is reflected by low critical values of the transitivity-related test statistics. When both the indegree and outdegree sequences are skewed in the same direction, there is a small number of vertices with large indegrees and outdegrees. This results in a clustering structure, in which transitive triples occur frequently; in such conditional uniform graphs, the critical values of the test statistics are rather high.

The powers of the tests are estimated against the Bernoulli transitive triple model, which assumes a simple random graph distribution in which the transitivity is high. The test based on density difference has the highest power in many cases. The tests are applied to a large set of classroom sociograms, and in this situation it is also found that uniform randomness is rejected in favor of transitivity most frequently when the test based on the density difference is used. However, the vast majority of these sociograms are so

The major part of this research was financed by the Department of Statistics at Stockholm University.
*Astra Arcus AB, Södertälje, Sweden

225

*far from the uniform distribution that the null hypothesis of uni-
form randomness is rejected regardless of which test is used. Nevertheless, the results imply that the density difference is the best
detector of transitivity related to the measures examined.*

1. INTRODUCTION

That transitivity in social networks is common, or, in the words of Davis,
Holland, and Leinhardt (1971), that "Interpersonal choices tend to be
transitive—if P chooses O and O chooses X, then P is likely to choose X,"
is a rather well-established fact. Wasserman and Faust (1994) discuss transitivity at length, stating that evidence has accumulated that transitivity is
indeed a compelling force in the organization of social groups. However,
numerous kinds of interpersonal relations are not transitive; whether a
certain kind of relationship is transitive must be confirmed, typically by
some kind of test.

Tests of transitivity hypotheses have been carried out for digraphs
by Holland and Leinhardt (1970,1975), who create indices of transitivity
and intransitivity using the observed counts of transitive and intransitive
triples of a social network, normalizing the counts using the expected values and variances under the uniform distribution (conditional on the null,
asymmetric, and mutual dyad counts); in the social networks examined,
the null hypothesis of uniform distribution is rejected due to high transitivity (and low intransitivity) in the majority of cases.

The testing of transitivity in undirected graphs is studied by Karlberg (1997), who in addition to triad-based transitivity indices uses the
densities of ego networks; in the social networks studied, the null hypothesis of uniform distribution is frequently rejected, both when using these
densities and when using the triad-based transitivity indices.

The purpose of this paper is to facilitate the testing of transitivity in
digraphs by performing a similar study for the digraph case. When testing
transitivity, it is undesirable that nontransitivity related irregularities in the
graph observed—such as a skewed degree distribution—lead to the rejection of the null hypothesis, although the graph does not have more transitivity than what is to be expected from the expansiveness/popularity
structure observed. This is avoided by conditioning on as many of those
irregularities as possible.

Wasserman (1977) summarizes many of the conditional uniform
distributions by plotting them after they have been arranged with respect

to the amount of conditioning made. Close to the top of the plot is the rather complex conditional uniform distribution of all graphs with the same indegrees and outdegrees. When Holland and Leinhardt (1970, 1975) tested transitivity, they were forced to refrain from using this highly nontrivial distribution, since no simple way was known for generating random graphs according to it; they merely conditioned on the numbers of null, asymmetric, and mutual dyads. Since then, Snijders (1991) has developed an algorithm (outlined in Section 3) for generating random graphs with fixed indegrees and outdegrees, which can be easily used to examine the properties of this conditional uniform distribution. Here, we make use of this algorithm by letting this conditional uniform distribution be our structural null hypotheses when testing transitivity; the large-scale application of this complex null distribution to transitivity testing is the most prominent contribution made in this paper to the previous research, in which (by necessity) considerably more trivial null distributions have been used.

Various triad- and triple-based indices of transitivity are provided in the literature for both undirected graphs (for instance, see Frank and Harary 1982) and digraphs (see Holland and Leinhardt 1970). We will consider two procedures—one test based on triple counts and one test based on local transitivity densities—for determining whether a graph is likely to be a realization of some transitive random graph distribution rather than of the uniform distribution conditional on both indegrees and outdegrees. In Section 2 we introduce the notation used in this paper, and proceed to define the two test statistics.

Transitive triples will obviously be more frequent in graphs with high transitivity than in uniform graphs, whereas the frequency of intransitive triples will be lower. We will therefore use the proportion of transitive triples out of all potentially transitive triples (i.e., the triples that are either transitive or intransitive) as the test quantity of the first of our tests. For example, this measure is used by Frank (1980), who expresses it as a ratio between linear combinations of triad counts.

Another measure of transitivity is the ego-network-based mean local transitivity density, which, as it is defined in Section 2, should not be high in relation to the overall edge density of the graph if the graph has no transitivity tendency. We will consequently use the density difference (the difference between the mean local transitivity density and the overall edge density) as the test quantity in our second test.

Due to the lack of formulas for the expected values and variances of our test quantities under the rather complex null distribution, we cannot provide even approximate formulas for the critical values of the tests treated. We have instead undertaken a simulation study, which is summarized in Section 3, in which critical values have been estimated for various combinations of indegree and outdegree sequences.

If we want to decide which of the tests is most suitable in a given situation, we would like to know how likely the test is to reject the null hypothesis of no transitivity, if the graph has been generated by some transitivity model. Karlberg (1997) uses the Bernoulli triangle model, which is a special case of the random hypergraph as described by Karoński and Luczak (1996); we define the Bernoulli transitive triple model, a digraph version of that model, in Section 4. This model is based on transitive triples and consequently generates graphs with a strong transitivity tendency. The results of another simulation study, in which we estimate the powers of the tests against the Bernoulli transitive triple model, are given in Section 5. The test based on the density difference is found to be the most powerful for the larger graphs, whereas the test based on the proportion of transitive triples out of all potentially transitive triples is often the most powerful one when graphs of a lower order are examined.

In Section 6, we apply the tests to a large set of classroom sociograms taken from the Metropolitan study presented by Janson (1975a, 1984). Karlberg (1997) uses these sociograms to create undirected graphs and is thus forced to symmetrize the originally directed friendship choices, although the data in the original digraph form may be used. Due to this, and the fact that a more complex distribution is used, our findings differ from the ones obtained for undirected graphs. We find that the null hypothesis of no transitivity is rejected in most cases at extremely low levels of significance regardless of which test is used. When there are differences between the tests, the test based on the density difference is the best one at detecting transitivity. In order to determine whether the extremely high rejection rates depend on the fact that the numbers of mutual dyads in most of the observed networks differ considerably from those in the random graphs, we also examine some of the smallest sociograms by applying the transitivity tests to them while using the even more complex uniform distribution over all graphs with fixed degree sequences and a fixed number of mutual dyads as the structural null hypothesis. When using this null distribution, slightly lower rejection rates are noted. We also discuss the potential benefit of a distribution under which not only the numbers of mutual dyads but the entire mutual-degree sequence of the vertices are fixed. The results are summarized in Section 7.

2. THE TRANSITIVITY TESTS

2.1. *Notation*

Let $G = (V, E)$ be a digraph without loops on the vertex set $V = \{1, \ldots v\}$, where v, the order of the graph, is known. If we let $V_{(k)}$ denote the class of all k-sequences (with no repetitions) of elements from V, we have for E, the edge set of G, that $E \subseteq V_{(2)}$. The elements of $\mathbf{X}$, the corresponding $v \times v$ adjacency matrix of G, are given by

$$x_{ij} = \begin{cases} 1 & \text{if } (i,j) \in E \\ 0 & \text{otherwise.} \end{cases}$$

We denote the size of the graph, which is the same as the number of edges, by

$$r = |E| = \sum_{i=1}^{v} \sum_{\substack{j=1 \\ j \neq i}}^{v} x_{ij} \ .$$

Letting $v_{(k)}$ denote $k!\binom{v}{k}$, we define the (edge) density of G, as

$$\Delta_E = \frac{r}{v_{(2)}} \ .$$

We define the outdegree and indegree of vertex i as

$$x_{i+} = \sum_{j=1}^{v} x_{ij}$$

and

$$x_{+i} = \sum_{j=1}^{v} x_{ji} \ ,$$

respectively. Further, we let

$$m_i = \sum_{j=1}^{v} x_{ij} x_{ji}$$

denote the number of mutual dyads adjacent to vertex i. The sequences of outdegrees and indegrees are denoted by

$$\mathbf{X}_{\bullet+} = (x_{1+}, \ldots, x_{v+})$$

and

$$\mathbf{X}_{+\bullet} = (x_{+1}, \ldots, x_{+v}) \ ,$$

respectively.

Consider a triple (i, j, k) of vertices from V in which there are edges from i to j and from j to k. Since the premises for transitivity are thus fulfilled in this triple, it is said to be potentially transitive. If there is an edge from i to k in a potentially transitive triple (i, j, k), it is said to be transitive; otherwise, it is said to be intransitive. The triples in which the premises are not fulfilled (and therefore neither can support a transitivity hypothesis by being transitive or contradict it by being intransitive) are said to be vacuously transitive.

The number of transitive triples in G is denoted by

$$T = |\{(i, j, k) \in V_{(3)} : (i, j), (j, k), (i, k) \in E\}|$$

$$= |\{(i, j, k) \in V_{(3)} : x_{ij} = x_{jk} = x_{ik} = 1\}| = \sum_{\substack{i=1 \\ j \neq i}}^{v} \sum_{\substack{j=1 \\ i \neq k \neq j}}^{v} \sum_{k=1}^{v} x_{ij} x_{jk} x_{ik}$$

and the number of intransitive triples is denoted by

$$I = |\{(i, j, k) \in V_{(3)} : (i, j), (j, k) \in E, (i, k) \notin E\}|$$

$$= \sum_{\substack{i=1 \\ j \neq i}}^{v} \sum_{\substack{j=1 \\ i \neq k \neq j}}^{v} \sum_{k=1}^{v} x_{ij} x_{jk} (1 - x_{ik}) \ ;$$

these sums are given, for example, by Fershtman (1985). We let the transitivity index

$$\Delta_T = \begin{cases} \dfrac{T}{I + T} & \text{if } I + T > 0 \\ 0 & \text{otherwise} \end{cases}$$

denote the proportion of transitive triples out of all potentially transitive triples.

2.2. *The Conditional Uniform Model*

As our stochastic null distribution, we will use $U(\mathbf{X}_{\bullet+},\mathbf{X}_{+\bullet})$—i.e., the uniform distribution conditional on the indegree and outdegree sequences, referred to as the $U|\{X_{i+}\},\{X_{+j}\}$ model by Holland and Leinhardt (1975). We let $N(\mathbf{x}_{\bullet+},\mathbf{x}_{+\bullet})$ denote the number of graphs for which $\mathbf{X}_{\bullet+} = \mathbf{x}_{\bullet+}$ and $\mathbf{X}_{+\bullet} = \mathbf{x}_{+\bullet}$. Under the $U(\mathbf{x}_{\bullet+},\mathbf{x}_{+\bullet})$ distribution, all graphs with those indegree and outdegree sequences have the same probability; the probability of a graph with the adjacency matrix $\mathbf{X}$ is defined as

$$
P(\mathbf{X}|\mathbf{X}_{\bullet+},\mathbf{X}_{+\bullet}) = \begin{cases} \dfrac{1}{N(\mathbf{x}_{\bullet+},\mathbf{x}_{+\bullet})} & \text{if } \mathbf{X}_{\bullet+} = \mathbf{x}_{\bullet+} \text{ and } \mathbf{X}_{+\bullet} = \mathbf{x}_{+\bullet} \\ 0 & \text{otherwise.} \end{cases}
$$

This distribution is discussed already by Katz and Powell (1954, 1957), who provide the formula for $N(\mathbf{x}_{\bullet+},\mathbf{x}_{+\bullet})$, but until recently, when Snijders (1991) developed an algorithm for generating random graphs with fixed indegree and outdegree sequences, it has not been possible to examine this distribution in detail. According to Wasserman and Faust (1994), however, it is extremely important in social network analysis, since it can be used to control statistically for both choices made by each actor (which in the data that we use in Section 6 are fixed in the experimental design) and choices received. As demonstrated by Wasserman and Faust (1994), distinctly different conclusions on the structure of a friendship network may be drawn, depending on the structural null hypothesis one adopts; when the reciprocity in the advice network of Krackhardt (1987) was tested using $U(\mathbf{X}_{\bullet+})$ (i.e., the uniform distribution conditional on the outdegree sequence) as the null distribution, the null hypothesis was not rejected, whereas when the $U(\mathbf{X}_{\bullet+},\mathbf{X}_{+\bullet})$ null distribution was used, the null hypothesis was rejected, since the number of mutual dyads was significantly greater than the expected number under the null distribution. When testing transitivity, it is equally wise to condition on both the expansiveness and the popularity of the actors of a network; if we do not, we may for instance find a high rate of transitivity that is an artifact of the popularity structure, or fail to discover that the transitivity observed is high when taking the popularity into account.

We thus use the hypothesis that G has been generated according to the $U(\mathbf{X}_{\bullet+},\mathbf{X}_{+\bullet})$ model as the null hypothesis in our transitivity tests. Generally, $N(\mathbf{x}_{\bullet+},\mathbf{x}_{+\bullet})$ can assume extremely large values since it increases faster than exponentially as $v \to \infty$ (cf. Snijders 1991), so when we in Sections 3 and 6 estimate the critical values of the test statistics under this distribution, we sample from the $U(\mathbf{X}_{.+}, \mathbf{X}_{+.})$ distribution instead of examining all graphs with outdegrees $\mathbf{x}_{.+}$ and indegrees $\mathbf{x}_{+.}$.

2.3. Testing Transitivity Using the Proportion of Transitive Triples

The alternative hypothesis of our transitivity tests is that G has been generated according to some transitivity model. Graphs generated according to a transitivity model are obviously more likely to have a higher proportion of transitive triples than random uniform graphs, whereas the proportion of intransitive triples is likely to be smaller. We therefore consider Test 1, which will reject the null hypothesis if the proportion of transitive triples (out of the potentially transitive triples) is high—that is, when

$$\Delta_T > c_{1;\alpha} \ ,$$

where $c_{1;\alpha}$ is the critical value of Test 1 at the significance level α.

2.4 Testing Transitivity Using Local Transitivity Densities

Like Karlberg (1998), we define the supported set of vertex i—that is, the vertices it is adjacent to, as

$$\alpha_i = \{ j : x_{ij} = 1 \} \ .$$

In the same manner, we define the supporting set of vertex i as

$$\beta_i = \{ j : x_{ji} = 1 \} \ .$$

We refer to $\alpha_i \cup \beta_i$ as the local set of vertex i. Obviously, $|\alpha_i| = x_{i+}$, $|\beta_i| = x_{+i}$, and $|\alpha_i \cup \beta_i| = x_{i+} + x_{+i} - m_i$. If we for two arbitrary vertex sets A and B denote the number of edges that go from members of A to members of B by

$$R(A, B) = \sum_{i \in A} \sum_{j \in B} x_{ij} \ ,$$

we may express the local transitivity r_i, the number of transitive triples in which vertex i is involved as

$$r_i = \sum_{\substack{j=1 \\ j \neq i}}^{v} \sum_{\substack{k=1 \\ i \neq k \neq j}}^{v} (x_{ij} x_{jk} x_{ik} + x_{jk} x_{ki} x_{ji} + x_{ji} x_{ik} x_{jk})$$

$$= \sum_{\substack{j=1 \\ j \neq i}}^{v} \sum_{\substack{k=1 \\ i \neq k \neq j}}^{v} (x_{ij} x_{ik} + x_{ki} x_{ji} + x_{ji} x_{ik}) x_{jk}$$

$$= R(\alpha_i, \alpha_i) + R(\beta_i, \beta_i) + R(\beta_i, \alpha_i) \ .$$

Each term of the local transitivity thus reflects one of the three aspects of transitivity: (1) friendship between individuals that are chosen by ego, (2) friendship between individuals that choose ego, and (3) direct friendship between individuals who are joined by a path via ego of length two. Each transitive triple (i, j, k) thus occurs in the local transitivity of each of the three vertices i, j and k, and consequently

$$\sum_{i=1}^{v} r_i = \sum_{i=1}^{v} \sum_{\substack{j=1 \\ j \neq i}}^{v} \sum_{\substack{k=1 \\ i \neq k \neq j}}^{v} (x_{ij} x_{jk} x_{ik} + x_{jk} x_{ki} x_{ji} + x_{ji} x_{ik} x_{jk}) = 3T \ .$$

This relationship is similar to the one (for undirected graphs) in Karlberg (1997) between the local size measure and the number of transitive triads.

We define δ_i, the local transitivity density of vertex i, as the local transitivity of i divided by the largest possible local transitivity of i given x_{i+}, x_{+i}, and m_i—that is,

$$\delta_i = \begin{cases} \dfrac{r_i}{(x_{i+})_{(2)} + (x_{+i})_{(2)} + x_{i+} x_{+i} - m_i} & \text{if } |\alpha_i \cup \beta_i| > 1 \\[2em] \dfrac{r - x_{i+} - x_{+i}}{(v-1)_{(2)}} & \text{otherwise.} \end{cases}$$

The denominator of the first ratio is equal to zero if $|\alpha_i \cup \beta_i| \leq 1$, which explains the need for another definition of δ_i in that situation. By defining δ_i as above, instead of, for example, just setting it to 0, the expected local transitivity density will be, as we show below, equal to the expected overall edge density in a couple of rather common random digraph models.

Let us first consider the Bernoulli distribution (described by Wasserman and Faust 1994, for example), where all edges (i, j) of the digraph are assumed to be independent Bernoulli(p_{ij}) random variables, and let us assume that the p_{ij} are equal to a certain p for all i and j. When the local set is larger than one, the local transitivity density δ_i simply measures the proportion of edge positions that are occupied out of the $(x_{i+})_{(2)} + (x_{+i})_{(2)} + x_{i+}x_{+i} - m_i$ positions considered; due to the independent identical distribution of the edges, the expected value of this proportion is equal to p. If the local set is of size 0 or 1, δ_i is equal to the edge density in the subgraph of G induced by $V - \{i\}$; the expected density of this graph is obviously p as well. We thus obtain

$$E(\delta_i | x_{i+}, x_{+i}, m_i) = p$$

and consequently

$$E(\delta_i) = E(E(\delta_i | x_{i+}, x_{+i}, m_i)) = E(p) = p = E(\Delta_E) \ ,$$

i.e., that the expected local transitivity density is equal to the expected overall edge density.

If we now consider the uniform distribution for all graphs of the size r (cf. for instance Wasserman and Faust 1994), we see that, given x_{i+} and x_{+i}, there are $r - x_{i+} - x_{+i}$ edges left to distribute in the $(v-1)_{(2)}$ edge positions between the members of $V - \{i\}$. The expected local transitivity is thus equal to

$$E(r_i | x_{i+}, x_{+i}, m_i) = ((x_{i+})_{(2)} + (x_{+i})_{(2)} + x_{i+}x_{+i} - m_i) \frac{r - x_{i+} - x_{+i}}{(v-1)_{(2)}} \ .$$

Using the above definition of δ_i, we obtain

$$E(\delta_i | x_{i+}, x_{+i}, m_i) = \frac{r - x_{i+} - x_{+i}}{(v-1)_{(2)}} \ ,$$

from which it follows that

$$E(\delta_i) = E(E(\delta_i | x_{i+}, x_{+i}, m_i)) = E\left(\frac{r - x_{i+} - x_{+i}}{(v-1)_{(2)}} \right)$$

$$= \frac{\Delta_E v_{(2)} - 2\Delta_E(v-1)}{v_{(2)} - 2(v-1)} = \Delta_E \ .$$

This differs from the result obtained for the Bernoulli model only in that the edge density is invariant and hence always equals its expected value.

A natural way of summarizing the local transitivity densities of G is the mean local transitivity density,

$$\bar{\delta} = \frac{1}{v} \sum_{i=1}^{v} \delta_i .$$

Under the Bernoulli and uniform (for all graphs of the same size) models, we obviously see that

$$E(\bar{\delta}) = \frac{1}{v} \sum_{i=1}^{v} E(\delta_i) = E(\Delta_E) .$$

By choosing the above definition of δ_i, the expected mean local transitivity density is thus equal to the expected edge density in at least two rather common random graph models. However, under the $U|\mathbf{X_{.+}}, \mathbf{X_{+.}}$ distribution, $\bar{\delta}$ is not different from most other nontrivial statistics in the sense that its expected value cannot be calculated. However, graphs that are more transitive than graphs likely to be generated by the conditional uniform distribution will, since the mean local transitivity density in essence is an increasing function of the numbers of transitive triples in which the vertices are involved, in general have a mean local transitivity density that is greater than the one expected under the conditional uniform distribution. We may thus consider Test 2, in which the null hypothesis of uniform randomness is rejected in favor of the alternative hypothesis of transitivity if the mean local transitivity density exceeds the overall edge density too much—that is, if

$$\bar{\delta} - \Delta_E > c_{2;\alpha} ,$$

where $c_{2;\alpha}$ is the α-level critical value of Test 2. In the sequel, we will refer to $\bar{\delta} - \Delta_E$ as the density difference.

3. CRITICAL VALUES

In this section, we will examine the distribution of the test statistics for different parameters of the null distribution. We will for each of the graph orders $v = 10,20,30$ study four different kinds of indegree and outdegree sequence combinations: (1) when both sequences are constant, (2) when one sequence is skewed and one is constant, (3) when both are skewed in different directions, and (4) when both are skewed in the same direction.

For each of the three orders, we have selected r so that it is a multiple of v (while the overall edge density is as close to .25 as possible); the average degree is thus an integer. We have defined the degrees in $D_{v;0}$, the constant degree sequence corresponding to order v, to all be equal to r/v. The degrees of the corresponding increasing sequence, $D_{v;+}$, which is divided into homogeneous fifths, range from $r/v - 2$ to $r/v + 2$. The corresponding decreasing degree sequence, $D_{v;-}$, is obtained by reversing $D_{v;+}$. The nonconstant sequences all have variance 2; the relative impact of the skewness (i.e., the variation coefficient of the degree sequence) thus decreases with the graph order. The nine different degree sequences (three for each value of v considered) are given in Table 1.

We have used the simulation algorithm of Snijders (1991) in order to generate random graphs with fixed $\mathbf{X}_{\cdot+}$ and $\mathbf{X}_{+\cdot}$. In essence, this algorithm generates random graphs using a stepwise procedure, where an initially empty adjacency matrix is filled; a randomized decision is taken for every matrix entry that is not fixed by the marginal conditions (i.e., that the sequence of row sums must be equal to the sequence of outdegrees and the sequence of column sums must be equal to the sequence of indegrees). Since the graphs generated according to this algorithm have unequal probabilities (proportional to the product of the probabilities of the randomized decisions), we have to adjust for these probabilities (by weighting each generated graph by its inverse probability) when estimating the critical values under the $U(\mathbf{x}_{\cdot+}, \mathbf{x}_{+\cdot})$ distribution.

For each combination of $\mathbf{x}_{\cdot+}$ and $\mathbf{x}_{+\cdot}$, we have generated $10\,000$ random graphs $G_1, \ldots, G_{10000}$ with these outdegree and indegree sequences,

TABLE 1
The Degree Sequences Used in the Simulation Study

Sequence Symbol	Sequence
$D_{10;-}$	(4,4,3,3,2,2,1,1,0,0)
$D_{10;0}$	(2,2,2,2,2,2,2,2,2,2)
$D_{10;+}$	(0,0,1,1,2,2,3,3,4,4)
$D_{20;-}$	(7,7,7,7,6,6,6,6,5,5,5,5,4,4,4,4,3,3,3,3)
$D_{20;0}$	(5,5,5,5,5,5,5,5,5,5,5,5,5,5,5,5,5,5,5,5)
$D_{20;+}$	(3,3,3,3,4,4,4,4,5,5,5,5,6,6,6,6,7,7,7,7)
$D_{30;-}$	(9,9,9,9,9,9,8,8,8,8,8,8,7,7,7,7,7,7,6,6,6,6,6,6,5,5,5,5,5,5)
$D_{30;0}$	(7,7,7,7,7,7,7,7,7,7,7,7,7,7,7,7,7,7,7,7,7,7,7,7,7,7,7,7,7,7)
$D_{30;+}$	(5,5,5,5,5,5,6,6,6,6,6,6,7,7,7,7,7,7,8,8,8,8,8,8,9,9,9,9,9,9)

recording for each random graph G_i the probability $P(G_i)$ that it will be generated by the algorithm used. In order to estimate $c_{k;\alpha}$, the critical value of Test k at a given significance level α, we have then sought a value $\hat{c}_{k;\alpha}$ such that the test statistic of Test k exceeds $\hat{c}_{k;\alpha}$ in a subset A of the 10 000 random graphs for which

$$\sum_{i \in A} \frac{1}{P(G_i)} = \alpha \sum_{i=1}^{10\,000} \frac{1}{P(G_i)} .$$

The estimates of the critical values of the two transitivity tests are given in Table 2.

Since the test statistics are discrete, we may—in particular in graphs with few edges, in which the number of possible values of each test statistic is low—have trouble finding critical values at the desired significance level. This problem could be worked around by randomized testing (cf. Pratt and Gibbons 1981), but in this paper we will take the conserva-

TABLE 2

Estimated Critical Values of the Two Transitivity Tests for Different Values of the Outdegree Sequence $\mathbf{x}_{.+}$, the Indegree Sequence $\mathbf{x}_{+.}$, and the Significance Level α^*

		Test					
		1			2		
		α			α		
$\mathbf{x}_{.+}$	$\mathbf{x}_{+.}$	.10	.05	.01	.10	.05	.01
$D_{10;0}$	$D_{10;0}$	.118	.139	.188	−.058	−.020	.035
$D_{10;+}$	$D_{10;-}$	.400	.444	.500	.021	.028	.085
$D_{10;+}$	$D_{10;0}$	.206	.235	.278	.060	.091	.156
$D_{10;+}$	$D_{10;+}$	.380	.400	.458	.205	.245	.293
$D_{20;0}$	$D_{20;0}$	.205	.210	.220	−.034	−.028	−.018
$D_{20;+}$	$D_{20;-}$	.245	.251	.263	−.018	−.013	−.002
$D_{20;+}$	$D_{20;0}$	.224	.229	.240	−.019	−.014	−.001
$D_{20;+}$	$D_{20;+}$	.246	.252	.264	.015	.021	.035
$D_{30;0}$	$D_{30;0}$	.200	.203	.209	−.025	−.021	−.015
$D_{30;+}$	$D_{30;-}$	.219	.222	.228	−.018	−.014	−.008
$D_{30;+}$	$D_{30;0}$	.210	.213	.219	−.017	−.014	−.008
$D_{30;+}$	$D_{30;+}$	.219	.222	.229	−.004	.000	.007

*10 000 random graphs were generated for each combination of the indegree and outdegree sequences.

tive approach, using a nonrandomized test with a critical value that makes the exact significance level as close to α as possible without exceeding α.

As we see from Table 2, the critical values are generally at their lowest (given the order, test, and significance level) when both $\mathbf{x}_{\cdot+}$ and $\mathbf{x}_{+\cdot}$ are not skewed, and at their highest when those sequences are skewed in the same direction. This is most likely a consequence of the clustering that occurs when a small number of vertices have both high indegrees and high outdegrees; many edges go between these vertices, and consequently the probability of transitive triples increases considerably in the subgraph of G induced by these vertices.

For Test 1, the highest critical values are sometimes obtained when $\mathbf{x}_{\cdot+}$ and $\mathbf{x}_{+\cdot}$ are skewed in different directions. This may be due to the fact that while T is smaller when $D_{v;+}$ and $D_{v;-}$ are used (compared with when $D_{v;+}$ and $D_{v;+}$ are used), I may also be smaller, in which case the ratio Δ_T is not affected in any particular direction.

For Test 2, the critical values are negative for many $\mathbf{x}_{\cdot+}$ and $\mathbf{x}_{+\cdot}$ parameters; for the conditional uniform distributions with those parameters, the overall edge density thus exceeds the mean local transitivity density in the bulk of the cases. This could be contrasted with the Bernoulli and uniform (over all graphs of the same size) models, in which the expected difference (although not necessarily the median difference) between the two types of densities is zero.

4. A TRANSITIVITY MODEL

Before we estimate the powers of the tests, we need an alternative random graph model against which we can test the uniform model. For this purpose, we define the Bernoulli transitive triple model below, in which transitive triples are the basic elements. Simply put, under this model, edges and transitive triples are randomly thrown into an initially empty graph; a Bernoulli "noise" of random edges is thus added to the basic transitive triple structure. The Bernoulli transitive triple model can be regarded as a digraph version of the Bernoulli triangle model of Karlberg (1997).

Consider an adjacency matrix $\mathbf{X}$ of a random graph, in which, for all ordered vertex pairs $(i,j) \in V_{(2)}$,

$$x_{ij} = 1 - (1 - e_{ij}) \prod_{\substack{k=1 \\ i \neq k \neq j}}^{v} (1 - t_{ijk})(1 - t_{ikj})(1 - t_{kij}) \ .$$

The e_{ij}:s are called edge indicators and the t_{ijk}:s are called transitive triple indicators; all these indicators are either 0 or 1. There is an edge between

i and j if and only if the edge indicator e_{ij}, or any of the $3(v - 2)$ transitive triple indicators involving (i, j), is nonzero. We assume that the indicators are independently Bernoulli(p_E) and Bernoulli(p_T) distributed, respectively, and we refer to p_E as the edge probability and to p_T as the transitive triple probability.

One way for us to generate a graph according to this model is to begin by generating a Bernoulli(p_E) graph, as in Wasserman and Faust (1994). We then proceed to generate t_{ijk} for each $(i, j, k) \in V_{(3)}$ and, if the outcome of t_{ijk} is 1, set x_{ij}, x_{jk}, and x_{ik} to 1, regardless of the previous values of these matrix elements. The expected density of the entire graph is equal to the expected edge density of any vertex pair $(i, j) \in V_{(2)}$:

$$E(\Delta_E) = P(x_{ij} = 1) = 1 - P(e_{ij} = 0) \prod_{\substack{k=1 \\ i \neq k \neq j}}^{v} P(t_{ijk} = t_{ikj} = t_{kij} = 0)$$

$$= 1 - q_E \prod_{\substack{k=1 \\ i \neq k \neq j}}^{v} q_T^3$$

$$= 1 - q_E q_T^{3(v-2)} \ ,$$

where $q_E = 1 - p_E$ and $q_T = 1 - p_T$.

For compactness, we define, for all triples $(i, j, k) \in V_{(3)}$, the indicator

$$\pi_{ij;k} = 1 - (1 - e_{ij}) \prod_{\ell \in V - \{i,j,k\}} (1 - t_{ij\ell})(1 - t_{i\ell j})(1 - t_{\ell ij}) \ ;$$

$\pi_{ij;k}$ is thus equal to 1 if any indicator involving the ordered vertex pair (i, j) but not involving vertex k is equal to 1. Any vertex triple $(i, j, k) \in V_{(3)}$ will be transitive if the transitive triple indicator t_{ijk} for that particular triple is equal to 1. It will also be transitive if all members of an appropriate combination of indicators corresponding to one or two of (i, j), (i, k), and (j, k) are equal to one—i.e., if (i) $t_{ikj} = t_{jik} = 1$, (ii) $t_{ikj} = 1$ and $(1 - t_{jki}) \times (1 - \pi_{jk;i}) = 0$, (iii) $t_{jik} = 1$ and $(1 - t_{kij})(1 - \pi_{ij;k}) = 0$, or (iv) $(1 - t_{jki}) \times (1 - \pi_{jk;i}) = 0$, $(1 - t_{kij})(1 - \pi_{ij;k}) = 0$, and $\pi_{ik;j} = 1$. Thus the probability of the triple (i, j, k) being transitive is equal to

$$E(T/v_{(3)}) = P((i, j), (j, k), (i, k) \in E)$$

$$= p_T + q_T(p_T^2 + 2p_T q_T(p_T + q_T \Pi) + q_T^2(p_T + q_T \Pi)^2 \Pi)$$

where $\Pi = 1 - q_E q_T^{3(v-3)}$ denotes the probability of an indicator of the type $\pi_{ij;k}$ being equal to 1; this relationship is more complicated than the corresponding one of Karlberg (1997), where it was easy to estimate the model parameters with the method of moments, using the edge and transitive triad densities of the observed undirected graph.

Assume that we want the expected density to be equal to some value δ_E. The maximum possible value of p_T would then be $1 - (1 - \delta_E)^{1/3(v-2)}$. We can express the parameter p_T in terms of the ratio between its actual value and its maximum possible value (given δ_E) by replacing it by a transitivity parameter τ, defined according to

$$p_T = \tau(1 - (1 - \delta_E)^{1/3(v-2)}) \ .$$

It thus follows that $0 \leq \tau \leq 1$. Since the parameter p_E is given by p_T and δ_E as

$$p_E = \frac{1 - \delta_E}{(1 - p_T)^{3(v-2)}} \ ,$$

this reparameterization of the model enables us to express it in terms of the desired density δ_E and the transitivity parameter τ. One should note that $E(\Delta_T/v_{(3)})$ is not necessarily a monotonically increasing function of τ (we can thus not exclude the possibility that there may be more than one value of τ that, given δ_E, yields the same expected value of $\Delta_T/v_{(3)}$). However, generally, a value of τ close to 1 implies that $E(\Delta_T/v_{(3)})$ is high.

The advantage of the Bernoulli transitive triple model is that it, like the Bernoulli triangle model of Karlberg (1997), is a very simple two-parameter model under which random graphs may be generated in a straightforward way, despite the fact that the expected proportion of transitive relationships can become rather high in relation to the expected density of the network.

5. POWER AGAINST TRANSITIVITY

We are now able to estimate the powers of the tests against transitivity, using the Bernoulli transitive triple model as our transitivity model. For each combination of $\mathbf{x}_{.+}$ and $\mathbf{x}_{+.}$, we have generated 10 000 random graphs according to the Bernoulli transitive triple model. We have then estimated the test power against the Bernoulli transitive triple model by simply computing the proportion of random graphs with test statistics exceeding the critical values obtained in Section 3; these powers are listed in Table 3.

From this table, we see that Test 2 is the most powerful one in the majority of cases, particularly for those graphs with no skewed degree sequences and in the larger graphs (for which the relative impact of the skewed degree sequences is smaller). For the smaller graphs, particularly for the graphs with skewed degree sequences, Test 1 is often the most powerful one. For each combination of test, v, τ and α, the power is the highest when $x_{\bullet+} = x_{+\bullet} = D_{v;0}$, and virtually always the lowest when $x_{\bullet+} = x_{+\bullet} = D_{v;+}$; this is the inevitable consequence of the pattern in Table 2, where the critical values are at their lowest when both degree sequences are equal to $D_{v;0}$, and (except for Test 1 when $v = 10$) at their highest when both degree sequences are equal to $D_{v;+}$ (in which case clustering, and thereby a large number of transitive triples, is already present in the null distribution). For both tests, the power, as expected, increases with τ, but the ranking of the tests with respect to power is rarely affected by this parameter.

6. APPLICATION TO CLASSROOM SOCIOGRAMS

6.1. *The Metropolitan Networks*

We will now see how the tests of transitivity behave when they are applied to actual data instead of Bernoulli transitive triple graphs. For this purpose, we have used classroom sociograms from the longitudinal study Project Metropolitan presented by Janson (1975a, 1984). In 1966, Project Metropolitan conducted the School Study, an extensive survey of youths in sixth form (born in 1953) in the Stockholm metropolitan area. Among the questions (listed in Janson 1975b) was one sociometric question, asking the children to select their three best friends in class. Several studies of the network structure of the data from this classroom survey have been performed, and some are described by Dahlbäck (1982), Stütz (1985), Pearson (1994), Jansson (1997), and Karlberg (1997).

From the sociogram data of each school class, we have constructed the adjacency matrix X so that x_{ij} is equal to 1 if pupil i has chosen pupil j as a friend and 0 otherwise. For the 554 school classes that we have data on, the number of pupils per school class ranges between 10 and 32. Due to the restriction on the number of choices, the edge densities of the school

TABLE 3

Estimated Powers Against the Bernoulli Transitive Triple Model with Transitivity Parameter τ of the Two Transitivity Tests for Different $U(\mathbf{X}_{.+}, \mathbf{X}_{+.})$ Null Distributions and Different Significance Levels α^*

					v										
				10				20				30			
				τ				τ				τ			
α	$\mathbf{x}_{.+}$	$\mathbf{x}_{+.}$	Test	.25	.50	.75	.95	.25	.50	.75	.95	.25	.50	.75	.95
.01	$D_{v;0}$	$D_{v;0}$	1	.73	.88	.97	1.00	.94	.98	.99	1.00	.98	.99	1.00	1.00
			2	.51	.76	.94	.99	.94	.99	1.00	1.00	.99	1.00	1.00	1.00
	$D_{v;+}$	$D_{v;-}$	1	.01	.02	.06	.13	.67	.81	.91	.96	.86	.95	.98	.99
			2	.29	.54	.81	.94	.79	.95	.99	1.00	.95	1.00	1.00	1.00
	$D_{v;+}$	$D_{v;0}$	1	.39	.59	.79	.92	.85	.93	.97	.99	.94	.98	.99	1.00
			2	.09	.23	.50	.76	.78	.95	.99	1.00	.95	1.00	1.00	1.00
	$D_{v;+}$	$D_{v;+}$	1	.02	.06	.14	.25	.65	.80	.90	.96	.86	.95	.98	.99
			2	.00	.01	.07	.23	.23	.52	.80	.93	.66	.92	.99	1.00
.05	$D_{v;0}$	$D_{v;0}$	1	.86	.95	.99	1.00	.97	.99	1.00	1.00	.99	1.00	1.00	1.00
			2	.77	.93	.99	1.00	.98	1.00	1.00	1.00	1.00	1.00	1.00	1.00
	$D_{v;+}$	$D_{v;-}$	1	.03	.07	.17	.29	.77	.88	.95	.98	.91	.97	.99	1.00
			2	.55	.79	.95	.99	.91	.99	1.00	1.00	.99	1.00	1.00	1.00

$D_{v;+}$	$D_{v;0}$	1	.56	.74	.91	.98	.91	.96	.99	1.00	.96	.99	1.00	1.00
		2	.27	.51	.79	.93	.92	.99	1.00	1.00	.98	1.00	1.00	1.00
$D_{v;+}$	$D_{v;+}$	1	.06	.15	.29	.46	.77	.87	.95	.98	.91	.97	.99	1.00
		2	.01	.04	.17	.41	.41	.72	.92	.98	.84	.98	1.00	1.00
.10	$D_{v;0}$ $D_{v;0}$	1	.90	.96	.99	1.00	.98	.99	1.00	1.00	.99	1.00	1.00	1.00
		2	.90	.98	1.00	1.00	.99	1.00	1.00	1.00	1.00	1.00	1.00	1.00
	$D_{v;+}$ $D_{v;-}$	1	.06	.15	.29	.46	.81	.91	.96	.99	.93	.98	.99	1.00
		2	.59	.81	.96	.99	.95	.99	1.00	1.00	.99	1.00	1.00	1.00
	$D_{v;+}$ $D_{v;0}$	1	.67	.83	.95	.99	.93	.97	.99	1.00	.97	.99	1.00	1.00
		2	.40	.65	.89	.97	.95	.99	1.00	1.00	.99	1.00	1.00	1.00
	$D_{v;+}$ $D_{v;+}$	1	.09	.20	.38	.56	.81	.90	.96	.99	.93	.98	.99	1.00
		2	.03	.10	.29	.57	.53	.81	.96	.99	.90	.99	1.00	1.00

*For each combination of outdegrees $\mathbf{x}_{\cdot+}$, indegrees $\mathbf{x}_{+\cdot}$, and transitivity parameter τ, 10 000 random Bernoulli transitive triple graphs have been used.

classes are generally equal to $3/(v - 1)$, in some classes slightly lower, since some pupils made fewer than three choices.

6.2. Results When Conditioning on Indegrees and Outdegrees

Since the number of choices made is fixed in the design, it is virtually mandatory to use a random distribution that conditions on the outdegree sequence to control for this—for instance, by using the uniform distribution conditional on the outdegrees. In order to also capture deviations in transitivity due to the school class popularity structures (and to facilitate comparison with the previous section), we have used the $U(\mathbf{X}_{.+}, \mathbf{X}_{+.})$ distribution as the null distribution. For each of the 554 Metropolitan school classes, we generated 1000 random graphs with degree sequences equal to the observed ones, using the algorithm of Snijders (1991).

For both tests, we can regard the proportion of uniform graphs with test statistic values greater than the test statistics of the observed graph as an estimate of the p-value (the smallest significance level at which the null hypothesis is rejected) of the test for that particular graph. Since the random graphs generated have unequal probabilities, we estimate the p-values by

$$\hat{p} = \sum_{i=1}^{1000} \frac{W_i}{P(G_i)} \bigg/ \sum_{i=1}^{1000} \frac{1}{P(G_i)} \, ,$$

where W_i is equal to 1 if the test statistic of G_i exceeds the one in the observed sociogram (and 0 otherwise). The distribution of the 554 p-value estimates of Tests 1 and 2 for the Metropolitan graphs is shown in Table 4.

As we see from Table 4, the smallest p-values are extremely frequent for both tests. The ranking of the tests is still the same as for the Bernoulli transitive triple graphs of the previous section—i.e., at a given significance level, the null hypothesis of conditional uniform distribution is rejected most frequently when Test 2 is used. One might argue that since the null hypothesis is rejected for a huge proportion of the graphs regardless of the test used, the choice of test is of no interest.

However, Test 1 does not reject the null hypothesis at the 5 percent level of significance for three (0.7 percent) of the Metropolitan networks, whereas Test 2 rejects the null hypothesis for all Metropolitan networks at that level. The density difference gives larger relative impact to transitive triples that are adjacent to vertices with small local sets (than to transitive

TABLE 4

Distribution of the 554 Estimates of p-Values for the Metropolitan Graphs Under the Null Hypothesis of $U(\mathbf{X}_{.+}, \mathbf{X}_{+.})$ Distribution

	Number of Metropolitan Graphs			
	Absolute Frequency Test		Relative Frequency Test	
Estimated p-Value	1	2	1	2
$\hat{p} > 10\%$	3	0	0.005	0.000
$5\% < \hat{p} \leq 10\%$	1	0	0.002	0.000
$1\% < \hat{p} \leq 5\%$	7	0	0.013	0.000
$0\% < \hat{p} \leq 1\%$	10	2	0.018	0.004
$\hat{p} = 0\%$	533	552	0.962	0.996
Total	554	554	1.000	1.000

triples adjacent to vertices with large local sets). The common denominator of these three Metropolitan networks may be that although the transitive triples are not extremely large in number, they are distributed so that they generally are adjacent to vertices with small local sets. When a social network analyst is about to test the transitivity of a relationship observed in such social networks (i.e., networks consisting of both small, close-knit, groups of pupils and larger groups of pupils with a more "normal" transitivity pattern), the generally high rejection rate of Test 1 is of little comfort; the analyst would indisputably be better off using Test 2 instead, since if there is a departure in transitivity from the conditional uniform distribution, the detection of it would be virtually certain if Test 2 is used at the 5 percent significance level.

6.3. Conditioning on the Total Number of Mutual Relationships

It would be interesting to see whether a random graph distribution controlling for even more of the not directly transitivity-related irregularities would result in a different distribution of the p-values. A conceivable candidate is the $U(\mathbf{X}_{.+}, \mathbf{X}_{+.}, M)$ distribution, under which, in addition to the outdegree and indegree sequences,

$$M = \sum_{i=1}^{v} \sum_{j=i+1}^{v} x_{ij} x_{ji} \; ,$$

—i.e., the number of mutual dyads—is fixed. This distribution is, as Wasserman (1977) states, perhaps the most important distribution in sociometric data analysis. An option of fixed number of mutual dyads is available in the program used by Snijders (1991). When selecting this option, the random graphs generated are checked during the generation procedure, and when it is clear that the value of M will deviate from the desired one, the graph is discarded. This approach can be very inefficient, since the desired value of M may be extremely unlikely under the $U(\mathbf{X}_{\bullet+}, \mathbf{X}_{+\bullet})$ distribution; for the Metropolitan graphs, it is by no means unusual that only one out of a thousand $U(\mathbf{X}_{\bullet+}, \mathbf{X}_{+\bullet})$ graphs has the number of mutuals equal to the observed M. Since the generation of random graphs with the desired attributes thus is very time-consuming using this algorithm, we confine ourselves to the 14 smallest Metropolitan graphs (of order 10–12). For these we have estimated the p-values under the $U(\mathbf{X}_{\bullet+}, \mathbf{X}_{+\bullet}, M)$ random graph distribution and displayed the distribution of these estimates in Table 5, along with the distribution obtained for those graphs when the $U(\mathbf{X}_{\bullet+}, \mathbf{X}_{+\bullet})$ distribution is used.

As shown in the table, the p-value estimates are slightly higher (i.e., slightly less extreme) when the $U(\mathbf{X}_{\bullet+}, \mathbf{X}_{+\bullet}, M)$ distribution is used. Some of the Metropolitan networks' departure in transitivity from the $U(\mathbf{X}_{\bullet+}, \mathbf{X}_{+\bullet})$ distribution could thus be explained by the number of mutual dyads. Test 2 is the most powerful transitivity test in this case as well.

TABLE 5

Distribution of the 14 Estimates of p-Values for the Smallest Metropolitan Graphs (of Order 10–12) Under Two Different Null Hypotheses of Conditional Uniform Distribution

	Null Distribution			
	$U(\mathbf{X}_{\bullet+}, \mathbf{X}_{+\bullet})$ Test		$U(\mathbf{X}_{\bullet+}, \mathbf{X}_{+\bullet}, M)$ Test	
Estimated p-Value	1	2	1	2
$\hat{p} > 10\%$	2	0	5	0
$5\% < \hat{p} \leq 10\%$	1	0	1	0
$1\% < \hat{p} \leq 5\%$	2	0	0	0
$0\% < \hat{p} \leq 1\%$	1	0	5	1
$\hat{p} = 0\%$	8	14	3	13
Total	14	14	14	14

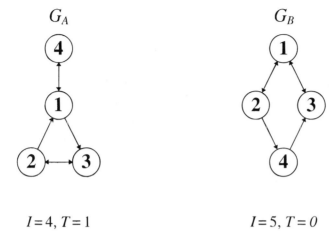

$I = 4, T = 1$ $I = 5, T = 0$

FIGURE 1. Two graphs with equal indegree and outdegree sequences, and total number of mutuals, but with different sequences of mutual-degrees.

6.4. Conditioning on the Sequence of Mutual-Degrees

We may increase the amount of conditioning even further by considering
the segmentation of $2M$, the number of mutual choices made and received,
into the sequence

$$\mathbf{M.} = (m_1, \ldots, m_v) \ ,$$

where m_i is the number of mutual dyads adjacent to vertex i, as defined in
Section 2. We refer to the uniform distribution resulting from the conditioning on the outdegrees, indegrees, and the above sequence of mutual-
degrees (i.e., the number of mutual relationships that each vertex is involved
in) as the $U(\mathbf{X.}_+, \mathbf{X}_{+\cdot}, \mathbf{M.})$ distribution. There are a number of reasons for
considering this conditional uniform distribution, which is a rather natural
extension of the $U(\mathbf{X.}_+, \mathbf{X}_{+\cdot}, M)$ distribution. In the transitivity testing
situation, it could be the case that the number of transitive triples is high
merely because of the configuration of the mutual relationships; we would
therefore like to take this configuration into account when testing transitivity. In Figure 1, two graphs, G_A and G_B, are displayed. Both have

$$(\mathbf{X.}_+, \mathbf{X}_{+\cdot}, M) = ((2,2,1,1),(2,1,2,1),2) \ ,$$

but they have different sequences of mutual-degrees; in G_A, we determine that $\mathbf{M.} = (1,1,1,1)$, whereas in G_B, $\mathbf{M.} = (2,1,1,0)$. This difference in the individual reciprocities also leads to differences in the numbers of transitive and intransitive triples. We cannot rule out that in our empirical networks, the transitivity is high compared with the transitivity commonly encountered under the $U(\mathbf{X_{.+}}, \mathbf{X_{+.}}, M)$ distribution merely because there are more subgraphs similar to G_A than there are subgraphs similar to G_B. We should therefore control for differences in transitivity due to $\mathbf{M.}$ by also conditioning on the sequence of mutual-degrees.

In this paper, we have not performed any transitivity test using $U(\mathbf{X_{.+}}, \mathbf{X_{+.}}, \mathbf{M.})$ as the null distribution. If random graphs are to be generated according to this distribution, the algorithm of Snijders (1991) must be slightly modified; this should however not present any insurmountable problems, since the major principles already are set out.

7. CONCLUSIONS

The results for random and observed data in Sections 5 and 6 imply that Test 2, the test based on the mean local transitivity density, is the most appropriate for transitivity testing, since its power is the highest in most situations. For the empirical data, the advantage of Test 2 is relatively small, since the test powers are extremely high for both tests. However, the power advantage of Test 2 could be of importance when transitivity testing is to be performed on graphs where the transitivity is most pronounced in small, close-knit, groups of vertices.

In Karlberg (1997), the p-value estimates for the Metropolitan graphs are, quite surprisingly, less extreme than the ones obtained in this paper, in spite of the fact that in that paper, the null distribution used conditions only on the network size. One explanation to this initially confusing result may be that by symmetrizing the Metropolitan networks, much information is lost; the resulting networks thus become more "mainstream"—i.e., closer to the center of the null distribution. Another conceivable explanation is that exactly because of the conditioning, the random graphs might become more homogeneous; although the random graphs generally may have higher values of the test quantities, very large (and very small) values of the test quantities may become less likely.

A question of interest is whether the p-values would be less extreme when the uniform distribution conditional on indegrees, outdegrees, and number of mutual dyads is used. The results of Section 6 imply that a slight increase in p-values occurs when this null distribution is used. Most of the

Metropolitan graphs have mutual dyad counts that differ considerably from the ones that are likely under the uniform distribution conditional on indegrees and outdegrees. For this reason, the algorithm used was extremely time-consuming for those graphs; they were thus not analyzed. It could not be ruled out that the increase in p-value may have been even more substantial for those graphs, precisely because of the extremity of their mutual dyad counts. The time efficiency of the algorithm of Snijders (1991) for the simpler distribution is in many respects due to the selection of probabilities for setting cell entries when they are not predetermined by the conditions; those probabilities are the key to reducing the number of failures (i.e., the number of graphs that are rejected by the simulation procedure). We have undertaken a preliminary study in which the number of failures was reduced so much that random graphs with the indegrees, outdegrees, and mutual dyad counts equal to those of Metropolitan graphs with an order of 20 could be generated within reasonable time. With some additional efforts, it may be feasible to examine the properties of the uniform distribution conditional on both indegrees, outdegrees, and mutual dyad count for a larger part of the 554 Metropolitan graphs.

It would also be interesting to investigate the conditional uniform distribution introduced in Section 6.4, under which, in addition to the indegrees and outdegrees, the entire sequence of mutual-degrees is held constant. The generation of random graphs according to this distribution may be problematic, but, as stated previously, it should not be overly difficult to adapt the algorithm used here to this situation.

The fact that a triple (i, j, k) is transitive could of course depend on other mechanisms, more related to balance theory, for example (in which, as Rapoport [1963] noted, "a friend of my friend is my friend" is one of the rules about combinations of friends and enemies among a triad of actors) than a tendency toward transitivity. On the one hand, it could be the case that since i is related to both j and k, j and k are likely to be related to each other. On the other hand, it might be that since both i and j are related to k, i and j are likely to be related to each other. By using Test 1, we are to some extent able to shift the focus from these alternative interpretations, since the test statistic is the number of transitive triples divided by the number of times the premises for transitivity (i.e., triples in which i is related to j and j is related to k) exist; the transitivity is thus contrasted against intransitivity rather than imbalance. Ideally, one would of course go further and separate transitivity from balance by either disregarding the transitive triples that have occurred due to the observed balance when computing the transitivity index or conditioning on the observed balance in the structural null hypothesis.

In the current paper, we have used the rather simple Bernoulli transitive triple distribution, which is a two-parameter distribution similar to the Bernoulli triangle distribution of Karlberg (1997), as our transitivity distribution when testing the power of the two transitivity tests. One might wonder whether other transitivity models that enable testing should be considered—for instance, one that also controls for the number of mutuals in the graph. However, for our purposes the Bernoulli transitive triple distribution is satisfactory, since the two tests exhibit similar power patterns (in relation to each other) regardless of whether they are applied to Bernoulli transitive triple graphs or to observed friendship data.

There exists a multitude of other graph attributes that are related to transitivity, and it would be interesting to extend this study by incorporating more test statistics. Ideally, one would like to have a test statistic that is optimal (most powerful) in some sense. However it is currently hard to see how this optimality could be ascertained, bearing in mind, among other things, the complexity of the conditional uniform distribution that ought to be used as the null distribution; likelihood functions of the test statistics may thus be very hard to obtain.

It would also be of interest to extend the current study to the case when a sample from the empirical network is observed. The appropriateness of the tests may depend on the sampling design; it might very well be the case that some network attributes, that one would like to use as test quantities, are unobservable for some designs. Karlberg (1998), who extended the triad count estimation formulas of Karlberg (1995) to the digraph case, treats a number of network observation schemes that are relevant in this context. When for instance only the labeled local sets (as defined by Karlberg [1998]) of a vertex sample are observed, the local transitivities of the sampled vertices will not be recorded; consequently, tests based on the local transitivity densities cannot be applied.

REFERENCES

Dahlbäck, Olof. 1982. "Choices of Contact, Attraction, and Social Relations." Report No. 19 from Project Metropolitan, Department of Sociology, Stockholm University.

Davis, James A., Paul W. Holland, and Samuel Leinhardt. 1971. "Comments on Professor Mazur's Hypothesis About Interpersonal Sentiments." *American Sociological Review* 36:309–11.

Fershtman, Meir. 1985. "Transitivity and the Path Census in Sociometry." *Journal of Mathematical Sociology* 11:159–89.

Frank, Ove. 1980. "Transitivity in Stochastic Graphs and Digraphs." *Journal of Mathematical Sociology* 7:199–213.

Frank, Ove, and Frank Harary. 1982. "Cluster Inference by Using Transitivity Indices in Empirical Graphs." *Journal of the American Statistical Association* 380:835–40.

Holland, Paul W., and Samuel Leinhardt. 1970. "A Method for Detecting Structure in Sociometric Data." *American Journal of Sociology* 76:492–513.

———. 1975. "The Statistical Analysis of Local Structure in Social Networks." Pp. 1–45 in *Sociological Methodology 1976*, edited by D.R. Heise, 1–45. San Fransisco: Jossey-Bass.

Jansson, Carl-Gunnar. 1975a. "Project Metropolitan: A Presentation." Report No. 1 from Project Metropolitan, Department of Sociology, Stockholm University.

———. 1975b. "The School Study: A Code Book." Report No. 3 from Project Metropolitan, Department of Sociology, Stockholm University.

———. 1984. "Project Metropolitan: A Presentation and Progress." Report No. 21 from Project Metropolitan, Department of Sociology, Stockholm University.

Jansson, Ingegerd. 1997. "Clique Structure in School Class Data." *Social Networks* 19:285–301.

Karlberg, Martin. 1995. "Triad Count Estimation in Graphs." Research Report, Department of Statistics, Stockholm University.

———. 1997. "Testing Transitivity in Graphs." *Social Networks* 19:325–43.

———. 1998. "Triad Count Estimation in Digraphs." *Journal of Mathematical Sociology* 23:99–126.

Karoński, Michal, and Tomasz Luczak. 1996. "Random Hypergraphs." Pp. 283–93 in *Combinatorics, Paul Erdös is Eighty*, vol. 2, edited by D. Miklós, V.T. Sós and T. Szönyi. Budapest, Hungary: Janos Bolyai Math Sci.

Katz, Leo, and J.H. Powell. 1954. "The Number of Locally Restricted Directed Graphs." *Proceedings of the American Mathematical Society* 5:621–26.

———. 1957. "Probability Distributions of Random Variables Associated with a Structure of the Sample Space of Sociometric Investigations." *Annals of Mathematical Statistics* 28:442–48.

Krackhardt, David. 1987. "Cognitive Social Structures." *Social Networks* 9:109–34.

Pearson, Frank S. 1994. "Peer Networks and Delinquency." Pp. 109–30 in "Studies of a Stockholm Cohort." Report No. 39 from Project Metropolitan, Department of Sociology, Stockholm University.

Pratt, John W., and Jean D. Gibbons. 1981. *Concepts of Nonparametric Theory*. New York: Springer-Verlag.

Rapoport, Anatol. 1963. "Mathematical Models of Social Interaction." Pp. 493–579 in *Handbook of Mathematical Psychology*, edited by D.R. Luce, R. Bush, and E. Galanter. New York: Wiley.

Snijders, Tom A.B. 1991. "Enumeration and Simulation Methods for 0–1 Matrices with Given Marginals." *Psychometrika* 56:397–417.

Stütz, Göran. 1985. "Kamratstatus (Peer status)." Report No. 23 from Project Metropolitan, Department of Sociology, Stockholm University.

Wasserman, Stanley. 1977. "Random Directed Graph Distributions and the Triad Census in Social Networks." *Journal of Mathematical Sociology* 5:61–86.

Wasserman, Stanley, and Katherine Faust. 1994. *Social Network Analysis*. Cambridge, England: Cambridge University Press.

🙢 8 🙠

LOGIT MODELS FOR AFFILIATION NETWORKS

*John Skvoretz**
*Katherine Faust**

*Once confined to networks in which dyads could be reasonably
assumed to be independent, the statistical analysis of network data
has blossomed in recent years. New modeling and estimation strategies have made it possible to propose and evaluate very complex
structures of dependency between and among ties in social networks. These advances have focused exclusively on one-mode
networks—that is, networks of direct ties between actors. We generalize these models to affiliation networks, networks in which actors are tied to each other only indirectly through belonging to
some group or event. We formulate models that allow us to study
the (log) odds of an actor's belonging to an event (or an event
including an actor) as a function of properties of the two-mode
network of actors' memberships in events. We also provide illustrative analysis of some classic data sets on affiliation networks.*

1. INTRODUCTION

Affiliation networks represent actors' ties to events. The events may refer
to well-defined collectivities like membership in country clubs or on corporate boards of directors or to more ephemeral collections like the guests
at a party or spectators at a sporting event. Much of network analysis,
including the statistical analysis of relational ties, focuses on one-mode

We appreciate the comments of two anonymous reviewers, the editors, and our
colleagues in the USC Structuralist Group: Vicki Lamb, André Mizell, and Shelley
Smith.

*University of South Carolina

253

networks—that is, networks in which the ties are from actors to actors or from collectivities to collectivities. In contrast, affiliation networks are two-mode networks because the ties link together different types of entities, actors, and collectivities. Affiliation networks have theoretical significance, despite the fact that they are not at the center of network analysis.

Social theorists have long recognized the importance of individuals' affiliations with groups, including both informal social encounters and more institutionalized memberships in organizations. Simmel (1950, 1955) forcefully contends that people are defined socially by the intersection of the various collectivities (family, occupation, neighborhood, voluntary organizations) to which they belong. Others have argued that participation in these collectivities heightens the likelihood of direct linkages emerging between pairs of individuals (Feld 1981, 1982; McPherson and Smith-Lovin 1982). Patterns of memberships not only define individual social identities and facilitate linkages between pairs, but overlapping memberships constrain individual action and provide the basis for social control (Breiger 1990).

From a different perspective, Homans (1951) argues that the identity of social groups emerges from the patterns of informal interactions among collections of people. Such groups can be located by examining patterns in people's participation in informal social activities. Variation in levels of participation and in comemberships among subsets of people indicates internal divisions defining important groups within a population (Breiger 1974; Davis, Gardner, and Gardner 1941; Doreian 1979; Freeman and White 1993; Homans 1951). From the perspective of the collectivities, individuals' overlapping memberships allow for flow of information between groups and for potential coordination of groups' activities. Common members who produce interlocks between organizations allow organizations to monitor one another's actions, to coopt potential competitors, or to coordinate multifaceted production activities by linking together different kinds of organizations.

Affiliation networks, consisting of a set of actors and a collection of "events" (or social occasions) with which subsets of actors are affiliated, have been used to investigate the empirical implications of these theoretical insights (Breiger 1974). They have been used in a wide variety of substantive studies, including the following: interlocking boards of directors (Allen 1982; Bearden and Mintz 1987; Levine 1972; Mariolis 1975; Mintz and Schwartz 1981a, b; Mizruchi 1982; Sonquist and Koenig 1975); voluntary organizations (Bonacich 1978; McPherson 1982); informal social gatherings (Bernard, Killworth, and Sailer 1980, 1982; Breiger 1974; Davis, Gardner, and Gardner 1941; Freeman and Romney 1987; Freeman, Romney, and Freeman 1987; Freeman, Freeman, and Michaelson 1989; Homans 1950); common political activities (Schweizer 1991, 1996); and ceremonial events (Foster and Seidman 1984; Schweizer, Klemm, and Schweizer 1993).

Affiliation networks—also called membership networks (Breiger 1974, 1990), hypernetworks (McPherson 1982), or dual networks (Berkowitz 1982)—differ in important ways from the usual social networks mapping linkages between pairs of actors. First, affiliation networks consist of two different kinds of entities: actors and events. Thus affiliation networks are two-mode networks. In addition, pairs of actors are not directly linked via dyadic ties; rather ties are recorded on subsets of actors (the members of the events or collectivities) and link these actors to the events or collectivities to which they belong. Because affiliation networks are two-mode, nondyadic networks, methods designed to study one-mode networks are not generally appropriate for studying affiliation networks. Furthermore, because of the duality in the relationship between actors and events, appropriate methods for affiliation networks permit one to study the linkages between people through shared memberships, the linkages between groups through common members, and the relationship between people and the groups to which they belong.

Although methodology for one-mode social networks has developed rapidly over the past several decades, there has not been similar development of methods for studying affiliation networks. Graphical displays using concept lattices have been proposed for studying the relationships between actors and events simultaneously (Freeman and White 1993; Schweizer 1991, 1996; Wasserman and Faust 1994). Centrality measures for affiliation networks have been explored (Bonacich 1991; Borgatti and Everett 1997; Faust 1997; Mizruchi, Mariolis, Schwartz, and Mintz 1986), as have methods for finding positions in two-mode networks (Borgatti and Everett 1992).

Despite the theoretical significance of affiliation networks, techniques for their statistical analysis have typically lagged behind those for the analysis of one-mode data. In an early generalization of models for one-mode networks, Snijders and Stokman (1987) extended Holland and Leinhardt's (1970, 1975) U|MAN model for triads to two-mode networks. One of the first statistical models for one-mode network data was Holland and Leinhardt's p_1 model (1981). It was an "independent dyad choice" model and it proposed that the probability of a tie from i to j depended on node level parameters measuring the expansiveness and attractiveness of nodes and on the tendency for choices to be reciprocated. It was well-known in the literature before similar models for two-mode network data were published by Galaskiewicz and Wasserman (1989), Iacobucci and Wasserman (1990), and Wasserman and Iacobucci (1991). These models, reviewed below, shared the p_1 model's assumption of dyad independence—that is, that the occurrence of a tie between i and j was independent of the occurrence of a tie between j and k, or i and k, or any other dyad.

More recent advances in the statistical analysis of one-mode data discard the assumption of dyadic independence in favor of more complicated and hence more realistic structures of dependency between dyads. These models, termed p^* models by Wasserman and Pattison (1996), can be expressed in logit form and estimated approximately by logistic regression techniques, as demonstrated by the pioneering work of Strauss and Ikeda (1990). Frank and Strauss (1986) provided one early type of p^* model that they called "Markov" graphs. More recently, Wasserman and Pattison (1996), Pattison and Wasserman (1999), Robins, Pattison, and Wasserman (Forthcoming), and Anderson, Wasserman, and Crouch (Forthcoming) have given general form and characterization to these models. In all of this recent development, however, little attention has been paid to two-mode networks.

We generalize these logit models to the analysis of affiliation networks. These models allow us to study the (log) odds (or *logit*) of an actor's belonging to an event or an event including an actor as a function of properties of the two-mode network of actors' memberships in events. We begin with a review of the "independent dyad choice" models for affiliation data and then introduce the basics of logit models for one-mode data. We then generalize the approach to two-mode data. Finally, we analyze some classic examples of affiliation networks using the new modeling techniques and demonstrate how properties of affiliation networks can be incorporated into these models to yield useful insights into the structural features of these networks.

2. INDEPENDENT DYAD CHOICE MODELS FOR TWO-MODE NETWORKS

Following the notation of Wasserman and Faust (1994), we denote the set of actors by G and the set of events by H where g and h denote the number of actors and events, respectively. The matrix representing the affiliation network is denoted by $\mathbf{X}^{(G\ H)}$. Actors may belong to events at c different levels of intensity or participation $m = 0,1,\ldots,c - 1$. We let $P(x_{ij} = m)$ denote the probability that actor i belongs to event j at level m. Following Iacobucci and Wasserman (1990), under the assumption that the dyads are independent, a simple dyad choice model has the following log-linear form

$$\log P(x_{ij} = m) = \lambda_{ij} + \theta_m + \alpha_{i(m)} + \beta_{j(m)} \tag{1}$$

for each m, subject to the constraints

$$\sum_{m=0}^{c-1} P(x_{ij} = m) = 1$$

$$\sum_{i} \alpha_{i(m)} = 0$$

$$\sum_{j} \beta_{j(m)} = 0 \ . \tag{2}$$

The parameters are also constrained as follows: when $m = 0$, $\theta_m = 0$, $\alpha_{i(m)} = 0$, and $\beta_{j(m)} = 0$. The parameter $\alpha_{i(m)}$ measures the tendency for actor i to belong to events at level m, net of other factors—i.e., holding the other parameters constant, larger values of $\alpha_{i(m)}$ increase the probability that actor i belongs to event j at level m. The parameter $\beta_{j(m)}$ measures the tendency for event j to be belonged to by actors at level m, net of other factors. The $\{\theta_m\}$ parameters measure general strength effects related to the overall frequency with which actors belong to events at level m. The $\{\lambda_{ij}\}$ parameters, finally, are technically required terms that ensure the first equality in equation set (2) is satisfied. This model is similar to the p_1 model in that it assumes the occurrence of a tie at level m between actor i and event j is independent of the occurrence of a tie at level m' between actor i' and event j'.

Certain special cases of equation (1) are immediately apparent. For instance, one could assume homogeneity (i.e., equality) of either the α parameters or the β parameters, or both, for a fixed level of participation at level m. An important simplification arises if actors or events or both can be "blocked" or partitioned into subsets within which equality of the relative parameters is assumed. Usually these subsets are defined *a priori* based on actor or event characteristics, as we illustrate below.[1] More importantly, though, all of these models are "independent dyad choice" models. This means that the joint probability distribution of the affiliation matrix is a product of the dyadic probabilities (recognizing that certain dyads— namely, all pairs of events and all pairs of actors—are constrained to take on value 0 with probability 1).

The assumption of dyadic independence is often regarded as suspect in analyses of one-mode networks. But, until the work of Frank and Strauss (1986) on Markov graphs, there was little choice but to make this assumption in order to have statistical models of network data. The assumption is equally dubious for affiliation networks, despite the much simpler structure of the basic independent dyad choice model. One can think of reasons why one actor's level of involvement in a particular event may not be independent of another actor's level of involvement in that event and vice-versa. One can also think of various reasons why an actor's level of involvement in one event may not be independent of his or her level of involvement in another event. These plausible but more complex dependency structures can be addressed within the framework of Markov graphs and logit models for network data. We now turn to a development of these ideas for affiliation networks.

3. LOGIT MODELS, MARKOV GRAPHS, AND PSEUDO-LIKELIHOOD ESTIMATION

Moving beyond "independent dyad choice" models required innovations in model building and in estimation. Both of these innovations are suggested, but not fully developed, in the work of Frank and Strauss (1986) on Markov graphs. Full development of the modeling approach is set out in Wasserman and Pattison's (1996) work on p^* logit models for social networks. Strauss and Ikeda (1990) provide the innovation in estimation, the use of pseudo-likelihood functions and logistic regression estimation procedures. We outline these innovations beginning with the p^* modeling framework.

The p^* modeling framework uses a log-linear model to express the probability of a graph G as a function of vector of parameters θ and an associated vector of graph statistics $x(G)$, and a normalizing constant $Z(\theta)$:

---

[1] Parameter estimates could also be used *a posteriori* to define subsets of stochastically equivalent actors (Wasserman and Anderson 1987).

$$P(G) = \frac{\exp(\theta'x(G))}{Z(\theta)} . \tag{3}$$

The normalizing constant simply ensures that the probabilities sum to unity over all graphs. The θ parameters express how various "explanatory" properties of the graph affect the probability of its occurrence. These parameters must be estimated. However, estimation via maximum likelihood techniques is very difficult because of $Z(\theta)$ in the denominator of equation (3). We first describe some p^* models, and then return to the problem of estimation at the end of this section.

The approach, proposed by Strauss and Ikeda (1990) and elaborated by Wasserman and Pattison (1996), first converts equation (3) into an expression for the log of the odds, or *logit*, a form that does not involve the normalizing constant. We use a mathematical identity that specifies the probability that $x_{ij} = 1$ given the rest of the adjacency matrix. We use G^{-ij} to denote this complement graph—that is, the graph including all adjacencies except the i,j^{th} one. The graph G^+ is defined as the adjacency matrix plus $x_{ij} = 1$ while G^- is defined as the adjacency matrix plus $x_{ij} = 0$. Then with $P(G^+)$ the probability of G^+ and $P(G^-)$ the probability of G^-, the identity is

$$P(x_{ij} = 1|G^{-ij}) = \frac{P(G^+)}{P(G^+) + P(G^-)} . \tag{4}$$

Basically this equation expresses the probability that $x_{ij} = 1$ conditional on the rest of the graph. Note that it does not depend on the normalizing constant because upon rewriting we get

$$P(x_{ij} = 1|G^{-ij}) = \frac{\exp(\theta'x(G^+))}{\exp(\theta'x(G^+)) + \exp(\theta'x(G^-))} . \tag{5}$$

If we consider the odds of the presence of a tie from i to j to its absence, we get

$$\frac{P(x_{ij} = 1|G^{-ij})}{P(x_{ij} = 0|G^{-ij})} = \frac{\exp(\theta'x(G^+))}{\exp(\theta'x(G^-))} . \tag{6}$$

From equation (6) we can then derive a simple form for the log of the odds or *logit* model:

$$logit\, P(x_{ij} = 1|G^{-ij}) = \theta'[x(G^+) - x(G^-)] . \tag{7}$$

The quantity in brackets on the right side is the vector of differences in the relevant graph statistics when x_{ij} changes from 1 to 0.

The specification of a p^* logit model requires a selection of network properties that are *a priori* assumed to affect the log odds of a tie being present to absent. A particularly simple case is the p_1 model expressed in logit form:

$$logit\ P(x_{ij} = 1 | G^{-ij}) = \theta + \rho x_{ji} + \alpha_i + \beta_j\ . \tag{8}$$

The parameters of this model include expansiveness parameters α and attractiveness parameters β. The expansiveness parameters relate to an actor's tendency to initiate ties and the attractiveness parameters relate to an actor's tendency to receive ties. In addition, the model includes a reciprocity parameter ρ that expresses any tendency for a tie from j to i to be returned by a tie from i to j at greater (or lower) than chance levels. Following Wasserman and Pattison (1996), the vector of parameters and the associated vector of graph statistics for this model are

$$\theta = (\theta, \alpha_1, \ldots, \alpha_g, \beta_1, \ldots, \beta_g, \rho)'$$

$$x(G) = (L, x_{1+}, \ldots, x_{g+}, x_{+1}, \ldots, x_{+g}, M)'\ . \tag{9}$$

L is the number of edges in the digraph, M is the number of mutual dyads, and the remaining graph statistics are the set of outdegrees and the set of indegrees. It is easy to calculate the difference vector of graph statistics for this simple model.

The same logic works for "dependent dyad choice" models, such as those proposed in the Markov graph framework by Frank and Strauss (1986). A Markov graph is a random graph with a particular kind of dependency structure among its possible edges. The dependency structure obeys the following rule: If two dyads are node-disjoint (that is, they do not share a node), then they are conditionally independent (Frank and Strauss 1986:835). The idea is that the presence or absence of tie in one dyad is independent of the presence or absence of a tie in another dyad only when the dyads have no nodes in common. If they share a node, then the presence or absence of a tie in one may depend on the presence or absence of a tie in the other. In contrast to the basic assumption of independent dyad choice models, only some dyads are assumed to be independent in a Markov graph—namely, those that are node-disjoint. The Markov property generalizes in an obvious way to digraphs (Frank and Strauss 1986).

One of the simplest models proposed by Frank and Strauss is the $\rho\sigma\tau$ homogeneous Markov graph model, also called the triad model. Homogeneous models assume that nodes are *a priori* indistinguishable and so no node-specific parameters are necessary. The triad model is a further simplification of the basic homogeneous Markov model for graphs. In the basic model, the probability of a graph is given by a log-linear function of effects pertaining to various tie configurations in which different ties have nodes in common. In particular for a nondirectional relation, the relevant tie configurations are triangles and stars from degree 1 up to degree $g - 1$. A triangle is a subset of three nodes where all three ties are present and a k-star is a subset of $k + 1$ nodes where one node has a tie to the remaining k nodes. The basic homogeneous Markov model is

$$P(G) = \frac{\exp\left(\tau t + \sum_{k=1}^{g-1} \sigma_k s_k\right)}{Z(\tau,\sigma_1,\ldots,\sigma_k)} , \tag{10}$$

where $Z(\tau,\sigma_1,\ldots,\sigma_k)$ is the normalizing constant, t is the count of triangles and s_k is the count of stars of degree k. The $\rho\sigma\tau$ model makes the simplifying assumption that stars of degree $k \geq 3$ have no effect on the probability of the graph beyond the effect of the $\binom{k}{2}$ 2-stars and the k 1-stars embedded in them. Specifically,

$$P(G) = \frac{\exp(\tau t + \rho r + \sigma s)}{Z(\tau,\rho,\sigma)} , \tag{11}$$

where r is the number of edges in G—i.e., 1-stars—and s is the number of 2-stars. The quantities r, s, and t are the sufficient statistics for the model. Frank and Strauss (1986:836) note that an equivalent set of sufficient statistics is any three of the set of triad counts of G—that is, the number of subgraphs of size 3 having 0, 1, 2, or 3 ties.

Strauss and Ikeda (1990:206) give the logit form of this model as

$$logit\, P(x_{ij} = 1|G^{-ij}) = \rho + \sigma\Delta S + \tau\Delta T , \tag{12}$$

where ΔS is the change in the number of 2-stars when x_{ij} changes from 1 to 0 and ΔT is the change in the number of triangles. For a directed graph, they note how this model can be made more complicated by including the expansiveness, attractiveness, and reciprocity parameters of the p_1 model

$$logit\, P(x_{ij} = 1|G^{-ij}) = \rho + \psi x_{ji} + \alpha_i + \beta_j + \sigma\Delta S + \tau\Delta T \,, \quad (13)$$

where ΔS and ΔT change interpretation now that the underlying graph is directed.[2] Finally, they propose a blockmodel form of the basic triad model in which 2-stars and triangles are counted within blocks and b is the block indicator:

$$logit\, P(x_{ij} = 1|G^{-ij}) = \rho + \sigma^{(b)}\Delta S_{ij}^{(b)} + \tau^{(b)}\Delta T_{ij}^{(b)} \quad (14)$$

Finally, Wasserman and Pattison (1996) propose entire family models, referred to as p^* models, with various structural aspects of networks as conditioning factors. Possible parameters for logit models of graphs include the triangles and stars already mentioned but, in addition, overall graph connectivity, various measures of graph centralization, and paths of varying length. In fact, any graph property is a candidate for inclusion. They note that some of these quantities assume a more complicated dependency structure than the simple Markovian one. For instance, a model with a parameter for k-paths assumes that all edges on paths of length k are conditionally dependent, even though pairs of these edges may have no node in common.

Estimation of the p^* models relies on pseudo-likelihood estimation, due to difficulty of maximum-likelihood estimation arising from $Z(\theta)$ in the denominator of equation (3). $Z(\theta)$ is a normalizing constant, given by the equation

$$Z(\theta) = \sum exp^{\{\theta'x(G)\}} \,, \quad (15)$$

where the summation is over all $2^{g(g-1)}$ graphs (Strauss and Ikeda 1990:205). For small values of g, $Z(\theta)$ can be calculated directly. However, as g increases (above about 6), direct calculation is all but impossible.

One possibility is to simulate a number of random graphs, each with the same number of nodes and lines as in the observed network, and estimate the θ parameters as a function of observed graph statistics, as sug-

[2]Note that Frank and Strauss's notation for the reciprocity effect and for the overall density effect differs from that of Wasserman and colleagues.

gested and illustrated by Frank and Strauss (1986) and Strauss (1986). However, given the computation intensity, this approach is not really practical (Frank and Strauss, 1986).

To estimate the p^* model, we use pseudo-likelihood estimation, a strategy hinted at by Frank and Strauss (1986) and elaborated by Strauss and Ikeda (1990) and Wasserman and Pattison (1996). The pseudo-likelihood function is defined as

$$PL(\theta) = \prod P(x_{ij}|G^{-ij}) \qquad (16)$$

The idea is to maximize equation (16) with respect to the parameters, θ, where the maximum pseudo-likelihood estimator (MPE) is a value of θ that maximizes equation (16) (Strauss and Ikeda 1990:207). As Strauss and Ikeda note, "the pseudolikelihood function is simply the product of the probabilities of the $[x_{ij}]$ with each probability conditional on the rest of the data" (p. 204). This strategy is analogous to the procedure proposed by Besag (1974) in the context of spatial models and rectangular lattices, where pseudo-likelihood estimation is widely used in estimations that also involve difficult normalizing constants (Hjort and Omre 1994).

The estimation method proposed by Strauss and Ikeda (1990) forms a pseudo-likelihood function for the graph in terms of the conditional probabilities for x_{ij} as follows:

$$PL(\theta) = \prod_{i \neq j} P(x_{ij} = 1|G^{-ij})^{x_{ij}} P(x_{ij} = 0|G^{-ij})^{1-x_{ij}} . \qquad (17)$$

Strauss and Ikeda prove that equation (16) can be maximized using maximim likelihood estimation of the logistic regression, equation (7), assuming the x_{ij}'s are independent observations. Thus the p^* family of models can be estimated, albeit approximately, using logistic regression routines in standard statistical packages.[3] However, since the logits are not independent, the model is not a true logistic regression model and statistics from the estimation must be used with caution. Goodness-of-fit statistics are pseudo-likelihood ratio statistics, and it is questionable whether the

---

[3]The data array has $g \times (g-1)$ rows, one column for the dependent variable x_{ij} and the remaining columns express the change in the graph statistics that constitute the independent variables in a model. The extraordinary flexibility of p^* models means that care must be taken that the vector of independent variables does not unintentionally have a logically determinate relationship to the dependent variable.

usual chi-square distributions apply; in addition, standard errors have only "nominal" significance (see Crouch and Wasserman 1998).

In sum, much progress has been made, and made recently, toward statistical models for networks that abandon the restrictive assumption of dyadic independence. More complicated dependency structures can be formulated and estimated approximately by logistic regression techniques. However, all of this development takes place in the context of one-mode graphs or digraphs. In the next section, we extend these models to two-mode affiliation networks.

4. MODELS FOR AFFILIATION NETWORKS

Our models for affiliation networks focus on simply the presence or absence of a tie rather than its strength. Hence, in terms of earlier notation the number of levels of intensity, c, equals two.[4] The first model we consider adapts the basic triad model of Frank and Strauss (1986). However, because an affiliation network is a bipartite graph—the nodes can be partitioned into two subsets and all ties are between the two sets, so that all triples of nodes are constrained to have at most two ties—the adaptation produces a model whose entire structure depends simply on the degree sequences—that is, on the marginals of the adjacency matrix (see footnote 5 later). This model has some merit as a basic "baseline" model from which to address the question of whether a particular affiliation network displays any "interesting" structure. This question of "interesting structure" was first framed by Holland and Leinhardt (1979) who argued that any network in which higher-order properties could be adequately modeled using only the properties of nodes or dyads had no social structure. By "adequately modeled" they meant that the higher-order properties took on values within the range expected given chance variation as constrained by the lower-order properties (Skvoretz, Faust, and Fararo 1996). Thus if a particular affiliation network is fit well by the triad model, its higher-order properties are simply expected consequences of the lower-order degree sequences. We then propose additional models that use higher-order properties as "explanatory" variables in predicting the log odds on the presence of a tie.

Frank and Strauss's triad model has as sufficient statistics the triad census of the graph. For an undirected graph, there are four triad equiva-

---

[4]We note that p^* models for one-mode networks have been extended to valued relations in Robins, Pattison, and Wasserman (forthcoming).

lence classes: the nonisomorphic three-subgraphs with zero, one, two, or three edges. But for an affiliation network (and bipartite graphs in general), the census has three, rather than four, equivalence classes since there can be no triads with three edges because there are no ties between actors or between events (Snijders and Stokman 1987). Furthermore, the triads in an affiliation network can be further distinguished by the number of actor and event nodes in the triad. All triads with three actors or three events are empty since ties cannot be present between nodes within the same set. Triads in which ties may be present must contain either two actors and one event or two events and one actor, and each triad may have zero, one, or two ties. Thus, once we distinguish between actors and events in an affiliation network, there are six equivalence classes of triads.

Our extension of the homogeneous triad model for an undirected graph (Frank and Strauss 1986) estimates separate parameters for the "two actor one event" and the "two event one actor" triads. As noted by Frank and Strauss (1986:836), for a given network, the sum of the counts of triads with zero, one, two, and three edges is a constant, the total number of triads in the network; therefore only three of four counts are needed as sufficient statistics. For an affiliation network, further dependencies among these counts mean that only a single count within each of the two sets is needed: We select the configurations with two edges depicted in Figure 1—2-stars with actors at their centers (actor 2-stars) and 2-stars with events at their centers (event 2-stars). Our model is homogeneous within each of the two sets because actors are interchangeable in one set and events in the other.

The direct generalization of the homogeneous triad model has the logit form

$$logit\, P(x_{ij} = 1 | G^{-ij}) = \theta + \sigma_a \Delta S_a + \sigma_e \Delta S_e \; , \tag{18}$$

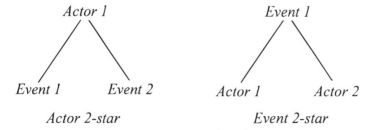

Actor 2-star   *Event 2-star*

FIGURE 1. Actor 2-stars and event 2-stars.

where θ is an overall density effect and the two σ parameters refer to the impacts that actor 2-stars and event 2-stars have on the logit.[5] A positive σ_a effect means that the log odds of x_{ij} being present are increased if the absence of the tie disrupts links between event j and other events that are created through actors' participation in events. A positive σ_e effect means that the log odds of x_{ij} being present are increased if the absence of the tie disrupts links between actors that are created through an event's inclusion of multiple actors. These parameters are responsive to the ideas that an actor's involvement in a particular event may depend on other actors' involvement in that event (captured by the event 2-star count) and that an actor's involvement in one event may depend on his or her involvement in another event (captured by the actor 2-star count).

As Wasserman and Pattison (1996) have noted, a wide range of network structural effects can be incorporated into p^* models. Even parameters in the relatively simple Markov random graph models embody important structural properties. Consider the frequent observation that in an affiliation network actors are linked to one another through joint membership in events, and events are linked through joint participation of actors (Breiger 1974). Joint membership for actors is captured in the event 2-stars (equivalently in the count of triads with two lines and two actor nodes). The parallel effect for event overlap is captured in the actor 2-stars (equivalently in the count of triads with two lines and two event nodes).

The event 2-star effect parametrizes how multiple shared memberships for actors affect the likelihood of a single actor-event tie. If actor i belongs to many events with other actors, we might hypothesize that these multiple memberships influence the probability of actor i's membership in

---

[5]As a reviewer pointed out, the number of actor 2-stars and the number of event 2-stars are simple functions of sums of degrees and sums of degree squares. It is easy to verify that

$$S_a = \sum_i \frac{x_{i+}^2}{2} - \sum_i \frac{x_{i+}}{2}$$

$$S_e = \sum_j \frac{x_{+j}^2}{2} - \sum_j \frac{x_{+j}}{2},$$

and since θ is a function of the number of edges in the graph, x_{++}, the probability distribution depends only on the average degree and the variance of actor degrees and the event degrees. Therefore the triad model for two-mode networks is a model about dispersion of degrees rather than about structure defined as pattern within the adjacency matrix conditional on the marginals.

the events shared by these other actors. As a general tendency for actors, this effect is captured in the parameter for event 2-stars. Similarly, we could consider the extent to which multiple overlapping members among a set of events would affect the probability of an event-actor tie. This is captured in the parameter for the actor 2-stars. All of these structural effects of actor comemberships and event overlaps are incorporated in the Markov graph model for affiliation networks with nonhomogeneous 2-star effects, or equivalently with nonhomogeneous triad parameters distinguishing between actor 2-stars and event 2-stars.

Some obvious extensions to the basic Markov model include the following ideas. First, we can investigate the effect of higher-order subgraphs on the presence/absence of tie. That is, we can add parameters that express the effects of various 3-stars, 4-stars, etc., following the full homogeneous Markov graph model proposed by Frank and Strauss (1986). But as Frank and Strauss note, since lower-order stars are embedded in higher-order stars, interpretation of the parameters is problematic.

Second, we can relax the homogeneity assumption to allow for specific actor and event effects related to the overall number of events an actor participates in and to the overall number of actors an event attracts. There are three possibilities:

$$logit\, P(x_{ij} = 1 | G^{-ij}) = \theta + \alpha_i + \sigma_a \Delta S_a \tag{19}$$

$$logit\, P(x_{ij} = 1 | G^{-ij}) = \theta + \beta_j + \sigma_e \Delta S_e \tag{20}$$

$$logit\, P(x_{ij} = 1 | G^{-ij}) = \theta + \alpha_i + \beta_j + \sigma_a \Delta S_a + \sigma_e \Delta S_e \tag{21}$$

where α_i parametrizes actor i's expansiveness and β_j parametrizes event j's attractiveness. However, these models are not well-formed and cannot be estimated since the logits will assume the value $+\infty$ for ties that are actually present and $-\infty$ for ties that are actually absent.[6]

[6]Echoing the caution in footnote 3, we note that in each case, there is a logically determinate relationship between the observed value of x_{ij} and the corresponding vector of graph statistic differences used as independent variables. For instance, consider equation (20). The vector of difference statistics is of length $h + 2$. If $x_{ij} = 1$, then the vector equals $(1, 0, \ldots, 1, \ldots, 0, x_{+j} - 1)$: the first position equals 1, the change in the overall number of ties as x_{ij} goes from present to absent; there are 0s in all but the jth location in the next h positions (corresponding to the fact that only the degree of the jth event changes—and by 1—as x_{ij} goes from present to absent), and the last position equals the degree of event j minus 1, the number of changes in event 2-stars as x_{ij} goes from present to absent. If $x_{ij} = 0$, then only the last entry changes. The last position now equals just the degree of event j, since if x_{ij} were to be present, x_{+j} additional event

Third, we may consider subgroup effects within the basic Markov model for affiliation networks. A specific model we estimate in the next section blocks only on events. This block diagonal model includes effects for actor 2-stars when the events are in the same block:

$$logit\, P(x_{ij} = 1 \mid G^{-ij}) = \theta + \sum_b \sigma_a^{(b)} \Delta S_a^{(b)} + \sigma_e \Delta S_e \tag{22}$$

Of course, one could add parameters of the off-diagonal blocks or make the assumption that the effect parameters for the various blocks are equal or build an analogous model for blocking on actors. The parameters capture the idea that it is the extent to which multiple overlapping members among a block of events, rather than the entire set of events, affects the probability of an event-actor tie.

Finally, we illustrate models that condition on higher-order properties of an affiliation network. We examine two properties of interest, both of which have been argued to be theoretically important features of affiliation networks. The first property is called "subgroup overlap," or in our context either "actor overlap" or "event overlap." We use a measure proposed by Bonacich (1972).[7] Events overlap to a greater degree when more actors participate in both of them. Actors overlap to a greater degree when they both jointly participate in many events. Bonacich's measure of overlap is logically independent of the size of the events or the number of events attended by the actors. Event overlap varies from 0 if no actors jointly participate in the two events, to 1 if all actors attending one event attend the other (and vice versa). Actor overlap varies from 0 if the two

---

2-stars would be created. We can select values for the parameters $\theta, \beta_1, \ldots, \beta_h$, and σ_e such that x_{ij} becomes a determinate linear function of the difference vector. For instance, if we let $\beta_j = \theta - x_{+j}$ and let $\sigma_e = -1$, it is easy to see that

$$x_{ij} = \theta + (\theta - x_{+j})(1) + \sum_{k \neq j}(\theta - x_{+k})(0) + (-1)(x_{+j} - x_{ij}).$$

[7]Bonacich's measure r is defined as

$$r = \frac{n_{11} n_{22} - \sqrt{n_{11} n_{22} n_{12} n_{21}}}{n_{11} n_{22} - n_{12} n_{21}} \qquad \text{if} \qquad n_{11} n_{22} \neq n_{12} n_{21}$$

$$= 0.5 \qquad\qquad\qquad \text{otherwise,}$$

where n_{11} is the number of actors belonging to both groups or events, n_{22} is the number belonging to neither group/event, n_{12} is the number belonging to the first group/event but not the second, and n_{21} is the number belonging to the second but not the first.

actors attend no events together, to 1 if the two attend exactly the same set of events. We explore models that condition the occurrence of a tie on the *average* amount of overlap between events and the *average* amount of overlap between actors. In logit form, the log odds of the presence of a tie is modeled as a function of the change in the average amount of overlap between events (or between actors) when the tie goes from 1 to 0.

The second property of interest also takes two forms depending on whether we consider paths from events to events or paths from actors to actors. We consider the path length between actors and between events as measured by the *average* number of events on the shortest path between two actors and by the *average* number of actors on the shortest path between two events. Prevalence of short paths between pairs of actors or pairs of events is indicative of system-level integration, whereas prevalence of long paths can indicate a tendency for segregation into subgroups with little connection between them (Granovetter 1973). In logit form, the log odds of the presence of a tie is modeled as a function of the change in the average path length when the tie goes from 1 to 0. Note that the change will always be zero or negative—that is, removing a tie will either leave the average path length unchanged or increase it. This is not true for the first property—removing a tie can increase the average amount of measured overlap.

One reason to examine these properties is that they are not determined by the degree sequences—i.e., by the marginals of the affiliation matrix. It is possible to construct two affiliation networks with the same degree sequences but with different values for average event or actor overlaps and for the average path lengths. Furthermore, both of these properties imply that the underlying graph is not Markovian: Models based on these properties postulate dependencies between dyads that do not share a node. However, such effects can be easily parametrized and approximately estimated by a logit model of the p^* family. Thus these properties give us an opportunity to illustrate the application of p^* models to affiliation networks.

5. TWO ILLUSTRATIONS

We illustrate various models on two data sets. The first is Davis, Gardner, and Gardner's (1941) classic affiliation network of the participation of 18 Southern women in 14 social events (see also Homans 1951 and Breiger 1974). The second is Galaskiewicz's (1985) data on the board and club

TABLE 1
Logit Models of Data for Davis, Gardner, and Gardner (1941)

Model	Number of Parameters	Pseudo-Likelihood Ratio Statistic
1. Choice	1	327.292
2. Choice + 2-stars	2	305.328
3. Choice + event 2-stars	2	308.273
4. Choice + actor 2-stars	2	325.618
5. Choice + event 2-stars + actor 2-stars	3	304.784

memberships of corporate executive officers (CEOs) in Minneapolis–St. Paul. We use the subset of data on 26 CEOs and 15 boards/clubs reprinted in Wasserman and Faust (1994). This second example includes a four-category subgrouping variable for the type of board or club: country club, metropolitan club, board of FORTUNE 500 firms or FORTUNE 50 banks, and board of cultural or religious organizations.

Table 1 presents the pseudo-likelihood ratio statistics for the fits of models to Davis, Gardner, and Gardner's Southern women data. The simplest interesting model has a homogeneous effect for 2-stars (model 2). Models 3 and 4 consider, separately, effects of event 2-stars and actor 2-stars (respectively) ignoring the other type of 2-star. Model 5 includes nonhomogeneous effects for type of 2-star. Interestingly, this model is not an improvement over the homogeneous effect of 2-stars (model 2). Thus for these data there is no advantage in distinguishing between actor-centered and event-centered 2-stars.

Table 2 gives the parameter estimates for models 2 and 5 for the Davis, Gardner and Gardner data. The parameter estimate for the effect of

TABLE 2
Parameter Estimates for Models 2 and 5 from Table 1

Effect	Parameter Estimate Model 2	Model 5
Choice	−2.503	−2.374
2-stars	0.175	
Event 2-stars		0.186
Actor 2-stars		0.131

TABLE 3
Logit Models for CEOs and Boards/Clubs Network (Galaskiewicz 1985)

Model	Number of Parameters	Pseudo-Likelihood Ratio Statistic
1. Choice	1	439.717
2. Choice + 2-stars	2	400.878
3. Choice + event 2-stars	2	391.940
4. Choice + actor 2-stars	2	429.746
5. Choice + event 2-stars + actor 2-stars	3	387.013
6. Choice + actor 2-stars within blocks	5	403.777
7. Choice + actor 2-stars between blocks	2	437.480
8. Choice + actor 2-stars within and between blocks	6	401.136
9. Choice + actor 2-stars within and between blocks + event 2-stars	7	369.700

2-stars is positive, indicating that the greater the number of 2-stars disrupted by the absence of a particular actor-event tie, the greater the log odds that the tie is present versus absent. Clearly the type of 2-stars that have this enhancing effect are event 2-stars. This indicates that it is coattendance at events over pairs of actors that is primarily responsible for the positive 2-star effect.

Table 3 presents fits of models to Galaskiewicz's CEOs and boards/clubs network. In this example we fit the same models as for the Davis, Gardner and Gardner data but also include models with a blocking of the events. This blocking operates on the actor 2-stars and captures whether or not the two events in the actor 2-star are in the same block (for blocks 1 through 4) or whether they are in different blocks (regardless of the specific blocks).

First consider the models without event blocking. In contrast to the results for Davis, Gardner, and Gardner's data, the addition of nonhomogeneous effects distinguishing actor 2-stars and event 2-stars provides an improvement of fit for Galaskiewicz's CEOs and boards/clubs network (compare models 2 and 5 in Table 3). Table 4 gives the parameter estimates for model 5 for these data. Actor 2-stars and event 2-stars have contrasting effects on the likelihood of a tie; actor 2-stars decrease whereas event 2-stars increase this probability. Comparing models 3 and 4 with model 1 suggests that event 2-stars provide more leverage than do actor 2-stars.

Models 6 through 9 in Table 3 add event blocking to the actor 2-stars. These event blockings are added separately for within block (model 6) and

TABLE 4
Parameter Estimates for Models 5 and 9 from Table 3

| | Parameter Estimate | |
	Model 5	Model 9
Choice	−1.338	−1.284
Event 2-stars	0.154	0.144
Actor 2-stars	−0.238	
Blocked actor 2-stars:		
Block 1		−7.210
Block 2		−0.512
Block 3		−1.102
Block 4		−0.031
Between blocks		−0.142

between block (model 7) actor 2-star effects and then for both within and between block actor 2-star effects (model 8). Finally event blocking of actor 2-stars is considered in combination with event 2-stars (model 9). Comparing model 8 with model 4, and model 5 with model 9 shows the additional effect that the event blocking has on the actor 2-stars. In both cases event blocking improves the fit of the model. Parameter estimates for model 9 are in Table 4.

Recalling that block 1 is composed of two country clubs, the large negative effect of actor 2-stars for this block of events means that membership in the clubs tends strongly to being mutually exclusive—that is, actors belong either to one club or to the other, but not both. The next largest effect is in block 3, which is composed of boards of Fortune 500 firms or Fortune 50 banks. Again the tendency here, although it is not as strong, is for memberships on some of these boards to depress the likelihood of membership on others. The negative effect means that the greater the number of actor 2-stars that would be created by a tie from an actor to a board, the lower is the probability of the tie being present. So there is a "ceiling effect" on total number of memberships on boards within a block—the more boards of a given type to which an actor belongs, the lower is the likelihood that he belongs to one more. That the effect of event 2-stars is positive indicates the tie connecting an actor to clubs or boards with relatively many members is a "stronger" tie than one connecting the actor to relatively small clubs or boards. The first tie creates relatively many event 2-stars and so, as compared with the condition in which it is absent, the log odds of it being present are increased substantially. The second tie creates relatively few event 2-stars and so the "force" of its presence (as measured by the log odds) is not as strong.

The next set of estimated models condition on the average overlap between events and between actors and/or the average minimum path length between actors and between events. Table 5 presents zero-order correlations between relevant variables for the two data sets. The cases here are the $(g \times h)$ dyads, and the variables are the dyad change scores corresponding to the independent variables in our models. In both data sets, there are substantial positive correlations between the change in actor 2-stars and the change in event overlap and between the change in event 2-stars and actor overlap. There is also a substantial negative correlation between the change in the average distance between actors and the change in actor overlap. The latter, however, is not paralleled by the correlation between the change in the average distance between events and the change in event overlap. While these correlations are substantial, they are not perfect, indicating that the overlap and distance measures are not simple linear functions of the 2-stars and the underlying degree sequences. Finally, we note that in both data sets there are moderate positive correlations between the presence of a tie (the dependent variable) and event 2-stars and actor overlap. In the Davis, Gardner, and Gardner data, there is a moderate positive correlation between the dependent variable and the average distance between events while in the Galaskiewicz data, this correlation is essentially zero.

The p^* models we estimate for these data sets are presented in Tables 6 and 7. We begin with the basic model that includes both actor and event 2-stars and then add the overlap and distance measures. The best fitting model for the Davis, Gardner, and Gardner data includes effects for event overlap and for the distance between events as measured by the number of actors on the shortest path between them. The best fitting model for the Galaskiewicz data only includes an effect for the distance between events. Parameter estimates corresponding to the basic model and the best-fitting models are present in Tables 8 and 9. Interpretation of these effects can be made either in terms of how the change in the corresponding independent variable affects the log odds on the presence of a tie or, preferably, in terms of the underlying p^* models in which the independent variable impacts the probability of a tie being present.

In the Davis, Gardner, and Gardner data, we find that event overlap has a negative effect on the presence of a tie. The size of the coefficient reflects the scale of the independent variable—in this data set the change score varies from -0.011 to 0.028. The negative effect means that as be-

TABLE 5

Zero-order Correlations for p^* models (Davis, Gardner, and Gardner [1941] above diagonal, Galaskiewicz [1985] below diagonal)

	Actor 2-stars	Event 2-stars	Actor Overlap	Event Overlap	e-on-a Path	a-on-e Path	Tie Present
Actor 2-stars	—	-0.11	0.12	0.81	0.36	0.19	0.08
Event 2-stars	-0.15	—	0.79	0.05	-0.55	0.15	0.28
Actor overlap	-0.08	0.86	—	0.21	-0.74	0.10	0.25
Event overlap	0.74	-0.20	-0.06	—	0.19	0.17	-0.06
e-on-a path	0.26	-0.77	-0.95	0.17	—	0.09	-0.12
a-on-e path	0.00	0.27	0.23	-0.01	-0.22	—	0.28
Tie present	-0.16	0.37	0.31	-0.16	-0.32	-0.03	—

TABLE 6
$p*$ Models for Davis, Gardner, and Gardner Data

Model	Number of Parameters	Pseudo-Likelihood Ratio Statistic
1. Choice + event 2-stars + actor 2-stars	3	304.784
2. 1 + actor overlap	4	304.698
3. 1 + event overlap	4	279.092
4. 1 + actor overlap + event overlap	5	279.035
5. 1 + a-on-e path	4	286.170
6. 1 + e-on-a path	4	304.783
7. 1 + a-on-e path + e-on-a path	5	285.835
8. 1 + event overlap + a-on-e path	5	263.979

tween two ties—say, x_{ij} and x_{kl}—the one that has the higher probability of occurrence is associated with a lower amount of event overlap. Net of other considerations, this effect has the consequence that an actor would be less likely to add a tie to an event if the actors already tied to that event are ones to whom the focal actor is not already tied via coparticipation in other events. Adding such a tie would increase overlap between events more than adding a tie to an event attended mostly by other actors to whom the focal actor is already tied via common participation in other events. The positive effect of average distance between events means that as between two ties, x_{ij} and x_{kl}, the one that has the higher probability of occurrence is associated with a longer average path length between events. In effect, these data exhibit an "anti-bridging" tendency—a tie from an actor to an event that would create shorter paths is less likely to occur than a tie

TABLE 7
$p*$ Models for Galaskiewicz Data

Model	Number of Parameters	Pseudo-Likelihood Ratio Statistic
1. Choice + event 2-stars + actor 2 stars	3	387.013
2. 1 + actor overlap	4	386.804
3. 1 + event overlap	4	386.711
4. 1 + a-on-e path	4	378.833
5. 1 + e-on-a path	4	386.989

TABLE 8
Parameter Estimates for Models 1 and 8 from Table 6

	Parameter Estimate	
Effect	Model 1	Model 8
Choice	−2.374	−4.238
Event 2-stars	0.186	0.232
Actor 2-stars	0.131	0.612
Event overlap		−158.177
a-on-e path		2.376

that would create longer paths. In the Galaskiewicz data, the effect of the average distance between events is negative, indicating that these data exhibit a "bridging" tendency. That is, in these data, as between two ties, the one with a higher probability of occurrence is associated with a shorter average path length between events.

We can explore this effect inspecting the event overlap matrices. In the Davis, Gardner, and Gardner data, there are 91 pairs of events; 25 have zero overlap—that is, there are no actors who attend both events—7 pairs overlap at just one actor, and the rest overlap from 2 to 9 actors. The zero and one overlap pairs are critical since a change in the value of a single tie could increase or decrease the distance between events. Since the zero cases are much more numerous than the one cases, there are more occasions where adding a tie would decrease path distance than there are occasions where deleting a tie would increase path distance. In addition, the zero cases predominately fall between two blocks of events. The fact that such critical ties are *not* present is the "anti-bridging" tendency, a tendency

TABLE 9
Parameter Estimates for Models 1 and 4 from Table 7

	Parameter Estimate	
Effect	Model 1	Model 4
Choice	−1.338	−1.837
Event 2-stars	0.154	0.180
Actor 2-stars	−0.238	−0.245
a-on-e path		−0.797

consistent with the frequently observed "clique" structure in these data (Homans 1951; Breiger 1974). In the Galaskiewicz data, there are 105 pairs of events; 35 have zero overlap, but 33 overlap at one actor; the zero cases do not appear to fall between entire blocks of events. Consequently, these data display a different tendency with respect to the probability of bridging ties, one where ties tend to create short paths or bridges between events.

6. CONCLUSION

We show that recent advances in the statistical analysis of one-mode network data can be extended to two-mode data from affiliation networks. The models we have proposed and evaluated do not exhaust the possible model structures. Our models begin with the basic idea of Markov graphs by postulating dependencies between dyads only if they share a node. Because of their nature, certain simple homogeneous Markov graph models simplify further when applied to affiliation networks. However, they become more complex in one respect—there is a natural heterogeneity between types of triads depending on whether they contain two actors and one event or one actor and two events. That these configurations can have empirically different effects is documented in our illustrative analyses.

Finally, by using measures for average path length and for actor and event overlap, we show how non-Markovian models can be proposed and estimated via the p^* framework. These models uncover both "bridging" and "anti-bridging" tendencies in the formation of affiliation networks. In the Davis, Gardner, and Gardner data set of Southern women, actors' ties to events appear to differentiate them and push them apart, whereas in the Galaskiewicz data set of CEOs, events appear to integrate actors and pull them closer together.

REFERENCES

Allen, Michael Patrick. 1982. "The Identification of Interlock Groups in Large Corporate Networks: Convergent Validation Using Divergent Techniques." *Social Networks* 4:349–66.

Anderson, Carolyn J., Stanley Wasserman, and Bradley Crouch. Forthcoming. "A p* Primer: Logit Models for Social Networks." *Social Networks*.

Bearden, James, and Beth Mintz. 1987. "The Structure of Class Cohesion: The Corporate Network and its Dual." Pp. 187–207 in *Intercorporate Relations: The Struc-*

tural Analysis of Business, edited by Mark S. Mizruchi and Michael Schwartz. Cambridge, England: Cambridge University Press.

Berkowitz, Stephen D. 1982. *An Introduction to Structural Analysis: The Network Approach to Social Research.* Toronto: Butterworths.

Bernard, H. Russell, Peter Killworth, and Lee D. Sailer. 1980. "Informant Accuracy in Social Network Data IV: A Comparison of Clique-level Structure in Behavioral and Cognitive Network Data." *Social Networks* 2:191–218.

———. 1982. "Informant Accuracy in Social Network Data V: An Experimental Attempt to Predict Actual Communication from Recall Data." *Social Science Research* 11:30–66.

Besag, Julian. 1974. "Spatial Interaction and the Statistical Analysis of Lattice Systems." *Journal of the Royal Statistical Society. Series B: Methodological* 36:192–225.

Bonacich, Phillip. 1972. "Technique for Analyzing Overlapping Memberships." Pp. 176–85 in *Sociological Methodology 1972*, edited by Herbert L. Costner. San Francisco: Jossey-Bass.

———. 1978. "Using Boolean Algebra to Analyze Overlapping Memberships." Pp. 101–15 in *Sociological Methodology 1978*, edited by Karl F. Schuessler. San Francisco: Jossey-Bass.

———. 1991. "Simultaneous Group and Individual Centralities." *Social Networks* 13:155–68.

Borgatti, Stephen P., and Martin G. Everett. 1992. "Regular Blockmodels of Multiway, Multimode Matrices." *Social Networks* 14:91–120.

———. 1997. "Network Analysis of 2-mode Data." *Social Networks* 19:243–69.

Breiger, Ronald L. 1974. "The Duality of Persons and Groups." *Social Forces* 53:181–90.

———. 1990. "Social Control and Social Networks: A Model from Georg Simmel." Pp. 453–76 in *Structures of Power and Constraint: Papers in Honor of Peter M. Blau*, edited by C. Calhoun, M. W. Meyer, and W. R. Scott. Cambridge, England: Cambridge University Press.

Crouch, Bradley, and Stanley Wasserman. 1998. "A Practical Guide to Fitting p* Social Network Models." *Connections* 21:87–101.

Davis, A., B. Gardner, and M.R. Gardner. 1941. *Deep South.* Chicago: University of Chicago Press.

Doreian, Patrick. 1979. "On the Delineation of Small Group Structures." Pp. 215–30 in *Classifying Social Data*, edited by H. C. Hudson. San Francisco: Jossey-Bass.

Faust, Katherine. 1997. "Centrality in Affiliation Networks." *Social Networks* 19:157–91.

Feld, Scott L. 1981. "The Focused Organization of Social Ties." *American Journal of Sociology* 86:1015–35.

———. 1982. "Social Structural Determinants of Similarity Among Associates." *American Sociological Review* 47:797–801.

Foster, Brian L., and Stephen B. Seidman. 1984. "Overlap Structure of Ceremonial Events in Two Thai Villages." *Thai Journal of Development Administration* 24:143–57.

Frank, Ove, and David Strauss. 1986. "Markov Graphs." *Journal of the American Statistical Association* 81:832–42.

Freeman, Linton C., Sue C. Freeman, and Alaina G. Michaelson. 1989. "How Humans
  See Social Groups: A Test of the Sailer-Gaulin Models." *Journal of Quantitative
  Anthropology* 1:229–38.
Freeman, Linton C., and A. Kimball Romney. 1987. "Words, Deeds and Social Struc-
  ture: A Preliminary Study of the Reliability of Informants." *Human Organization*
  46:330–34.
Freeman, Linton C., A. Kimball Romney, and Sue C. Freeman. 1987. "Cognitive Struc-
  ture and Informant Accuracy." *American Anthropologist* 89:310–25.
Freeman, Linton C., and Douglas R. White. 1993. "Using Galois Lattices to Represent
  Network Data." Pp. 127–46 in *Sociological Methodology 1993*, edited by Peter V.
  Marsden. Cambridge, MA: Blackwell Publishers.
Galaskiewicz, Joseph. 1985. *Social Organization of an Urban Grants Economy*. New
  York: Academic Press.
Galaskiewicz, Joseph, and Stanley Wasserman. 1989. "Mimetic Processes within an
  Interorganizational Field: An Empirical Test." *Administrative Science Quarterly*
  34:454–79.
Granovetter, Mark. 1973. "The Strength of Weak Ties." *American Journal of Sociol-
  ogy* 81:1287–1303.
Hjort, Nils Lid, and Henning Omre. 1994. "Topics in Spatial Statistics." *Scandinavian
  Journal of Statistics* 21: 289–357.
Holland, Paul W., and Samuel Leinhardt. 1970. "A Method for Detecting Structure in
  Sociometric Data." *American Journal of Sociology* 70:492–513.
———. 1975. "The Statistical Analysis of Local Structure in Social Networks." Pp.
  1–45 in *Sociological Methodology 1976*, edited by D. R. Heise. San Francisco:
  Jossey-Bass.
———. 1979. "Structural Sociometry." Pp. 63–83 in *Perspectives on Social Net-
  work Research*, edited by P. W. Holland and S. Leinhardt. New York: Academic
  Press.
———. 1981. "An Exponential Family of Probability Distributions for Directed Graphs"
  (with discussion). *Journal of the American Statistical Association* 76:33–65.
Homans, George C. 1950. *The Human Group*. London, England: Routledge & Kegan
  Paul.
Iacobucci, Dawn, and Stanley Wasserman. 1990. "Social Networks with Two Sets of
  Actors." *Psychometrika* 55:707–20.
Levine, Joel. 1972. "The Sphere of Influence." *American Sociological Review* 37:14–
  27.
Mariolis, Peter. 1975. "Interlocking Directorates and Control of Corporations: The
  Theory of Bank Control." *Sociological Quarterly* 56:425–39.
McPherson, J. Miller. 1982. "Hypernetwork Sampling: Duality and Differentiation
  Among Voluntary Organizations." *Social Networks* 3:225–49.
McPherson, J. Miller, and Lynn Smith-Lovin. 1982. "Women and Weak Ties: Differ-
  ences by Sex in the Size of Voluntary Organizations." *American Journal of Sociol-
  ogy* 87:883–904.
Mintz, Beth, and Michael Schwartz. 1981a. "The Structure of Intercorporate Unity in
  American Business." *Social Problems* 29:87–103.
———. 1981b. "Interlocking Directorates and Interest Group Formation." *American
  Sociological Review* 46:851–69.

Mizruchi, Mark S. 1982. *The American Corporate Network 1904–1974*. Beverly Hills, CA: Sage.

Mizruchi, Mark S., Peter Mariolis, Michael Schwartz, and Beth Mintz. 1986. "Techniques for Disaggregating Centrality Scores in Social Networks." Pp. 26–48 in *Sociological Methodology 1986*, edited by Nancy B. Tuma. San Francisco: Jossey-Bass.

Pattison, Philippa, and Stanley Wasserman. Forthcoming. "Logit Models and Logistic Regressions for Social Networks: II. Multivariate Relations." *British Journal of Mathematical and Statistical Psychology*.

Robins, Garry, Philippa Pattison, and Stanley Wasserman. Forthcoming. "Logit Models and Logistic Regressions for Social Networks: III. Valued Relations." *Psychometrika*.

Schweizer, Thomas. 1991. "The Power Struggle in a Chinese Community, 1950–1980: A Social Network Analysis of the Duality of Actors and Events." *Journal of Quantitative Anthropology* 3:19–44.

———. 1996. "Actor and Event Orderings across Time: Lattice Representation and Boolean Analysis of the Political Disputes in Chen Village, China." *Social Networks* 18:247–66.

Schweizer, Thomas, Elmar Klemm, and Margarete Schweizer. 1993. "Ritual as Action in a Javanese Community: A Network Perspective on Ritual and Social Structure." *Social Networks* 15:19–48.

Simmel, Georg. 1950. *The Sociology of Georg Simmel*, edited by K. H. Wolff. Glencoe, IL: Free Press.

———. 1955. *Conflict and the Web of Group Affiliations*. Glencoe, IL: Free Press.

Skvoretz, J., K. Faust, and T. J. Fararo. 1996. "Social Structure, Networks, and E-State Structuralism Models." *Journal of Mathematical Sociology* 21:57–76.

Snijders, Tom A. B., and Frans N. Stokman. 1987. "Extensions of Triad Counts to Networks with Different Subsets of Points and Testing Underlying Graph Distributions." *Social Networks* 9:249–75.

Sonquist, John A., and Thomas Koenig. 1975. "Interlocking Directorates in the Top U.S. Corporations: A Graph Theory Approach." *Insurgent Sociologist* 5:196–230.

Strauss, David. 1986. "On a General Class of Models for Interaction." *Society for Industrial and Applied Mathematics, Review* 28:513–27.

Strauss, David, and Michael Ikeda. 1990. "Pseudolikelihood Estimation for Social Networks." *Journal of the American Statistical Association* 85:204–12.

Wasserman, Stanley, and Carolyn J. Anderson. 1987. "Stochastic *a posteriori* Blockmodels: Construction and Assessment." *Social Networks* 9:1–36.

Wasserman, Stanley, and Katherine Faust. 1994. *Social Network Analysis: Methods and Applications*. New York: Cambridge University Press.

Wasserman, Stanley, and Dawn Iacobucci. 1991. "Statistical Modelling of One-Mode and Two-Mode Networks: Simultaneous Analysis of Graphs and Bipartite Graphs." *British Journal of Mathematical and Statistical Psychology* 44:13–43.

Wasserman, Stanley, and Philippa Pattison. 1996. "Logit Models and Logistic Regressions for Social Networks: I. An Introduction to Markov Graphs and p^*." *Psychometrika* 61:401–25.

9

A NEW MODEL FOR INFORMATION DIFFUSION IN HETEROGENEOUS SOCIAL NETWORKS

Vincent Buskens*
Kazuo Yamaguchi†

This paper discusses a new model for the diffusion of information through heterogeneous social networks. In earlier models, when information was given by one actor to another the transmitter did not retain the information. The new model is an improvement on earlier ones because it allows a transmitter of information to retain that information after telling it to somebody else. Consequently, the new model allows more actors to have information during the information diffusion process. The model provides predictions of diffusion times in a given network at the global, dyadic, and individual levels. This leads to straightforward generalizations of network measures, such as closeness centrality and betweenness centrality, for research problems that focus on the efficiency of information transfer in a network. We analyze in detail how information diffusion times and centrality measures depend on a series of network measures, such as degrees and bridges. One important finding is that predictions about the time actors need to spread information in the network differ considerably between the new and old models, while the predictions about the time needed to receive information hardly differ. Finally, some cautionary remarks are made about using the model in empirical research.

Stimulating comments and discussions with Jeroen Weesie and Werner Raub are gratefully acknowledged. The authors are also grateful to Diana Gillooly for her editorial assistance. Financial support was provided by the Netherlands Organization for Scientific Research under Grant PGS 50-370.
*Utrecht University
†University of Chicago

282   BUSKENS AND YAMAGUCHI

1. INTRODUCTION

A considerable amount of research has been devoted recently to studying
the efficiency of diffusion of different kinds of goods through networks.
Models of processes such as epidemics of infectious diseases, diffusion of
innovations, information diffusion, and influence of actors on others are
all based on contacts between actors organized in a social network. We
concentrate in this paper on the efficiency of information diffusion. The
term "efficiency" refers to how fast information is expected to flow through
a network with a particular structure. The major question is how efficiency
of information diffusion depends on network measures such as density,
degrees, centralization, and number of bridges. This question can be addressed at different levels. On the dyadic level, what is the expected time
for information to go from a specific transmitter of information to a specific receiver? On the individual level, what is the expected time for an
actor to receive or to diffuse information in a network? On the global level,
what is the expected time for information to diffuse in a network starting
from an arbitrary actor in the network? Yamaguchi explained (in)efficien-
cy of information diffusion at the global (1994a) and dyadic (1994b) levels
with the network measures mentioned above. In this paper, we compare
the model used by Yamaguchi and earlier by Friedkin (1991) with a new
model for the diffusion of information in heterogeneous networks.

Our new model avoids a problematic assumption by Yamaguchi
(1994a) that is not made explicit and discussed substantially in the paper:
namely, that information is handed from one actor to another like some
kind of package. Two centrality measures that Friedkin (1991) introduced
and the measure of inefficiency in information flow through networks that
Yamaguchi (1994a) introduced rely on mean first passage time and the
related assumption in the Markov chain model (Kemeny and Snell 1960)
that the actor who transmits information loses it at the time he transmits.[1]
However, this assumption is inconsistent with "[the] peculiar feature of
information as a resource, in contradistinction to other sorts of resources
. . . . , that it is not consumed or lost in exchange but becomes 'possessed'

[1]It has to be noted that Friedkin models opinion formation, not information
diffusion. Although Friedkin's model resembles Yamaguchi's information diffusion
model, Friedkin's interpretation of the elements in the model is different. Although
Friedkin's model is equivalent with a Markov chain, it cannot be interpreted in the
sense that influence probabilities are transition probabilities between separate states in
a Markov chain.

by both the transmitter and the receiver" (Laumann and Knoke 1987:192). We believe that it is a crucial property of the transfer of information that the transmitter does *not* lose the information by giving it to somebody else.

The new model makes the information transfer assumption more realistic. This paper also searches for differences in predictions between the old and new models. In this way, we can distinguish between situations in which the unrealistic assumption is truly problematic and leads to unreliable predictions and other situations in which the predictions of the different models are comparable.

If the information diffusion process is compared with the diffusion of an infectious disease, the model used by Yamaguchi assumes that an actor is infectious only for a short time and infects at most one other actor. In the new model, it is assumed that an actor who is infectious remains infectious permanently. This is of course another extreme, and in the research on epidemics there exist intermediate models (see, for example, Bailey 1975; Bartholomew 1982). Still, in relatively small networks where information spreads in a short time, the assumption that actors do not forget information during the diffusion of the information in the network seems sensible. To distinguish between the two models compared in this paper, the model used by Yamaguchi is referred to as the "transit" model and the new model as the "contagion" model. Both are variants of diffusion models, and with the introduction of these terms the word "diffusion" is reserved for situations that do not refer to one of the two models specifically.

Among several centrality measures that Friedkin (1991) described, two of them—namely, *immediate effects centrality* and *mediative effects centrality*, which are respectively centrality measures of closeness centrality and betweenness centrality (Freeman 1979)—are related to the transit model. Friedkin did not investigate in detail how his centrality measures depend on particular existing network measures. He only showed examples of networks with five actors. Yamaguchi (1994a) used mean first passage time, thereby implicitly assuming the transit model, to derive global measures of the inefficiency of information flow through networks, and he related these inefficiency measures to descriptive measures of networks such as density and number of bridges. In another paper, Yamaguchi (1994b) introduced a new group of accelerated failure-time regression models for diffusion processes and then applied the models to simulated network-diffusion data using the logarithm of the mean first passage time between two actors in a network (a measure based on the transit model) to estimate the determinants of information diffusion time between the actors. In both models the results were plausible. Efficiency of information diffusion increased with network density and decreased with number of bridges. Actors with more ties needed less time to reach each other than actors with fewer ties.

Thus far, the results obtained with the transit model seem plausible, and it is possible that the unrealistic assumption is not problematic. However, the investigation of the consequences of this assumption has been limited, and the results of the transit model have not been compared with those of other models. We think that more extensive investigation is needed. Therefore, some intuition is offered to demonstrate that the "transit" assumption probably has undesirable implications. For example, the role of bridges is likely to be much more important in the case of a package that is passed from one actor to another than for the case of information that is transmitted. If a package reaches one side of a bridge but does not immediately cross the bridge, it will drift back into the part of the network from which it came and it can take a long time before the package returns to the bridge. Under the new assumption, once the information reaches one side of a bridge it will stay and can cross the bridge in every subsequent time period. Even more important is the role of the crucial variable network density. In Yamaguchi's article (1994a) global network density has a negative effect on the time it takes for information to spread through the network. The negative effect of density is expected to be larger under the new assumption, because if information stays with the transmitter, the total amount of information will build up quickly in a dense network and everybody will soon be informed. If information is sent around like a package, it can "get lost" in the large number of network ties in a dense network and the package may need a long time to reach certain actors.

Section 2 describes the new model for the diffusion process in two slightly different versions. Section 3 presents formal definitions of the dependent and independent variables used in the models and states conjectures about the effects of the different variables. In Section 4, we regress diffusion times generated with the different models at the global, dyadic, and individual levels on the network measures defined in Section 3 using a set of networks with seven actors. Section 5 argues that one has to be quite cautious using the model in cases when only dichotomous data about network ties are available. This section also gives a possible generalization of the model if more continuous values for tie strengths are available. Finally, Section 6 summarizes the results.

2. THE MODEL

The wide range of models describing diffusion processes includes over-views by Bailey, (1957, 1964, 1975), Bartholomew (1982), Mahajan and Peterson (1985), and Valente (1995). Especially in research on epidemics of infectious diseases, diffusion processes are studied in considerable de-tail, although the attention to effects of social structure has largely been ignored until recently (see Morris 1993). During the last decade, the mod-eling efforts in this area have been extended considerably toward explain-ing epidemics using structural properties of social networks (for example, Altmann 1993; Kretzschmar and Morris 1996). For spatial diffusion, struc-tural factors were often introduced by assuming lattice and related models (Harris 1974; Mollison 1977). More recently, lattice models have been also used in the studies of evolutionary ecology for such topics as the speed of spatial invasion and the emergence of cooperation through spatial contacts (for example, Nowak and May 1992; Ellner et al. 1998).

Furthermore, in recent years a number of studies using hazard rate models have expanded the research on diffusion models (for example, Diekmann 1989; Strang 1991; Hedström 1994; Strang and Tuma 1994; Yamaguchi 1994b; Greve, Strang, and Tuma 1995). The Strang-Tuma model, in particular, explicitly takes into account the effects of relations between transmitters and receivers of information on the rate of diffusion. While hazard rate models are very useful in general for empirical research on diffusion, most of the previous studies were not directly concerned with the effects of network structure and network positions on the rate of dif-fusion except for the studies of Yamaguchi (1994a, 1994b). Yamaguchi used simulated network data to derive hypotheses about the network-structural determinants of diffusion efficiency. After describing the new contagion model, which differs from the old transit model, we also employ simulated network data to compare the network-structural predictors of diffusion efficiency between the new and old models.

2.1. Definitions, Assumptions, and Main Theorem

Consider a network with n actors. The $n \times n$ incidence matrix of this net-work is given by N with $n_{ij} = 1$ if a tie exists between actor i and actor j, and $n_{ij} = 0$ otherwise; $n_{ii} = 0$.[2] Only undirected networks are considered ($n_{ij} = n_{ji}$ for all i, j), although the model can be generalized to directed networks.

[2]Boldface is used to denote matrices (uppercase) and vectors (lowercase).

A second assumption is that the network is connected: a path exists from every actor in the network to every other actor. For disconnected networks, the diffusion process can be solved by applying the model to the different connected components of the network. For the calculation of diffusion times, we need more than just the network of ties. It would be preferable if contact probabilities w_{ij} were known between every pair of actors i and j per unit of time. However, this paper is based on the situation in which only N is given. Yamaguchi (1994a) discussed theoretical considerations that allow contact probabilities to be deduced from the interests of the actors in the network. Assuming that an actor is equally interested in communicating with each of his neighbors and that he divides all his resources equally among these actors, the contact probabilities are chosen such that

$$ w_{ij} = \frac{n_{ij}}{\displaystyle\sum_{j=1}^{n} n_{ij}} \ . \tag{1} $$

For a connected network $\sum_{i=1}^{n} n_{ij} > 0$ and, thus, w_{ij} is well defined.[3] Note that the fact that N is symmetric does not imply that W is symmetric. At the end of the paper it will be shown that this definition of the contact probabilities is not self-evident. However, because this paper emphasizes the influence of the information transfer assumption on the implications of the model, the same definition is used for the contact probabilities as was used by Yamaguchi before, to avoid any suggestion that the implications change because of changes in this definition.

Knowing the probability that actor i communicates to another actor j in a given time period, we want to calculate expected diffusion times under different assumptions. Expected diffusion time refers to a number of distinct events in a network. These events will be discussed in detail later on. Examples are the expected time necessary to transmit information from actor i to actor j (dyadic diffusion time) or the expected time needed for information to reach every actor in a network if the information starts from one randomly chosen actor in the network (global diffusion time). Yamaguchi described how to calculate what is called *mean first passage time* (MFPT) at the global and dyadic levels for the transit model. Similarly, *mean contagion time* (MCT) will refer to the diffusion time for the con-

---

[3]Friedkin (1991) defined the diagonal elements of N to be equal to one in his example and then also used (1) to determine W.

tagion model.[4] Friedkin's *immediate effects centrality* (IEC) and *mediative effects centrality* (MEC) are based on mean first passage time in a model equivalent with the transit model. For these centrality measures too, comparable measures will be introduced based on the contagion model.

The transit model is based on a Markov chain directly described by W. This Markov chain has n states, and each state represents one actor who is able to *give* information to others. Each entry in W gives the probability that one actor will provide information to somebody else while *not* retaining the information himself. Thus the process represented by this Markov chain resembles passing a package between the actors in the network according to the probabilities in W. The expected time for information to go from one actor to another is based on the expected number of steps this package needs to travel from one actor to another, including the possibility that the package will return to the original actor. Another way to observe that these models use Markov chains in a problematic way is by recalling the *Markov property*, which defines Markov chains (Kemeny and Snell 1960:24). The Markov property implies that to predict the state of a chain at time $t + 1$, one need only know the state at time t; the transition does not depend on what happened before time t. However, to predict how a diffusion process will proceed, one actually wants to know all actors who have been informed before; therefore, these Markov chains should have more than n states.

This does not imply that Markov chain theory cannot be used to describe the contagion model. On the contrary, it is a very useful theory if the necessary assumptions are made explicit. First, we assume that each actor in a network is either informed (i.e., he obtained the considered information at any time in the past) or not informed. Second, we assume that nobody ever forgets information once obtained. This assumption is not necessary to define the Markov chain, but it seems a plausible assumption for the process under study.[5] Now, a Markov chain is defined in which the states are elements of the power set of actors in the network; i.e., each subset of actors in the network that is informed forms a state in the new

[4]Although we prefer the term "mean diffusion time," we are forced to use consistent terminology to compare the different models and need the term "diffusion" in cases that do not refer to one of the two models specifically.

[5]Of course this is not a suitable assumption in, for example, the study of epidemics in which the time that an actor is infectious is short compared with the time the disease takes to spread through the population. Including the possibility that actors forget information or stop transmitting information is possible, but in that case all states have to be included and the diffusion process becomes considerably more complex.

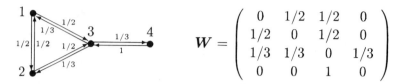

FIGURE 1. Example network.

Markov chain. We consider the example of the network in Figure 1. The power set S for this example has $2^4 = 16$ elements,

$$S = \{\varnothing,\{1\},\{2\},\{3\},\{4\},\{1,2\},\{1,3\},\{1,4\},\{2,3\},\{2,4\} ,$$

$$\{3,4\},\{1,2,3\},\{1,2,4\},\{1,3,4\},\{2,3,4\},\{1,2,3,4\}\} , \qquad (2)$$

where each element represents the set of actors who are informed in this state of the Markov chain. S has 2^n elements for a network with n actors. Fortunately, it is not necessary to consider all states in every analysis of such networks. For example, there is no need to consider the empty set $\varnothing$, because if nobody has information, nobody will obtain information. At least one actor has to have information to start the information process. The assumptions imply that the originally informed actor is always informed. Thus, we need only consider the states in which this actor is informed, which reduces the number of essential states to 2^{n-1}. Because the index of the actor where the information starts is only a label, this actor can always be given the number 1 without loss of generality. For special situations the number of states can be reduced even further.[6]

[6]E.g., for the network in Figure 1, if the information starts from actor 1, then actor 4 can be reached only through actor 3. Therefore, the states $\{1,4\}$ and $\{1,2,4\}$ will never occur during a diffusion process starting from actor 1. This implies that they do not play a role in the diffusion process and can be omitted. Furthermore, if there are groups of structurally equivalent actors—i.e., actors with identical contact probabilities with all other actors—only the number of these equivalent actors who are informed is important and not exactly which actors are informed. In the example network, actor 1 and actor 2 are structurally equivalent. This paper does not elaborate on this issue, although it is very relevant if one wants to apply the method to larger networks. Note that we assume in this paper that one actor is informed by an external source and that external sources of information do not play a role in the process of information diffusion. One can also assume that every actor with a certain probability is informed by an external source at each point in time. In that case one cannot omit, for example, the states $\{1,4\}$ and $\{1,2,4\}$ in the example.

To analyze the model, a transition matrix T has to be calculated that contains the transition probabilities between the states of the Markov chain at every point in time. However, some additional assumptions are necessary. Table 1 summarizes two sets of assumptions for MCT and compares them with assumptions for MFPT. In the multinomial version of MCT, we try to stay as close as possible to MFPT by allowing only one contact for an actor in every time period.[7] Except for the assumption that actors never forget information, the only additional assumption needed is that different actors act independently (*between-actor independence*). This version of MCT implies that the sum of w_{ij} equals one where we can choose $w_{ii} = 1 - \sum_{j \neq i} w_{ij}$. Thus, in this case W is stochastic. The advantage of calculating T in this way is that the model stays as close as possible to the transit model. However, the disadvantage is the restriction that the w_{ij} add up to one. Therefore, we introduce a second version in which *within-actor independence* is assumed as well; i.e., whether an actor communicates with one of his neighbors in a certain time period does not depend on whether he communicates with one of his other neighbors. In this version, the sum of w_{ij} need not to be equal to one. This implies that if W is given, this matrix can be used directly. To compare the two versions of the contagion model a stochastic W is always used, defined with the help of N, although a stochastic W is only necessary for the multinomial version.

The calculation of the transition matrix for the new Markov chain T is rather straightforward, although it becomes tedious for larger networks. We start with the assumption that an actor informs at most one other actor in each time period. Consider two states S_1 and S_2. Denote the probability that the process goes from S_1 to S_2 by $Pr(S_1 \rightarrow S_2)$. Then $Pr(S_1 \rightarrow S_2) = 0$ if $S_1 \not\subset S_2$, again because actors cannot forget information, which implies that the set of actors who have information can only increase. If $S_1 \subset S_2$ holds,

$$Pr(S_1 \rightarrow S_2) = \sum_{f:S_1 \rightarrow S_2} \prod_{i \in S_1} w_{i,f(i)} , \qquad (3)$$

where we sum over all functions f with domain S_1 and a range $f(S_1)$ for which holds $S_2 \backslash S_1 \subset f(S_1) \subset S_2$.[8] In words, we enumerate all possible

---

[7]This version is called "multinomial" because the selection of receivers by the transmitter of information follows a multinomial distribution. In the second version the selection follows a product-binomial distribution.

[8]$S_2 \backslash S_1$ is the notation for the set of elements that includes all elements of S_2 that are not elements of S_1.

TABLE 1
Overview of the Key Assumptions for Different Diffusion Time Models

Mean first passage time (MFPT)	Mean contagion time, "multinomial" version (MCT^M)	Mean contagion time, "product-binomial" version (MCT^{PB})
1. The informed actor informs at most one actor in every time period with probabilities w_{ij}.[a]	1. Each informed actor informs at most one actor in every time period with probabilities w_{ij} that are independent for all i (between-actor independence).	1. Each informed actor informs the other actors with probabilities w_{ij} that are independent for all i and j (within- and between-actor independence).
2. For every actor i, it holds that $\sum_j w_{ij} = 1$ and w_{ii} is the probability that actor i does not inform anybody if he is informed.		2. For all i,j, it holds that $0 \leq w_{ij} \leq 1$.[b]
3. An actor who informs another actor loses his information afterward.	3. An actor who is informed at any time will never forget the information.	
4. The w_{ij} are independent of the history of the diffusion process.		

[a] Because of assumption 3, there is always exactly one actor in the network informed under this set of assumptions.

[b] To compare this set of assumptions with the other two, the w_{ij} are chosen to be the same for all three cases in this paper. However, under this set of assumptions, the w_{ij} can be chosen less restrictively to represent, for example, empirical contact probabilities in certain time periods.

ways for the informed actors in S_1 to inform exactly the uninformed actors in $S_2 \backslash S_1$. Informed actors can also transmit information again to each other. $Pr(S_1 \rightarrow S_2) = 0$ if the number of actors in $S_2 \backslash S_1$ is larger than the number of actors in S_1, because for a function (as it was assumed to be) one element in the domain is assigned to exactly one element in the range.

For the network in Figure 1 using the probability matrix W, this results in the following transition matrix T_M (the subscript M indicates the multinomial version):

$$T_M = \begin{array}{c|cccccccc} & \{1\} & \{1,2\} & \{1,3\} & \{1,2,3\} & \{1,4\} & \{1,2,4\} & \{1,3,4\} & \{1,2,3,4\} \\ \hline \{1\} & 0 & 1/2 & 1/2 & 0 & 0 & 0 & 0 & 0 \\ \{1,2\} & 0 & 1/4 & 0 & 3/4 & 0 & 0 & 0 & 0 \\ \{1,3\} & 0 & 0 & 1/6 & 1/2 & 0 & 0 & 1/6 & 1/6 \\ \{1,2,3\} & 0 & 0 & 0 & 2/3 & 0 & 0 & 0 & 1/3 \\ \{1,4\} & 0 & 0 & 0 & 0 & 0 & 0 & 1/2 & 1/2 \\ \{1,2,4\} & 0 & 0 & 0 & 0 & 0 & 0 & 0 & 1 \\ \{1,3,4\} & 0 & 0 & 0 & 0 & 0 & 0 & 1/3 & 2/3 \\ \{1,2,3,4\} & 0 & 0 & 0 & 0 & 0 & 0 & 0 & 1 \end{array}$$

(4)

From this matrix and the graph that illustrates the Markov chain belonging to T_M in Figure 2, one sees that the states $\{1,4\}$ and $\{1,2,4\}$ could have been omitted. Markov chains constructed in this way have simple characteristics. As long as the network is connected, all the states are *transient* states, except the state in which everybody is informed, which is the unique *ab-*

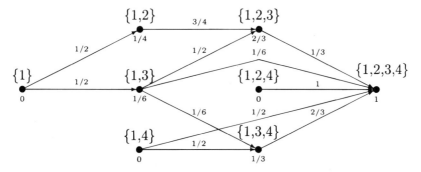

FIGURE 2. Markov chain belonging to the example network. (The probability at each node is the probability of staying at that node.)

sorbing state. Furthermore, once the process leaves a transient state, it can never return. The theory on absorbing Markov chains (Kemeny and Snell 1960:60, theorem 3.5.4.) is used to formulate the following theorem.

Theorem 1

Let Q be a matrix containing the rows and columns of T without the row and column for the absorbing state, and let actor 1 be the actor who obtained the information first and whose transition probabilities are given in the first row of T. Let I be the identity matrix of appropriate order. Then the following properties hold:

1. $(I - Q)_{1j}^{-1}$ is the expected number of times the process is in the j-th state before reaching the absorbing state.
2. $(I - Q)_{1+}^{-1}$ is the expected total number of steps the process needs to reach the absorbing state.
3. The sum of the first row entries of $(I - Q)^{-1}$ over all states in which a certain actor k is not informed is the expected number of steps the process needs to inform actor k.

Proof

Proofs for parts 1 and 2 can be found in Kemeny and Snell (1960, theorem 3.5.4). Part 3 is not true for absorbing chains in general, but it is true in this case because returning to any state is impossible. We will not present a formal proof here. The following intuition can be translated in a formal proof quite easily. To calculate the time needed to inform actor k, one considers the set of states in which actor k is informed as the new absorbing state. This implies that only a part of $(I - Q)$ has to be inverted. However, because the probability of going from a state in which k is informed to a state in which k is not informed is always 0, the inverse of the suitable part of $(I - Q)$ is exactly equal to the corresponding part of $(I - Q)^{-1}$. ∎

For the example network the first row of $(I - Q_M)^{-1}$ using W becomes

$$\begin{array}{ccccccc} \{1\} & \{1,2\} & \{1,3\} & \{1,2,3\} & \{1,4\} & \{1,2,4\} & \{1,3,4\}. \\ 1 & \frac{2}{3} & \frac{3}{5} & \frac{12}{5} & 0 & 0 & \frac{3}{20} \end{array} \tag{5}$$

This implies that the expected time to reach actor 2 from actor 1 equals $1 + \frac{3}{5} + \frac{3}{20} = 1\frac{3}{4}$; to reach actor 3 equals $1\frac{2}{3}$; to reach actor 4 equals $4\frac{2}{3}$; and to reach all actors equals $4\frac{49}{60}$.

The diffusion process as described above differs only in one aspect from MFPT—i.e., that information conveyed by the transmitter is also kept by the transmitter. Furthermore, actors communicate at most (exactly, if $w_{ii} = 0$) to one actor in every time period. This was a necessary assumption to treat W directly as a Markov chain. We can change that assumption now. If it is assumed that one actor i communicates with the other actors in one time period independently, T_{PB} can be calculated for every W with $0 \leq w_{ij} \leq 1$ for all i and j.

Consider two states: S_1 and S_2. Denote the probability that the process goes from S_1 to S_2 by $Pr(S_1 \rightarrow S_2)$. Then $Pr(S_1 \rightarrow S_2) = 0$ if $S_1 \not\subset S_2$, because actors cannot forget information, which implies again that the set of actors who have information can only increase. For $S_1 \subset S_2$,

$$Pr(S_1 \rightarrow S_2) = \prod_{j \in S_2 \backslash S_1} \left(1 - \prod_{i \in S_1}(1 - w_{ij})\right) \prod_{j \notin S_2}\left(\prod_{i \in S_1}(1 - w_{ij})\right) . \quad (6)$$

This is quite easy to understand. The first part expresses the probability that for each actor j who will be one of the newly informed, at least one of the already informed actors informs him. The second part expresses the probability that none of the informed actors in S_1 informs any actor not in S_2. Because all these events are independent and must be true at the same time, their respective probabilities have to be multiplied. Furthermore, it is important to see that the diagonal elements of W are not used to calculate T_{PB}. Thus the extent to which an actor "talks to himself" does not influence the diffusion process.

For the network in Figure 1, this results in the following transition matrix:

	{1}	{1,2}	{1,3}	{1,2,3}	{1,4}	{1,2,4}	{1,3,4}	{1,2,3,4}
{1}	1/4	1/4	1/4	1/4	0	0	0	0
{1,2}	0	1/4	0	3/4	0	0	0	0
{1,3}	0	0	2/9	4/9	0	0	1/9	2/9
{1,2,3}	0	0	0	2/3	0	0	0	1/3
{1,4}	0	0	0	0	0	0	1/2	1/2
{1,2,4}	0	0	0	0	0	0	0	1
{1,3,4}	0	0	0	0	0	0	1/3	2/3
{1,2,3,4}	0	0	0	0	0	0	0	1

$T_{PB} =$ (for the matrix above)

$$(7)$$

Theorem 1 applies also to this case. For the example network, the first row of $(I - Q_{PB})^{-1}$ becomes

$$
\begin{array}{ccccccc}
\{1\} & \{1,2\} & \{1,3\} & \{1,2,3\} & \{1,4\} & \{1,2,4\} & \{1,3,4\}. \\
\frac{4}{3} & \frac{4}{9} & \frac{3}{7} & \frac{18}{7} & 0 & 0 & \frac{1}{14}
\end{array}
\tag{8}
$$

According to Theorem 1, this implies that the expected time to reach actor 2 from actor 1 equals $\frac{4}{3} + \frac{3}{7} + \frac{1}{14} = 1\frac{5}{6}$; to reach actor 3 equals $1\frac{7}{9}$; to reach actor 4 equals $4\frac{7}{9}$; and to reach all other actors equals $4\frac{107}{126}$. Thus the expected contagion time is somewhat larger for the product-binomial selection of receivers than for the multinomial selection.

2.2. *Some Analytic Results for the New Model*

With the methods and theorem described above, it is possible to calculate contagion times for the contagion model. To find relations between contagion times and simple network measures, the first approach is to calculate these relations analytically. In this subsection, we give some illustrations showing that analytic results are complex and hard to interpret even for small networks.

The first analytic results are related to the comparison between the multinomial and product-binomial versions of the contagion model. In Section 4, it will be shown that the two models hardly differ in their implications. In all the networks we calculated, contagion time in the multinomial version is equal to or marginally smaller than it is in the product-binomial version. We could not prove that this result holds for all networks, but two related results are presented below. First, for trees—i.e., connected graphs with n nodes and $n - 1$ vertices (for example, see Wasserman and Faust 1994:119–20), the two versions result in exactly the same contagion times. The reasoning behind the proof is the following. In a tree exactly one possible path exists for information to travel between a pair of nodes. We can disregard paths in which information goes back and forth between actors because that does not occur in the information diffusion process as defined in the contagion model. For a certain tie in the network, say between actor i and actor j, the expected time needed for information to cross that tie after information has reached actor i equals $1/w_{ij}$ for the multinomial as well as for the product-binomial selection of receivers. The expected time needed for information to be transferred between i and j does not depend on which other actors are or have been informed during the diffusion process. Therefore, the expected time needed to traverse a certain path is the sum of the expected times for each tie in that path. Consequently, the expected time needed for information to travel from actor i to actor j in a tree is equal for both versions of the contagion model

$$\text{MCT}_{ij} = \frac{1}{w_{ik_1}} + \frac{1}{w_{k_1 k_2}} + \cdots + \frac{1}{w_{k_t j}} , \qquad (9)$$

where $k_1, \ldots, k_t$ are the nodes that necessarily have to be passed to reach j from i.[9] This is an appealing result because it closely fits the intuition that the diffusion process is straightforward if only one path for information diffusion exists. Results are not this simple for the transit model because information can go back and forth, even in trees.

For networks more complicated than trees, analytic expressions become fairly complex. For a three-actor network in which information starts from actor i, the expected time to reach actor j equals for the product-binomial distribution

$$\text{MCT}_{ij}^{PB} = \frac{1}{1 - (1 - w_{ij})(1 - w_{ik})}$$

$$+ \frac{w_{ik}(1 - w_{ij})}{(1 - (1 - w_{ij})(1 - w_{ik}))(1 - (1 - w_{ij})(1 - w_{kj}))} , \qquad (10)$$

where k is the third actor in the network. For the multinomial distribution, the expected time equals

$$\text{MCT}_{ij}^{M} = \frac{1}{w_{ij} + w_{ik}} + \frac{w_{ik}}{(w_{ij} + w_{ik})(1 - (1 - w_{ij})(1 - w_{kj}))} . \qquad (11)$$

Straightforward calculation shows that $\text{MCT}_{ij}^{PB} \geq \text{MCT}_{ij}^{M}$ and that equality holds if and only if $w_{ij} = 1$ or one of the ties in the triad does not exist—i.e., if the graph is a tree.

The two foregoing analytic results enable us to calculate directly expected contagion times for the network in Figure 1. For example, because the only way for information to reach actor 4 is through actor 3, MCT from actor 1 to actor 4 equals MCT from actor 1 to actor 3 plus the time needed for information to go from actor 3 to actor 4. Both contagion

---

[9]This implies that if we would approximate contagion time for W in a "neighborhood" of I with the help of linearization, we obtain similar expressions using the shortest paths, because probabilities of longer paths tend to zero. Note also that these expressions do not hold if information may start with more than one actor at the same time.

times are independent and are deduced from contagion times for the smaller subnetworks. This implies that MCT from actor 1 to actor 4 in the example network for the version using the multinomial distribution equals

$$\text{MCT}_{14}^M = \frac{1}{w_{12} + w_{13}} + \frac{w_{12}}{(w_{12} + w_{13})(1 - (1 - w_{13})(1 - w_{23}))} + \frac{1}{w_{34}} .$$

(12)

Thus for networks without loops other than triads, we can calculate contagion times easily. However, for a cycle with four actors the situation is complex enough to refrain from presenting it here. For a complete four-actor network, the expressions exceed one page; it resisted and discouraged attempts at interpretation.

The examples given above show that analytic expressions for contagion times become complex for small networks. An additional step is needed to link these expressions to simple network measures, such as density or degree. Therefore, in Section 4 we will use an approach that has been used before by Yamaguchi (1994a, 1994b) and Buskens (1998). We will calculate contagion times and network measures for a given set of networks. Then, with the help of statistical models, we will try to find comparative statics for the relations between contagion times and network measures.

3. VARIABLES AND MODEL COMPARISONS

In this section we formalize the dependent and independent variables to compare the different models. Conjectures are presented about the effects of the independent variables on the diffusion time and about the differences in these effects between the different diffusion models.[10]

3.1. *Dependent Variables*

We introduce comparable dependent variables in this section to compare the models distinguished in Section 2. The dependent variables will be defined at three levels: (1) global, (2) dyadic, and (3) individual.

---

[10]We use the term "conjecture" here because we discuss intuitions about the mathematical implications of theoretical models. This is in contradistinction to the term "hypothesis," which is used for a theoretical prediction about an empirical situation. Only if the analyses below show that the conjectures actually follow from the model do the conjectures become hypotheses.

3.1.1. Dependent Variables for the Transit Model

We define dyadic MFPT from actor i to actor j: MFPT_{ij}. This is the expected time it takes to transmit information from actor i to actor j in the transit model. For the exact way to calculate MFPT_{ij}, we refer to Yamaguchi (1994a). By definition $\text{MFPT}_{ii} = 0$ for all i. *Individual mean first passage time* is the average of MFPT_{ij} over all j:

$$\text{MFPT}_i = \frac{\sum_{j=1}^{n} \text{MFPT}_{ij}}{n-1} \, . \tag{13}$$

If W is not symmetric, MFPT_i is not equal to the average time needed for actor i to receive information, which we call *individual mean first receiving time*. Formally,

$$\text{MFRT}_i = \frac{\sum_{j=1}^{n} \text{MFPT}_{ji}}{n-1} \, . \tag{14}$$

Friedkin (1991) defines *immediate effects centrality* (IEC_i), which equals the inverse of MFRT_i. Furthermore, Friedkin defines a betweenness centrality measure based on the transit model called *mediative effects centrality* (MEC_i), which "indicates the extent to which an actor transmits the total effects of other actors" (p. 1490). We will define a similar measure for the contagion model later on. To obtain *global* MFPT, we average all MFPT_{ij} over i and j:

$$\text{GMFPT} = \frac{\sum_{i=1}^{n} \sum_{j=1}^{n} \text{MFPT}_{ij}}{n(n-1)} = \overline{\text{MFPT}_i} = \overline{\text{MFRT}_i} \, . \tag{15}$$

3.1.2. Dependent Variables for the Contagion Model

We now turn to the contagion model. For the multinomial and product-binomial versions, the definitions of contagion times are the same. We call the expected time it takes to diffuse information from actor i to actor j in the contagion model *dyadic mean contagion time* (MCT_{ij}), which is a measure of the distance between two actors in the network. The exact way to calculate MCT_{ij} is presented in Section 2. The calculation of MCT_{ij} implies that actor i is the first actor to be informed and then the expected time to reach actor j is determined. Because other starting situations, in which more actors are informed initially, are possible, one might ask whether this is the best starting position. For the transit model, only one actor is informed at any time; therefore, starting with one informed actor seems to be most closely related to dyadic mean first passage time. Moreover, it is the best building block for constructing individual and global contagion times. Namely, for these contagion times, we are interested in what happens with the information if it starts from a particular or a random actor.

For an actor i, one can average MCT_{ij} over all other actors. This is called *individual mean contagion time*:

$$\text{MCT}_i = \sum_{j=1}^{n} \frac{\text{MCT}_{ij}}{n-1} . \tag{16}$$

A straightforward alternative to this diffusion measure is the expected time needed for information to reach the absorbing state in which everyone is informed, when information starts from a certain actor. The disadvantage of this alternative measure is that one cannot determine whether many actors are informed early in the diffusion process and few at the end or the other way round. The intuition is that individual mean contagion time should be smaller for an actor who informs many actors early in the diffusion process. This problem could be cured by weighting a period of time before absorption with the expected number of actors not informed in that time period. Thus, a "second" definition of individual mean contagion time would be the following:

$$\widehat{\text{MCT}}_i = \sum_{j=1}^{2^{n-1}-1} \frac{u_j q_{1j}}{n-1} ,$$

where q_{1j} is the j-th element of the first row of the matrix Q and u_j is the number of actors who are not informed in the state that corresponds to the j-th column in the matrix Q. However, it can be proven that this alternative definition is equivalent to the first one—i.e., $\text{MCT}_i = \widehat{\text{MCT}}_i$. The reason is that each $q_{1j}/(n-1)$ occurs exactly u_j times in MCT_{ij}. Because of the parallel with the transit model, we refer mostly to the first definition of MCT_i.

Again, if W is not symmetric, the expected time for transmitting information is not equal to the expected time for receiving information, and we again need a reciprocal concept, *individual mean receiving time*:

$$\text{MRT}_i = \sum_{j=1}^{n} \frac{\text{MCT}_{ji}}{n-1} . \tag{17}$$

Global diffusion time based on the contagion model is *global mean contagion time* and is the average of all dyadic contagion times:

$$\text{GMCT} = \frac{\sum\limits_{i=1}^{n}\sum\limits_{j=1}^{n}\text{MCT}_{ij}}{n(n-1)} = \overline{\text{MCT}_i} = \overline{\text{MRT}_i} \ . \tag{18}$$

Individual mean contagion time and individual mean receiving time are measures of a certain actor's ability to transmit and receive information quickly through the network. We use these measures directly to introduce related centrality measures, *contagion transmitter centrality* and *contagion receiver centrality*:

$$\text{CTC}_i = \frac{1}{\text{MCT}_i} \ , \tag{19}$$

$$\text{CRC}_i = \frac{1}{\text{MRT}_i} \ . \tag{20}$$

Both centrality measures are closely related to closeness centrality as defined by Freeman (1979) and immediate effects centrality as introduced by Friedkin (1991).[11]

The concept of betweenness centrality is somewhat more difficult to address via the contagion model. We define W^{-i} as the contact probability matrix in which actor i does not communicate with any of the other actors. Thus $w_{ii}^{-i} = 1$ and $w_{ij}^{-i} = 0$ if $i \neq j$. In all other rows W^{-i} equals W.[12] We now define MCT_{jk}^{-i} as dyadic mean contagion time for W^{-i} from j to k. The difference between contagion time if actor i does not inform others and contagion time if actor i does inform others is a measure of the dyadic betweenness of actor i. We define

$$p_{ijk} = \frac{\text{MCT}_{jk}^{-i} - \text{MCT}_{jk}}{\text{MCT}_{jk}^{-i}}, \quad i \neq j \neq k \tag{21}$$

[11]The new closeness centrality measures can be considered generalizations of Freeman's closeness centrality, because CTC_i and CRC_i are exactly Freeman's measure if $W = N$. Note that Freeman defines his closeness measure only for symmetric networks, which means that CTC_i and CRC_i are identical in that case.

[12]Although W^{-i} is not related to a symmetric N, it is related to a network in which the ties between actor i and the others are directed toward actor i.

as the extent to which actor i affects the flow of information from actor j to actor k; $p_{ijk} \in [0,1]$. It is possible that actor j can no longer reach actor k if actor i ceases to transmit information. In that case we define $p_{ijk} = 1$. Now we define *contagion betweenness centrality* as the mean dyadic betweenness of actor i,

$$\text{CBC}_i = \frac{\displaystyle\sum_{j \neq i} \sum_{k \neq j, k \neq i} p_{ijk}}{(n-2)(n-1)}. \tag{22}$$

CBC_i has some nice properties. For the central actor in a star network, this betweenness measure equals one. The betweenness measure is zero for an actor who has only one tie and thus does not take a position between any two actors. All other actors will obtain values between zero and one. Table 2 presents an overview of the dependent variables.

3.2. Independent Variables

This subsection discusses the independent variables used in the different analyses. All the independent variables are relatively simple network measures. We will make conjectures about the effects expected from the network measures on the different dependent variables. The independent variables are all based on N, such that almost all network measures correspond to the measures used by Yamaguchi (1994a, 1994b). Because the network measures are explicitly defined in terms of n_{ij}, it is possible to generalize them in terms of w_{ij}. The discussions in Section 5 will show why that can be preferable. We present not only conjectures about effects of the independent variables on the different diffusion times but also conjectures about the differences between the transit model and the contagion model.

The independent variables can be divided in three levels: (1) dyadic, (2) individual, and (3) global.

3.2.1. Independent Variables at the Dyadic Level
At the dyadic level we have only one independent variable—namely, the *distance* between the two actors involved. The distance between two actors is the shortest path length between these two actors. We assumed that all actors are connected. Formally, the distance from actor i to actor j can be defined in terms of the product-binomial version of the contagion model:

$$\text{Distance}_{ij} = \text{MCT}_{ij}^{PB} \text{ if we choose } W = N.^{13} \tag{23}$$

---

[13]Note that this independent variable is not equal to dyadic contagion time, which is calculated with a W that is certainly not equal to N.

TABLE 2
Overview of Diffusion Times at Different Levels

MEAN FIRST PASSAGE TIME

Global level	Global mean first passage time	$\text{GMFPT} = \dfrac{\sum_i \sum_j \text{MFPT}_{ij}}{n(n-1)}$
Dyadic level	Dyadic mean first passage time	MFPT_{ij}
Individual level	Individual mean first passage time	$\text{MFPT}_i = \dfrac{\sum_j \text{MFPT}_{ij}}{n-1}$
	Individual mean first receiving time	$\text{MFRT}_i = \dfrac{\sum_j \text{MFRT}_{ji}}{n-1}$
	Immediate effects centrality	$\text{IEC}_i = \dfrac{1}{\text{MFRT}_i}$
	Mediative effects centrality	MEC_i

MEAN DIFFUSION TIME

Global level	Global mean contagion time	$\text{GMCT} = \dfrac{\sum_i \sum_j \text{MCT}_{ij}}{n(n-1)}$
Dyadic level	Dyadic mean contagion time	MCT_{ij}
Individual level	Individual mean contagion time	$\text{MCT}_i = \dfrac{\sum_j \text{MCT}_{ij}}{n-1}$
	Contagion transmitter centrality	$\text{CTC}_i = \dfrac{1}{\text{MCT}_i}$
	Individual mean receiving time	$\text{MRT}_i = \dfrac{\sum_j \text{MCT}_{ji}}{n-1}$
	Contagion receiver centrality	$\text{CRC}_i = \dfrac{1}{\text{MRT}_i}$
	Contagion betweenness centrality	$\text{CBC}_i = \sum_j \sum_k \dfrac{\text{MCT}_{jk}^{-i} - \text{MCT}_{jk}}{(n-1)(n-2)\text{MCT}_{jk}^{-i}}$

The reason is that by setting all contact probabilities equal to one, information will traverse all ties connected to informed actors in all time periods; therefore, the expected dyadic contagion time for information transmission from actor i to actor j equals the minimal number of steps needed between i and j.

This variable applies only in analyses where the dependent variable is at the dyadic level. The conjecture about the effect of distance does not need extensive elaboration. The farther two actors are apart, the longer it will take to convey information from one to the other. For both models, we expect distance to be a predominant predictor of dyadic diffusion time. Nevertheless, in the contagion model the probability that the shortest path will be used for diffusion is relatively high, while in the transit model this probability is relatively low, for in the transit model every deviation from the shortest path generates a completely different path to reach an actor. Therefore, we predict that the effect of distance is larger for the contagion model than for the transit model.

Conjecture 1 *Dyadic diffusion time increases with the distance between the two actors involved.*[14]

Conjecture 2 *The positive effect of distance on dyadic diffusion time is larger in the contagion model than in the transit model.*

3.2.2. Independent Variables at the Individual Level

We use four individual independent variables. For the dyadic dependent variables, these network measures form pairs of independent variables, because the measures for both actors are relevant. These independent variables do not apply to global diffusion times. The first variable is the *degree* of the actor. Degree is defined as the proportion of actual ties among possible ties:

$$\text{Degree}_i = \frac{\sum_{j=1}^{n} n_{ij}}{n-1} . \tag{24}$$

Because the networks used are undirected, indegree and outdegree cannot be distinguished. For directed networks, the above formula gives the outdegree, and the indegree can be obtained by summing over i. For both transmitting and receiving information, we think that a large degree is advantageous.

Conjecture 3 *Individual and dyadic diffusion time decrease with, respectively, the degree of the focal actor and the degree of an actor of the dyad.*

---

[14]If we write "diffusion time" without direct reference to a comparison between the contagion model and the transit model, we refer to diffusion time in general, including mean contagion time and mean first passage time.

The second individual variable is *individual local density*. This variable is defined for each actor as the extent to which ties exist between two actors connected to the focal actor:

$$\text{Local density}_i = \frac{\sum\limits_{j=1}^{n} \sum\limits_{k \neq j} n_{ij} n_{ik} n_{jk}}{\sum\limits_{j=1}^{n} \sum\limits_{k \neq j} n_{ij} n_{ik}} . \tag{25}$$

Individual local density is only defined by this formula if actor i has more than one tie. If an actor has only zero or one tie, individual local density is defined to be zero. There is one important effect of local density. High local density has the potential to trap information in a "corner" of the network and can therefore hinder information diffusion to other parts of the network. Because of the difference between the transit model, in which information really travels around, and the contagion model, in which information builds up, we expect that the effect of trapping information will be more severe for the transit model than for the contagion model. We expect that trapping information in the region of the transmitter will increase diffusion time, while the possibility of trapping information in the region of the receiver will decrease diffusion time. The following conjectures are consequences of this reasoning.

Conjecture 4 *Individual mean contagion time, individual mean first passage time, and dyadic diffusion time increase with the individual local density of the transmitter of information.*

Conjecture 5 *Individual mean receiving time, individual mean first receiving time, and dyadic diffusion time decrease with the individual local density of the receiver of information.*

Conjecture 6 *All predicted effects of individual local density are larger (in the absolute sense) for the transit model than for the contagion model.*

The third individual variable is *degree quality*, which is closely related to prominence measures (Burt 1976). The measure is formally defined for actor i as the covariance of whether actor i has a tie with actor j and the degree of actor j over all other actors j:

$$\text{Degree quality}_i = \sum_{j \neq i} \frac{n_{ij} n_j}{n-1} - \sum_{j \neq i} \frac{n_{ij}}{n-1} \sum_{j \neq i} \frac{n_j}{n-1} . \tag{26}$$

Because degree quality is an indication of the number of actors an actor can reach in two steps, relative to his own number of ties, we think that high degree quality is also advantageous for information diffusion.

Conjecture 7 *Individual and dyadic diffusion time decrease with, respectively, the degree quality of the focal actor and the degree quality of an actor of the dyad.*

The final independent variable at the individual level is the number of bridges at which an actor is located. A bridge is a tie in the network that satisfies two conditions. First, if this tie is removed, the network is not connected anymore; thus, information can no longer be communicated between these two parts of the network. Second, the two parts that are created by removing the tie both contain at least two actors. Because actors at bridges have direct access to different parts of the network, they will be faster at transmitting information. Moreover, actors at bridges have to be passed in order for information to travel from one part of the network to another; therefore, they will receive information earlier than others. In the introduction we already argued that this effect is larger for the transit model than for the contagion model.

Conjecture 8 *Individual and dyadic diffusion time decrease with the number of bridges at which the focal actor(s) is located.*
Conjecture 9 *The negative effect of the number of bridges at which an actor is located on individual and dyadic diffusion time is larger (in the absolute sense) for the transit model than for the contagion model.*

Of course, the number of bridges at which an actor is located is closely related to the concept of betweenness centrality and structural holes (Burt 1991), although Burt emphasizes essential actors, while we emphasize essential ties. We did not develop any conjectures about the effects of other independent variables on betweenness centrality measures, because for most variables it is not straightforward. For the number of bridges at which an actor is located it is almost obvious.

Conjecture 10 *Betweenness centrality increases with the number of bridges at which an actor is located.*

3.2.3. Independent Variables at the Global Level
Finally, we use five independent variables at the global level. The first one is *global density*, the proportion of ties in the network:

$$\text{Global density} = \sum_{i=1}^{n} \sum_{j=1}^{n} \frac{n_{ij}}{n(n-1)} . \qquad (27)$$

If all ties have equal probability of transferring information, the conjecture that global density increases efficiency of information transfer is straight-forward. However, for W in which the expected number of information transfers for each actor is one in each time period, this conjecture is not self-evident. The choice of W implies that global density is not a measure of the amount of information circulating through the network but of the number of possible ways for information to be transferred between all the actors in the network. Nevertheless, Yamaguchi (1994a, 1994b) obtained negative effects for global density. However, because Yamaguchi (1994b) did not include distance, it is questionable whether we will replicate his result. We expect that global density promotes diffusion if we take the average over all diffusion times—i.e., for GMCT and GMFPT. But for individual and certainly dyadic diffusion times the effects are less clear. More ties provide additional possibilities for the transmission of informa-tion, and information can choose paths other than the shortest path. This effect will be larger for the transit model than for the contagion model, because in the transit model deviating from the shortest path really means taking a detour, while in the contagion model it only means waiting for the moment when the shortest path can be continued.

Conjecture 11 *Global, individual, and dyadic diffusion time decreases with global density.*
Conjecture 12 *The negative effect of global density on global, individual, and dyadic diffusion time decreases (in the absolute sense) with the level of aggregation of diffusion time—i.e., going from global diffusion time via individual diffusion time to dyadic diffusion time.*
Conjecture 13 *The negative effect of global density on global, individual, and dyadic diffusion time decreases (in the absolute sense) if we move from the contagion model to the transit model, especially for individual and dyadic diffusion time.*

The second global variable is *transitivity*—the proportion of all or-dered triads i, j, k for which the ties (i,j), (i,k), and (j,k) exist among all ordered triads for which the ties (i,j) and (i,k) exist.[15] Formally,

---

[15]Unfortunately, this definition is different from the two definitions for system-level local density given by Yamaguchi, although it correlates highly (.975 in the data

$$\text{Transitivity} = \frac{\displaystyle\sum_{i=1}^{n}\sum_{j=1}^{n}\sum_{k=1}^{n} n_{ij}\, n_{ik}\, n_{jk}}{\displaystyle\sum_{i=1}^{n}\left(\sum_{j=1}^{n}\sum_{k \neq j} n_{ij}\, n_{ik}\right)} \,. \tag{28}$$

In a network in which no actor has more than one tie (for connected net-works this can only be a network with two actors), transitivity is zero. By an argument similar to that for individual local density, transitivity will cause trapping of information in some parts of the network. Therefore, transitivity will slow down information diffusion for global diffusion time, and the effect will be larger for the transit model. Similar effects are expected for individual and dyadic diffusion time.

Conjecture 14 *Global, individual, and dyadic diffusion times increase with transitivity.*

Conjecture 15 *The positive effect of transitivity on global, individual, and dyadic diffusion times is larger for the transit model than for the contagion model.*

The third global variable is the *number of bridges* in the whole network. Because bridges form bottlenecks for information transfer through the network, we expect diffusion times to increase with the number of bridges in the network. As we explained in the introduction, we expect this effect to be larger for the transit model than for the contagion model.

Conjecture 16 *Global, individual, and dyadic diffusion time increase with the number of bridges in the network.*

Conjecture 17 *The positive effect of bridges on global, individual, and dyadic diffusion time is larger for the transit model than for the contagion model.*

---

used later in the paper) with the "1994b" definition. One advantage of this definition is that it is more easily expressed in terms of the n_{ij}. A second advantage is that it is a weighted sum of the individual local densities, which will be defined later, and in this sense it is an improvement on Yamaguchi's "1994a" definition because it weights the individual local densities in such a way that all ordered triads contribute equally to transitivity. All these definitions lead to virtually the same results in the analyses. Because the new definition differs slightly from earlier definitions of system-level local density and to avoid confusion with individual local density, we use the term "transitivity," which is certainly appropriate.

The fourth global variable is *diameter*, which is defined as the maximum of the distances between all pairs of actors in the network:

$$\text{Diameter} = \max_{i,j} \text{distance}_{ij} \ . \tag{29}$$

We use the diameter only to explain individual and global diffusion measures. It does not add explanatory power beyond that provided by the distance between two actors for dyadic diffusion times. We expect that for larger diameters diffusion times are larger because the actors are more dispersed. By an argument similar to that for number of bridges, we expect that especially for the transit model information has many possible ways to wander around if the diameter is large.

Conjecture 18 *Global and individual diffusion time increase with the diameter of the network.*

Conjecture 19 *The positive effect of diameter on global and individual diffusion time is larger for the transit model than for the contagion model.*

The last global variable is *coefficient of variation in centrality* (CVC) used by Yamaguchi (1994a). CVC is formally defined as

$$\text{CVC} = \frac{\sqrt{\sum_{i=1}^{n} \left(n_i - \sum_{i=1}^{n} \frac{n_i}{n-1} \right)^2}}{\sum_{i=1}^{n} \frac{n_i}{n-1}} = \frac{\sqrt{V(n_i)}}{E(n_i)} \ , \tag{30}$$

where $n_i = \sum_{j=1}^{n} n_{ij}$ is the number of ties of actor i, and $E(n_i)$ and $V(n_i)$ are the mean and variance of n_i over actors in the network. CVC, rather than the standard deviation of n_i, is employed because the latter is affected by the density. CVC is closely related to the degree variance defined by Snijders (1981). Conjectures about CVC are not straightforward, but we will include this variable because of its relevance in Yamaguchi's papers.

4. THE SIMULATION

4.1. *Design*

As discussed in Section 2, it seemed infeasible to obtain relations between diffusion times and network measures analytically. First, diffusion times can be expressed in terms of w_{ij}, but for most networks these are complex expressions even for quite simple networks. Second, we did not define the network measures in terms of w_{ij} but in terms of n_{ij}. Thus, an additional step is needed to express diffusion times as a function of these network measures.[16]

Therefore, we use a simulation method that has also been used by Yamaguchi (1994a, 1994b) and, in a slightly adjusted way, by Buskens (1998) to compare the different diffusion models. We use the set of 218 networks containing all nonisomorphic connected networks with 7 actors and 6, 7, 8, or 9 ties. We computed the expected diffusion times and the network measures discussed in Section 3 for each of these networks. In the next step, we used ordinary statistical methods to "explain" the diffusion times from the network measures. With the linear regression models, we estimate diffusion times as a linear function of the network measures. This linear function will not fit the diffusion times perfectly, but because any "smooth" function can be approximated by a linear function, the coefficients found in the regression are estimates for the partial derivatives of the involved network measures. The explained variance of these models provides an indication for how well the diffusion times can actually be approximated by such a linear function.

There are two main reasons why we chose this particular set of networks. First, the variance of the network measures is large enough. Choosing denser networks—i.e., with more than 9 ties—causes higher correlations between the network measures we want to use in the analyses. With fewer than 6 ties, a network with 7 actors cannot be connected. Second, diffusion times are still computable in a relative short time for networks with 7 actors.[17] The population of networks for which we want to estimate the regression analyses is the population of all networks with 7 actors and 6, 7, 8, or 9 ties. This population consists of considerably more than 218 networks; however, there are only 218 different networks that are nonisomorphic. Some groups of isomorphic networks are larger than other groups. Because isomorphic networks lead to equivalent calculations, we calculate diffusion times for each group of isomorphic networks only once. In the analyses, we weight each network in proportion to the number of

---

[16]Buskens (1998) expressed the network measures in terms of the w_{ij} and was able to deduce with linearization some first-order results for the relation between a comparably complex dependent variable and density and outdegree.

[17]At the moment we can handle networks of size at most 12 and certainly up to size 10. Diffusion times can be calculated in a few seconds for networks of size 7, but computation time increases rapidly to minutes and hours for larger networks. The Pascal and FORTRAN computer programs used are available from the authors.

isomorphic networks it represents. The weighting is done in such a way that the total number of networks still adds up to 218.[18] We do not claim that we use in this way a representative set of networks as they occur in the real world. How the results depend on the specific choice of the set of networks will be a subject of later investigations.

4.2. Analyses

4.2.1. Global Diffusion Time

We start by presenting the analyses for global mean contagion time compared with global mean first passage time. For these global diffusion times, we apply ordinary linear regression. There were no strong indications that we could obtain a considerably better fit by transforming the dependent variable by the logarithm transform (Yamaguchi 1994a) or using another transformation of the dependent variable.[19]

Table 3 (Panel A) shows the correlations between the different global diffusion measures. We use superscripts M and PB to distinguish between the multinomial and product-binomial version of the contagion models. It becomes immediately clear that the contagion times of these two versions are extremely highly correlated. Furthermore, although all measures are highly correlated, the measures of the transit and contagion models are certainly not perfectly correlated.

---

[18]In fact, the weighting is based on a representation of social networks as *labeled* graphs. If networks would be considered as *unlabeled* graphs, such weighting should not be used. We think that the representation by labeled graphs is preferable because actors are clearly distinguishable in a social network. Because substantive results do not differ whether or not the weights are used in the analyses, this choice is not essential for our results.

[19]More precisely, we did Box-Cox regression (Box and Cox 1964) in Stata 5.0 around the mean and the origin, estimating one parameter for the transformation of the dependent variable. Although the transformation parameter was significant in many analyses, it was not consistent, depending on whether the transformation was done around the origin or around the mean. Moreover, the substantial consequences did not differ from those obtained from the untransformed regression in all analyses. Also, the logarithm transform was not chosen. The largest differences with the untransformed dependent variables occurred for dyadic diffusion times. However, equation (13) shows that the distance between the two actors has an additive effect on the dependent variable. Because the distance is the most important explanatory variable, the logarithm transform is less suitable. Furthermore, the substantial differences between the untransformed and logged dependent variables were marginal at the global and individual levels. Thus, we preferred to keep all dependent variables comparable and did not use any transformation.

TABLE 3

Global Diffusion Variables: Weighted Correlations and Weighted Linear Regression
with Huber Standard Errors and Standardized Coefficients ($N = 218$)

A. Correlations		GMCT ^{M}	GMCT ^{PB}	GMFPT
GMCT^M		1		
GMCT^{PB}		0.996	1	
GMFPT		0.916	0.911	1

B. Regression results		Contagion		Transit
	Conjecture	GMCT ^{M}	GMCT ^{PB}	GMFPT
Global density	−	−0.51**	−0.48**	−0.35**
Transitivity	+	0.36**	0.41**	0.40**
Number of bridges	+	0.46**	0.43**	0.48**
Diameter	+	0.01	0.03	0.26**
CVC	?	0.36**	0.38**	0.14**
Explained variance		0.95	0.94	0.95

** and * represent significance at respectively $p < .001$ and $p < .01$ (two-sided tests).

Table 3 (Panel B) presents the regression results for the global dependent variables. We present β-coefficients to compare the sizes of similar effects in the different models. The standard errors are Huber standard
errors that are consistent under heterogeneity in the residual variables.[20]
These can be generalized for clustered observations (Rogers 1993), which
we will need to do for the other dependent variables.

The density effect is negative for all dependent variables as was
expected in Conjecture 11. As a matter of fact, the effects of all independent variables are in the expected directions. Only the effect of diameter is
not significant for the contagion models. The differences or similarities
between the transit model and the contagion models are more interesting to
look at. As Conjecture 13 stated, the effect of density is indeed larger for
the contagion models than for the transit model. In the contagion models,
it is the largest effect of all, and that is certainly not the case for the transit
model. Furthermore, we expected in Conjecture 15 that the effect of transitivity would be smaller for the contagion models. However, the coeffi-

[20]The Huber estimator of variance was independently discovered by Huber
(1967) and White (1980) and is also called the White, sandwich, or robust estimator of
variance. Note that the standard errors do not have an interpretation in the classical
sense because we analyze a complete population and not a sample. Nevertheless, we
provide the standard errors to indicate the "importance" of the effects.

cients are very much alike. What can be noted is that GMCT ^{M}, which was considered to be closest to the transit model because under the multinomial selection of receivers only one actor at a time could be informed, has indeed a smaller coefficient. This coefficient becomes larger again if we change to GMCT ^{PB}. From the analytic results, we know that GMCT ^{PB} is larger than GMCT ^{M} for the three-actor network. Because transitivity measures the number of "closed" triads compared with "open" triads, this is an indication that the difference between the contagion times for the multinomial and the product-binomial versions depends on the number of closed triads in the network.

The number of bridges has a larger effect on GMFPT than on GMCT, although the difference is marginal. Thus, we do not obtain strong confirmation of Conjecture 17, which stated that bridges would hinder information diffusion more severely in the transit model. On the other hand, similar reasoning holds for diameter, which led to Conjecture 19. In the transit model, information is much more able to wander around especially if the diameter of the network is large. In the contagion model, diameter does not affect information flow, while it has a strong effect on GMFPT. In addition, number of bridges and diameter are the two dependent variables with the highest correlation (.66). If we drop diameter from the analyses, the results for GMCT hardly change, but for GMFPT the coefficient of the number of bridges increases sharply. All these observations confirm that GMFPT increases much faster than GMCT with number of bridges and/or size of diameter.

The results for global diffusion times show that substantive predictions do not change between the transit and contagion models—i.e., all predicted directions of effects are the same. The only difference is that the contagion model does not predict an effect of diameter in addition to an effect of number of bridges, while the transit model predicts that diameter has a positive effect on global diffusion time above and beyond the positive effect of number of bridges.

4.2.2. Dyadic Diffusion Time

In the previous section, we already found differences in the magnitude of effects of the network measures between the transit model and the contagion model at the global level. However, we will now see that the differences become larger at the more detailed dyadic level.

Table 4 (Panel A) shows the correlations between the dyadic diffusion measures. Again, the correlation between the two different versions of the contagion model is nearly one. The correlations between the contagion

TABLE 4

Dyadic Diffusion Variables: Weighted Correlations and Weighted Linear Regression with Standardized Coefficients and Huber Standard Errors Modified for Observations Clustered Within the Networks ($N = 9156$, number of clusters is 218)

A. Correlations		MCT_{ij}^{M}	MCT_{ij}^{PB}	$MFPT_{ij}$
MCT_{ij}^{M}		1		
MCT_{ij}^{PB}		0.999	1	
$MFPT_{ij}$		0.884	0.875	1

B. Regression results		Contagion		Transit
	Conjecture	MCT_{ij}^{M}	MCT_{ij}^{PB}	$MFPT_{ij}$
Global network measures				
Global density	−	0.03*	0.03*	0.08**
Transitivity	+	0.06**	0.06**	0.12**
Number of bridges	+	−0.03*	−0.04**	0.10**
CVC	?	0.10**	0.09**	0.10**
Individual network measures				
Degree transmitter	−	0.19**	0.20**	0.19**
Degree receiver	−	−0.26**	−0.24**	−0.48**
Local density transmitter	+	0.02**	0.03**	−0.02**
Local density receiver	−	−0.07**	−0.06**	−0.06**
Degree quality transmitter	−	0.05**	0.05**	0.12**
Degree quality receiver	−	0.02**	0.03**	−0.23**
Bridges transmitter	−	0.03**	0.04**	0.05**
Bridges receiver	−	0.03**	0.03**	−0.05**
Dyadic network measure				
Distance	+	0.88**	0.90**	0.55**
Explained variance		0.93	0.93	0.90

** and * represent significance at respectively $p < .001$ and $p < .01$ (two-sided tests).

models and the transit model are a little bit lower than for the global diffusion variables.

Table 4 (Panel B) presents the regression results for the dyadic dependent variables. The dyadic dependent variables have the problem that the cases are nested within networks. For each network we have forty-two cases. Therefore, a straightforward generalization of the Huber standard errors is used that takes explicitly into account the clustering of observations and the expected correlations between residuals (Rogers 1993).

Arguments to explain the effects on dyadic diffusion time have to start with distance. In the contagion model, distance is by far the most important explanatory variable, and in the transit model it is, with the degree of the receiver, one of the most important variables. The interpretations of all the other variables are based on whether they cause information to make detours away from the shortest path or whether they help information reach the receiver. In comparing the models, the reasoning will be analogous to that outlined earlier. Possibilities for detours increase diffusion time to a larger extent in the transit model than in the contagion model. Possibilities for trapping information in the neighborhood of the receiver decrease diffusion time to a larger extent in the transit model than in the contagion model.

Distance has the effect expected in Conjecture 1 and is indeed more important in the contagion model than in the transit model, as was stated in Conjecture 2. Global density clearly does not have the effect expected in Conjecture 11. High global density causes information to go in many directions, and most of them turn out to be wrong. This implies that the argument for Conjecture 12 about the decreasing effect of density for dependent variables at lower aggregation levels is even stronger than expected. The effect of information drifting away to unfavorable parts of the network is larger than the opportunity provided by information paths; and, therefore, the effect turns in the other direction. In correspondence with Conjecture 13, this effect is even stronger for the transit model. In the contagion models, the effect of density is in the wrong direction but hardly significant. Related to this effect is also the definition of W, which implies that increasing density does not increase the amount of information going through the network but only the number of possible ways to transfer information.

Transitivity has the effect of trapping information away from the receiver, and this effect is stronger in the transit model (Conjectures 14 and 15). In the transit model, number of bridges has the effect expected in Conjecture 16, which reasons that bridges hinder information flow. However, we find a different prediction for the contagion model—namely, that number of bridges decreases diffusion time. This shows clearly that information diffusion turns out to be hindered less by bridges in the new model, as stated in Conjecture 17. The fact that bridges force information to take the shortest path is even more important in the contagion model resulting in a negative effect of number of bridges on contagion time. CVC has similar effects in all models.

The effect of degree is in the direction expected in Conjecture 3 for the receiver. Larger receiver degree reduces diffusion time. However, larger transmitter degree increases diffusion time. Comparable with the argument explaining why a higher density could have a positive effect on diffusion time, transmitter degree has a positive effect on diffusion time because the transmitter has more possible ways to transmit the information in the *wrong* direction. The origin of this effect also lies in the definition of W. We will be more specific about that problem in the next section. We did not formulate conjectures about differences between the effect of degree for the transit model and the contagion model. Still, degree is more important in the transit model than in the contagion model. This can be seen most clearly if the degree qualities of the transmitter and receiver are taken into account. Degree quality indicates the "second-order" degree—namely, the number of contacts that can be reached in two steps. High transmitter degree quality increases diffusion times. Again, in this situation information has a higher probability of taking routes other than the direct route to the receiver, and this effect is stronger in the transit model. Moreover, receiver degree and degree quality help considerably to accelerate information diffusion toward the receiver in the transit model, but in the contagion model, receiver degree quality increases contagion time slightly.

Concerning individual local density, we run into collinearity problems that affect the analyses. Correlations between independent variables are often low, but in some cases they are as high as 0.6—for example, between number of bridges and global density. Fortunately, in most cases this does not seem to be a problem. Nevertheless, it is a problem for degree quality and individual local density. The correlation is about 0.52 and the two measures seem to explain about the same part of the variation in the dependent variable. If we include only one of the two pairs of variables, the explained variance decreases only marginally. In that case, Conjecture 7 is confirmed for receiver degree quality but rejected for transmitter degree quality. The trapping effects of individual local density as stated in Conjectures 4 and 5 are confirmed for the contagion model. Only if we add the coefficients of degree quality and individual local density is some confirmation found for the assertion that trapping of information is more important in the transit model than in the contagion model (Conjecture 6). This is indicated especially by the fact that receiver degree quality has a large negative effect on the dyadic diffusion time for the transit model.

The effect of number of bridges at which an actor is located mostly rejects Conjecture 8. The conjecture is only confirmed for receiver bridges in the transit model. All effects are relatively small, and we are still puzzled about what explains these effects. Nevertheless, the effects of receiver bridges moves in different directions for the transit model and the contagion model. Thus we do find essential differences between the transit and contagion models in this section. Not only is the effect of distance between two actors much more important in the contagion model, but also opposite effects were found most prominently for number of bridges in the network and for degree quality of the receiver.

4.2.3. Individual Diffusion Measures

All analyses in this paper were done for both the multinomial and the product-binomial selection of receivers. The correlations between the corresponding diffusion times were always higher than 0.995, and substantive implications did not change. A plausible reason for this is that at every time point, the "marginal" probability of information being provided to actors is the same in both versions of the model: only probabilities for simultaneously informing others differ. We have already shown in Section 2 that the assumptions led to exactly the same results for trees. In the last two subsections, we presented results for both versions for dyadic and global diffusion time to show how small the differences are. From now on we use only the product-binomial version because this version places less stringent restrictions on W.

In considering the efficiency of information transfer in a network from the actor's point of view, there are actually three things that matter. First, if an actor obtains information, how quickly can he transmit that information throughout the network? Second, if information enters the network at some random place, how long will it take before the information reaches the focal actor? Third, if somebody wants to transmit information to a specific other actor in the network, to what extent can a third actor influence the time it takes to transfer information between these two actors? For all three concepts, we developed diffusion and/or centrality measures. In this subsection, diffusion times for transmitting and receiving and the centrality measure for betweenness are analyzed. We did not analyze closeness centrality measures related to the diffusion times for transmitting and receiving because they are the inverses of the diffusion times.

Table 5 (Panel A) presents the correlations between the dependent variables of this section. Note that we expect negative correlation between diffusion times and centrality measures. In Table 5 (Panel A), we are immediately struck by the correlations in the second column. All diffusion measures should give an indication of the lack of centrality of a certain actor. However, individual mean first passage time correlates negatively with the other diffusion times, while it correlates positively with the betweenness centrality measures. The implications of the model are not convincing for mean first passage time: for example, in a chain of seven actors the most peripheral actors (those at the ends of the chain) reach the other

TABLE 5

Individual Diffusion Variables: Weighted Correlations and Weighted Linear Regression with Standardized Coefficients and Huber Standard Errors Modified for Observations Clustered within the Networks ($N = 1526$, number of clusters is 218)

A. Correlations

	MCT_i^{PB}	$MFPT_i$	MRT_i^{PB}	$MFRT_i$	CBC_i	MEC_i
MCT_i^{PB}	1					
$MFPT_i$	0.52	1				
MRT_i^{PB}	0.63	−0.10	1			
$MFRT_i$	0.60	−0.17	0.95	1		
CBC_i	−0.21	0.38	−0.63	−0.54	1	
MEC_i	−0.44	0.34	−0.93	−0.90	0.81	1

B. Regression results

	Conj.[a]	Transmitting		Receiving		Betweenness	
		Contagion MCT_i^{PB}	Transit $MFPT_i$	Contagion MRT_i^{PB}	Transit $MFRT_i$	Contagion CBC_i	Transit MEC_i
Global network measures							
Global density	−	−0.23**	−0.43**	0.12**	0.19**	−0.27**	−0.29**
Transitivity	+	0.18**	0.32**	0.14**	0.12**	0.13**	0.04**
Number of bridges	+	0.51**	0.45**	0.21**	0.21**	−0.19**	−0.11**
Diameter	+	0.06*	0.24**	0.01	0.06**	0.04**	−0.01*
CVC	?	0.45**	0.04	0.19**	0.18**	0.10**	−0.08**
Individual network measures							
Degree	−	−0.27**	0.31**	−0.88**	−0.78**	0.73**	0.94**
Individual local density	+/−	0.34**	0.07**	−0.01	−0.03	−0.11**	−0.10**
Degree quality	−	−0.38**	0.23**	−0.18**	−0.37**	−0.16**	0.21**
Individual bridges	−	−0.31**	−0.05*	−0.12**	−0.14**	0.52**	0.19**
Explained variance		0.88	0.91	0.94	0.89	0.89	0.97

** and * represent significance at respectively $p < .001$ and $p < .01$ (two-sided tests).

[a] The conjectures hold only for transmitting and receiving information. If there are two signs, the first holds for transmitting information and the second for receiving. For betweenness, the only conjecture we had is that the number of bridges at which an actor is located increases betweenness centrality.

actors in the shortest time and should be considered central. These kinds of results do not follow from the contagion model. There are two factors responsible for these peculiar results. First, the transit model implies that if an actor in the center of the chain starts the diffusion process in the wrong direction, he has to wait until the information comes back to him before he can transmit to the other half of the network. The actors at the end of the chain will always transmit their information in the right direction. Second, the definition of W implies that everybody communicates with others to the same extent. The definition is built on the assumption that every actor has the same amount of resources to transmit information and divides these resources equally among his contacts. Thus, an actor at the end of the chain will communicate at every time period to his neighbor and as soon as he obtains information the neighbor will know it at the next time period. In this way, actors are restricted by their own contacts, but they are hardly restricted by the resources of their neighbors; in other words, neighbors will always "listen." On the other hand, if we examine the time it takes before an actor obtains information, he is restricted by his own contacts as well as by the time other actors invest in communicating with him. Therefore, for the diffusion time of an actor it seems better to define W in such a way that actors divide their resources among the actors who are communicating with them. Formally, this would imply that we transpose W and interpret w_{ij} as "actor i receives information from actor j." The resulting diffusion times are exactly MRT_i and $MFRT_i$. Furthermore, as was mentioned before, $MFRT_i = 1/IEC_i$, for which the results are still reasonable.

Table 5 (Panel B) shows that most of the conjectures about MCT_i are supported. Density, degree, degree quality, and the number of bridges at which the transmitter is located promote information diffusion. Local density, bridges, diameter, and centralization (CVC) inhibit information diffusion. Note that this does not imply that centralization of the network is disadvantageous for information diffusion in general. It is only disadvantageous on average if each actor is equally likely to be the starting point of the diffusion process. However, due to the degree effect, a centralized network will diffuse information fast if the central actor always receives information first.

$MFPT_i$ is clearly a problematic measure. The coefficients for degree and degree quality imply that peripheral actors often turn out to be the most central actors. This is a good example of how a number of plausible assumptions can combine to lead to an implausible conclusion. Furthermore, it is the clearest example that the contagion and transit models can have different implications in certain situations.

In contrast with the measures for transmitting information, it is also remarkable that the results for receiving time for the transit and contagion models are so similar. To receive information soon, degree and degree quality are the important indicators, which confirms Conjectures 3 and 7. Density is again a disturbing factor. Large density increases information diffusion time in both models, refuting Conjecture 11. Again, the background of this effect lies in the definition of W, which implies that larger density only influences the number of possible ways to transfer information, not the amount of information in the network. Trapping information in the area around the focal actor is, as stated by Conjecture 6, more important in the transit model. The similarity between the transit and contagion models in this case indicates that the immediate effects centrality introduced by Friedkin (1991) is less sensitive with respect to the information transfer assumption in this situation.

We did not make many conjectures about the betweenness measures. The only conjecture about betweenness centrality we formulated is confirmed: actors located at more bridges have higher betweenness centrality. It is not in accordance with our intuition that this effect is larger in the contagion model than in the transit model. Nevertheless, we observe some other interesting results. In dense networks, actors will find other routes relatively easily if one actor stops diffusing information. As a result betweenness centrality is smaller, on average, in dense networks. In a network with areas that are locally dense, there will be actors with high betweenness centrality between these areas, while actors that are in the locally dense areas will have lower betweenness centrality. An actor who has more ties will also be more influential in the diffusion of information through the network. Moreover, contagion betweenness centrality is much more strongly related to number of bridges at which an actor is located than is mediative effects centrality. Two effects point in opposite directions for the two models. Namely, in the transit model degree quality has a positive effect on betweenness centrality, while in the contagion model it has a negative effect. And CVC has a positive effect on betweenness in the contagion model, while it has a negative effect in the transit model.

Summarizing, we encountered a number of essential differences related to the assumptions made in the models under research. At the highest aggregation level, the models do not differ that much. However, at the individual and dyadic levels, we find that the implications of the transit model differ from those of the contagion model. First, we obtained predictions of effects of variables that point in opposite directions for some variables—for example, for the effect of number of bridges on dyadic diffusion time and for the effects of degree and degree quality on individual diffusion time for transmitting information. For betweenness centrality, two effects of network measures were found that went in different directions. Second, effects of some variables were found to be consistently smaller for one model than for the other. In the transit model the effect of bridges and/or diameter is much larger than in the contagion model. Also, the effect of trapping information in certain parts of the network is larger in the transit model. These effects are due to the unrealistic information transfer assumption in the transit model; and, therefore, it can be stated that the transit model actually overestimates these effects. Third, we discovered that the implementation of W can have large effects on centrality measures. For example, the positive effects of density on dyadic and individual diffusion times are related to the assumption that all actors invest the same amount in communicating with others. We found especially undesirable results for the combination of the transit model and the W chosen for individual mean first passage time. The results turned out to be less problematic for individual mean contagion time using the improved information transfer assumption. Thus we found differences between different centrality measures not only because they have different substantive meanings but also because of assumptions we do not want to have such effects— among others, the assumption that information is transmitted between actors as a kind of package.

5. USING THE MODELS IN EMPIRICAL ANALYSES

Discussions about the choice and use of W in the model would have shifted the focus of the paper too much away from the key assumption we wanted to discuss—namely, the information transfer assumption. However, the influence of the choice of W seems to be essential in the empirical use of the model. Therefore, we summarize some points of that discussion without new analyses in this section.

Some cautionary remarks about using the model discussed in this paper in empirical analyses are necessary. Network data often are dichotomous, and, therefore, we made the model applicable to cases in which only dichotomous data are available. We "estimated" contact probabilities in W from the dichotomous data based on theoretical considerations (see

Yamaguchi 1994a). In Section 4, we argued that the way we obtained these contact probabilities would probably be less suitable if MCT_i or $MFPT_i$ were the dependent variable. The mere fact that we have to pay attention to this discussion, because the definition of W can have large effects on the implications of the model, shows that one has to be careful using the model when only dichotomous network data are available. Moreover, we highlighted in Subsection 4.2.3 only one part of the problem—namely, that the theoretical reasoning behind the choice of contact probabilities does not correspond directly to the dependent variable involved. The other side of the problem is that we use only the dichotomous data to define the network measures in the analyses. One can argue that we are analyzing a valued network and should deduce network measures that are related to the values of the ties and not only to whether a tie does or does not exist. For example, one can ask who has a larger degree: an actor with many friends whom he sees rarely or an actor with fewer friends whom he sees frequently. According to the former definition, the actor with many friends has a larger degree, but it is certainly arguable that degree depends not only on the number of contacts but also on the frequency.

It is relatively easy to change the definitions of most network measures to make them applicable to valued networks. In fact, almost all definitions were formulated in a way that would make this change straightforward. All the network measures that were formulated in terms of n_{ij} can be reformulated by changing n_{ij} to w_{ij}. One point that needs some more attention is that in some of the formulations of the network measures we used the fact that $n_{ii} = 0$ so we could sum over all i and j without having to exclude the cases where $i = j$. If we want to choose w_{ii} to be different from zero, we need to be more explicit about how these diagonal elements have to be treated. Another point that needs attention is that when W is used the networks are not necessarily symmetric. For instance, indegree and outdegree need not have the same value and should be calculated separately, but these generalizations are straightforward. The only measures that need some adjustment are bridges, distance, and diameter. For bridges one can define the "bridgeness" of a valued graph as

$$\text{Bridgeness} = \sum_{\text{bridges}} \frac{1}{w_{ij}} , \qquad (31)$$

which implies that a bridge that is very "small" adds more to the bridgeness than a bridge between two actors with a strong tie. Note that this definition is in fact a generalization of the number of bridges in the dichotomous network; namely, changing w_{ij} to n_{ij} results in a value for bridgeness that is equal to the number of bridges. The number of bridges at which an actor is located can be generalized in a similar way by summing over the bridges connected to that actor. The new distance measure we propose is inspired by the new diffusion measure:

$$\text{Distance}_{ij} = \min_{R} \sum_{(k,l) \in R} \frac{1}{w_{kl}} , \tag{32}$$

where R contains all paths that go from actor i to actor j and (k, l) are all dyads on these paths. This definition implies that for all trees, $\text{MCT}_{ij} = \text{distance}_{ij}$ (see Section 2). The diameter was defined in terms of distances in the network, and this definition can still be used.

Further research is necessary to investigate how the results of this paper change if the network measures are based on valued networks. Nevertheless, using the model based on contact frequencies that are measured as such in empirical research will lead to more convincing results due to the model's sensitivity to an indirect theoretical estimation of W based on dichotomous network data.

6. CONCLUSIONS AND DISCUSSION

This paper introduced a contagion model for information diffusion in heterogeneous networks and compared that model with the transit model used by Yamaguchi (1994a). The main difference between the two models is that, information is given from one actor to another as a kind of package in the transit model, while in the contagion model every actor who ever obtained information will have that information at any time in the future. With analyses of networks with seven actors, we compared the implications of the two models for substantive questions, such as efficiency of information diffusion in networks and centrality of actors in networks.

The analyses show that the implications of the transit model and the contagion model are partially different. Bridges hindered global information diffusion more in the transit model than in the contagion model. Moreover, trapping of information in certain parts of the network was more severe in the transit model than in the contagion model. We assert that these difference are due to the unrealistic information transfer assumption in the transit model and, consequently, that the transit model overestimates these effects. Individual mean first passage time based on the transit model turned out to have undesirable implications when taken in combination with the contact probabilities used. Individual mean contagion time based on the contagion model seemed to be less sensitive to the choice of the contact probabilities; at least the results for individual mean contagion time made much more sense.

For individual mean first passage time, increases in degree and degree quality had large positive effects on the time needed to transmit information through the network, while these effects were negative and, consequently, much more plausible for individual mean contagion time. Furthermore, concerning centrality measures, this paper shows again that the determination of who is central in a network depends on whether centrality is about transmitting, receiving, or betweenness. Somebody who can transmit information quickly in a network is not necessarily a good receiver of information in the network. Still, we assert that contagion receiver centrality and contagion betweenness centrality measure similar concepts as Friedkin (1991) measured, respectively, with immediate effects centrality and mediative effects centrality. Both pairs of measures are defined for valued networks W. However, comparing the measures using the same W showed that there were considerable differences. As said before, for receiving information the effects of the different network measures varied only in the size of effects; therefore, the new model does not provide different hypotheses about the effects of certain network measures on centrality. This result makes it questionable whether it is necessary to use the more complex model to estimate closeness centrality. On the other hand, betweenness centrality predictions of two network measures went in opposite directions, which increases the value of using our more complex model for this centrality measure.

Besides the differences found in the regression analyses, we studied the ordering of centrality inside the networks. For connected networks with fewer than six actors there were hardly any differences in the ordering,[21] but for networks of size 7, changes in the ordering were omnipresent, especially as can be expected from the foregoing results, for betweenness centrality. We expect that these differences will increase with the network size and, therefore, investing in the increasing calculation effort of the new model for larger networks is reasonable. Of course, only

[21]This set of networks consists of only 30 networks and could easily be checked by hand.

empirical tests can provide evidence about whether the models produce different predictions in empirical situations and which one is better in a particular situation.

This brings us directly to a discussion about the use of the new model for larger networks. For larger networks, it is essential that only reachable states are included in describing the diffusion process. Also, network equivalence concepts can be used to reduce complexity. We do not exclude the possibility that there are far more efficient methods to calculate the new diffusion times, because there seems to be a lot of structure in the Markov chain that we could not use directly to reduce computation time. For example, in the case of trees, the contagion times turned out to be simple, but this was a result of the discovery of a straightforward way to calculate these contagion times. If we had constructed the Markov chain and calculated contagion times that way, these relations would be hard to reproduce. Besides trying to find faster methods to calculate contagion times exactly, one can develop approximation methods. A first example is what we did in this paper: finding relations between simple network measures and contagion times. For the networks with seven actors, we were able to explain about 90 percent of the variance in diffusion times with relatively simple network measures. One could use the regression equations to approximate contagion times in other networks. The problem is that the accuracy of these equations for larger networks is highly uncertain. Another way of approximating contagion times is to summarize a large network structure in a simpler stochastic block design. Then expected contagion times can be calculated within and between the blocks. Thereafter, these results can be brought together to estimate contagion times between actors in different blocks.

REFERENCES

Altmann, Michael. 1993. "Reinterpreting Network Measures for Models of Disease Transmission." *Social Networks* 15:1–17.

Bailey, Norman T. J. 1957. *The Mathematical Theory of Epidemics*. London: Charles Griffin.

———. 1964. *The Elements of Stochastic Processes with Applications to the Natural Sciences*. New York: Wiley.

———. 1975. *The Mathematical Theory of Infectious Diseases and Its Applications*, 2nd ed. London: Charles Griffin.

Bartholomew, D. J. 1982. *Stochastic Models for Social Processes*, 3rd ed. New York: Wiley.

Box, G. E. P., and D. R. Cox. 1964. "An Analysis of Transformations." *Journal of the Royal Statistical Society*, ser. B, 26:211–43.

Burt, Ronald S. 1976. "Positions in Networks." *Social Forces* 55:93–122.

———. 1991. *Structural Holes*. Cambridge, MA: Harvard University Press.

Buskens, Vincent. 1998. "The Social Structure of Trust." *Social Networks* 20:265–89.

Diekmann, Andreas. 1989. "Diffusion and Survival Models for the Process of Entry into Marriage." *Journal of Mathematical Sociology* 14:31–44.

Ellner, Stephen P., Akira Sasaki, Yoshihiro Haraguchi, and Hirotsugu Matsuda. 1998. "Speed of Invasion in Lattice Population Models: Pair-Edge Approximation." *Journal of Mathematical Biology* 36:469–84.

Freeman, Linton C. 1979. "Centrality in Social Networks: Conceptual Clarification." *Social Networks* 1:215–39.

Friedkin, Noah E. 1991. "Theoretical Foundations for Centrality Measures." *American Journal of Sociology* 96:1478–504.

Greve, Henrich R., David Strang, and Nancy B. Tuma. 1995. "Specification and Estimation of Heterogeneous Diffusion Models." Pp. 377–420 in *Sociological Methodology 1995*, edited by Peter V. Marsden. Washington, DC: American Sociological Association.

Harris, T. E. 1974. "Contact Interactions in a Lattice." *Annals of Probability* 2:969–88.

Hedström, Peter. 1994. "Contagious Collectivities: On the Spatial Diffusion of Swedish Trade Unions, 1890–1940." *American Journal of Sociology* 99:1157–79.

Huber, Peter J. 1967. "The Behavior of Maximum Likelihood Estimates under Non-Standard Conditions." *Proceedings of the Fifth Berkeley Symposium in Mathematical Statistics and Probability* 1:221–33.

Kemeny, John G., and J. Laurie Snell. 1960. *Finite Markov Chains*. New York: D. Van Nostrand.

Kretzschmar, Mirjam, and Martina Morris. 1996. "Measures of Concurrency in Networks and the Spread of Infectious Disease." *Mathematical Biosciences* 133:165–95.

Laumann, Edward O., and David Knoke. 1987. *The Organizational State: Social Choice in National Policy Domains*. Madison: University of Wisconsin Press.

Mahajan, Vijay, and Robert A. Peterson. 1985. *Models for Innovation Diffusion*. Beverly Hills, CA: Sage.

Mollison, Denis M. 1977. "Spatial Contact Models for Ecological and Epidemic Spread." *Journal of the Royal Statistical Society*, ser. B, 39:283–326.

Morris, Martina. 1993. "Epidemiology and Social Networks: Modeling Structured Diffusion." *Sociological Methods and Research* 22:99–126.

Nowak, Martin A., and Robert M. May. 1992. "Evolutionary Games and Spatial Chaos." *Nature* 359:826–29.

Rogers, W. H. 1993. "Regression Standard Errors in Clustered Samples." *Stata Technical Bulletin* 13:19–23.

Snijders, Tom A. B. 1981. "The Degree of Variance: An Index of Graph Heterogeneity." *Social Networks* 3:163–74.

Strang, David. 1991. "Adding Social Structure to Diffusion Models: An Event History Framework." *Sociological Methods and Research* 19:324–53.

Strang, David, and Nancy B. Tuma. 1994. "Spatial and Temporal Heterogeneity in Diffusion." *American Journal of Sociology* 99:614–39.

Valente, Thomas W. 1995. *Network Models of the Diffusion of Innovations.* Cresskill, NJ: Hampton Press.

Wasserman, Stanley, and Katherine Faust. 1994. *Social Network Analysis: Methods and Applications.* Cambridge, England: Cambridge University Press.

White, Halbert. 1980. "A Heteroscedasticity-Consistent Covariance Matrix Estimator and a Direct Test for Heteroscedasticity." *Econometrica* 48:817–30.

Yamaguchi, Kazuo. 1994a. "The Flow of Information through Social Networks: Diagonal-Free Measures of Inefficiency and the Structural Determinants of Inefficiency." *Social Networks* 16:57–86.

———. 1994b. "Some Accelerated Failure-Time Regression Models Derived from Diffusion Process Models: An Application to a Network Diffusion Analysis." Pp. 267–300 in *Sociological Methodology 1994*, edited by Peter V. Marsden. Washington, DC: American Sociological Association.

NAME INDEX

SUBJECT INDEX